A
VISION
OF
ORDER

A man, I suppose, fights only when he hopes, when he has a vision of order, when he feels strongly there is some connection between the earth on which he walks and himself.

V.S. Naipaul in *The Mimic Men* (André Deutsch, 1967)

A
VISION
OF
ORDER

A Study of Black South African
Literature in English (1914–1980)

Ursula A. Barnett

SINCLAIR BROWNE: LONDON
UNIVERSITY OF MASSACHUSETTS PRESS: AMHERST

For Shelley
in appreciation

First published in Great Britain 1983 by
Sinclair Browne Ltd, 10 Archway Close,
London N19 3TD.
First published in the United States of America 1983 by
The University of Massachusetts Press,
Amherst, Massachusetts 01002.

Copyright © Ursula A. Barnett 1983.

British Library Cataloguing in Publication Data
Barnett, Ursula A.
A vision of order.
1. South African literature (English)—Black
authors—History and criticism
I. Title
820.9'968   PR9359.6

ISBN 0-86300-007-X

Library of Congress Cataloging in Publication Data

Barnett, Ursula A.
A vision of order.
Bibliography: p. 329
Includes index.
1. South African Literature (English) – Black authors –
History and criticism. I. Title.
PR9358.2.B57B37 1983   820'.9'8968   83-9296
ISBN 0-87023-406-4

Book designed by Richard Kelly

Printed in England by Photobooks (Bristol) Ltd

Contents

Acknowledgements

The Editor, *Contrast*, for 'Be Gentle' by N.S. Ndebele; André Deutsch Ltd for extracts from *The Mimic Men* by V.S. Naipaul and *Zulu Poems* by M. Kunene; Mr Desmond Dhlomo for extracts from the works of H.I.E. Dhlomo and R.R.R. Dhlomo; Ad. Donker (Pty) Ltd for extracts from *Hurry up to It* by S.S. Sepamla, *Yol'Iinkomo* by M.P. Gwala, *Yakhal 'inkomo* by M.W. Serote and *It is Time to Go Home* by C. van Wyk; Heinemann Educational Books for extracts from *Letters to Martha*, *A Simple Lust* and *Stubborn Hope* by Dennis Brutus, *The Marabi Dance* by M. Dikobe, *Maru* and *The Collector of Treasures* by Bessie Head, *Emperor Shaka the Great* by M. Kunene, *A Walk in the Night*, *In the Fog of the Season's End*, *The Stone Country* and *The Time of the Butcherbird* by Alex la Guma, *Dead Roots* by Arthur Nortje, *Mhudi* by S.T. Plaatje, *Hill of Fools* by L. Peteni, quotations from *Quartet*, *Seven South African Poets*, *Black Poets in South Africa*, *Ten One-Act Plays*, *Nine African Plays for Radio*, *The Will to Die* by Can Themba and *Robben Island* by D.M. Zwelonke; Hickey Press Ltd for an extract from *Present Lives Future Becoming* by C. Pieterse; John Johnson for an extract from *A Question of Power* by Bessie Head; lines from *A Simple Lust* by Dennis Brutus, copyright © Dennis Brutus 1963, 1968, 1970, 1971, 1973, reprinted by permission of Hill and Wang, a division of Farrar, Straus and Giroux, Inc.; the author for extracts from *Pass me the Meatballs, Jones* by James Matthew; Oxford University Press for extracts from *Sounds of a Cowhide Drum* by O. Mtshali; Ravan Press (Pty) Ltd for extracts from *Staffrider*, *The Rainmaker* by F. Johanesse, *Call Me Not a Man* by M. Matshoba and *Just a Little Stretch of Road* by A. Williams; extracts from *Ezekiel Mphahlele* by Ursula Barnett copyright © 1976 by Twayne Publishers Inc., a division of G.K. Hall & Co., Boston; The University of Texas Press for extracts from *Poems from Algiers* and *China Poems* by Dennis Brutus.

Introduction

THE DEFINITIONS OF black or African writing are as many as the writers defining it. They range from distinction according to colour or birth, to a loose description of African writing as writing in Africa based on the contention that 'you can't carve up the country of the imagination';[1] from the meticulous classifications of Janheinz Jahn according to 'stylistic features or pattern',[2] to the definition of the Freetown Conference on English Language literature of Africa in 1963, reported by Ezekiel Mphahlele, as literature with 'an African setting authentically handled and to which experience originating in Africa are integral'.[3]

With the present preference for the term 'black' rather than African, further nuances of meaning have been added to attempts at definition. In South Africa, the white establishment sees 'black' negatively as non-white and denies it a culture. For the indigenous African, the term 'black' signifies pride in African culture and history and commits him to a struggle to cast off the non-African yoke. In literary critical terms, this means on the one hand that a yardstick of Western European literature is used against which to measure black South African writing, and on the other a demand for rejection of falsely labelled universal standards and a substitution of purely African values. The South African black writer is caught between. He is accused by white South African critics, at one extreme, of persisting 'in using almost every possible occasion to castigate the prevailing system of government without regard for any of the basic precepts of poetry',[4] and by black critics of being 'a kind of Afro-Saxon or Euro-African who can't be trusted to speak for Africa',[5] at the other.

A criterion for judging writing by black South Africans will have to be found within the works themselves. The achievement must be measured against the aims. A time will surely come when each culture will acknowledge that it has something both to give and take. This can only be achieved by communication through literature, the encouragement of which I consider to be one of the chief tasks of the critic, literary historian and observer.

The area under consideration is the Republic, formerly Union, of South Africa. Although the black literature in this area has elements in common with that in neighbouring countries, the effects of the apartheid laws of South Africa, those for instance assigning people to live in a particular district according to their racial group, are the very substance on which black South African literature is built. Growing up in 'Second Avenue'—the title of Ezekiel Mphahlele's auto-biography—is very much like growing up in District Six or in Fordsburg. Each of these three areas is assigned to a different racial group: one black, one 'coloured' and one Indian. Their writers are united in opposition to the apartheid laws which deprive them of any say in the government of their land, and relegate them to an inferior status in every sphere of life. A common black South African literature is the result.

Also included are those writers who have gone into voluntary or enforced exile. They are still held by a 'tyranny of place'—a term coined by Ezekiel Mphahlele—and their concern in their writing is their native land.

Only writing in English has been included in this study, a language which is progressively developing into an African language in South Africa. Although not all black South Africans speak English, they are the largest group of English users in the land. It is the *lingua franca* of commerce, industry and officialdom, and of urban blacks belonging to different language groups. The demand for its reinstatement as a free choice of language medium in education is an explosive political issue. The only publishing houses producing books in the vernacular are government controlled. English is therefore the most effective way of communicating ideas.

It is no easy task to study black writing comprehensively inside South Africa. At every turn one is frustrated by the ever-changing censorship laws. Works may not be read, or they may not be distributed, or the author may not be quoted, or they are simply not available. Permission has to be obtained, undertakings and guaran-tees have to be signed. Acquiescence means that one is in the invidious position of cooperating with a system one abhors. On one occasion, unable to obtain a particular banned work, I asked the author for a copy. He directed me to a friend. Had he kept it at home a police raid could have led to a heavy fine. Another time, in order to photocopy a paper *I had written myself*, I was required by a university library to leave my identity documents at the desk until I had brought it back.

Without the cooperation of friends abroad this work could not have been written. I would like to thank particularly the writers who are the subjects of this study, many of whom were never too busy to answer my many questions and discuss their work.

Ursula A. Barnett
Cape Town

A History of Black Writing in English in South Africa

A STUDY OF the history of black writing in English in South Africa requires an investigation into the reasons why some began to write in English rather than in the African languages, why some continued to do so, and why others continued to write in the vernacular.

Black creative writing in South Africa began in the middle of the nineteenth century with the missionaries, whose primary purpose was to publish reading matter for, rather than by, the black man. It did not matter whether the translations of the Bible and religious works were written by whites or blacks, provided that the writers were proficient in the language in which they were writing and likely to reach the largest number of potential converts. When black writers did begin to produce work they were certainly encouraged to do so, and many works were published by the mission presses. The Paris Evangelical Mission press at Morija and the Church of Scotland mission station press at Lovedale became the centres of early black literature in the African languages.

The Rev. R.H.W. Shepherd, at Lovedale, was one of the first to see the importance of expanding African literature written by the black man himself, and he eventually envisaged an 'all-African publishing house', 'asking no favours, seeking no patronage or props from others . . .'. He felt that 'there is that in Bantu culture and language which is well worthy of preservation, something unique, the loss of which would be a loss to the world at large'.[1] By publishing books, he also wanted to counter the frequent complaint made against missionaries that they had taken away the games, dances and other recreations of the people, without providing substitutes.

While Shepherd was doubtlessly acting in the interests of the Church and endeavouring, as he said, to counteract any tendency to writing 'in wildness of passion and protest',[2] to which he felt 'Bantu' writers were prone as a people still at an 'adolescent'[3] period, his enthusiasm in encouraging writers over a period of many years clearly superseded the call of the cross. 'It is nothing short of romantic,' he said, 'to find every week several manuscripts by African authors in the vernacular or in English . . . (on) one's desk'.[4]

The missions began to encourage the preservation of folklore and also the writing of novels, naturally with a religious or Christian moral background. The earliest work to be published in English was by John Knox Bokwe, *Ntsikana, The Story of an African Convert*.[5] This story of one of the first Christian converts is dramatically told and reads like a novel. Bokwe at this time had had considerable experience in journalism, after editing *The Kaffir Express* from the age of fifteen in 1870. Later, as the *Christian Express* and subsequently as the *South African Outlook*, this journal used both Xhosa and English. Other publications were also appearing partially in English, and black journalists took an active part in their editorial production. *The Bechuana Gazette (Koranta ea Becoana)*, established in 1901 by Silas Molema, was one of these. Sol Plaatje and others also launched bi- or multi-lingual journals. Towards the end of the century C. John Tengo Jabavu was contributing to the *Cape Argus* under a pen-name. His life-work became the journal *African Opinion (Imvo Zabantu-undeu)*, and in Natal John L. Dube pioneered *Ilanga Lase Natal* which still today publishes large portions in English. Many of the leading black creative writers, like H.I.E. Dhlomo and Jordan Ngubane, have been among its contributors in English, and R.R.R. Dhlomo was its editor for many years. He and H.I.E. Dhlomo began to contribute short stories, poems, critical essays and columns in English to journals such as *The Sjambok, Bantu World, The African Observer* and *South African Outlook*.

The first novel in English by a black writer was *An African Tragedy*, by R.R.R. Dhlomo. As a teacher and a journalist of wide experience (he was at one time even on the editorial staff of a white publication, *The Sjambok*, something unheard-of in those days) R.R.R. Dhlomo was used to writing in English, and doubtlessly wanted to reach the same readership he addressed through the press. The mission press was only publishing books suitable for schools, and, according to his brother H.I.E. Dhlomo, R.R.R. Dhlomo did not want to 'water them down to the tone and requirements dictated by the selection committee'.[6] Thus three historical plays which he wrote in Zulu were never published, and after the Christian-orientated *African Tragedy* he wrote no further books in English.

Sol Plaatje's novel *Mhudi* was published in 1930, though written some ten years earlier. Plaatje wrote in English because he aimed deliberately at an English-speaking, mainly white, readership, not because he scorned the vernacular. On the contrary, he hoped to cultivate a love for art and literature in the vernacular by collecting and printing Bechuana folk-tales which, he felt, were fast being forgotten, with the spread of European ideas. One of the aims of the publication of *Mhudi*, as expressed in the introduction, was to collect money for this purpose. Earlier, he had compiled a collection of *Bechuana Proverbs* ('with Literal Translations and their European Equivalents') which was published in London in 1916.

Solomon Tshekiso Plaatje was born in 1876 in the Boskop district while his family was moving to Priel on the banks of the Vaal river. He went to school there and reached the fourth standard, which enabled him to teach. In 1894 he became a postman in Kimberley, and at the same time studied for a civil service certificate. He topped the list of all candidates. He moved to Mafeking where he became an interpreter and magistrate's clerk to the Court of Summary Jurisdiction under Lord Edward Cecil. During the siege of Mafeking, and later during the war years, he interpreted for the British officers. He saw duty at the siege of Mafeking between October 1899 and May 1900, and acted as war correspondent during that period. The Tshidi-Barolong tribesmen had been enemies of the Boers for many years, and Plaatje felt that the blacks would best be served by making common cause with the British.

Some years ago his diary of the siege of Mafeking was discovered by chance by a grandson, under the back cover of a scrapbook. He presented it to John L. Comaroff who had asked for old documents while researching for an anthropological study of the Barolong. Comaroff published the notes as *The Boer War Diary of Sol. T. Plaatje—An African at Mafeking.*[7]

Plaatje continued to study and became proficient in eight languages: English, German, Afrikaans, High Dutch, Tswana, Sotho, Zulu and Xhosa. In 1904, he persuaded Chief Silas Molema of Mafeking to finance the first Tswana-English weekly, the *Koranta ea Becoana* mentioned earlier, which he edited, and in Kimberley he established another newspaper, *Tsala ea Batho* (Friend of the People). In 1912 he became first Secretary-General of the African National Congress under John L. Dube.

He was a member of a deputation which went to London in 1914 to protest against the Native Land Act of 1913. War broke out and the deputation was recalled. His first published work, *Native Life in South Africa before and since the European War and the Boer Rebellion*, appeared in London in 1916. In a scathing attack on the Land Act, it gave the reasons for the deputation and appealed to the British public for help. In 1918 he led another deputation, this time to the Peace Conference at Versailles to get recognition, but was ignored. He remained in Europe to attend the first Pan African Congress in Paris, then travelled to the United States and Canada, lecturing about conditions of the black man in South Africa and explaining his political status. In 1921 Plaatje founded the Brotherhood Society, which strove to bring about racial harmony. He represented the African National Congress at a conference in Pretoria in 1927.

Plaatje's range of knowledge was tremendous. This almost completely self-taught man translated several Shakespeare plays into Tswana. A recent collection of his non-fiction writing in *English in Africa*[8] shows that he wrote with authority, wit and great readability on subjects as varied as Setswana phonetics and spelling, history and Shakespeare. He died in 1932.

Mhudi will be evaluated later as a novel, but I have gone into detail about Sol Plaatje's life at this stage in order to show that not all the early writers were mouthpieces of the missionaries or the Europeans, as has often been claimed. Plaatje was a member of early black political organisations, and wrote of the conditions of his people with bitterness. Despite his Western-orientated education he did not turn away from Africanism, but found it necessary to seek the aid and assistance of a European readership in helping Africa emerge.

The Lovedale Press published several other early works in English, and by 1945, in his 'Supplementary to the Main Thesis' for the degree of Doctor of Literature at the University of the Witwatersrand, Shepherd was predicting that African writers would be writing more and more in English. Among works in the nineteen-twenties and thirties were D.D.T. Jabavu's *Native Disabilities in South Africa* (1932), his *The Black Problem*, H.I.E. Dhlomo's play, *The Girl Who Killed to Save* (1936), and a volume of poems by J.J.R. Jolobe.

H.I.E. Dhlomo was a prolific writer. We know of one published play, a large collection of unpublished plays carefully preserved in the Library of the University of Natal, his published long poem 'Valley of a Thousand Hills', and numerous articles and poems in various journals. An abortive attempt was made to preserve some of the latter in the Killie Campbell Museum in Durban, in an anonymous collection of clippings and typescripts probably made by Mrs Campbell herself. More recently, N.W. Visser and T.J. (Tim) Couzens obtained permission from Mr Desmond Dhlomo to edit all existing material for publication, a project sponsored by the Institute for the Study of English in Africa at Rhodes University, and the Human Sciences Research Council. They intend publishing a complete edition eventually. Selected collections have appeared in the periodical published by the Institute, *English in Africa*.

Herbert Dhlomo was born in 1903 in Simyamu near Pietermaritzburg in Natal, the son of a preacher. He was educated at Adams College, a Church school in Amanzimtoti, which has also educated other well known writers, for instance Peter Abrahams and Ezekiel Mphahlele. Dhlomo became a teacher and journalist. At the time of his death in 1956 he was assistant editor of *Ilanga Lase Natal*.

Dhlomo has sometimes been criticised for being too strongly influenced by English literature in his writing. It must be remembered, however, that black students who received a high school education before the Bantu Education Act, mostly attended missionary and other church schools run and staffed by British teachers, and therefore received an education even more English-orientated than that of English-speaking white students at this time. It was never Dhlomo's aim to westernise African literature or to discard African heritage. As early as 1939, he advocated the formation of an African archives department for African scholars planning to write on African historical and anthropological subjects, and the granting of research funds and scholarships for delving into the background of African drama. He made various suggestions in this respect, such as the collection and reconstruction of the Bantu 'Izibongo', the collection (for dramatic purposes) of biographical material of Bantu kings, heroes and other outstanding figures, the study of Negro drama, the organization of an African national drama movement. Yet he also advocated a study comparing African life and literature with Greek, Hebrew and Egyptian life and literature, and the translation of Shakespeare and Attic drama.

'Art is understanding and expressing the feeling and experiences around you,' he wrote. 'An artist must come out of himself and enter into the general emotion, thought and opinion of the people. He must express not only himself, but the thought and feeling of the people.'[9] His work is steeped in tradition. In some of his poetry he foreshadows the fiercely conscious pride of the black poets of the seventies. 'Sound the Drum', one of these poems begins, some forty years before Oswald Mtshali took up the beat. He sums it up in an article entitled 'Why Study Tribal Dramatic Forms?':

> If our literature is to hold its own among the literatures of the world; if it is to offer something distinct and unique; if it is to reflect the soul of Africa, it must spring from indigenous, tribal culture; it must treat of our history, customs and our great tribal heroes . . . We cannot build by forsaking our origins. We must go back to go forward . . .[10]

These are ideas generally attributed to a movement of black consciousness which reached South Africa some 30 years later.

Yet art, for Dhlomo, was for all people, and perhaps in that spirit he wanted to reach as wide an audience as possible, whether black or white.

> Great art or thought (art is thought-feeling) is more than national, it is universal, reflecting the image—the spirit of the All-Creative Being who knows neither East nor West, Black nor White, Jew nor Gentile, time nor space. The tragedy of a Job, a Hamlet, a Jean, a Nonqause, is the tragedy of all countries, all times, all races.

A reader of the publication *South African Outlook*, T. Makiwane, writing to the editor in 1935, tells the story of how he met two Basuto graduates of Fort Hare. 'We could only discuss in English, and if they should ever venture to write, I should be glad if they did so in English, so that I also, a Xhosa-speaking man, might enjoy their thoughts and ideas'.[11] The idea of English as a *lingua franca* in literature for Africans in South Africa, or even in the whole of Africa south of the

Sahara, like Latin for Europe of the Middle Ages, had been born and subsequently found its exponents everywhere.

An interesting publication appeared in 1944. Entitled *Bantu Babel*, and subtitled 'Will the Bantu Languages Live', it appeared in the Sixpenny Library edited by Edward Roux and was published by The African Bookman. The author, Jacob Nhlapo, was principal of the Wilberforce Institute, and was a great admirer of H.I.E. Dhlomo.

> We ought not to let our feelings blind us to the truth. The truth is that language is just a tool for letting other people know what we think. If a language is a bad tool, there is no reason why we ought not to make it better by putting words from other languages into it, or if need be, by throwing it away altogether.[12]

Here again was a man in advance of his time in South Africa, foreshadowing the way in which black writers today adapt the English language to African usage. However, calling English 'the educated Africans' Esperanto', he looks upon it as a second language, useful for communicating with the rest of Africa. For a first language he suggests amalgamating all the Bantu tongues in South Africa into two only, Zulu and Xhosa into one Nguni language and Southern Sotho, Tswana and Pedi into a Sotho language.

By this time black academics, such as Z.K. Matthews, were beginning to stress the importance of a Western language as a basis for learning. It would be impossible, they felt, to understand and appreciate the machinery of western civilisation through languages which were not equipped to deal with it. Opposed to these ideas were the active exponents of African literature in the vernacular. The most explicit in this respect was the Zulu poet Benedict Wallet Vilakazi, who engaged in literary arguments with H.I.E. Dhlomo in the columns of *Outlook*. 'I do not class English or Afrikaans dramas on Bantu themes, whether these are written by Black people, I do not call them contributions to Bantu literature [*sic*],' he wrote to the editor on 1 July, 1939 in reply to Dhlomo's essay 'African Drama and Poetry'.

> I have an unshaken belief in the possibilities of Bantu languages and their literature, provided the Bantu writers *themselves* can learn to love their language and use them as vehicles for thought, feeling and will. After all, the belief, resulting in literature, is a demonstration of people's 'self' where they cry: *Ego sum Quod sum*. That is our pride in being black and we cannot change creation.[13]

But it was Vilakazi who advocated the adoption of Western techniques in Zulu literature, whereas Dhlomo emphasised African tradition, and about this they argued even more heatedly. The apparent contradiction is still a subject of controversy in Africa today: How can one reconcile the cultures of the conqueror and the African, and, if this is not desirable, may one still use the conqueror's language to voice African traditional culture?

The missions were still encouraging vernacular writing. A conference of African authors was convened by Shepherd on behalf of the Committee on Christian Literature at Florida, Transvaal, in October 1936, to encourage African writers in the Bantu languages. Yet the authors, who included Vilakazi, H.I.E. Dhlomo, D.D.T. Jabavu, R.V. Selope Thema and the two Basuto graduates mentioned by Makiwane above, now identified as D.M. Romoshoana, and S.S. Mafoyana, were now beginning to question the motives of the whites in encouraging the vernacular. They stressed that they desired complete freedom to use whatever language they wanted.

The conference adopted the following resolution:

> While this Conference is particularly concerned to encourage and assist the production of literature in the Bantu languages, the Conference expresses its conviction that African authors should be entirely free to use any language medium they desire and those who use English or Afrikaans are fully entitled to help and encouragement in their efforts to produce works of merit'.[14]

English as a medium for black writing in South Africa suffered an almost killing blow when the Bantu Education Act of 1955 became law. The Act put into practice the government policy of separate development—*apartheid*—by transferring the control of black education from the provincial education department to central government, and within the government from the Department of Education to the Department of Native Affairs. In higher education, training schools and institutions were now required to take students only from their own ethnic groups. Colleges were set up under the University of South Africa in half a dozen main regions, and were soon referred to disparagingly as the 'tribal colleges'. The medium of instruction was the vernacular of the particular area. There was an immediate outcry from all sections of the population and black writers voiced their opposition. Z.K. Matthews, as acting principal of Fort Hare University College, called the forced use of a language which is confined to a small area or is spoken by too small a number of people a 'cruel imposition which can only be perpetrated upon a voiceless and defenceless people'.[15] '. . . the Government is trying so hard to legislate the African back to the past', Lewis Nkosi wrote in a letter to the author. Writing in *The New Statesman* in 1960, Ezekiel Mphahlele said that black writers in South Africa were on the 'threshold of a dark age'[16] because Bantu education hindered their writing creatively in English.

Yet it would appear that the legislation had the very opposite effect. It became an impetus rather than a hindrance. Whereas in other African countries south of the Sahara thinking men were beginning to stress a pride in blackness and tradition, black writers in South Africa, in opposition to Government policy, used the medium in which they could stress the universality of literature.

A new generation was now living in the towns, where members of different tribes and language groups intermingled. The black man in the towns heard all these languages as well as English and Afrikaans, and had a smattering of many of them. C.L.S. Nyembezi, then Professor of Bantu languages at the University College of Fort Hare, told a conference of African writers held at Atteridgeville, Pretoria, in 1959, that as examiner in Zulu for the Orange Free State Bantu Teachers' Examination he often found papers with Zulu, Xhosa and Swazi words in the same sentence 'with a Sotho construction thrown in'. 'Imagine someone in that position trying to write a Zulu book'.

The books—or rather the stories, poems and essays—coming from the townships were being written in English, not merely as a vehicular language but as a symbol of equality. 'In their joint use of English,' wrote Nat Nakasa, a writer himself, 'Africans reach with greater ease the various levels of common ground which are of importance in the process of eliminating tribal division with all its unwelcome consequences. To the African, English has become a symbol of success, the vehicle of his painful protest against social injustice and spiritual domination by those who rule him.'[17]

Books in the various vernaculars continue to be written, and are encouraged by publishing houses often run by a semi-official government group, like Perskor. The readership is mainly in the schools, however, and writers have to fulfil certain requirements of conforming to the government's specific moral and political standards to pass the board responsible for literature.

For the English writers, Sophiatown in Johannesburg became the centre of literary activities until this area ceased to exist in 1953. Writers, including Todd Matshikiza, Ezekiel Mphahlele, Lewis Nkosi and Bloke Modisane, formed a coterie which met to discuss literature. They met at each other's houses or, more often, at a shebeen. When Lewis Nkosi compared the shebeen with an English club he was not being facetious. The shebeen was the centre of African life in the townships.

Nkosi, in his collection of essays, *Home and Exile*,[18] calls this period 'The Fabulous Decade'. Everything that went before in African literature was discarded as being crusadingly Christian or unacceptably romantic. The writers revolted against what they conceived as the naïve and simple-minded generation personified, according to Nkosi, by Alan Paton's character in *Cry the Beloved Country*, Stephen Kumalo, just as the black Americans had revolted against the concept of Uncle Tom many years earlier.

The idea of a journal for black readers in English was conceived by Bob Crisp, a white journalist and broadcaster well-known at the time. He envisaged a vehicle for all black art forms, with separate editions not only for South, East and West Africa but also for the western hemisphere and Europe, including the West Indies, and its many black students and emigrants. Since he lacked the necessary funds, he asked Jim Bailey to finance him. This was in 1951 and Bailey, a younger son of Sir Abe Bailey, a Rand gold millionaire and race-horse owner, is still connected with the magazine *Drum* today. Bailey's aim, as he once wrote to one of his editors, Tom Hopkinson, was to 'do a great deal by the inhabitants of this continent',[19] and although his methods of achieving this were varied, often the subject of controversy, the results sometimes debatable, and led to the resignation of his editors from time to time, he has adhered to this purpose for the past thirty years.

Bob Crisp left the magazine because, as he put it, Bailey had 'Johannerburged' it. *African Drum* was in fact moved from Cape Town to Johannesburg where its name was changed to *Drum*. Crisp's place was taken by Anthony Sampson, who had been at Oxford with Bailey. Sampson had already been working under Crisp in Cape Town and Johannesburg. Sampson had little journalistic experience, but he was full of enthusiasm. Four numbers had appeared when Sampson first arrived and he gives the following account of their content in a book of reminiscences.[20]

> It was a sixpenny monthly magazine, written in English, printed on cheap yellow newsprint; the bright cover showed two Africans facing each other, symbolically across the continent: one in a Western hat and suit, the other with African skins and assegai.
>
> The first numbers contained poems and stories, articles on 'music of the Tribes' and 'Know Yourselves' recounting the history of the Bantu tribes, instalments of *Cry the Beloved Country*: features about religion, farming, sport and famous men; and strip cartoons about Gulliver and St Paul.[21]

He quotes a poem by Countee Cullen from one of these issues in which Cullen describes his Africa as one of 'Jungle Star' and 'Jungle Track'. 'This,' says Sampson, 'was *Drum*'s Africa; it was as exotic and exciting as I had hoped Africa to be, unspoilt by the drabness of the West.'[22]

There were some African contributors. They supplied stories in the form of legends and variations on the hackneyed theme of the dangers of the town as opposed to the simple life of the country. A story entitled 'Nomoya of the Winds' by Randolph Ben Pitso[23] is told in the Biblical style used by Paton in *Cry, the Beloved Country*. Nomoya is murdered in Johannesburg while 'Far away in Swaziland, the serenade of the wind was low and wild the sway of the bush; for no more, no more, would the jingle of anklebands sound to the mellow tread of lovely Nomoya.'[24]

It did not take Sampson long to find out that while a story with a sub-heading 'True story of How a Brave Man loved an African Chief's Favourite daughter', with its explanation of African custom, might appeal to the white reader, it held no interest whatsoever for the black people around Johannesburg whom he was learning to know. *Drum* was making the mistake of stressing the exotic which meant little to the black man at that time.

Bailey and Sampson thereupon proceeded to give their readers what they now believed that they wanted. *Gulliver's Travels* and the Bible were replaced by American comic strips featuring black heroes, and all tribal references were eliminated. More black journalists were taken on the staff. One of these was Todd Matshikiza, a graduate teacher born in Queenstown in 1922, who was later to gain fame as the composer of the black musical *King Kong*. According to Sampson it was mainly Matshikiza who transformed *Drum*. 'He wrote as he spoke, in a brisk tempo, with rhythm in every sentence. He attacked the typewriter like a piano.'[25] They called his style 'Matshikese' and this became the style of *Drum*, often, however, degenerating into American-style 'tough' prose.

Drum became, as Lewis Nkosi put it in *Home and Exile*, not so much a magazine as a symbol of urbanised Africa. It represented African literature in English in South Africa for almost a decade. While attempting to compete for black readership with the *Daily Mirror* in providing pin-up pictures, crime and sentiment, it also gave a voice to writers who then had no other outlet: Todd Matshikiza, Arthur Maimane, Can Themba and others, most of whom were also on its staff at one time or another. Many teachers at this time had refused to accept the provisions of the Bantu Education Act. Those of them who campaigned against it were dismissed and prevented from working in any government-controlled school. Ezekiel Mphahlele was one such teacher. He joined *Drum* and became its fiction editor. Nkosi worked as a reporter for *Drum* and its sister publication, the newspaper *Post*, until he left South Africa in 1961 to study journalism at Harvard University on a Nieman Fellowship. Can Themba joined *Drum* after he won a prize in its first short story contest in 1953, and eventually became its assistant editor. The crusading spirit of the journal appealed to these writers.

In *Home and Exile* Nkosi explains what was expected of a *Drum* man, apart from his responsibilities as a writer. He took 'sex and alcohol in his stride . . . and stayed in the front line of danger so long as there was danger to be endured'.[26]

There was certainly no lack of danger when *Drum* took up the cudgels on behalf of its readers. *Drum* became well-known and widely quoted abroad for its crusading articles and exposés. The best known of these were an article entitled 'Bethal Today',[27] which exposed the contract system of farm labour and recorded cases of flogging and torture, and one showing photographs of naked prisoners taken secretly with a telescopic lens.[28] These were years of protest, boycotts, demonstrations, marches, arrests and bannings, of the removal of Sophiatown and the formation of dissident organisations which came together to form a Freedom Charter, of the Treason Trials of the late fifties, and finally of Sharpeville.

In *Drum* the black man could give expression to what one of its contributors, Peter Clarke, called a very virile, passionate, conscious entanglement with living our lives. Can Themba's reply to people who queried the cheeky abuse of English in *Drum* was: 'Confound the cultural ideas of those men! All we seek is the fullest expression of the bubbling life around us and the restless spirit within us'.

In 1957 the editorship fell to Tom Hopkinson, who was essentially a professional journalist of vast experience. He worked hard to 'make a magazine which the African reader would take to with enthusiasm, and then, having captured his interest, to use it to give him a much fuller picture of the outside world, to break down his isolation, to widen his tiny location-bound horizon'.[29] But later he felt that in this he had failed, and when Bailey proposed to lower the price and the standard ('the magazine needs a youthfulness, hard stories and a rapport with its public—so for the next 6–12 months can we avoid being highbrow and work out the strong, sensational stories which our public go for?'[30]) Hopkinson resigned. He was followed by a succession of editors. In 1969 *Drum* had its first black editor. Although short story contests were still occasionally held, very little fiction was published. Sensational articles on sex and crime, pin-up pictures and photo-picture novellas made up the contents of the magazine.

As far as black short story writers were concerned, *Drum* had served its purpose of introducing them, and was now dead.

Black short story writers now needed a more serious platform, and South Africa of the nineteen-sixties was ready to give it. A spate of literary and other journals appeared almost all of which, in varying degrees, were anxious to include black writing; *Africa South, Contrast, The Classic, Ophir, Izwi, New Coin, Bolt, The Purple Renoster, New Nation.*

The aim of *The Classic* was specifically to seek black writing of merit, according to its first editor, Nathaniel (Nat) Nakasa, when introducing the new publication. It was named after a shebeen at the back of a laundry of that name and arose out of a discussion between Nakasa and Can Themba. It was partially funded by the Fairfield Foundation. At the beginning the contributors, like its editor, were black. Later, however, stories, poems, and articles by white writers were also accepted.

Anthologies including reprints from these publications were beginning to appear in Britain, the United States and in other English-speaking African countries, as well as in translation in Germany and Sweden. British publishers vied with each other to publish full-length books from Africa. The prospects looked good. But the appeal of the writing lay mainly in its expression of protest against the position of the black man in South African society; it therefore clashed with the policy of the South African Government, which was not prepared to stand by and watch such influence spread.

Within a few years almost all the writers mentioned above and their group, who still constituted the leading exponents of black writing in English in South Africa, could no longer be read in that country. This was the result of the Amendment of 1966 to the Suppression of Communism Act, followed later by similar acts, which put a blanket ban on all the work of many of these authors. Forty-six authors were banned by a Government Gazette Extraordinary of April 1, 1966, among them Ezekiel Mphahlele, Mazisi Kunene, Lewis Nkosi and Bloke Modisane all of whom left the country, Todd Matshikiza and Can Themba who also left and died abroad, and Nat Nakasa who committed suicide in New York. The Act prohibited the reading, reproduction, printing, publication or dissemination of any speech, utterance, writing or statement (or any extract therefrom) made or produced by such writers. It did not prohibit the possession or perusal of the material. This is controlled by censorship acts which have changed over the years, without altering their purpose of preventing South Africans from reading freely what the Government does not wish them to know. Its effect is to keep South Africa immune from ideas opposing the Government stand, whether they come from abroad or from within. The first was the Publications and Entertainment Act of 1963, which extended the Customs Act of 1955 the latter dealing only with imported literature. Under the new Act, a Censorship Board responsible to the Minister of the Interior decided which foreign works may be imported, and could also ban publications produced within the country. The Act allowed appeal against banning by the Publications Control Board to the Supreme Court, a body which still enjoyed independence from politics. In 1974 a parliamentary commission of enquiry proposed the abolition of this right of appeal. In spite of protests from the Bar Council and bodies representing publishers, the book-trade and others, the Publications Act No. 42 of 1974 duly became law. There was now a directorate appointed by the Minister of the Interior which formed a Publications Appeal Board. Censorship was therefore now solely in the hands of the Government executive, a powerful political weapon. The Government made full use of it in silencing protest in black literature.

Literature in South Africa was experiencing a polarisation. Black literature became more and more committed to the cause of liberation, while the government became more and more afraid of literature as a weapon and took steps to protect itself. There were other, more subtle forms of censorship. Publishers of books and periodicals knew they ran the danger of economic loss by publishing a work that courted banning, so that it took courage to go ahead. Authors themselves had to wrestle with their consciences, or even with unconscious self-censorship. Ezekiel Mphahlele, in a discussion with an interviewer for the periodical *English in Africa*, said: 'One of the painful things that I experienced when I was abroad was that I was writing and the books that I was writing were read by people outside, whereas I was really writing out of my South African experience . . . And then I ask myself, "What is the use, if the people you write about don't read what you're writing?"[31]'

The magazines continued to publish contributions by black writers with varied enthusiasm. *Contrast* is still today a prestige literary magazine. In its editorials Jack Cope, its editor for many years, wrote about current literary matters, hitting out at censorship and bannings, and proclaimed anti-racism. But *Contrast* was the voice of white liberalism, which was beginning to be stigmatised as paternalism by black writers. Recounting the history of *Contrast* in *English in Africa*, Cope asks: 'Does one . . . make allowance for the fact that the manuscript being read comes from a black junior teacher in the Ciskei as against another by an English graduate from Rhodes and Cambridge? The answer', he says:

> . . . is yes and no. No, if it means leaning over backwards, making an 'ethnic' decision in favour of the under-privileged and thus inflicting on him/her the patronising shroud of condescension. Yes, if the less sophisticated work contains somewhere deeply, even if not yet brought to greater refinement, the true frisson which is vision or originality or whatever one may wish to call it.

He goes on to describe the hypothetical example as possibly a 'view through startled eyes as expressed in an unaccustomed medium'.[32]

The Purple Renoster, which began publication in 1956, laid even greater emphasis on a non-aligned stance and insisted that there was no black writing, only writing, in South Africa. Its editor, Lionel Abrahams, campaigned fearlessly against bannings of black writers. More than most other literary figures, he was personally responsible for the encouragement of black writers. His faith in the poet Oswald Mtshali, and his publication of a collection of Mtshali's poems, contributed towards a new era in black South African literature. Among other names which *Purple Renoster* introduced to South African readers in the sixteen years of its existence were Mongane Wally Serote, Arthur Nortje and Ahmed Essop.

New Coin, first published in January 1965, was the outlet for the

South African Poetry Society, under the auspices of the English Department of Rhodes University in Grahamstown. It recognised the talent of Oswald Mtshali by publishing three of his poems as early as 1968, in the same year as he appeared in *The Classic* and *Purple Renoster*. *Ophir*, which began publication in 1967, was produced by a small group of writers for the publication of their own poetry, and poetry which interested them. It included a poem by Wally Serote in 1969, 'What's this black S . . .',[33] and later some poems by Mtshali. The Bulletin of the Department of English of the University of South Africa, *UNISA*, and *De Arte*, published by its Department of Fine Art, also contained poems by Mtshali. *Izwi* published contributions by many black writers but this was later, well into the seventies, by which time the situation had changed. In all the journals the contributions were sparse, and there was none of the group spirit and the excitement of outpourings which existed in the nineteen-fifties. In a scathing attack on the English-speaking liberal stance, Mike Kirkwood, addressing the Poetry 74 Conference at the University of Cape Town said:

> The Afrikaner will lay down the limits of contact—sport, in politics, in poetry (let us get our priorities right)—and we (English-speaking South Africans) will exercise our diplomatic gifts, our endless connections, and not least our pious liberal 'it's-not-our-fault' composure to build the bridges, Lee and Eddie will turn up some presentable Black batsmen, Guy, Jack and Lionel, Stephen Ridley and Robert, Chris, Mike and Tony will edit and publish the township bards who haven't been banned; Big Harry will talk it over with Barney and young Harry will entwine thumbs with Gatsha—you could call it Athenianism, but TIMEO DANAOS; especially when bearing carrots.[34]

The few writers of the *Drum* days left in South Africa who were still allowed to publish appeared in *The Classic*: Casey Motsisi, Webster Makaza, Stanley Motjuwadi and a few others. Can Themba's Tribute to Nat Nakasa had to be torn out of Volume II, No. 1, before distribution, because he was banned. There were one or two newcomers in the pages of *Classic*, notably Njabulo Simakahle Ndebele. Contributions of protest were also welcome in *Fighting Talk*, *Guardian* (later *New Age* and *New Era* as each was proscribed), *Africa South* and *The New African*, but soon these publications were either banned or went into exile.

The only book by a black writer resident in South Africa during this period was Dugmore Boetie's *Familiarity is the Kingdom of the Lost*, a novel in a category of its own, though in many ways foreshadowing the fiction of the seventies and eighties. We shall have a close look at it later.

The so-called coloured writers were still producing and being published during this period. Though few were banned under the Suppression of Communism Act they were being driven further and further into a black literary stance by legislation and events. In a short story entitled 'Azikwelwa' (we will not ride) about the boycott of buses by black workers protesting against an increase in fares, James Matthews's character Jonathan, asked by his boss why he was late says:

'I walked.'
'All the way?' The White man in the white coat looked at him in surprise.
'All the way.'
'But why? You're not one of them.'
He could not tell the white man of the feeling inside him, that when he was with them he knew it was good.[35]

Matthews was the earliest of the writers to enjoy wide readership in translation from the English. A volume of his short stories appeared in Sweden in 1963. He has been involved in almost every phase of Black writing in South Africa. His stories appeared in the early *Drum*. He has been active in various writers' associations, has published his own work and that of others under the name of Blac Publishing Company, his writing has often been banned and he has been detained in jail. Short of stature and fiercely independent, at once proudly black in his writing and defending his right to form literary associations with whomever he wishes, Matthews will allow no one to put him into a niche. During the decade following the bannings of black writers and the shootings at Sharpeville, he continued to write stories in the *Drum*-school style. His stories deal with the hypocrisy of white liberalism and with all the vicious aspects of apartheid. His writing, though sparse during these years, forms a tenuous link with the seventies. Whether his story 'The Park', about a small coloured boy chased out of a park for whites only was read by Oswald Mtshali or not matters little: one of Mtshali's best-known poems describes a similar incident.

Alex La Guma was born in Cape Town in 1925. As the son of a one-time President of the South African Coloured People's Congress, he was involved in politics from an early age, joining the Young Communist League in 1946. He was a member of the party till its banning in 1952 and at one time a Councillor of the City of Cape Town. He was arrested with 155 others in 1956. He appeared in the famous Treason Trial and was acquitted in 1960. Later he was placed under house arrest for five years and also detained without trial several times. He escaped from the country in 1966.

While he was still in South Africa and before his banning, his stories appeared in *Africa South* and overseas publications such as *Flamingo* and *Black Orpheus*, as well as in a collection entitled *Quartet*, edited by Richard Rive. *Quartet* also contained stories by

Matthews and by Rive himself. A collection of La Guma's stories, together with a short novel, *A Walk in the Night*, was first published by Mbari Press in 1962 and later reprinted by Heinemann. His stories present a powerful and realistic portrayal of the violence and suffering of the black man in South Africa. They are etched in stark and naturalistic terms. Wole Soyinka in *Myth Literature and the African World* describes *Walk in the Night* as 'a near obsessive delineation of the physical, particularised reality of a South African ghetto existence . . . a total statement both about the reality of that situation and on the innate regressive capacity of man in a dehumanised social condition'. An early story, 'A Glass of Wine' tells poignantly how simple human emotion is destroyed by apartheid. The normal good-natured teasing by a drunk of two shy lovers becomes grotesque when we know that by associating they court jailing under the Act which forbids black and white to marry or cohabit. In other stories he shows his characters in the Cape Town slum of District 6, 'a human salad' often 'sucking at the disintegrating, bitter, cigarette-end of life'.

Dennis Brutus came into even greater conflict with the authorities than La Guma. He was arrested in 1963, escaped and was shot at and re-imprisoned, this time on Robben Island. He left the country in 1966 on a one-way ticket. By this time his first collection of poems had been published, but since in the bulk of his work he is essentially the black South African poet in exile, we shall speak about him later in that context.

Richard Rive wrote a novel, *Emergency*, and several short stories in South Africa during the decade under discussion, though he was out of the country a great deal of the time, travelling in East, West and Central Africa, as well as the United States on a Fairfield Foundation Fellowship Grant. Rive, interviewed by Lewis Nkosi[36] in 1963, expressed his belief in a South African literature regardless of colour. He felt at that time that there was almost nothing to distinguish writing by black and white. A synthesis was developing, he said, and quoted as an example the novel *Episode*, by Harry Bloom. He did not see himself as part of an ethnic group, and felt no sense of belonging to Africa. 'I am nothing other than a South African,' he said. His play *Make Like Slaves*, originally a short story called 'Middle Passage', is described by Wole Soyinka as a fortunate example of a credible creative expression of the longing for humane resolution along the lines of reconciliation. The play won first prize in a radio play competition of the BBC.

In an essay entitled 'No Common Factor' Rive says: 'The African literary experience is incomplete unless the contributions of white Africans are also taken into consideration . . . And we are a synthesis of all this experience and more. It would be as ridiculous for me to deny the influence of Plomer and Bosman as it would be to deny the existence of my white and black forefathers'.[37] And he finds the exciting thing about African literature is its diversity, its difference and lack of a common factor.

Yet his writing is 'black' in the same way as that of the *Drum* writers: it arises out of and is deeply rooted in the milieu in which he was forced to live in District Six, the slum of his childhood, which comes to life as an integral part of his short stories like 'Rain' and 'Willieboy'. His theme is often conflict as in 'The Bench', and he writes of characters which would be beyond the pen of most white South African writers. The fact that Rive's irony is often piercingly directed at the coloured characters who deny their blood, as in 'Resurrection', or have an apartheid of their own directed at darker members of the community, as in 'Street Corner', only serves to emphasise the iniquities of the South African system where such situations can develop.[37] *Cry the Beloved Country* has never been accepted by black readers as a true portrayal of the black man. Writers of the stature of Nadine Gordimer and Athol Fugard accept the limitations of the white writer in South Africa and indeed have often made the lack of communication and understanding the theme of their writing. Significantly the one white writer with whom black writers like to identify is Ingrid Jonker, united in death with others who took their own life: Nat Nakasa and Arthur Nortje.

These writers did not form a group. They were published mainly abroad, and there was little contact between them. By 1966, when most of the bannings occurred, James Matthews had stopped writing to avoid self-censorship and Rive says that he was so disillusioned— 'books banned, surveillance and all the pressures that work on one in South Africa'—that he went into the academic stream, 'and I kind of collected degrees and lectured and wrote books about writers instead of writing myself . . .'.[38] Black writers had been effectively silenced, with hardly a ripple being felt of what was happening abroad. Black South African literature had gone mainly into exile.

While some of the writers in South Africa were occasionally published in journals abroad, those who had left the country had to rely on these outlets. Essays by Mphahlele on African Literature appeared in *Twentieth Century, The New Stateman*, and *Encounter* and Lewis Nkosi contributed to the *Observer* and *Guardian*. A story by Bessie Head appeared in *The New Statesman*. Publications were being established in other parts of Africa, some of which included creative writing. Most important of these was *Black Orpheus*, which was founded in 1957 as a 'platform for creative writing'. The contributors were the leading writers in Africa and its editors some of the best known literary figures in African literature. Contributions by Mphahlele were appearing as early as 1958 ('The Suitcase', October 1958). Occasionally there were special publications and one of these was Mphahlele's collection of short stories *The Living and the Dead and Other Stories*. Similarly *Transition*, published from Kampala, Uganda, with East and West African editors, encouraged young writers. A few stories by South Africans began to appear in its pages, such as Arthur Maimane's 'The Day After' and one or two stories by Bessie Head. Papers by Mphahlele appeared both in *Black Orpheus* and *Transition*, as well as in *Presence Africaine*, published from Paris. The *West African* published an article by Modisane in its issue of 30 June, 1962.

The African Studies Departments of American Universities and other organisations devoted to the study of African culture established journals. In the first issue of *Research in African Literatures*, in Spring 1970, John Povey, then Assistant Professor of English at the University of California at Los Angeles, reported on a Conference of South African writing held in July 1969 in Grahamstown, South Africa, under the auspices of the English Academy of Southern Africa, and concluded: 'It was . . . depressing, though of course in no way surprising, that many of the major contemporary South African writers, La Guma, Mphahlele and Brutus, were not mentioned at all, as they were in exile'.[39] Publications for Black Americans began to include contributions by South Africans living in the States. *Negro Digest*, for instance, in its July 1968 issue included poems by Keorapetse Kgositsile.

Contributions by these writers began to be included in anthologies, and many of these were then promptly banned in South Africa. The first anthology was a German one, *Schwarze Ballade* by Janheinz Jahn. Jahn included an extract from *Mine Boy* by Peter Abrahams, one of the earliest writers to leave South Africa. Next came Peggy Rutherford's *Darkness and Light*, but she had done her research inside South Africa, so her contributions came from writers still living in the country. Stories by two writers in exile, Mphahlele and Maimane, were included in an anthology published in East Germany, *Following the Sun, 17 Tales from Australia, India and South Africa*. These two writers, as well as Can Themba, Modisane, Kunene Mazisi, Alfred Hutchinson, Lewis Nkosi and others, were included in a spate of anthologies of African writing from 1960 onwards. A list of such anthologies will be found in the bibliography at the end of this work. The literary scramble for Africa had begun, but, with few exceptions, no writers within South Africa participated.

First to leave South Africa were the writers of the *Drum* period, such as Mphahlele, Modisane and others. There followed an exodus of poets who were still mainly unknown in their homeland: Dennis Brutus, Mazisi Kunene, Keorapetse Kgositsile, Arthur Nortje. Why did these writers leave? The bannings were one reason. Understandably the writers saw little point in compiling literature which no one was going to read. Furthermore, they could not create in the stifling atmosphere of censorship and harassment, a combination of literary and political reasons, sometimes more of the one, sometimes of the other.

Most of the *Drum* writers went to England except for Mphahlele, who spent some time in Nigeria, Kenya, Zambia and France and eventually settled in the United States. The poets, except for Nortje who left for England, went to the United States, where they were often welcomed at Universities as visiting or permanent lecturers. Mphahlele, who held a Master's degree in England when he left, and later gained a doctorate, became professor of English at the Universities of Denver and Philadelphia. The authors continued to write; some were published, as we have seen, in American, African and other journals and included in anthologies.

Soon after arriving in the countries of their choice they began to have full length books published. Several autobiographies appeared: Mphahlele's *Down Second Avenue*, Modisane's *Blame Me on History*, Matshikiza's *Chocolates for my Wife* and Alfred Hutchinson's *Road to Ghana*. La Guma had smuggled *A Walk in the Night* out of the country while under house arrest. He had hidden the pages under the carpet in case of a search and then posted them to London in small batches. This was followed by a steady output in exile. Nkosi published two volumes of essays. Not one of these books could be read in South Africa.

The poets, too, had collections published. Volumes appeared by Dennis Brutus, Arthur Nortje, Keorapetse Kgositsile and Mazisi Kunene. Editors, critics and publishers began to look upon the writers in exile more and more as representative of South African writing.

Few of the writers were happy in exile or able to become absorbed into the literature of their adopted countries. In a fictionalised essay on the experiences of a black academic visiting the United States, Noel Chabani Manganyi, Professor of Psychology at the University of Transkei, says:

> Even in the United States with its motley of tribes, the refugee tends to stay afloat relentlessly trying to elude the melting pot. In the thriving refugee subcultures, refugees indulge in wild anniversary flings recreating social atmospheres whenever they can get together, if only to eat, drink and make love the way they know how.[40]

Apart from the wild social flings they got together at conferences and seminars. They wrote, and still write, almost only about South Africa, and South Africa is their concern.

Nat Nakasa, in one of his tongue-in-cheek provocative columns which he wrote for a general daily newspaper, gives a strange reason for the exiles' inability to adapt, and their occasional nostalgia for the country they fled:

After a lifetime of illegal living in the Republic's shebeens, the exiles are suddenly called upon to become respectable, law-abiding citizens. Not a law to break in sight. For my part, it would be an act of providence if I survived under such circumstances. I have broken too many curfew laws and permit regulations to change so easily. Even if I did change, I would miss the experience of illegal living.[41]

As in all his columns, there is a serious undertone, all the more poignant in this instance since Nakasa himself did not in fact survive the change from the life he knew. The 'darkness and despair' into which his experience at home had dragged him, overwhelmed him when the challenge was removed, and he took his own life.

Arthur Nortje, in his poems, most of them collected under the telling title *Dead Roots*, sings lyrically and poignantly of the loneliness of the exile whose roots have been transplanted and wither on strange soil. He, too, succumbed to despair. One of his last poems, entitled 'All hungers pass away', contains the following lines:

> Fat hardened in the mouth
> famous viands tasted like ash:
> the mornings-after of a sweet escape
> ended over bangers and mash.
>
> I gave those pleasures up,
> the sherry circuit, arms of a bland girl
> Drakensberg lies swathed in gloom,
> starvation stalks the farms of the Transvaal.
>
> What consolation comes
> drops away in bitterness.[42]

Coupled with the nostalgia for home is guilt at being out of the fray and leaving others behind. To choose as one's task to 'define the happening' rather than 'storm the castles',[43] as Nortje does according to the poem 'Native's Letter', or to write poems and stories of protest, is not enough. Timi, the narrator in Mphahlele's novel *The Wanderers* says: 'Eventually I would have to decide whether to stay and try to survive: or stay and pit my heroism against the machine and bear the consequences if I remained alive: or stay and shrivel up with bitterness; or face up to my cowardice, reason with it and leave'.[44] Mphahlele himself says that his friends tried to dissuade him from leaving: '"Stay on in the struggle!" they kept saying, "I'm contributing nothing," I told them. "I can't teach and I want to teach, I can't write here and I want to write."'[45] He never ceased to feel a sense of guilt at having left, and eventually, as we shall see later, he returned. In exile he found himself unable to create. In a discussion arranged by the Institute for the Study of English in Africa he explained why. 'The problem for me as a writer was that as long as I refused to strike roots, I was going to continue to write about home, but at the same time I was away from home.'[46] Paradoxically, or perhaps just because they are not part of the fray, the writings, especially some of the poetry, embody not just hope but faith in the future. In a paper delivered at Rhodes University and published in the March 1979 issue of *English in Africa*, Mphahlele describes South African poets like Mazisi Kunene, Kgositsile and Brutus, just like the prose writers, as being 'prophets whose voices float from the wilderness of exile to the ears of an indefinable audience'. Their works, he says, are banned, and so their 'very continuance in this task is an act of faith that only prophets can sustain'.[47]

These are some of the tensions to which the writers in exile reacted in their work. It is sometimes suggested that no distinction should be made between writers within and without South Africa because such distinction, when made by South African publishers, is looked upon as a submission to censorship. However, there is no doubt that while many of the themes and aims are similar, several emotional factors motivating the writers in exile are sufficiently different to have created two separate literatures. There was also the influence of contemporary black writers in other parts of the world, which was far more accessible to the writers in exile and therefore reached them earlier than it did those in South Africa.

As movements for independence developed, so the black man's image of himself changed. In the French African territories especially, where black intellectuals were encouraged by the colonial power to become integrated, they began to take an African direction in their culture and to spurn being turned into black Frenchmen. In his famous work *Black Orpheus*,[48] Jean Paul Sartre calls the new Negro poetry 'evangelic, it comes bearing glad tidings, negritude is found again'. Negritude stood for a pride in blackness and especially in African culture, history and philosophy. Writers in the English colonies however felt that the French were striking a pose, and tended to reject negritude as a label. Mphahlele endorsed Wole Soyinka's famous argument that a tiger had no more need to proclaim his tigritude than a Negro does his negritude, and felt that diversity in definition and interpretation of the African personality opposed the concept of negritude. It was, however, an argument mainly of degree. Writers in the British colonies and former colonies were also becoming consciously aware of the positive side of being black Africans. In South Africa, on the other hand, there was a definite resistance towards emphasis on blackness, and this was in direct reaction to the apartheid policy of the Government. It was the National Party in power whose policy it was to legislate Africans back to their roots by separating the races and forcing them into tribal allegiance at every level of their lives. It is therefore understandable that black intellectuals fought against these attempts to differentiate in terms of colour. They continued their efforts to be first recognised as equal human beings before they could indulge in the luxury of pride in blackness. Non-racialism in literature was therefore still the ideal.

This did not apply to the writers in exile. In 1969 Mazisi Kunene wrote an introduction to Aime Cesaire's *Return to My Native Land*,[49] in which he said that the black man must find a new definition of man, i.e. he must redefine his reality in his own terms rather than in the role allotted to him by the white man.

In South Africa Noel Chabani Manganyi, in a work entitled *Being Black in the World*,[50] explores the African personality in psychological terms. An African ontology is obscured, he finds, by the domination of the white man. Once we look underneath we find many differences. Manganyi sees one of the greatest in the relationship between the individual and his fellow men. At this level, he says, we recognise a 'polarity of approaches. The white approach is characterised by the primacy of the individual' (individualism) while the black approach is characterised by 'the primacy of the community'.

Gradually these ideas which Manganyi describes began to seep into South Africa. In his later work, *Mashangu's Reverie and Other Essays*,[51] now by N. Chabani Manganyi, since significantly, like many writers at that time, he was using his African name, he describes the emergence of black consciousness as the antithesis of the white dominant culture. The dynamic involved, he says, seems to be one in which 'a colossal attempt is made to help the victim of racialism to arrive at a more profound appreciation of their alienation, to unmask the limits of the false consciousness by unleashing for constructive purpose the welter of their "unconscious resources".'[52] And of its effect on literature he says:

> The unconscious as part of and mediator of the black experience (or any other for that matter) comes to constructive life in the literature, theatre and other arts of a people. This should remain true even at a most superficial level of analysis for it is art at its best that explodes for our usually mundane consciousness those resonances which lie buried in a man's innermost being.[53]

The black consciousness movement in South Africa was spread by the black student organisations, SASO and SASM in the late sixties and early seventies. They helped to set up a Black Communities Programme, with its own annual journal, the aim of which was to make the black community aware of its own identity. It encouraged the Arts and especially theatre, and as a result various drama groups arose. On the 19 October 1977 all these organisations were banned, but this time banning was not synonymous with silence. Black awareness had become articulate and had begun to speak in too many voices to be stifled. It echoed the Black American Renaissance in poetry and strains of negritude were heard. 'Africa I Love You,' Bonsile Joshua Motaung sang, in the April 1977 issue of *Donga*. 'And like Senghor, Diop, Cesaire and Serote / I'll sing my love song to you.'

The tone of writing began to take on a new note. There was still protest against the conditions under which the black man lived but now there was an optimism not heard before, a new confidence that the future of South Africa belonged to the black African. The white man is no longer seen as an all-powerful disembodied force, but as contemptible and pathetic. In a story by Mango Tshabangu, 'Thoughts in a Train',[54] two boys, Msongi and Gezani, investigate why they always experience a feeling of uncanny fear when they walk through white suburbs. An incident when the whites-only coach of a train passed them gave the answer:

> On this day Msongi stared at the shut windows. He looked at the pale sullen white faces and he knew why.
>
> He felt tempted to throw something at them. Anything . . . an empty cigarette box, an orange peel, even a piece of paper; just to prove a point. At that moment, and as if instructed by Msongi himself, someone threw an empty beer bottle at their train.
>
> The confusion: they ran around climbing onto seats. They jumped into the air. They knocked against one another as they scrambled for the doors and windows. The already pale faces had no colour to change into. They could only be distorted as fear is capable of doing that as well. The shut windows were shattered wide open, as if to say danger cannot be imprisoned. The train passed swiftly by, disappearing with the drama of the fear the like of which Msongi and Gezani had never known.

Some poets sound a warning note. 'Without calling people to a sermon I do wish to point out that Black Consciousness does not mean politics disguised as literature,' says Mafika Gwala in *Staffrider* July/August 1979. Eventually he feels it will become redundant: 'I do not think I would have to worry about the term "black" if I went to live in Mozambique or Angola'.

Mphahlele, as we have seen, sees the black personality as subject to a diversity of definitions and interpretations. His own African-ness tells him, he says in *African Image*,[55] to turn away from the Christian-Hebrew God, and the Islamic God, towards his own ancestors, forces that are closer to him. This aspect, and an African direction and relevance in cultural education, he sees as the essentials. Elsewhere, he told a television interviewer that he himself had no sleepless nights wondering if he would eat or dress African the next day. His African values continued to remain a solid thing inside him, he said: the

African humanism and the sense of wanting to be one with a community. But at the same time he feels that it is neither possible nor desirable to switch back the clock and reject all western culture. His individualism he feels is the European part of him.

This attitude met with disapproval among militant writers elsewhere, especially in the United States, where African writing was now being measured according to a black aesthetic. While in South Africa reviewers of black poetry could still say in *Contrast* in 1977 that those who had participated in 'a rush to indiscriminate celebration' (of black poetry) had tended to lose sight of accepted criteria of criticism, black reviewers, editors and critics abroad were asking 'criteria accepted by whom?' and discarding Western preference as a standard for judgement.

Black South Africans, even those in exile, were therefore taken to task for leaning towards the West. I. Tagbo Nwogu, for example, in the *West African Review*, accused Mphahlele of being unrepresentative of independent Africa. At a conference on African Literature in French and the Universities in 1963, Mphahlele said that his body itched from the number of labels that had been stuck on him, and he felt he had been misunderstood.

Traditional literature is becoming increasingly important to black writers. Jordan K. Ngubane, a former South African newspaper editor and writer now living in the United States, attempted to write an adaptation of *umlando*, a Zulu vehicle which has 'been "reconditioned" to convey into the English milieu ideas conceived in a Zulu framework'. He says in the 'Foreward' [*sic*] to *Ushaba*:

> In my search for a satisfying vehicle through which I could tell at least part of the tragic story behind the vicious power-struggle between the African and the Afrikaner in my country, I eventually turned to the patterns of story-telling which my missionary teachers had condemned and rejected as heathen and barbaric. In the pages which follow I have adapted the *umlando* form of narrative as used by the ancient Zulus when they talked to themselves about themselves. *Umlando* was a vehicle for developing the collective wisdom or strength of the family, the clan or the nation. It is the form of narrative the Zulus employed to translate into action the principles . . . that (the) king rules by the grace of the people, and that the collective wisdom of the citizens leads to the truth. . . .[56]

Mazisi Kunene has produced an epic poem of more than 300 pages dealing with the life of Shaka. Written first in Zulu, he has translated it himself, keeping almost literally to the original text to emphasise the traditional heroic style. Much earlier A.C. Jordan, a Xhosa novelist, critic and lecturer, collected and wrote down the oral tales with which he grew up and formed them into a unique volume of written stories in English. After his death they were published in the United States in 1973, under the title *Tales from Southern Africa*.

These were mainly the attempts of the academic and established writers to foster pride in African history and culture, but for the less erudite Oswald Mtshali beat the *Sounds of the Cowhide Drum*.

His epoch-making volume of that title[57] was published by Lionel Abrahams's Renoster Books in 1971. Mtshali had previously given several poetry readings in Johannesburg. His poems had been appearing in literary magazines since 1968, after Mtshali had seen Lionel Abrahams's remarks in *The Rand Daily Mail* that blacks were noticeably absent among South African poets in the literary journals, and had sent him several of his poems. Abrahams allowed these to appear first in *The Classic* because of its greater black readership, then published several in *Purple Renoster* in the same year, to be followed by publication in *New Coin, Ophir, De Arte, UNISA English Studies, Star, Natal Daily News* and so forth. The subject matter of the poems is usually, though not always, some area of African life, whether it is urban as in 'The Moulting Country Bird', the country as in 'Reapers in a Mieliefield' or mines as in 'The Miner'. Mtshali does more than present the African in a situation. He reveals the urban South African experience in all its aspects: the horror of slum life, the tenderness and compassion, the sophistication and learning, the simplicity and all the overtones between. Mtshali becomes one with all black men. In Soweto, he says in 'Nightfall in Soweto':

Man has ceased to be a man
Man has become beast
Man has become prey.[58]

and the poet, on behalf of all those who suffer, becomes the helpless victim:

I am the prey!
I am the quarry to be run down
by the maurauding beast,
let loose by cruel Nightfall
from the cage of death.[59]

Mtshali is essentially the urban poet; his importance lies in having brought Africa in literature to the townships, and thus making black literature once again an independent medium in South Africa. When I interviewed him in Johannesburg in 1973,[60] I asked him how he would answer the rhetorical question which Nadine Gordimer asks in the Foreword to his poems:

Is he an African poet because he is black? Is he an English poet because he writes in English? Does he belong alongside Leopold Sedar Senghor of Senegal, Tchicaya U Tam'si of the Congo, Wole Soyinka and Christopher Okigbo of Nigeria, Jean-Joseph Rabearivelo of Madagascar, Mazisi Kunene, K.A. Nortje and Dennis Brutus of South Africa? Or do his songs of innocence and experience place him somewhere along with Blake, and his gifts of colloquial irony with the tradition of Auden, and his almost surgical imagery along with Sylvia Plath?

He replied:

> I belong to myself. I have read many poets, Black and White, English, African, American, Russian, French and German; but I cannot identify myself with any particular school or poetry movement. I am Black. I write in English. I draw upon the experiences of my life and those around me.[61]

But he knew where his purpose lay:

> I once thought I could evangelise and convert Whites to give us back our dignity. But now I have abandoned that line of approach. It is *naïveté* at its highest. I have now turned to inspire my fellow blacks to be proud, to strive, to seek their true identity as a single solid group.[62]

He ended the interview by saying:

> My poetry embodies many facets of life here. It also captures the moods of such diverse things that I do not only regard it as art but as a vehicle to carry the messages of the people. It is poetry committed to their struggle to be free. As such it has to be committed and carry a message.[63]

He has therefore succeeded in combining the two main streams that feed black literature in South Africa: black consciousness and struggle for freedom.

When Lionel Abrahams published *Sounds of a Cowhide Drum* as the first volume of Renoster Books it immediately became a phenomenal success. The first edition of 1600 copies was soon sold out and in less than two years there were five more editions. It was the first time a volume of poems had made a profit for a publisher in South Africa. A British edition (Oxford University Press) and an American one (Third World Press) followed. The poems began to appear in anthologies published in Britain and the United States.

Mtshali was interviewed by newspapers in South Africa and abroad. *The Rand Daily Mail* in Johannesburg invited him to write a fortnightly column, which he did until the end of 1972. An Australian television team filmed him and his family and the BBC invited him to read poems. He was invited to read his poetry during Poetry International 1973, Britain's famous annual festival of spoken poetry, in 1974 he was awarded the Olive Schreiner Prize and in 1975 the United States State Department brought him to the United States with a Fellowship in an International writing programme at the University of Iowa.

We will examine Mtshali's poetry later with a view to discovering why it was so tremendously popular and whether its success was deserved or whether, as many critics felt, the acclaim was exaggerated.

Few people doubt, however, that the publication of *Sounds of A Cowhide Drum* had begun a new era in black South African poetry. Asked why he chose the title of the collection from the last poem Mtshali explained that the cowhide drum is a symbol which can be used to express many moods and different occasions of his life. 'When war is declared, drums are beaten in a particular way; and when a baby is born, another tune is played on the drum.'

These were the sounds which were now echoed repeatedly by contributors to literary magazines. Since only a literature which made art part of the totality of living was felt to have meaning within an African context, it was only a small step in South Africa from black awareness to a militant expression of protest. It was a more deliberate form of protest than that of the Drum period, in that writers were now consciously committed to a cause. They believed that all writing must be relevant to the situation of the Black man in South Africa. This, then, became the black aesthetic in South Africa. Mbulelo Mzamane, as associate editor of the magazine *Donga*, in an essay entitled 'The Short Story Tradition in Black South Africa',[64] says that since writers can't say in Parliament that they want the white man off their backs they shout their message loudly and clearly. 'It doesn't pay to be too subtle, too many people choose to misunderstand you; there's little good in being too artistic either, very many people neglect the message and applaud the art.'

Mtshali was followed very soon by other poets whose work had appeared in the journals and who now had collections published, such as Serote, Gwala, Sipho Sepamla and Njabulo Ndebele, and also James Matthews who, during the silent period had turned from prose to poetry which he now published.

What was the reason for the spurt of poetry in place of prose works? At first the reason might have been one which Nadine Gordimer brought forward: that poems were less likely to fall foul of censorship because of their more intellectual appeal. This, however, only applied in the beginning. Some felt that the urgency of the situation was not conducive to more protracted writing, that a poem was the shortest route to the truth. It was also a more traditional form of art than the novel, for instance. Art for the African was always a community activity and never a matter for private contemplation. Thus many of the writers began by reading their poetry in groups. The element of sharing in art applies to drama, too, which also blossomed during this period. One reason which is sometimes overlooked is the fact that Mtshali and Serote were poets, and not writers in another genre, and as Sipho Sepamla put it: 'I think the writing that is happening today is an extension of what those guys started around here'.[65]

Once again the question arises of how these writers reconcile the expression of African ideals and values with the use of English, a Western language. It does not mean that they no longer take pride in their African home language. Asked about his impeccable use of English, as though it were his first language, Mtshali replied firmly: 'English is not my language. My home language is Zulu'. At one time he considered seriously writing only in Zulu. Since, however, there is no outlet for independent writing in that language in the only country in which it is spoken, he, Mazisi Kunene and others who are writing or want to write in the vernacular must keep their output for a future time. Writers justify their use of English also because the use of the vernacular would be tribally divisive; they have, in fact, adapted English as an African language. It is a new language with symbols and terms of its own. Mphahlele explains this as follows:

> They are doing something different with the English language. There is some African song at the back of their minds distilling itself into what they are writing. When a person writes a conversation piece, you hear that African music coming through. It's a residue of their memory. It isn't anything they've heard from their mother's lap; it's something that is accumulated over the many generations, and it comes through, so that when a person writes in English something happens in his mother tongue, in his own mind, and when it gets into print, it sends out something quite different from English English. We're seeing this happening all the time, which is incidentally part of a whole pattern of African literature throughout the continent.[66]

The poets were first published in the literary journals like *New Coin, Bolt, Ophir, Wurm, New Nation, Izwi* and *Donga*, some of which we have already discussed. *Donga*, first published in 1976, proclaimed in its first editorial that it aimed to break the isolation existing among writers of various cultural groups, and continued in future issues with an editorial policy which attempted to make the publication relevant to what was happening in South Africa. The final issue in 1977 had two articles on the teaching of literature in Africa, advocating African literature for the Africans. Its sixth issue, that of July 1977, announced the magazine's liaison with the black writers' group Medupe. This did not last long as Medupe was banned in the same year; its chairman, Damakude kaNdlovu, who was also an editor of *Donga* (for No. 7) left the country. Several issues were banned and when No. 8 was banned along with all future publications, *Donga* obviously came to an end. It was followed by

Inspan with an interest in critical work, but this survived for only two issues before it was banned. *Donga* had given a voice to many black writers, and some became guest editors. Mzamane was chief editor of No. 4.

In 1975, Sipho Sepamla was investigating the possibility of filling the gap in the area of writing for budding black writers, when Barney Simon suggested he take over the slender assets of *The Classic*. He duly launched *New Classic* which he still edits. He described the aims of the magazine as follows:

> We [Mbulelo Mzamane, Njabulo Ndebele, who gave him 'strength to go on' and he himself] were clear about art for art's sake. That was never our thing; nor the bit on universality. My black experience in the arts was something taken for granted. What remained was the ability to articulate my thoughts and feelings. *New Classic* existed to manifest this part of the black man's life. Contributions from non-blacks had to satisfy my kind of existence first: an unfair prerequisite, perhaps, but absolutely understandable under the circumstances.[67]

Under its new editorship of Jeffrey Haresnape, *Contrast*, on the other hand, emphasises 'artistic conscience' as opposed to ideology; but it includes a note for its twentieth anniversary from Nadine Gordimer in which she says: 'If the new editors can adapt Jack's (Cope) conscientious open-mindedness to a time when ideas of what South African literature *is* are being questioned as never before, *Contrast* could go on a long time past its 20th birthday, along with *Staffrider*, *Wietie*, *The Bloody Horse* and other welcome additions . . . .'[68]

The journals she mentions are the newcomers and of these *Staffrider* revolutionised periodical publishing in South Africa. It took writing out of its intellectual setting and brought it to the people. Its publishers were Ravan Press, owned after the banning of Peter Randall by Mike Kirkwood. The name of the magazine sets its tone: Kirkwood explains it as follows: '. . . a staffrider is somebody who rides "staff" on the fast, dangerous and overcrowded trains that come in from the townships to the city, hanging on to the sides of the coaches, climbing on the roof, harassing the passengers. A mobile, disreputable bearer of tidings. The idea had a certain flavour that made it right for the magazine.' The actual term 'staffrider' is derived from a way of boarding a train so as to get a free ride—usually whereby the prospective passenger jumps aboard at the last minute, and hangs on by a method usually practised by conductors, i.e. *staff*, of railways.

Staffrider began auspiciously by having its first issue banned. The Publications Directorate took the unusual step of giving reasons for the banning which were published in the second issue, May/June

1978. One of them was the purported undermining of 'the authority and image of the police, as the persons entrusted by the State with maintaining law, internal peace and order', of which several examples were given. One poem and one article were named as examples of material considered calculated to harm black/white relationships, and there was also objection to 'offensive language—such as the use of "f---" and its derivations, "p---" and "s----".'

Undaunted, *Staffrider* continued. The effect of reading several issues in succession is overwhelming. One gets the impression that here gathers a crowd of people who have been waiting to release a flood of pent-up emotions in words. *Staffrider* opened the sluice-gates and out it poured, good bad and indifferent. The stories and poems express life in the raw and speak of survival. The aim of *Staffrider* is simply to be read. 'To be published in *Staffrider* is to be *read*—more widely than literary artists have ever been read in South Africa.' And its definition of a literary artist: 'a producer of literary works'. If one is looking for literary quality in the Western sense one will find it. If one is looking for the voice of black Africa it is there. Established writers like Mphahlele and Rive rub shoulders with youthful members of small regional writers groups, published for the first time. Freedom songs alternate with serious literary essays. A profusion of pictorial art appears between the stories, columns and poems and an increasing number of reports on music groups. The individuality of the writer is played down: there are no biographical notes. There is little attempt to edit, even where necessary. The editors are doubtlessly in agreement with one of their reviewers, who excused flaws in a play as being due to cultural malnutrition. *Staffrider* is there to provide the nourishment. It lists no editors because various art groups linked to particular township communities provide the access of the producer to the reader. The art group puts forward the work it wants to be published and then assists in the distribution of the magazine to the community. Editorial control is therefore, as it were, in the hands of the readers. This is explained in a note at the end of the July/August 1978 issue. It continues:

> Those who suggest that *Staffrider* should appoint an editor whose task is to impose standards on the magazine are expressing—consciously or unconsciously—an elitist view of art which cannot comprehend the new artistic energies released in the tumult of 1976 and after. Standards are not golden or quintessential: they are made according to the demands different societies make on writers, and according to the responses writers make to those demands.

Notwithstanding the emphasis on community art several writers have become well-known through the pages of *Staffrider*, such as Ingoapele Mandigoane and Mtutuzeli Matshoba, or it has helped them expand the scope of their writings as in the case of Miriam Tlali who had already had a novel published. Just as the writers of the fifties were known as the *Drum* generation, so today's writers are beginning to be referred to as the *Staffrider* generation.

As the media became available, so fiction writers as well as poets emerged once again. Writers like Mbulelo Mzamane and Ahmed Essop found outlets for their work and subsequently had volumes published.

Academic publications began to pay attention to black writing as a reflection of efforts to put African literature into University syllabuses. *English in Africa* published by the Institute for the Study of English in Africa at Rhodes University leads the field. The entire September 1980 issue was devoted to 'the little South African Magazines', with editors and former editors of these journals relating the life-story of their publication. *UNISA English Studies*, the Journal of the Department of English Studies of the University of South Africa, published contributions by black writers.

Black South African writers were also included in anthologies published in South Africa. *Quarry* is an annual publication edited by Lionel Abrahams, and Stephen Gray edited a collection of short stories, *On the Edge of the World* and one of Poetry, *A World of their Own*, subtitled 'Southern African Stories', and 'Poets of the Seventies' respectively. Mtshali, Serote and Sepamla are well represented in the poetry anthology, and Peter Clarke, Ahmed Essop, Bessie Head, James Matthews, Mothobi Mutloatse, Sepamla, Serote, Mzamane and Adam Small feature in the prose work. *To Whom It May Concern* is an anthology of only black South African poetry edited by Robert Royston. *Forced Landing*, edited by Mutloatse, was published in the Ravan Staffrider Series and therefore reflects the work of *Staffrider*'s leading writers.

These anthologies, it will be noted, were published by independent publishers who had come into existence in the seventies. South African writers no longer had to aim at the African series of British publishers to appear in book form. Renoster Press, Ravan Press, Ad. Donker, Bateleur Press, David Phillip and others were all keen to publish black writing, both from a sense of conviction of their value and importance to South Africa and as a commercial proposition. The challenges were great. The writers were unknown, the price of the books had to be kept low for popular appeal; most of all the books were often banned resulting in enormous financial losses. In an effort to free themselves of what they still considered to be white patronage, however, a few black writers established their own publishing firms. Leading among these was the Blac Publishing Company of James Matthews.

On the surface things once again looked bright but then came the unrest of 1976 followed by ever-increasing bannings and detainments. Literature was in the forefront in the struggle between authority and the people. Many works were banned. Writers were banned, detained and harassed. The guest editor appointed by *Donga* for the second issue of September 1976, Jakes Gerwel of the University of the Western Cape, noted in his editorial that searching for the poets of that institution who had promised contributions for the magazine, he found that the poets were gone: the only poetry he could find was chanted at a mass meeting: *Jan Pierewiet, Jan Pierewiet staan stil, sodat ek jou in jou moer kan slaan* parodying an Afrikaans folksong (the words mean: 'Jan Pierewiet stand still so that I can kick you in the guts!).

Poetry was found at the graveside of those shot during the riots when young boys and girls, boycotting their schools, would declaim their 'freedom songs'. Again some of the writers began to leave. Mtshali went to the United States on a study programme. A group of writers including Serote established themselves in Swaziland. Others went underground. In South Africa groups were formed and banned. The Federated Union of Black Arts was split into factions and the Johannesburg branch of PEN was disbanded because many of its members insisted on an all-black organisation. This is where South African black writing stands today. It is summed-up succinctly by Achmed Dangor in a poem entitled 'The Voices That Are Dead'. It begins:

> There is a silence
> upon the river tonight
> No great floods of song
> flow out into the darkness,
> our voices are dead.

and continues later

> Oh, my brothers—
> you too are dead,
> your voices rage barrenly
> within the august halls
> of the doomed,
>
> but are not heard
> by the cowherd who treads
> his unknowing peace,
> nor is it heard
> in the ashen townships
> where soon your memory
> will flit unlovingly
> from one darkness to the next.

But underneath it all there is a rumble of defiance and hope, a vision of order:

though the voice I hear
in the icy dawn
is still frail and tremulous,
and the mists are a portend
of a familiar and savage storm

I can sing a hymn
to the glory of my land
from the ashes something stirs
new voices are being heard.[69]

Poetry

POETRY IS THE only form of literature by black writers in South Africa which has led in an almost direct line from the oral vernacular to the modern in either the vernacular or English. In introducing *Zulu Poems*, a volume of his poetry in English published in 1970, Mazisi Kunene pointed out that these were not English poems but poems directly evolved from a Zulu literary tradition. He said:

> Zulu literature, like most African literatures, is communal. This has fundamental stylistic and philosophical implications. The communal organisation in Africa is not just a matter of individuals clinging together to eke out an existence, as some have claimed . . . It is a communal organisation which has evolved its own ethic, its own philosophical system, its own forms of projecting and interpreting its realities and experiences . . . It believes, for instance, that the highest virtue is . . . heroism, that is, self sacrifice on behalf of the community. Accordingly, it has developed a highly sophisticated heroic epic. Where individual-istic societies read 'I', this philosophy requires one to read 'I on behalf of'.[1]

Here lies the crux of the difference between Western poetry of the past two centuries and African poetry.

Oswald Joseph (Mbuyiseni) Mtshali, in some of the poems in *Sounds of a Cowhide Drum*[2] demonstrates the use of the concept of 'I' in the collective sense. In a poem entitled 'The Master of the House', for example, he says:

> I am a faceless man
> who lives in the backyard
> of your house.
> I am the nocturnal animal
> that steals through the fenced lair
> to meet my mate
> and flees at the break of dawn
> before the hunter and the hound
> run me to ground.[3]

Rarely do we find deeply personal emotions in the poetry of those writers who consciously follow African traditions. This is not because they are incapable or even unwilling to express their inner feeling. They simply do not see this as the purpose of poetry. H.I.E. Dhlomo, in 'Valley of a Thousand Hills', becomes deeply introspective in the fourth section in which he derides himself as a failure and asks why he should live 'If Life no rich gifts I can give', but he finds the answer in the beauty of nature and chides himself for being too 'encased in self'. It is only when he can stand 'beyond space and time' that he can create.

Protest in poetry does not appear as an alien element to the traditional African poet, since traditional poems usually had a purpose, often to express a message or glorify war. Vilakazi, the Zulu poet, it is true, condemned 'a reactionary attitude of bitterness' when discussing Dhlomo's poems, and chides the younger writers for producing second-rate and negligible controversial matter on political subjects, thus delaying 'the development of purely artistic expression'.[4] He has sometimes been accused by black critics of being insufficiently conscious of the sufferings of his people, yet this is disproved by some of his own poems such as 'In the Goldmines',[5] which gives a compassionate picture of just such suffering. H.I.E. Dhlomo's early poems are often variations on the theme of 'we who believe that human souls, like Art are one in God'.[6] In 'Not for Me' he protests against the breaking of political promises made to the black man during World War II:

Not for me
Ah! not for me
the celebrations
The peace Orations,
Not for me,
Yes not for me
The victory
And liberty!
Of the Liberty I died to bring in need;
And this betrayal wounds and sears my soul.
I bleed.[7]

Again we find in these poems, as in Mtshali's 'The Master of the House', that the protest is made not on behalf of the poet, but in the name of 'the faceless man', the anonymous black man.

Often we find in the imagery of black poetry a complicated system of symbols which works on several levels and requires a knowledge of history, myth and legend. These poets are not trying to create African versions of a 'Waste Land' but are following African traditional poetry. In Mazisi Kunene's 'The Proud'[8] for instance, it is necessary to know who Nodongo and Domndeni are, in order to understand the poem. This type of reference he explains in his collection *Zulu Poems*. Proper names in Zulu poetry, he says, are often part of a system of ideas or personifications. This is because the names bear meanings expressive of events. Thus the name 'Mpindelela' means 'recurrent' which in the following lines is the name of a fountain and at the same time describes the action of the fountain and symbolises recurrent yearnings:

> May I when I awake
> Take from all men
> The yearnings of their souls
> And turn them into the fountain of Mpindelela
> Which will explode into oceans.[9]

Njabulo S. Ndebele, a South African at the then University of Botswana and Swaziland at Roma, advocated the use of African imagery in *Expression*, a journal of the University's English Society, of which he was co-editor. In his poetry he consciously makes use of such imagery to convey his meaning. In 'Five Letters to M.M.M.'[10] he expresses love in terms of 'the moon as the Holy Missile of Love rather than the rose', thus, according to the editorial of the issue in which this poem appears, carrying out the journal's aim of drawing inspiration from African myths, superstitions and moral codes. This means, the editorial continues, recognising to the fullest extent 'the interdependence of man and the earth', which Ndebele demonstrates again in a poem about 'Little Dudu'[11] who 'slid off a cheek of God / And was born into the world' where he '. . .lay on his belly / On the dome of the hippo's mouth'.

Keorapetse Kgositsile, writing in the United States, also goes back to his roots in choosing his symbols but his choice is more stylised. His entire collection *My Name is Afrika*[12] is based on a system of certain key symbols associated with collective human consciousness. The words 'memory', 'dream', 'rebirth', occur again and again. Words like 'mother' and 'baobab', for instance, signify Africa. 'Fire' represents the fight for freedom, and in words like 'pulse' and 'dance' or in sexual symbolism, lies hidden a fiercely passionate protest explicit only to the initiated. These are the militant black Americans with whom he has made common cause, and who recognise him as one of their leading poets. He speaks, for example, of Meadowland and Harlem in the same breath.

The beginnings of African poetry in English in South Africa go back to 1937. The previous year James J.R. (James [*sic*] Ranisi) Jolobe, a Presbyterian Minister, educationalist, poet, novelist, playwright and translator into Xhosa, had won the May Esther Bedford prize for a poem entitled 'U-Mthithula'. This prize was awarded annually under the auspices of London University for poems in an African language, and a translation into English had to be submitted with the entry. Jolobe translated the poem himself as 'Thuthula', and it was published in London in 1937. Jolobe continued to write poetry in Xhosa and received many honours for it. In 1952 he received the Vilakazi Memorial prize, in 1953 the Afrikaanse Pers Boekhandel first prize for a collection of poems, and in 1957 he won the Margaret Wrong Memorial Medal and Prize for outstanding services to literature in South Africa. Apart from his ministerial duties, Jolobe taught English, Child Psychology, and School Method at the Lovedale Training College. He assisted with a Xhosa-English-Afrikaans Dictionary project at Fort Hare, and became a member of the Advisory Council when the University College became a full University. The University bestowed the doctoris honoris degree on him in 1974 in recognition of his contribution to Xhosa literature. He was on the editorial board of *Outlook*.

In *Bantu Literature and Life* Shepherd tells us that Jolobe was convinced of the distinctive contribution Africans would make to literature in the realm of poetry. They would arise, he said, and make known the soul of Africa. It must have become obvious to him that in order to do so they would have to aim at a wider audience through an English medium. Thus, in 1946, Lovedale Press published his *Poems of an African*. They were translations by the author of his own Xhosa poems which had appeared in a volume of the Bantu Treasury series of the University of the Witwatersrand. The collection includes 'Thuthula',[13] extracts of which have also appeared in several anthologies.

'Thuthula' is founded on a well-known incident in history which led to war between two Xhosa tribes. The chief of one tribe had fallen under the influence of Christianity through the seer Ntsikana, and, in order to discredit Ntsikana and his disciple, the chief of the other tribe, Nqgika, was encouraged by members of his tribe to raid the territory of his rival chief, Ndlambe, and abduct his wife Thuthula. Thuthula, who had known and loved Nqgika in the past and had been forced to marry the much older Ndlambe, makes '. . . her awful choice / With sigh both deep and sad from troubled soul'.[14] She goes to her beloved, thus losing 'the crown of womanhood' to become 'a husk without a character'.[15] Her dreadful deed can perhaps be explained but not excused:

> For marriage vows are precious far beyond
> all other pleasures that may win the heart.
> Perhaps 'twas love that tempted thee, poor dame,
> The pain of being weaned from thy soul twin,
> On altar of *lobola* sacrificed.
> Forsooth, that was a death in life, but this
> Is death, and yes, a death seven times o'er.[16]

Justice and morality triumph, however, when 'the kindlers of the fire'—those who had suggested the plan to Chief Nqgika—are killed and become 'the food of vultures wild',[17] and Thuthula is returned to Ndlambe's kraal where 'she was pardoned for her lapse'.[18]

The other three poems in this collection are a sonnet, 'To Light, An Ode To The Fallen',[19] and an elegy, 'In Memory',[20] with the refrain 'Mother mine, beauty of the Thembu clan'.

It is strange that this poet, who wrote mainly in the language of his forebears and at a time when the sound of traditional oral literature was still to be heard around him, should have written poetry which is so utterly derivative in thought, construction and style, in everything in fact except subject matter. One can only conclude that he was so completely under the spell of his missionary surroundings as to make him an undiscriminating admirer of all the literature he absorbed there. How could he speak of the soul of Africa when he was suppressing all genuine sentiment under a conglomeration of everything artificial and sentimental in English nineteenth-century literature? Some of the lines from Thuthula quoted above read like a parody of Tennyson. Less than ten years, but a great deal more of worldly experience, lie between H.I.E. Dhlomo's poem 'Not for Me' quoted earlier and Jolobe's 'To the Fallen'. While Dhlomo's soul bleeds for the betrayal of African soldiers, Jolobe sees them as looking 'beyond and seeing the fruit / . . . vast gains / To their own race, to mankind and the world'.[21] He gives 'Sweet comfort, Heaven's gift' to their mourners and exhorts the 'Divine Restorer' to 'wipe away all tears'.[22] As a writer in Xhosa, Jolobe is generally recognised as a man of deep philosophy and sensitivity. These qualities emerge in his Xhosa novels, which are described by B.E.N. Mahlasela[23] as being direct and unornamented in style, often moving in content and flowing with natural ease and dignity. His Xhosa poems, too, appear to be devoid of undigested Western literary trappings. In Imbongi yesizwe particularly, Mahlasela tells us, where Jolobe 'has written in praise of Mqhayi, the Xhosa poet laureate, . . . he seems to have completely abandoned every trace of foreign influence and poured out his soul in strict Xhosa verse forms of expression'.[24] Even in his religious poems he makes use of African imagery and tradition. To a large extent this appears to be true of 'Thuthula' in its original Xhosa version. It would perhaps be kinder, then, to eliminate Jolobe from a study of English writing, since he translated his poems mainly for the conditions of the prize entry.

It cannot be denied, however, that Jolobe is as proficient as Dhlomo in English, and that he handles the poetic forms he uses competently. His metrical skill is shown in lines such as:

Closed are the eyes to what we can see,
Dull is the ear to sounds of this world.

Still is the mouth and cold are the hands.
Mother mine, beauty of the Thembu clan.[25]

His passage in the sonnet 'To Light', from the particular in the first
eight lines to the general in the last six, shows his understanding of
this form of poetry.

Like Jolobe, Dhlomo also considered the question of the
contribution of the African to literature, and came to the conclusion
that rhythm was the greatest gift the black man had brought to it. In a
treatise on 'African Drama and Poetry', published in *Outlook* in
1939, he carefully laid out his argument in favour of a flexible form in
poetry and arrived at rhythm as a solution, a rhythm which 'is more
than a physical sensation. It is inspired by uniformity in motion,
giving birth to thought and emotion and vision'.[26] One suspects,
however, that his arguments were chiefly designed to provoke
Vilikazi who at the time was experimenting with rhyme in Zulu, and
who replied in a letter to the effect that Dhlomo did not understand
the forms which he was attempting to discuss.

These quarrels, fascinating as they may be to us from a distance of
forty years, are purely theoretical and bear little relationship to
Dhlomo's poetry, except for his comment on blank verse as most
suitable for African poetry, a form which he used largely in his best
known and longest poem, 'Valley of a Thousand Hills'. It was
published in Durban in 1941 and was so popular that it went into two
further printings, in March 1942 and March 1944. In 1962 it was
republished and the proceeds of this edition went to a childrens'
feeding fund.

In this poem, Dhlomo attempts to find himself as an African in an
alien society—through God as expressed in the beauty of nature on
the one hand, and through a pride in his past on the other. At the very
beginning, both themes combine when he calls upon his ancestral
spirits to give him power:

This magic sight to hold, imprison, sing!
This myriad beauty of the Thousand Land.[27]

The Valley becomes 'the skipping playing ground of tribal gods',[28]
and he sings songs of praise and supplication to some of these gods,
such as 'sweet Phunga', to whom he appeals:

Give us the mind
To soar above our present days
Of crippling strife.[29]

He then proceeds to paint a romantic picture of tribal life where 'god-
like wrinkled men—great sages, hunters, warriors'[30] are gathered
around 'The frothing choc'late, warm *utshwala* pots',[31] discussing
philosophy and law.

In the second section, the poet becomes more personal and tells how he came back to the country to see 'The arum-lily of my native streams'[32] long after 'to a foreign devil beast / In female form myself had tied'.[33] He cannot pluck the flower, because he dare not shirk those ties that are strangling him. He and the flower fail to understand each other and when finally understanding dawns, the flower droops and is plucked by a passer-by. Now the poet identifies himself with the flower and sings a song of pain. This continues into the third and fourth section, in which he craves for the freedom and beauty of the land to which he feels he no longer belongs. Fate is a whim of the gods and 'not good but power is worshipped everywhere'.[34] Death is the consummation, and there seems to be no reason why the poet should continue to live. The answer comes in a long section in which he states his belief:

> Awake! Arise! and see the beauty of
> The Valley of a Thousand Hills—and live.[35]

Having come to terms with himself and God through beauty, he now sees a vision of past, present and future. The past becomes part of the peacefully beautiful moonlight night, the present is a tortured vision of 'twanging tunes of clashing colour themes'. The future gives a varying picture of 'the broken people of the land',[36] the hopeful calm note of the soul of the past, a blunt voice exhorting the people to rise and fight.

In the final section, the Valley fills with a different vision, one in which life begins anew, 'Buds burst into a flower of peace', birds 'Take to the skies in song! It is our soul!'[37] A new dawn is about to emerge. The epilogue calls upon the creator to let beauty reign supreme.

The theme of the poem expresses his conviction that if we can feel external beauty as representing both God and the individual soul, which are as one, then there is hope for a world of love and truth without pain. The graves will have burst agape and the ancestral spirits will have arisen. No longer will the African be an outcast in his land, and 'lie and rot / Beneath a foreign yoke . . .'[38]

Now

> all earth is purged and we enthroned
> The picture from the Hills is painted full.[39]

The poem is carefully constructed. The beauty of the land introduces the former might of the Zulu nation and then carries us through the poet's attempts to find himself. Through the inspiration of the vision of the past we are led to a message of hope.

In its style the long poem often demonstrates a curious mixture of control and ineptitude. Dhlomo's descriptions of nature aim at a quiet classical pastoralism but he is often provoked into romantic outpourings. While some of these are full of descriptive vitality and vivid movement, for example:

> Silent a bird floats past, and far away
> A drunken whisk of smoke staggers about
> This way and that, and wastes itself to naught![40]

Other lines are less felicitous and far too effusive.

It is the heavy leaning on English romantic poetry which often leads him from the path of simple and direct communication of his African ideals and this detracts from the poem. Moreover, it has led to a misunderstanding among critics of the late nineteen-fifties who wrote him off as a romantic escapist. They saw only the romantic poet, extolling nature in the style of Tennyson and Scott, putting the Western ideals of the individual soul before that of the collective black nation. Among the rhetoric of descriptions of nature and the poet's pain they missed the directive lines such as: 'No longer mine but tortured visions of / The race I see . . .',[41] in which he puts into words his conviction that in communal life all things are one and that man is God and God man; and the exhortation, in the name of the heroes of old:

> We'll strike and take! If others will not give.[42]

It is interesting to note that Dhlomo himself quotes these lines and those preceding them in an article entitled 'Masses and the Artist' to illustrate the contention that 'Our tribal Heroes were dauntless practical men who faced problems of their times and place fearlessly', and that 'Today, wherever they be, they would like to see us facing our Day as courageously, actively, militantly'.[43]

Dhlomo's shorter poems were published mainly in *Ilanga Lase Natal* and *Bantu World*. Recently research into these and other newspapers has been undertaken under the sponsorship of the Institute for the Study of English in Africa at Rhodes University, Grahamstown, and it is to be hoped that a collection will be published soon. T.J. Couzens has unearthed a great many poems, even to the extent of identifying those written under pseudonyms. He and N.W. Visser came across a manuscript table of contents of a projected volume of Dhlomo's shorter poems which listed 133 titles.[44] There are several, such as 'The Nile', voicing the agony of the African as an outcast in his land:

> This beauty's not for me! My
> home is not
> My home! I am an outcast in my land![45]

lines which he repeats in 'Valley of a Thousand Hills'.

Very little poetry was published during the next years. Peter

Abrahams, better known later for his novels, wrote poetry while still in South Africa. He was influenced by the Marxist movement and contributed poems, all radical in their protest, to *Cape Standard* between 1938 and 1939. A collection of his poems, *A Blackman Speaks of Freedom*,[46] appeared in about 1940. Poems by other black contributors are still buried in the stacks in publications such as *Bantu World*, *Ilanga Lase Natal* and *The Voice*, but research is under way to collect and assess them.

I have shown in chapter 1 how the nineteen-sixties saw the introduction of a spate of South African literary journals, many of them devoted to the publication of poetry; how, by 1968, they were beginning to include contributions by black poets, and then how the publication of Oswald Mtshali's volume of poems *Sounds of a Cowhide Drum* began a new era in South African literature. Let us now look somewhat closer at the man and his poetry and examine why it was so successful. Could it have been a matter of the right man being there at the right time? Perhaps events in the early life of the poet formed a basis for his subsequent success. Mtshali is a Zulu and therefore born to a people with a strong tradition of poetry. Although his parents were teachers in a Catholic mission school and his mother particularly saw to it that he received a good English education, Zulu tradition formed an early influence. In a paper on black poetry in South Africa, delivered at the University of Iowa, he tells the story of how a friend of the family, a woman in her nineties, took him on a tour of a row of caves in the Lebombo Mountains in the Northern part of Zululand. The caves had been used as a hiding place during the wars between the Zulus and Swazis and the Zulus and whites. He says:

> Some of the dwellers in those caves were my ancestors who fled Shaka's wrath and vengeance after he and his army invaded Ntabankulu (Big Mountain), the ancestral home of the Mtshali clan. Later on some of my forbears settled in Northern Zululand and Swaziland.
>
> Though I was quite young when I was told this exciting bit of my history, I still remember it as vividly as if that old crone had related it to me last night. I remember seeing the timeless relics of my past, like claypots, crude iron tools and a kiln where iron was smelted to forge assegais [imikhonto], battle axes [izizenze], hatchets [ocelemba], and of course hoes [amageja] for tilling the soil.[47]

Born in Vryheid, Natal, in 1946, Mtshali moved to the Transvaal townships around Johannesburg. When the volume was published he was a scooter-messenger for a pharmacy. The readers of *Sounds of a Cowhide Drum* therefore believed that they were witnessing a romantic success story of the slum child making good. Yet it was not quite like that. Mtshali had matriculated and had the opportunity of obtaining a University education like his older brothers. By that time, however, the Bantu Education Act had been passed and he was refused entry to the white institution in Johannesburg, the University of the Witwatersrand. He refused to go to the black university allocated to him in protest against the act. Political feeling therefore also played an important part in his youth. When fame drew to him the attention of the Security Police, and he was pulled in several times for questioning, he had run the full gamut of black township life.

He succeeded because of his genius in putting this experience into words. White readers found his poetry fascinating because it gave them a window into black life, and black readers identified with his projection of their thoughts. 'I am convinced that my poetry echoes the feelings, aspirations, hopes, disappointments of many Blacks here in South Africa',[48] he told me. Mongane Wally Serote, addressing a conference at the University of Texas in 1976, recalling the popularity of the book after the long silence of black writers, said: 'God knows, the ghettoes, starved like that, devoured that book'. Mtshali makes his impact by his astounding capacity for absorbing and reflecting impressions and reproducing these, not instinctively— the simplicity is deceptive—but with the deliberate awareness of the craftsman. His much-quoted poem 'Boy on a Swing'[49] is a good example. The first two stanzas are a simple description of the boy swinging. Only in the last line of the second stanza, worked in as part of the visual action, do we realise that this is not just any child but a deprived one:

> His blue shirt
> billows in the breeze
> like a tattered kite.

In the next stanza the whirling motion is no longer visual but becomes transformed into the child's thoughts. The reader is suddenly brought up short in the last stanza, when he realises that this is not a little boy experiencing the unthinking joys of childhood. *His* world which whirls by, contains questions no boy on a swing should have to ask in the same breath with the more normal pursuits of childhood:

> Mother!
> Where did I come from?
> When will I wear long trousers?
> Why was my father jailed?

Not all black readers were happy with Mtshali's work. Mbulelo Vizikhungo Mzamane, in an article entitled 'The 50s and Beyond: An Evaluation'[50] holds against him mainly the impact he made on whites: the paternalism of Nadime Gordimer, for instance, in overemphasising his Blake-like simplicity and innocence. Black writers were suspicious of his appeal to white readers who, even in South Africa, bought his book by the thousands, awarded him prizes and lionised him personally. Some of the younger writers were disappointed at the lack of revolutionary fire.

Several white critics accused Mtshali's poems of being prosaic, too contrived, producing crude rhythms, lack of subtlety and poetic tension. This may be true at times, but essentially the critics were looking for something remote from Mtshali's aims. He was trying to make a direct approach so that the appeal of the poems was immediate, and this he achieved by etching his images with bold and well-defined strokes. The following lines are typical of what Nadine Gordimer in the Foreword to his collected poems describes as 'almost surgical imagery'.

> The cow cuts
> The shiny coat
> as a child would
> lick a toffee
> with a tongue as pink as
> the sole of a foot.

The calf sways

> . . . on legs
> filled with jelly and custard
> instead of bone and marrow.[51]

These earthy, almost rollicking, images create an impact as surely as do the more sophisticated similes which he handles with equal confidence, as for instance in one of his most striking descriptions:

> The sun spun like
> a tossed coin
> It whirled on the azure sky.
> It clattered on the horizon.
> It clicked in the slot
> and neon lights popped
> and blinked 'Time Expired'
> as on a parking meter.[52]

He likes to use direct comparisons rather than symbols. The Newly Born Calf in the poem of that title

> Is like oven baked-bread
> Steaming under a cellophane cover,

and 'An old man in church' 'hits . . . God's heart with screams as hard as stones / flung from the slingshot of the soul'.[53] Again, in the first stanza of a poem entitled 'The Shepherd and his Flock'[54] he compares the rays of the sun with 'a pair of scissors / cutting the blanket / of dawn from the sky'. This is followed by a description of a young shepherd driving his sheep into the veld. The pastoral scene of the reed-flute-playing boy amid the 'marvels / of a summer morning' is broken only at the end when the boy expresses his envy of children going to school. As in 'Boy on a Swing' and many other of his poems, the last line scores a direct hit.

This direct approach enables the reader, or better still the listener, since these poems are meant to be recited, to identify with the poet's varying moods: his scorn for hypocrisy in a world where

Love and Truth
are sugar-coated words
offered to Sunday school children[55]

or his despair when he sees a train going 'on its way to nowhere carrying six men shorn / of all human honour',[56] handcuffed, manacled, devoid of hope; his irony when watching pigeons trespassing on private property and defying the Immorality Act[57]; his compassion for all who suffer, especially child victims of deprivation ('The Face of Hunger') or racial hatred; his horror at the sordidness of township life where dogs tear at the mutilated corpse of an abandoned baby ('An Abandoned Bundle')—a scene which Nadine Gordimer has described as surely one of the most shocking poems ever written; or his song of soaring hope expressed in the approaching rumble and roll of the sounds of the drum.

Mtshali's greatest asset, therefore, was his ability to communicate, at a time when blacks were eager to find a spokesman and still willing to communicate with whites who were prepared to listen. By looking upon poetry as a form of communication, rather than as the intellectual pursuit of crystalising individual thought, Mtshali became an exponent of African culture. Moreover, Mtshali's writing moves with the rhythm of feeling to provide a particular emotional atmosphere which Dhlomo saw as essentially African. Looking again at 'Boy on a Swing', we find that he starts on a quiet note of routine living and works towards a climax like the increasing rise and fall of a swing until 'the four cardinal points / meet in his head', and the very essence of human and black life is questioned.

His bold rhythms, combined with an ease of phrasing, are often achieved by splitting a sentence into two lines in such a way that the important part—usually the subject of the sentence—is emphasized by standing alone, for example:

Handcuffs
have steel fangs.[58]

The deliberate slow-moving gait of the poem 'Amogoduke at

Glencoe Station'[59] seems almost like prose until it is read aloud, for which indeed all Mtshali's poetry is designed.

Mtshali rarely uses rhyme, usually only to emphasise an irony hidden behind the preceding lines. The washerwoman in 'A Washerwoman's Prayer', for instance, who has on 'frost-freckled mornings / In sun-scorched afternoons', drudged 'murmurless', shouts to God when she collapses with weariness one day:

'My child! Dear child,' she heard,
'Suffer for those who live in gilded sin,
Toil for those who swim in a bowl of gin'.[60]

Regular metre, too has been discarded, but like many black poets in English and the vernacular, he finds assonance and alliteration a method of creating a phonic pattern; for example:

The Marble Eye
is an ornament
coldly carved by craftsmen
to fill an empty socket
as a corpse fills a coffin.[61]

We will meet the poet again, a different Mtshali, ten years later after he had spent several years abroad. In 1971, when *Sounds of a Cowhide Drum* was first published, he was the herald of a new poetry.

Whereas Mtshali is the declamatory poet aiming at rapport with an audience, Mongane Wally Serote is the poet who sings spontaneously. In other circumstances he might have been a lyrical poet of joy and beauty. Much of his poetry falls easily on Western ears because it follows English poetry both in the flow of the verse and in the imagery. Like Mtshali he was prepared to address a white readership at the beginning. In the poem 'City Johannesburg', he reveals to the white man that he has a stranger in his midst who sees his city with very different eyes. Serote's appeal for communication in his poem 'Ofay-Watcher, Throbs-Phase',[62] is often quoted:

White people are white people,
They are burning the world.
Black people are black people,
They are the fuel.
White people are white people,
They must learn to listen.
Black people are black people,
They must learn to talk.[63]

But Serote does not really see as his function the teaching of the races to speak to each other. His poetry tells what he himself feels. He absorbs and articulates his surroundings. There is a gentleness and understanding in his poetry. Silence, watchfulness, intuition, are often the keynotes. The predominant mood is one of sadness. It is the horror of what is happening around him that forces his mood to change and almost to wring the anguished words from him and force them into lines.

> i sit here,

he writes in *No Baby Must Weep*

> bursting words between my wringing fingers
> like ripe boils.[64]

> 'God,'

he says in 'A Wish to Eye God'

> May it happen that one day
> . . .
> I will no longer write about people
> dying in the street and bleeding through the ears and eyes
> and babies suffocating in suitcases in muddy dongas.[65]

He is driven to a helpless and often almost incoherent rage. But it never turns to hate. In the poem 'Waking up, the Sun, the Body' he says:

> For what do you do when, again and again,
> Things around and in you beg you with a painful embrace to hate,
> And you respond with a rage and you know,
> That you can never hate.
> This is a waking deep as the distance of the sun,
> Mind-defying as the knowledge of God.[66]

Even in the horrifying 'Poem on Black and White', based on a true incident in which a white train driver poured petrol on a black child's face and set it alight, he cannot envisage any sweetness in revenge, were the position to be reversed:

> I wonder how I will feel when his eyes pop
> and when my nostrils sip the smell of his flesh
> and his scream touches my heart
> i wonder if i will be able to sleep.[67]

Serote's poems, like Mtshali's, were first published in the literary journals *Purple Renoster*, *Bolt*, *New Coin* and *Contrast*, during 1971 and 1972. Again it was *Purple Renoster* which introduced him, with what was in fact the first poem by a black contributor in these journals. It made its impact immediately, with its title 'What's in this Black "S---"' and its graphically outspoken condemnation of white inhumanity to black. It is included in Serote's first collection,

Yakhal' inkomo, also published by Renoster Books, in 1972. At this time Serote was living in Alexandra and working as a copywriter in an advertising firm. Born in Sophiatown in 1944, he reached Form IV in high school education. In June 1969 he had been detained under the Terrorism Act and released nine months later without having been charged. He tells how his first reading of the writers of the nineteen-fifties came as a revelation to him, and how he realised that his generation was being cheated out of its literary heritage. The arrests, bannings, exiling and the brutal laws were what shaped him, he told an audience at a conference on South African writing at the University of Texas in 1975.

Critics naturally compared his work with that of Mtshali and generally found him the more accomplished poet, though it was felt that the work was very uneven. The title of the collection represents the cry of cattle at the slaughter house, as Serote explains in the preface and again in the August 1973 issue of *Bolt*. It is based on a story told him by a sculptor friend who saw people kill a cow near a kraal, and in the kraal were cattle looking on and he heard them cry. 'He said they cried, they raged, they stabbed each other with their horns, they cried and thought they would bring their shelter to the ground, and they cried, just *mooed* the pain into his heart, they dug the ground with their hoofs, they saw their kind die at the hands of human beings, they saw the blood and they saw it fall . . .'.[68] Serote compares the sound with the music of a tenor saxophone player, expressing the same cry of fear and rage.

Serote echoes the cry of his people. In the poem 'Alexandra', for instance,[69] he speaks of his own intense feelings that link him to the township:

You throb in my inside silences
You are silent in my heart-beat that's loud to me,[70]

but he is also identifying with his birthplace as one of its sons. When he returned to it '. . . amid the rubble I lay / Simple and black'.[71]

The poems in *Yakhal' inkomo* throb with the poet's heartbeat, against a background of dim lights, shadows, dust, dongas, mud, barbed wire fences, fears, tears, blood and death. Some of the poems are slow and contemplative, others pace with the rhythm of urgency.

I do not know where I have been,
But Brother,
I know I'm coming.
I do not know where I have been,
But Brother
I know I heard the call.[72]

These are the first lines in a poem entitled 'Hell, well, Heaven', which describes the poet's arousal from the depth of despair. Serote is at his best when he encapsules the welter of emotions in clear images; for instance in these lines in the poem 'During Thoughts after Ofay Watching':[73]

> We are caught up in a turning tide,
> Slow; taking its pace, slow;
> Throbbing like the pulse of one dying,
> The turning tide, we are caught up there
> Where the waves break before they ripen,

or when the poem is a simple and lyrical expression of deep thought as in 'I Will Wait' which I quote in full:

> I have tasted, ever so often,
> Hunger like sand on my tongue
> And tears like flames have licked my eye-lids
> Blurring that which I want to see,
> I want to know.
> But Oh! often, now and then, everywhere where I have been,
> Joy, as real as paths,
> Has spread within me like pleasant scenery,
> Has run beneath my flesh like rivers glitteringly silver;
> And now I know:
> Having been so flooded and so dry,
> I wait.[74]

Sometimes however, the meaning is obscured behind symbols too personal to be accessible. At other times the pronouncements on the meaning of life are too pat and immature.

Tsetlo, his second collection, was published by Ad. Donker in Johannesburg in 1974. Whereas *Yakhal' inkomo* was the agonising cry of the cattle watching their kind being slaughtered, *Tsetlo*, more subtly, is the tiny bird with the 'weird sweet whistle which it plays while it flies from branch to branch in the bush, luring people to follow it . . . And then it stops. It may lead you to sweet honey, to a very dangerous snake or to something very unusual'.[75] Serote's concept of the world has widened and the mood has deepened. Sadness is still predominant but it has become firmer. He no longer speaks of returning to the bosom of Alexandra and lying amid the rubble, but mourns its passing and remembers it, in 'Amen Alexandra', like '. . . a thunder clap / that froze in our hearts'.[76] There is less talk of tears and desolation.

> If you stop weeping, you may see
> because that is how knowledge begins,

he says in 'Near the Hole'.[77]

Yet the tragedy of black life seems to have seeped even deeper into his being. 'Even screams don't come into dreams like this', he says in

'Death Survey',[78] where a man is chased by knife-wielding thugs, a
boy has his brains beaten out and a bulldozer razes a house to the
ground. Reality and nightmare blend into one. In 'Eyes Over my
Shoulder' he switches from sleep to wakefulness, from inside a room
to the outside world of the township, almost in a trance. Mostly the
poet is in control. He sees himself almost objectively, holding his
heart in his 'right hand / like a jacket' or wearing his life 'which covers
my heart with a leaping flame',[79] but sometimes nightmare inevitably
leads to melodrama as the images of spilt blood, leaping flames,
screaming whores, gaping graves, accumulate. Again, he is at his most
powerful when he transforms his experience into vivid simple images,
and especially when these are sustained throughout the poem. One of
the most successful in this respect is 'The Seed and the Saints'[80] in
which the poet—the black man—is a tree growing from seed,
nurtured by the heroes—saints and prophets—of Africa through the
seasons of the earth, until the wish dream of his saints come to
fruition in him.

There is new militant hope in some of the poems. Serote attempts
to shake off his lethargy, he covers his eyes to shade away horror while
he prepares himself, for he knows that the 'dry white season' will
come to pass,[81] that 'the pulse of time'[82] rushes ahead. But his vision
of a future, where 'black child's laughter will ring in the dark sky' still
holds no joy in vengeance for him. He ends the poem 'Sunset':

I wonder where I'll cleanse my hands.[83]

Although Serote's poetry is always the expression of powerful
emotion, there is a strong cerebral strain throughout. The poet
explores the world around and inside him and delves ever more
deeply into its meaning. Except for a few of the early poems, his
stance is one of humble questing without an attempt to supply facile
answers.

The world that God wrote with his big fingers
were they hesitant fingers?

he asks in 'A Poem' which salutes 'Mother and Child sculpture by
Dumile'. He continues:

They wrote a story that we do not understand.[84]

His probing continues in his subsequent two volumes, *No Baby
Must Weep*[85] and *Behold Mama, Flowers*.[86] By this time Serote had
left South Africa on a fellowship to go to the United States. He
attended and addressed the inaugural conference of the African
Literary Association in Austin, Texas, and toured the United States
under the auspices of the African Studies Center of Boston
University. He was awarded a scholarship to the University of
Columbia where he received a degree in Fine Arts. In South Africa he

was awarded the Ingrid Jonker prize for poetry, and his work was
included in many anthologies.

Serote's quest for truth and meaning takes on a new impetus in
exile. He has walked far, and hopes that the road will lead him
somewhere other than into nightmare, that it 'can whisper wisdom'
to him.[87]

His search is for the moment which:

> must be brand new
> like a baby
> so our broken tongues
> and long-soiled lips
> can grope for new words because the old ones have broken this
> earth to pieces.[88]

No Baby Must Weep is a single long poem on a theme of contrast
between the darkness of life and the bright hope of birth:

> i came into this earth
> bundled in blood and flesh and an immense love.[89]

The poem is strongly autobiographical. The first pages tell of his
childhood in the township and this theme recurs, but later events
take place within the poet himself. The world is real only in as far as
he experiences it, and he expresses his experience symbolically. The
mother becomes Africa and the poet, if he can succeed in throwing off
all physical trappings, even that of fear, will become one with the
earth, with Africa. Black life is represented by a river, deep and dark,
where the horrors of life and death form only little ripples on the
surface. The sea represents a free Africa into which the poet longs to
emerge.

> Let me seep into Africa
> let this water
> this sea
> seep into me own me.[90]

Neither this poem nor the long title poem in the collection *Behold
Mama, Flowers*, is entirely successful. There is many a pure burst of
poetry that goes right to the centre of the meaning such as the lines
expressing futility:

> and in time blood has been rendered to the sand
> the deep, deep sand
> which keeps sipping and sipping leaving its surface clean.[91]

But there are also too many banal passages, and repetitions of phrases
and moods that become monotonous. In *Behold Mama, Flowers*
Serote loses sight of the theme introduced in the foreword, of a child

seeing pieces of human flesh and bones floating down a river and saying 'behold mama, flowers', though he picks it up again at the end where the agony is tinged with hope:

> behold the flowers, they begin to bloom.[92]

The remaining poems in this collection are dedicated to various writers and friends. Most of the poems in this collection were written in the United States but some in Botswana where he is living at the time of writing.

With less restless striving and introspective search for life's answers than Serote, and less need to break new ground than Mtshali, Sydney (Sipho) Sepamla (after his first collection like several other writers he dropped the English Christian name) has a surer voice than either of these poets. Sepamla was older than Serote and Mtshali when he began writing, and his poetry is more mature. He is more selective when it comes to publication, and his first two volumes, *Hurry Up to It*[93] and *The Blues is You in Me*[94] are more even in quality. Sepamla is positive and affirmative in his approach. 'There has always been a purpose in life,' he states in 'Now is the Time', 'Living being the greatest'. He faces life squarely and expresses his views without frills:

> Now is the time
> To know words
> Not shut out their meaning
> Nor dress them in gaudy clothes.[95]

Like Mtshali, but in more subtle and sophisticated terms, he presents facets of black life as they are, often without intrusion as commentator. He grapples with the things that matter in the life of the black man: the crowded trains with its passengers like sheep herded into a kraal on their way to a loneliness beyond, families waking up in the early hours of the morning to the drone of bulldozers for forced removals, the many laws that rule the black man's life, and later the Bantu Education Act, censorship, the uprisings. It is a distorted world where 'time is just a little bit unnerved' and existence is 'tilted'.[96]

Sepamla is not happy about the limitations that black circumstances impose on a poet's subject-matter. As he remarked in an address at the United States Information Service Writers' Seminar in Johannesburg in May 1975:

> . . . I sometimes wonder how much growth in the broader artistic sense we miss as a result of our fixation on protest. We seem incapable of communicating the insights of man and nature because we are forced to remind other people about their undesirable deeds towards us. I long for that day when this will not be my priority.[97]

Sepamla takes nothing for granted. He has thought deeply about his commitment to the black cause, as evidenced in the poem 'I tried to say'[98]

> For days I've pondered the reality
> that lives with us
> . . .
> whether to sit by the window
> watching shadows turn to night
> or make those little noises
> that affirm our tilted existence.[99]

We know the inevitable conclusion he reaches, but he too, like Serote, finds it difficult to hate, because it is foreign to his nature. In 'Nibbling'[100] he says:

> I hate lies
> one of which tries
> to explain my bitterness
> as anti-whiteness.
> of course i do hate
> some people—
> i am in love
> with mankind![101]

A serious undertone is there even in his humorous poems for which Sepamla is perhaps best known. 'Ja meneer', 'The Applicant' for a job says in a poem of that title,[102] 'I qualify', and then lists as his qualifications all those attributes with which the white man burdens the black. The applicant says he has been 'measured for (his) swart gevaar / And (his) tolerance rating / Has been declared well above average / By the S.A. Bureau of Standards'.[103] Satire and irony are Sepamla's weapons, and he achieves the desired effect with great skill. His sharp wit makes it a most effective means of bringing home his point. In 'The Will'[104] the meagre effects of the dead person are divided up, but:

> The cat spotted black and white
> you will have to divide
> for that you'll need God's guidance.

In 'The Odyssey',[105] the tourist brochure lines beginning:

> explore the beauty of our land
> discover where the sun shines
> where shadows linger eternally

lull the reader until he realises with a shock that he is no longer looking at sunshine, mountains, rivers and wild game:

discover the hope that lives with despair
discover the rats gnawing at this hope
discover the concern of all non-tribal people
discover the land that has gone sulky to a vision.

This poem, as published in *Ophir* No. 23, before the collection appeared, was awarded the Pringle Award of the English Academy of South Africa in 1976. Sepamla's best known poem, 'To Whom It May Concern' is a brilliant satire. It gives Robert Royston's anthology of black poetry its title[106] and was Sepamla's first poem to be published abroad—in the May 1972 issue of *Playboy*. It is the black man's life history in the form of a typical official document, the officialese covering up for the inhumanity of the contents. It begins:

Bearer
Bare of everything but particulars
is a Bantu
The language of a people in southern Africa
He seeks to proceed from here to there
Please pass him on
Subject to these particulars.

It ends

Please note
The remains of R/N 417181
Will be laid to rest in peace
On a plot
Set aside for Methodist Xhosas
A measure also adopted
At the express request of the Bantu
In anticipation of any faction fight
Before the Day of Judgement.[107]

The title poem of his first collection, 'Hurry Up to It'[108] is a bitter, yet very funny, condemnation of the laws controlling the black man's life. A father's good advice to his son, who is choosing a bride, is to make certain 'she is a desirable person':

For love is:
 Knowing the girl's homeland,
Knowing her papers are right,
Knowing she has permission to marry,
and above all
Love is:
Knowing if you can make children;
For remember, son,
You will be required
To buzz thoughts of manhood

In a men's hostel;
She will be expected
To nurse the ache
Of an ill-used womb
In a women's hostel.
Hurry up
You need to register
for a certified permit
To have sex—
In good time![109]

Sepamla's diction gives his poems an often startling originality. He has a flair for memorable phrases. 'In those days of unsaid commentaries', begins a poem titled 'Zoom the Kwela-Kwela', 'thoughts moulding under our armpits'. And later in the same poem:

my head spins on a tilted fulcrum
resting on one illusion after another.[110]

Even much-used ideas become fresh when he uses phrases like 'rhythms of my street ways' and 'whizz of bullet words'.[111] It is never simply for effect, always to add meaning or emphasis.

Sepamla makes much use of African language in his poems, often to the point of incomprehensibility to the white English-speaker. Reading one such poem, 'Come Duze, Baby', to the National Conference of the 1820 Settlers National Monument Foundation in July 1974, Sepamla said: 'If you don't understand it, it's just perhaps you have not been a true South African'.[112] Sepamla's poetry is aimed at the new South African English-speaker who has made English an African language. This is further emphasised by his rhythm. The beat always runs concurrently with the meaning or the purpose of the poem, as the title of the second collection, *The Blues is You in Me* indicates. The title poem[113] begins:

when my heart pulsates a rhythm
off-beat with God's own scintillating pace.[114]

Besides poetry Sepamla has also written short stories, reviews, commentary, and a novel which will be dealt with later.

He became editor of *New Classic* in 1975 and also edited *S'ketsh*, a publication dealing with black drama. In 1977 his passport was withdrawn, so that he was barred from attending conferences, workshops, and other activities abroad to which he was invited. In the same year his third collection, *The Soweto I Love*[115] was banned. This volume was written immediately after the harrowing events in Soweto in 1976 and these events still have Sepamla in their grip. In some of the poems, such as 'I Saw This Morning'[116] he describes and articulates the terror which the riots brought in their wake. In others,

for instance 'At the Dawn of Another Day'[117] he gives an account of
the actual uprising, and with emphasis in printed pattern explains the
causes and aims:

    at the height of the day
    youth rage spilled all over the place
                        unleashing its own energy
                        confounding the moment
                        exploding the lie
    take away
            your teachings
    take away
            your promises
    take away
            your hope
    take away
            your language
    give
        me
            this
                day
                    myself
    i shall learn myself anew
    i shall read myself from the trees
    i shall glean myself from all others
    i shall wean myself of you.[118]

Sepamla reveals his deep personal shock in 'How a Brother Died'.[119]

    I want to remember these things
    because I had never known
            such hate before.[120]

The mood is grim, and the images are of violence, death, destruction
and inhumanity. The humour of subtle satire has been driven out of
him:

    nobody really sees the storm raging within us
    nobody cares to know that we've reached our own bottom,

he says with despair in his heart. He continues:

    laughing has become agonizing.[121]

Besides the Soweto uprisings he writes of suicide, murder and
rape in prison, and Robben Island is the metaphor for the authorities' attempts to break the black man's spirit. He has nothing
but contempt for the white way of life,[122] and he expresses pride in
the action of the youth of today. The careful poet of the telling
phrase, the subtle and witty lines, and well constructed verse, has

given way to a writer standing too close to events, sick with
abhorrence and giving way to a need to let the words pour out of
him.

It is no coincidence that in three collections of four main poets of the
nineteen-seventies cattle form part of the title. After Mtshali's
Cowhide Drum and Serote's cattle crying in death agony, come the
Natal poet Mafika Pascal Gwala's cattle being brought home to the
safety of the kraal: *Jol'iinkomo*.[123] That is also to say, Gwala tells us in
the introduction to the volume, 'I should bring some lines home to
the kraal of my Black experience'. Cattle have always played an
important role in traditional African life, and the use of this symbol is
part of the revival of African history and tradition in literature. The
title poem of the collection[124] is dedicated to the 'Children of
Namibia'. In it he looks forward to a time when black Southern
Africa maps out its own destiny. Only when the people recognise
their heroes will it be the time when

> The cattle shall have herded home
> to our ancestral kraal.
> Jol'iinkomo!
> Africa shall be one in her past.
> Jol'iinkomo!
> Africa shall have one Soul.
> Jol'iinkomo![125]

Gwala reveals the past of Africa as a glorious one, and tries to make all
Africa's children aware of 'the black giant / that always had been /
even yesterday'.[126] He is clear about the function he has assigned
himself: 'I'm the African Kwela instrumentalist whose notes / profess
change',[127] he says in the long poem 'Getting off the Ride'.[128] The
change he envisages is a total one, to a life where 'Dreams and hopes
. . . are Black'.[129] The picture of black life in South Africa, which he
paints with bitterness and anger in this and other poems, is a grim one
in which the black man is taken for a ride at every turn. Yes, he
concludes his tale of commercial trickery, wasted and faked
education, wasteland Bantustans:

> . . . I'm made to feel motherless, fatherless, shitless
> Me with enough shit in my guts to blackshit
>   any officiated shit,
> Me wishing for a gun
> When I know some pig will wish to collar me
> for the 3-Star knife I've bought at the shop
> down the street.[130]

The end of the poem is an even more frantic explosion of anger. In the
ghetto, a jungle he is learning to know, he hears 'the sound of African

drums beating to freedom songs' and hears 'the voice that moves with the Black Thunder':

> I'm the Wrath of the Moment
> I strike swift and sure
> I shout in the West and come from the East
> I fight running battles with enemy gods
>   in the black clouds
> I'm the watersnake amongst watersnakes
>   and fish amongst fish
> I throw missiles that outpace the SAM
> I leave in stealth
>   and return in Black anger.
> O- - -m! Ohhhh- - -mmmm! O- - -hhhhhhmmmmmmm![131]

Gwala makes it clear that for him there is no middle path. The man who shouts 'You're going too far!' or 'You're running too fast!' is a hypocrite and a 'stuntist fraud in a dead / and mighty fall',[132] he says in 'Paper Curtains'.[133] He finds little in white civilisation on which it can pride itself. A list of attributes set out in a pattern of print tell their story without comment in the poem 'Perspectives', for example:

> Auschwitz and babiy yar
>   hiroshima and nagasaki
> sharpeville
>   my lai
> pollution and thalidomide
>   pornography
>   immorality act
> tv   satellites   revolving restaurants
>   dracula   vampirebat   werewolf
> bankaccounts   instalments   chemistbills
>   junk and the gutter
> prison and death
>   masturbation and suicide
>   better-than-thou
>   psycho-analysis.[134]

In 'Grey Street',[135] he shows more graphically its corruption, desolation and hypocrisy, as symbolised by Durban's main city street.

While he is a poet of the township like the others, Gwala tries to draw his images also from a more traditional and unpolluted Africa.

> Let me drink from the khamba of the elders
> Let me blow my nose into kraalmis
> Let me seek through life
> the sons and daughters of yesterday

The waters of the Inyalazi
have crocodiled me to Umthunzini
Where men received the drilled patience
of a root doctor
When shall I inhale once more the gardenia fragrance
of the Umngeni Valley in mid-Spring?[136]

he asks in 'Beyond Fences'.[137] The contrasts between Durban and its
townships are as great as those between Johannesburg and Soweto—
'aren't Tin Town and Reservoir Hills / under the same sun?' he asks
in 'Grey Street'[138]—but Durban and its surrounding towns are still
close to the countryside which obtrudes even into the slums. Gwala is
therefore more aware of nature than the Soweto poets.

Beauty we still have in plenty though,[139]

he writes in a 'Letter to a Friend in Exile',

Except that we no more look
at the beauty of flowers.[140]

Yet like the earlier Natal poet, Herbert Dhlomo, he cannot resist the
call of the beauties of the land and speaks of:

Mist shadows
cloaking the rich bush hills
and waterfresh mountains;
Rivers flooding their wiry course
through growth covered forests
and age-old villages.

But it only serves to remind him how these rivers

. . . bite into the darkness
of distance;
Spilling the vicarious dreariness
of colonialist history
into the oceans.[141]

Although Gwala himself says 'that Black Consciousness does not
mean politics disguised as literature'[142] some of the later poems tend
to hold little other than political interest. His earlier poetry—those
poems published in journals before the collection, and those in the
collection which appear to have been written earlier—is never dull.
His inventiveness of phrase like 'ontoed curiosity', 'Auntie's cool
mama-look' or 'a whitelonely suburb', and his play on words makes
the poems vivid. The cleverness is not for its own sake. 'Cutex'
playing 'mommon games / on their faked finger nails' for instance, is a
picturesque example of 'Black Status Seekers'[143] in a poem of that
title.

Mafika Gwala—he too dropped the English Christian name—has been deeply involved in all aspects of black cultural life. Vocationally, he was a high school teacher and later became variously a factory worker, legal clerk, personnel assistant and publications researcher. He edited the 1973 edition of *Black Review*, published by the Black Community Programme, an organisation the aim of which was to help the black community become aware of its own identity. The organisation was later banned. Gwala himself was detained in 1977 and released nine months later without being charged.

If the Black Consciousness call is the predominant note in black literature of the nineteen seventies and eighties, and if it is based on a pride in black culture and history, why is it that a writer of mixed blood like James Matthews identifies with and is accepted by the proponents of contemporary black South African literature? Obviously the philosophy underlying that literature is much more complicated and varied than would at first appear.

'I am Black', James Matthews says in one of his own poems in *Black Voices Shout!*, an anthology which he edited and published. He continues:

> my Blackness fills me to the brim
> like a beaker of well-seasoned wine
> that sends my senses reeling with pride.[144]

Matthews is regarded as the doyen of the new black writers, because he provides a link with the writers of the previous period when he was writing short fiction, and because of his fearless expression of opposition to repression through the years, weathering bannings, withdrawn travel documents and imprisonment. True, he was silent during most of the sixties, but he had been writing poetry for several years and was waiting for an opportune moment to publish. But while his first volume *Cry Rage* enjoyed publication in America, Holland, France and Germany, it was banned in South Africa in 1973, the first book of poetry to suffer this fate. *Black Voices Shout* also fell victim to censorship, and so did his last volume to date, *Pass Me the Meatballs, Jones*.

It took Matthews a long while to feel at ease in the new medium. 'Living in our land is a political action',[145] he begins a poem in *Black Voices Shout*, but rarely does he translate 'the rage that / burns from living in a / white man's hell'[146] or the 'wail of a land / hideous with open graves'[147] into cohesive or effective poetry.

The school in which James Matthews eventually learnt to speak from his heart was a hard one. In 1976 he was jailed in the Victor Verster maximum security prison, then released after four months without being charged. During confinement he wrote the poems he published in the collection *Pass Me the Meatballs, Jones*. He calls it a

'gathering of feeling' and succeeds in conveying to the reader the
sensation of being deprived of freedom in all its nuances. The effect of
imprisonment is one of utter desolation. The whole world becomes
distorted to him:

hopes are aborted
dreams become nightmares
a serene face
twisted into distraught mask
my ears are invaded
by the silent clamour
of a defeated army
of dispirited souls
manifesting their anguish
in a paean of pain
to a disinterested god
trees drip blood
and birds sport
garments smeared in gore
flowers mourn crushed petals
as earth reveals raw wounds
man robbed of belief
looks at a sky
patterned with ebony stars
and a carrion crow
emotes a cynical call
'the world's end is now!'[148]

Time becomes meaningless 'as a faceless clock' and normal patterns
are turned inside out. The poet faces disintegration and becomes
frantic at the loss of identity, as memories:

dissolved in damp patches
leaving haunted traces
aglitter like silvered streaks
that i cannot place in
patterned form to picture my past.[149]

The long periods of solitary confinement turned the poet in upon
himself and he lost the need to posture and declaim from what
Nadine Gordimer calls 'a public address system for the declarations
of a muzzled prose writer'.[150] He shows that he has the ability to
condense feeling into effective image, as for instance one where the
disintegration of a prisoner is compared with a leaf in autumn:

yellow-serried as autumnal leaves
my spirit turns brittle
as days fade into night

with time meaningless
as a faceless clock
I feel the slow
disintegration of self
particles of my being
float leisurely to the
cement-grave bottom of
my keep to curl up
withering into dust.[151]

One must remember that the stimuli to which a poet normally responds, the life around him, are almost totally lacking in prison. The few things he sees from his cell window become a mockery, and accentuate his loneliness:

sky taunts me as
lace veils break apart
dazzling my eyes with a
garment of heart-breaking blue
birds parading the grass
rehearse a mocking serenade
its notes sharp-edged
adding to my torment.[152]

But the true black poet cannot keep his eyes turned inward, even in despair. After all, he went to prison because of communicating his thoughts and ideals to his fellowmen. The difficulty of such communication between man and man in such circumstances is expressed thus in one of his poems in the collection: '. . . my smile / cannot break into blossoms—sufficient to spread around'.[153] In prison one can communicate only through pain, the barrier excludes anything more.

As *Meatballs* was the first volume of poetry to be banned there was a considerable outcry. Today, undaunted, Matthews continues to write prose and verse but mainly for publication abroad.

These five are the most prominent among the poets who started a new wave in black poetry in South Africa. An important contributing factor to the flood of poetry which was released, was the new black organisations with black awareness as their aim—SASO, BPC and BCP—with meetings and publications through which the poets could speak. An influential poet among these was Don Mattera, of mixed black and Italian descent, who also appeared in *Izwi*, and led many poetry readings by *Izwi* contributors. His poems were among the first to sound a note of 'black power' which, in terms of literature, can perhaps be best described as confidence in a black future and an exhortation to bring it about. The black voices were no longer merely shouting with rage, but sounding a battle cry. In Cape Town James Matthews encouraged the younger writers, such as Christine Douts and Ilva Mackay both of whom left the 'Coloured' University of Western Cape in protest during the student crisis of 1973. Their poetry appeared in Matthews's anthology *Black Voices Shout*, together with that of several other writers; when the volume was banned in South Africa, Dennis Brutus's Troubadour Press published it in the States.

In a poem entitled 'To You' Christine Douts exhorts those 'bound / to plastic walled cells / of white ignorance' to:

> thrust your clenched fist
> in the face of their foolishness
> laugh at the naked fear
> that lines their feverish deeds.[154]

Hate for her

> . . . is a slow
> unwinding rope in me
> curling and swirling unleashing
> spasms of energy
> that ripples away
> into cul-de-sacs all around us.[155]

Ilva Mackay in '. . . and liberty' knows and accepts that

> There will be
> bangs, blood, bruises, bodies
> corpses, children crying, clenched
>   fists, furious, fervent fighting.[156]

before there can be liberty. In 'Beware', she warns her contemporaries against letting their ideas be smothered by 'eager fretting parents' and 'fear-filled folks'.[157] 'The future is ours / unite' she calls out in her last poem in the volume.[158]

The imagery is of wild beasts, rape, blood and decay. There is only one aim: to express the immediacy of oppression and prescribe its remedy. Such poetry lies outside the realm of literary criticism because its purpose it not to be read or listened to but acted upon. The authorities paid tribute to the success of the poets and their groups in this respect by banning them. SASO, BPC and BCP were banned as were Mattera, Achmed Dangor, Douts and Mackay. Douts was detained and later released. Mackay now lives partly in Britain and partly in Zambia and is on the staff of the Anti-Apartheid movement.

In the meanwhile the literary journals were still interspersed with black writing, and here the main feature was the increasing awareness and pride in being black. Poems had titles like 'Notes from an Afrikan

Calabash'.[159] In a poem entitled 'Be Gentle' N. (Njabulo) S. Ndebele, pleads for Africa to be left alone to find its own roots:

> do not crowd my mind
> with studied images of my past;
> let me feel it first:
> do not display my carved rituals
> at the British Museum,
> for little do they say;
> let me feel them first.[160]

The poets mourn the disappearance of a black identity and culture to be replaced by a dubious white civilisation. 'Sir',[161] writes Andrew Mothobi Mutloatse in a poem of that title,

> re: INDIGENOUS LANGUAGE (*sic*) (italics, brackets and
> Alas, 1, 2, 3   sic the poet's)
> the Bantu has, a, e, i . . .
> to forsake his own
> indigenous language
> his beloved mother's
> his old-fashioned forefathers'
> (What an unforgivable sacrilege)
> for the sake of passing lily-white
> a, b, c . . . exams!
> 'but this IS literacy'
> or, whatever . . .
> ModiMO! . . . thusa, tlhe.
> Yours obediently,
> Mothobi A. Mutloatse.[162]

Pride is taken not only in an ancient culture of the past but in a living tradition. The banned writers of the late fifties are exhumed from the pits to which the authorities had assigned them, and are admired and loved as masters of their art.

> . . . my wife fetches the water
> (Down Second Avenue)
> We drink and we eat.[163]

says Ndebele, in a reference to Mphahlele's autobiography and its poignant chapter on communal water taps. And Mutloatse begins a poem 'On Marriage'

> If
> death
> is a bastard
> like good old Themba says.[164]

A longing for the traditional ways of the country comes as a complete reversal of the former longing for acceptance in a common urban world, and is due to a desire by the black man to cry for his own beloved country and not have it done for him.

> I don't want all this cement smoothness,
> for my open toes need must smell the green blades,[165]

Winston (later Zinjva Winston) Nkondo says in an untitled poem in *New Classic*. In a poem entitled 'I Hid My Love' Ndebele rises to lyrical heights when he mourns his lost identity:

> I was king,
> I was king of the bees,
> I ruled over the honey
> I ruled over the milk pail
> Full of white bubbles.
> Ha! Ha! I held my hollow belly,
> In laughter when a hen dropped an egg.
> My arms akimbo,
> I knew the secrets of the world,
> I knew the secret pleasures.[166]

But in the city he hid his love 'in the sewerage' and there, 'below the bottom of life' it 'drowned in the stench'. Now he asks:

> I who am I? Who am I?
> I am the hoof that once
> Grazed in silence upon the grass,
> But now rings like a bell on tarred streets.[167]

The same idea of being one with nature, he expresses most beautifully in the symbolic poem 'Little Dudu'[168] about a child which will never again 'play with the whisk of God'.[169] The symbol for the world is the 'dome of a hippo's mouth' on which Dudu forms a small speck. Once the hippo's mouth snaps Dudu is imprisoned 'behind bars of teeth'.

But in the meanwhile, life in a white South Africa must be endured. It is a bitter experience and must either be faced stoically or treated with contempt. The poets do both. 'When Love is Banned'[170] by Mutloatse, is a bitter narrative of how two banned people attempt to have a love affair and describes minutely the frustrations of their lives.

Irony becomes a weapon. Mutloatse often sets his ironic tone by using sophisticated language, and either twisting the meaning of the words or misusing them slightly. 'We are the devils / may care', he says in 'Train Roof Jive',[171] and 'our men are cool aids' someone declares in 'Don't Lock Up Our Sweetshearts'.[172]

There is a marked increase in the use of African languages, intermingled with English and Afrikaans. In Mutloatse's poem 'Don't Lock Up Our Sweetshearts', the community coming together to voice their grievances answer the question: 'Ke basadi ba bo mang?' with:

'Dus ours. Ke basadi ba rona
Ke basadi ba rona'
Some interlarding: 'Ja ja.
Hulle is onse susters; onse ousies.'[173]

It meant that white readers of the journals and anthologies were often at a loss, and it indicated very clearly that the black poets were now addressing a black readership.

The published work often grew out of poetry readings. Such a poem was 'Black Trial', by Ingoapele Madingoane, which was widely known as a Soweto epic long before it was published (and immediately banned) by Ravan Press with other poems by Madingoane under the title *Africa My Beginning*,[174] in 1979. It was inspired by Wole Soyinka's poetry and the poet calls it a cry for Africa's exploited soul. It has a pan-African theme—'in the heart of Africa / Africans shall meet as one'[175]—and calls for courage for the African to awaken and find his destiny.

In Cape Town, Cosmo Pieterse asked aspirant writers to his home, among them Arthur Nortje and Richard Rive, but this came to an end when Pieterse left South Africa. On the Rand, the poetry group Medupe was formed in 1977 and at one time had 200 members, but it was banned soon afterwards.

There were still too few outlets for publication, and those that existed were almost exclusively in white hands. The new creative force in South Africa was in dire need of a new literary outlet that would respond to it. It found the answer in *Staffrider* with its policy of giving the various groups as well as individuals a voice (see above, pp. 37–39).

The contributions came from all parts of the country and increasingly all sections of the black community. Indian writers especially were coming to the fore, men like Achmed Dangor, Farouk Asvat and Essop Patel. The older, well-known writers like James Matthews and Gwala sent contributions or gave their help. Serote was given prominence with a long poem in Volume II, No. 4, with a double-page spread and a photograph of the poet.

Staffrider's editorial policy means that good writing sometimes appears to be lost in a morass of mediocrity, but this will concern critics and posterity rather than *Staffrider*'s present readers. Anthologies of the 'best of *Staffrider*' will probably emerge when the time is right. Its editors will find plenty of material and not only among the established writers.

The subject matter of the writers are those we have already seen expressed elsewhere. Black awareness is voiced in its many phases and themes. Several poets proclaim pride in history and the heroes of old, such as 'The Battle of Isandhlwana', by Mandla Ndlazi which ends:

> It is more like a hut*
> Like a song in my heart
> With lines of a lesson
> To guide its heritage
> Into history's next page.

*the Zulu word *isandhlwana* means 'more like a hut'.[176]

Present-day political leaders are celebrated: Steve Biko, Nelson Mandela, and the young heroes of the uprisings. Tribute is paid to writers of earlier periods: such as Casey Motsisi and also the newer writers like Zinzi Mandela. Poets have been studying the literature of other parts of Africa and make references to Achebe and others.

Inevitably most of the poems protest against the state of things in the land. The tone of protest varies. There is the deep hatred of Morena King Monare, in the ominously simple poem 'A Gossip' in which a 'nannie's' son confides to the white parents:

> Did you know
> that my Christian mother
> Daily chokes your little one
> Just for a second
> Wishing it was the zero-zero hour,[177]

and 'Family Planning', by James Twala which describes in bitter detail the whole ugly system of housing men in single quarters in which their wives and families are not allowed to join them. There is a patient and sorrowful hope for a better future as in 'So Well Tomorrow',[178] by Bonisile Joshua Motaung. There are freedom songs with titles like 'Power', 'Tribute to the Martyrs', and 'Tokologo' (the Pedi word for freedom). The latter, by Muhammad Omar Ruddin, ends:

> Sing me a Song of Freedom
> that I may rise
> from the quagmire of debasement
> and take my rightful place
> among free men.[179]

The poems which were listed by the Publications Board as being among the 'undesirable parts', and thus contributing to the banning of the first issue of *Staffrider* were: 'Change' by Mandla Ndlazi (because it was 'calculated to harm black/white relations'); 'At the Window' by Mike Nicol and 'Stray Bullet' by Hanyane Nelson Shikwambane because they 'undermined the authority and image of the police'; and 'Petition to my Interrogaters', by Keith Gottschalk, 'Nineteen Seventysix' by Oupa Thando Mthimkulu and 'For Fatima

Meer' by Shabbir Banoobhai, because they were considered 'prejudicial to peace and good order'. 'At the Window' is one of the finest pieces ever published in *Staffrider*, with its poignant contrast between love and the peace of sleep. It begins:

> Seeing you deeply asleep
> In the night's dead hours
> I slip from bed to stand
> At the window. So young
> And beautiful you be.

But his thoughts are bitter and angry as he thinks of what is in store. 'What place', he asks, 'has love?':

> . . . What
> Meaning and what promise
> In these suspicious days.[180]

'Nineteen Seventy-Six', like many *Staffrider* poems, deals with the Soweto risings. 'We do not boast about you', the poet says, but only because 'you were not revolutionary / enough'.[181] The 'Stray Bullet'[182] of the poem of that title killed an unborn child. Similar reasons led to the banning of Volume II No. 1, and one poem particularly drew the ire of the censors for ostensibly approving of subversive deeds, presenting Communist victories as laudable, giving a foretaste of what is to come in South Africa and accusing the police of murder. Entitled 'Tribute to Mapetha', the poem, by Bafana Buthelezi,[183] is about a detainee under the Terrorism Act who was found hanged in his cell.

Irony is still a weapon when writing about the black man in South African society. Timothy Motimeloa Makama makes good use of this in a poem entitled 'For Existence Sake', with the lines:

> I jump no higher than a hop,
> To climb and never reach the top,
> Like who and what am I, full stop;
> A fruitless search for peace of mind
> Has left me chasing miles behind
> For truth was never mine to find.[184]

And so, since not a single step he takes makes any difference, the poet exists for existence [sic] sake. Again satire is emphasised by the interspersal of African language as in Peter Setuke's poem 'The Marathon Runner', in which he sees the black man as a runner chased by the white man through every sphere of life, for example:

> for i romped over the highlands
> from the newlands
> to the meadowlands

to the so-called homelands
i was dubbed a kudu
while man was phudufudu.[185]

Many of the inclusions are totally in African languages.

Although individual themes inevitably tend to be repetitive, styles, allusions and symbols are for the most part varied and original, and make the reading of the issue exciting. A quick glance through a couple of issues will reveal the following lines, for example:

You've pinched the last moon-
ray; he now karate-chops the swollen cocoon,[186]

Nape 'a Motana, one of the most outspoken of the poets, writes in an untitled poem. A three-lined poem, 'Freedom' by Makhulu waLedwaba reads:

If the freedom I cry for
is beneath the big Marula tree
I'll use my hands to dig it free.[187]

Melissa King, in 'One Teaching Day', sees

Children scamper into
Bare peeling classrooms
Like shiny black beetles
Seeking shelter,

and, while the rain 'beats out an / Ancient endless rhythm / On the tin roof',

Ebony limbs stir and
Murmur,
Moved by an older and wiser
Teacher
Than I.
Western education trickles down the walls,
and seeps away,
Unheeded.[188]

Some phrases, however, tend to get repeated: too many poets, for instance, see the faces of their forefathers.

There is an urgency of rhythm in much of the poetry. Since the poems originated mainly at readings, often alternating with musical items or even accompanied by music, the beat of the drums can often be heard in the background. Music became more and more important in *Staffrider* and the artwork is as prominent as the literature.

The minimum of editorial intervention which was the policy of *Staffrider* also appears to be followed by Ravan Press when publishing collections of poetry in volume form. The poems are presented without introduction and, one sometimes feels, with a lack of selection. *The Rainmaker*, by Fhazel Johennesse,[189] appeared in 1979 in one volume with *Just a Little Stretch of Road* by Alwin Williams. 'My writing is a confirmation of my humanity, a celebration of my blackness', Johennesse is quoted as saying in a brief biography on the back cover, although in the title poem he stresses rather the futility of a false celebration of black beauty in place of looking closely at black pain. In a poem entitled 'bombs' he expresses the purpose of his poetry in clear and unambiguous verse:

> . . . i have a bomb
> a grey one
> that lurks beneath my skull
> waiting for the fuse to burn up
> from the ink that flows out of my pen
> and the nuclear explosion that follows
> will spurt out of my ears and mouth
> and afterwards we will all ponder
> white sensitivity to
> black radiation.[190]

In other poems the protest often takes the reader almost unawares, thus making all the more impact. A white soldier on the border is bored with the repetitiveness of army life. He misses his sweetheart, his family, work, city life, because all he does now:

> . . . is write letters
> tune in to radio highveld
> shine my boots shoot kaffirs and clean my gun.[191]

The long title poem takes the reader on a Dantesque tour of the black man's inferno. The poet identifies with all aspects of black life which become his own suffering. The pulse of this song of exhortation is often strong, and startlingly fresh images are often introduced, but it is too repetitive and would have benefited from trimming. Several of the shorter poems could have been excluded, and the volume would perhaps have gained from the inclusion of two or three more young writers.

Shabbir Banoobhai's poetic approach to the world he lives in is somewhat different. He begins his quest for truth from its fundamentals:

> prying open the oyster of my soul
> prayed to find
> the moon-perfect pearl
> of deep internal knowing
> cultivated
> from the grain of truth

god places
deliberately, delicately
in the heart
of every newborn child.[192]

We are warned in this first poem of the collection *Echoes of my Other Self* that 'too much life' has shrunk his youthful idealism. His universe is an ordered one where 'the moon, sun and earth / sea, grain and day / are at god's command',[193] but he, the poet, is part of a centre of powerful impulse:

god is ecstatic heart
and i
his wild, wild pulse.[194]

He fulfils: 'steadfastly that formidable task / of being the eyes of a nation / the heart, the blood, the pulse of your fellow men', under a surface of lyric calm, all enfolded, by a 'many-faceted, all encompassing, overwhelming love / for the whole of mankind', based on the teachings of the Quran.[195] Banoobhai reaffirms his faith in Islam, and in a long poem addressed to the Pakistani poet and philosopher Muhammed Iqbal, he prays for the will and strength to face the storms and recreate the possibilities of life by

Making our every thought, our every act
A searching, a sharing, a striving without end.[196]

The widening of the concept of black pride is shown by the development of many South African Indian poets and other writers. Farouk Asvat sees the writer as 'the medium of the creative source, the fountain stemming from underground streams of loneliness, laughter and longing into the rivers of everyday struggle towards the vibrant oceans of Justice lashing against the stationary statues of suppression', and he sees 'our people' as being those of 'Azania' (the Pan-African Congress name for South Africa.)[197] Achmed Dangor, in a poem which follows Asvat's essay in *Wietie*, hears new voices replacing those that have been silenced, singing 'a hymn / to the glory of my land'.[198]

For Essop Patel who wrote some of his poems in South Africa and others after leaving the country, black consciousness represents 'not only self-realisation of one's humanity, but also an assertion of one's identity'. It is a rallying-spirit among the people of colour, he says in a letter quoted on the back-cover of his collection *they came at dawn*.[199] He continues later:

Black consciousness is not a destructive force . . . it is a positive realisation which unites man at a universal level, free of racial or colour prejudices and also free from exploitation. That is the level of *human consciousness*; that is what we are seeking as writers.

Patel uses the word 'colourful' both to identify the people he writes about and to describe this world. It covers a wide spectrum of black life, from the mixed parties where '. . . a dance is / dance . . . howsit Mister Black . . . I am / Miss White . . . lets jingle jangle but / no tingle tangle. tog please man'[200]—to the prison cells, shabby tenements of the prostitute and meths drinker, the 'pulsating artery / of Durban's Grey Street' with its beggars and charitable ladies in saris. He takes us to the courts which, as a lawyer in Johannesburg, he knows only too well, and introduces us to his client Baby Thembisa who sits 'on the concrete floor like a lotus-flower' and quotes Langston Hughes:

> Justice is a blind goddess
> is a thing to which we black are wise . . .[201]

For all these the woes of oppression:

> harmonise
> our blackness
> all over Azania.[202]

Patel is capable of forceful explosive images such as: 'The stark vision cauterizes / the retina of our lives',[203] as he describes with anger, contempt and sometimes hatred the injustice in his land. Too often however, the images are hackneyed and the scenes described in prosaic terms, thus failing to make impact. Again, a briefer volume would have been more effective.

One of the most promising and versatile of the younger poets is Christopher Van Wyk, born in Johannesburg in 1957, whose first volume of poetry, *It is Time to Go Home*[204] appeared in 1979, published by Ad. Donker and jointly won the Olive Schreiner prize in 1980. His poems had previously appeared in journals such as *Donga*, *New Classic*, *Staffrider*, *The Voice* and others. He has also written a number of short stories of which two particularly indicate a possible future novelist. 'Twenty Years of Experience'[205] was published in *Heresy*, and 'Aunt Molly and the Girls[206] in *Wietie* of which he was an editor.

Much of Van Wyk's poetry has a lack of pretence and a simplicity which he applies to a vast range of subjects and styles. He writes a joyful love poem 'for Kath', entitled 'Portrait', in which he explains why, if he painted her portrait, he could 'create a new old master':

> Because you have a smile
> that is luminous in a room of dark faces
> and a laugh that's boisterous as a binge
> and a heart so big
> I can splash it all over the canvas
> crazy as Van Gogh,
> until the easel topples.[207]

With the same lyrical ease of expression, in a poem entitled 'Candle', he urges people to educate themselves before it is too late:

> Read brother read,
>> though the wax lies heaped
>> in the saucer
>> and the silhouettes of gloom
>> grow longer.

> Read brother read.
>> Only the wick shines red now.
>> But it is not yet dark.
>> Remember brother,
>> it is not yet dark.[208]

Political commentary is couched in fresh metaphor:

> My dreams these days are policed
> by a million eyes
> that baton-charge my sleep
> and frog-march me into a
> shaken morning,[209]

and his satire has been brought up to date. In 'My Name is Chris Ruthless'[210] the hypocrisy of Western youth with its phony message of showing the world 'just what a deplorable, disgusting, sickening / loathesome bloody mess it is in', is exposed when a member of a punk rock group called 'Sperm', which performs at the 'Raped Virgin', is forced to explain a misunderstanding:

> You see we're a punk outfit
> out to spread a message about the ills of the world
> and no ways do we wanna get involved with racism.[211]

The fact that van Wyk's poetry is often reminiscent of black poets who preceded him, Mtshali and Arthur Nortje for instance, is encouraging in that it shows that a line of black literature has been re-established in South Africa and is being given a fresh and youthful note.

What of those writers who stand outside the current trend of protest poetry and who possibly feel that they have no place in a study of South African poetry labelled black? The choice is the poet's whether he wishes to celebrate his blackness, accept it or ignore it. It is undeniable however, that what primarily makes him a black person and therefore a black writer is the fact that he lives or has lived in South Africa with a black skin, and that wherever he goes he is made to carry with him the mark of his blackness.

Jennifer Davids, whose collection *Searching for Words*[212] was published by David Phillip in 1974 after her poems had appeared in many of the literary magazines since 1966, follows in the footsteps of some of the poets who were important to her: Rilke, cummings, Hopkins, Sylvia Plath and, in South Africa, Sydney Clouts, Ingrid Jonker and Ruth Miller among others. She is an intensely self-contained poet. This does not mean that her poetry is an expression only of her inner self, but of a self which has absorbed the world around her. As she puts it:

> To be a poet is the clearest way I can live. It has been very difficult reaching this point at which it's becoming more and more interwoven with everything I do. I think living for me is a sort of distillation process and the poems are like crystals I've formed.[213]

It is therefore not self-centred poetry in which the artist attempts to purge her soul, but one such as she herself admires, where 'the creative artist, as well as revealing and clarifying aspects of a situation, can in a sense provide a climate which encourages . . . greater awareness and creativity within the situation, both individually and socially'.[214] Davids neither ignores nor denies realities. In the only poem in the collection with a dedication, 'For Albert Luthuli',[215] she says:

> Bounded
> you gave me
> knowledge of freedom
>
> Silenced
> you taught me
> how to speak.

Her world view is a wide one and when a man of the dimension of Luthuli comes into her orbit she places him for us clearly within her vision. Referring back to the first stanza:

> You a fragment of the sun
> go turn the world
> in the long strength
> of your fingers,

she ends the poem:

> Somewhere a train
> has reached a destination
> and tonight
> the cold fist of winter
> clenches around the world
> But beyond it
> the endless pulsations of space
> grow louder
> and stars breaking the dark
> grow large

Walk now father
unchecked
from sun to sun.

In order to release reality she must first transform it. 'Myths
release reality', she says in 'Living',[216] the last poem of the collection.
She feels that before people can reach out to each other and convey a
meaning they must first find a way of stretching beyond the
confinement of words. In 'A Possibility of Speaking', she sees herself
as 'perched precariously / for one moment / at the tip of a continent
listening / to the turning / of a particle' and continues:

Listen
even here
it is brightening

And in this groping
striving through darkness
to reach the edges
where brightness holds

in the turning
to meet the sun
and the singing

of this time this place

there is
as the morning challenges
grains of sand
a possibility
of speaking.[217]

The experiences from which she draws her themes are usually
mental experiences but sometimes we get a glimpse of her as teacher,
factory worker, dweller in present-day South Africa as a background
to her inner life as for example in 'Classroom S.E. 5, 4 P.M.'[218] and in
'Factory Canteen, Lunchtime',[219] and 'Location Fires'.[220] In each of
these poems the experience is indeed distilled into crystals of
meaning.

Where are the fires
for me to believe in
where are the tongues of flame
to lick and conquer the dark,

she asks in 'Location Fires', after describing the landscape from
Langa to Nyanga as 'flattened / frightened and silenced'. In answer:

. . . the black body
of the sky rears up

loud with roaring
voices of the stars.

'The stars tonight', she ends the poem:

are blue backyard fires
studding the black
location of the sky.[221]

Before Adam Small began to write in English he was well-known as an
Afrikaans poet and an important contributor to Afrikaans literature. When he turned to English the change was more than one of
language, it was also a political gesture. He could no longer identify
with the Afrikaner even in sharing his language in literature.
Interviewed by John Pank on television for the South African
Broadcasting Corporation in 1978, Small said that he would go back
to Afrikaans when the time came. He had already written a couple of
poems in English in the late nineteen-sixties, including one which was
later often used against him when black writers felt that no black man
should promulgate a doctrine of turning the other cheek. Entitled
'There's Somethin''[222] he, as a black man, tells the white man that he
can stop him from sharing his life in every sphere, such as, for example
in 'Goin' to Groote Schuur / in the same ambulance', or 'trying to go
to Heaven / from a Groote Kerk pew', but:

there's somethin' you can
never never do—
you can't
ever
ever
ever stop me
loving
even you!

Small was wrong. Although neither hate nor bitterness ever took
the urbane lecturer in philosophy in its grip, his love for all mankind
underwent a metamorphosis. He found himself anew in Africa. He
fell under the spell of Leopold Senghor and the Negritude
movement, while engaged in a comparative study of this poet and of
the Afrikaans poet Van Wyk Louw, whom he much admires and has
translated into English. He had also met Stephen Biko and was much
impressed. He expressed his new ideas in *Black Bronze Beautiful*:
'Moments in the Creation of a Myth'.[223] Small, who has studied in
London and Oxford as well as in Cape Town, is as fluent in English as
he is in Afrikaans. His theme is still the communion of man with man
through love, but he is no longer prepared to accept this with
Christian humility. He aligns and identifies himself with Africa.
The myths, the images of the poem are of Africa. But while this is a

departure for Small, in Africa it harkens back to the Negritude period, which in the South African context was ceasing to have meaning. The black poets used African imagery to awaken the black man to his inferior position in his land, rather than emphasise blackness for its own sake. The drum was beating to the rhythms of freedom songs, while Small's drum, 'The black drum of my [Africa's] soul beat' was making the music grow, 'beauteous and black now / like a black child / grows into a tall black man'.[224]

The emotion-laden imagery, the heavy metaphors, the over-emphasis and almost nineteenth century romantic classicism give the work an air of artificiality. The exaggerated protestation of beauty in blackness is indeed reminiscent of the excesses of some of the French-speaking Negritude poets, and this is significant when one remembers that the French-speaking Africans wanted to prove that they were not black Frenchmen. Small has taken pains to assure us that he is no longer a brown Afrikaner, and can now get back to work. He does so, as we shall see later, by turning to drama.

Most of the writers who left South Africa had begun to write while still in the country. Arthur Kenneth Nortje's poems had appeared, though sparsely, from the early nineteen-sixties in such varied publications as *Black Orpheus*, *African Arts/Arts d'Afrique* and *Purple Renoster*. He took part in poetry readings in Cape Town, and met other writers there: Cosmo Pieterse, Richard Rive. Dennis Brutus he met in Port Elizabeth, where Nortje was educated and where he lived in Schauder township (which he describes as one of the worst slums in South Africa). Brutus had been one of his teachers and they remained life-long friends. Nortje was a brilliant all-round student and excellent sportsman. He won a scholarship to the University of the Western Cape and, after qualifying, went back to Port Elizabeth where he taught at the South End High School. In 1962 he won the Mbari literary prize sponsored by the Congress for Cultural Freedom based in Paris. Then, in 1965, he was awarded a scholarship to Oxford where he read successfully for a B.Litt. degree in English at Jesus College. He then emigrated to Canada where he also taught English. He wanted to further his studies, and, when the University of Toronto insisted that he complete Honours courses there before being allowed into graduate school, decided to return to Oxford. He spent some time in London, then went to Oxford to read for the B.Phil. degree. There, one day in 1970, he was found dead in his room from an overdose of drugs. Those are the outlines of events in his life. A diary which he kept from 1965, but even more his poems, fill in the details of the inner life of a brilliant student, deep thinker and inspired poet, a life which was rarely evident to his many friends who found him a happy companion, and many of whom were surprised as well as devastated by his death. At the time a brilliant future awaited him. His poetry was being more widely published—several poems were included in an anthology edited by Cosmo Pieterse, *Seven South African Poets*,[225] poems had been read over the BBC, and Heinemann were considering his poems for the collection which they eventually published in 1973.

To find clues to an author's life in his writing is an interesting exercise, and will certainly be rewarding in working on a much overdue biography of Nortje. For us, in this work, it is significance only in throwing light on the writing of the poet himself and of writers in exile from South Africa generally. Few are more sensitive in absorbing their surroundings and impressions, and even fewer have Nortje's skill in reproducing them accurately and honestly. His poems roughly trace his movements because most are datelined, but the contents are autobiographical less in description of events than in their atmosphere of mood and their preoccupations.

Why did Nortje kill himself at the age of twenty-eight? Although he had a grudging admiration and even love for London—'Despite the irony, she, city, / suckled my exile', he writes in 'Return to the city of the heart',[226] like all the black writers who left South Africa, he never thought of himself as anything but an exile.

There is a sadness and nostalgia running throughout his poems. His longing for South Africa never leaves him. The isolation of exile he sees as 'a gutted / warehouse at the back of pleasure streets'. In this poem, 'Waiting',[227] he refers to the Cape as Cabo de Esperancia and writes of 'the loneliness of lost / beauties' there. Not world events, not 'cosmic immensity or catastrophe' is what terrifies him but:

> it is solitude that mutilates,
> the night bulb that reveals ash on my sleeve.[228]

Everything reminds him of home.

> Open skies flare wide enough
> to make me vaguely anxious.
> Nimbus wisps
> trace patterns of the past,[229]

he says in 'In Exile'. But such dreams are not for him, he can never return. The smooth rhythm of the above lines is jarred:

> But wrong pigment has no scope
> so clot the blue channel of memory.

He tries not to indulge in self-pity. 'Tears are pointless', he says in 'September poem', they:

> . . . merely reassemble
> deep ghosts in appropriate solitudes.[230]

Yet while Nortje's mood is often one of depression, and even his love poems are almost invariably about the absence of the loved one, his outlook on life is not an entirely pessimistic one. Dennis Brutus, who knew him well, tells us he 'lived life fully, relishing it'.[231] He believes in the ultimate triumph of humanity even if at the present time there is little sign of it:

> Drops of compassion in the oceans
> of humanity are bitterly invisible:
> The rice-field and the rose-garden must blend
> before the hand that sowed can waft in harvest,

he says in a poem entitled 'Asseverations'.[232] Invisible, it is true, but there nevertheless. It is this aspect of his work and, according to his friends, of his life—the tone of affirmation and purpose—that makes his suicide difficult to accept.

Even when signs of the disintegration of his personality increase in the later poems, his intellect rarely loses control. He is at once lyrical and highly cerebral. His sensitive mind is wide open to that of other poets, Yeats, Sylvia Plath, and the 'flame-soft bitterness of love'[233] of the unnamed teacher in 'Autopsy'[234] who is obviously Dennis Brutus. It is 'freshened into / lovesong tenderness, cool and lyrical' by the breath of summer, and in 'The drifting seeds of summer',[235] the sweet clear call of a bird, singing 'contrapuntally against the roar of traffic', is heard.

Although the poems are intensely personal, it is not merely his own feelings, however poignant, which he wants to communicate to the reader. He examines the stimuli giving rise to these feelings and, by distilling them, creates their significance for us all. The poet carries the burden of all men: 'was it me eating horse in 1916 / in the first great universal terror / or dealing out poison chocolates at Belsen?' he asks,[236] after finding that 'Infinities of images' clash in his mirror and thus give him many identities.

He is never at ease about those left behind. A prison warder kicking open the stitches of a man shot in the stomach, a man in a helmet watching prisoners break stone, such scenes are never far from his mind even if not many of the poems are explicitly political. Rather, he explores his own anguish, as a man of mixed blood, in relation to his native land and expresses it in the poem 'Dogsbody half-breed'[237] and again in 'Questions and Answers'.[238] He tries to justify his departure in '*Affinity* TO MAGGIE':

> lack of belonging was the root of hurt
> the quick child, he must travel
> new views of greening trees alert
> my sensitivities and why
> should I deny them.[239]

Not everyone can be there 'at fire hour' to 'storm the castles'. Some, he says in 'Native's Letter',[240] 'define the happening'.

All of Nortje's senses absorb impressions of the world around him, and this means also that his ear is finely attuned to the nuances in the meaning and sound of language. The right words come easily to his bidding and he dispenses them with confidence, both to express his thoughts with clarity and to paint a mood. This he does often by contrast as in the poem 'Stream, beach and shadow scene',[241] where the heavily putrescent atmosphere is only occasionally interrupted by such sudden movement as 'I flick sunlight off my toes'. In a poem entitled 'Night Ferry',[242] he lulls us with the smooth movement of the vessel through the water:

Black bows
cleave water, suffer the waves . . .

while his mind travels into the tortured regions of the infinite in space and time.

There is a fine economy of words in Nortje's poetry which he achieves by unusual combinations, and by using a kind of image shorthand as in the lines quoted earlier from 'September poem', where he describes tears as pointless, merely reassembling 'deep ghosts in appropriate solitudes'. The relationship between the vivid image and the subjective mental state at the beginning of the same poem, hits one with the force of the volleyed ball he describes:

September tennis: a twang of racquets.
The sun is a gypsy among white frantic figures.
Balls lobbed and smashed volley their senses
but lose fur skimming the courts of my brain.[243]

The images are defined with razor sharpness in terms of sight, sound or movement. His 'broken sentences', he says in 'Poem, South Africa', for instance:

stumble to heaven on the hill despite
the man with the whip who beats my
emaciated words back.

Sometimes the images and metaphors in his poetry seem excessive, but even when he launches the reader into sharing a trip into the realms of alcohol and drug-induced terror, with lines like:

in the small hours push
a probe through the pus into wounded flesh,
through the scalded membrane or the soul blister,
feel for the trauma, expel the black-toothed beast
there entrenched, hacking at the fibre,
or the thirteen satans strumming on my lifeline
mutinous dissonances,[244]

it is all done with design and control. In an entry in his journal dated January 25 1970, and quoted in the introduction to an issue of *New Coin* devoted to a collection of his poems and to tributes from those who knew him, he writes: 'I want poetry to be more professional. I think it should be more vigorous, disciplined . . . You don't wait for inspiration, you make it. Hard work'.[245] And in another entry he says that he spent hours carefully chiselling, paring, elaborately balancing words.

Dennis Brutus, calling him 'perhaps the best South African poet of our time',[246] says that the total impression of his work 'is of an intricate texture woven with great skill with an assured and masterful handling of language which gave a feeling of almost muscular strength: often his line could sing and be simple: but mostly he preferred the reasoned line: developed statement: was interested in *constructing* a poem which moved and convinced and delighted'. Often, however, what overwhelms one is not the fine craftsmanship but the sheer beauty of the lines.

In what direction would Nortje have proceeded had he lived? This is not idle speculation but a question very pertinent to the writing of South Africans in exile. Ezekiel Mphahlele described the impossibility of creating in exile as the tyranny of place, and had to return to South Africa to give meaning to his life and work. Arthur Nortje called his collection of poems *Dead Roots*. Yet by 1970 the sap was still running. Once it had dried completely what would there have been to say? Perhaps these are the only solutions: return and take your chance with the rest, be silent and await a new dawn, or, in exile, the leap from the window, the overdose of drugs.

When reading Dennis Brutus's work, more than that of any other black South African writer, one becomes aware of the contrast between the essential nature of the poet and what the South African situation has forced him to become. Inexhaustible in his political endeavours to procure a just South Africa to which all South Africans can return, Brutus yet can rarely suppress his natural gentleness in his poetry.

> I must come gently to gentleness,
> obliquely, almost by stealth,

he says in a poem in the volume *Strains*.[247] One feels that this is the real Brutus, one who lugs his 'crumpled sac of / tenderness turned to pain',[248] but steels himself against the temptation of giving rein to his personal feelings, his own 'simple lusts', 'the thin thread of agony / that runs through the veins / after the flesh is overspent—in over-taxing acts of love', and speaks instead of 'the others' woe', '*their* unarticulated simple lust' (italics mine).[249]

Brutus's devotion to his fellow men led him to clashes with the authorities early in his career. Neither imprisonment nor physical danger could daunt him. Born in Salisbury, Brutus, like Nortje, was brought up and educated in Port Elizabeth. He continued his studies at Fort Hare, where he gained his B.A. in 1946 with distinction in English. He taught English and Afrikaans at High schools in Port Elizabeth. In 1961 he was banned and dismissed from teaching, and began to study law at the University of the Witwatersrand. In 1963 he was arrested for contravening his banning order by attending a sports meeting, but was released on bail. He sought refuge in Swaziland, but while trying to get to Germany *via* Mozambique in connection with his activities for the South African non-racial Olympics committee, he was arrested by the Portuguese police and handed over to the South Africans. While attempting to escape in Johannesburg he was shot in the back. He was sentenced to eighteen months on Robben Island. After his release in 1965, he was allowed to leave with his wife and seven children (later there were eight) on a one-way exit permit. He first lived in London, between 1966 and 1970, where he taught, wrote poetry and served in various anti-South African organisations. He travelled a great deal for this purpose. In 1971, he was appointed professor of English at Northwestern University in Evanston, Illinois, a post which he still holds today. He was president of the South African Non-Racial Olympic Committee (where he was mainly instrumental in keeping South Africa out of the Olympic games), Director of the World Campaign for the Release of South African political prisoners, and he represented the International Defence and Aid organisation at the United Nations. In South Africa his writing continues to be banned.

With such a career one naturally expects his poetry to be strongly political. It is certainly a condemnation of the South African political situation, but he writes as a poet and not as a politician. Interviewed by Bernth Lindfors, Ian Munro, Richard Priebe and Reinhard Sander at the University of Texas in 1972,[250] Brutus said that he firmly believed in artistic integrity and that one should not turn art into propaganda.

> By reporting a simple experience I ask people to make up their own minds. But I don't try to persuade them as to how they ought to make up their minds. I don't think I myself would call this protest. I would say it functions as protest; it has the effect of protest. But I think it's poetry and not protest; it's not propaganda. The politics is not imported into it.[251]

He expresses a similar view in a poem entitled 'I must Speak', where he hopes that his 'words will reverberate' in his listener's 'silent moments' and then:

. . . when your heart answers
some strong assertion of the truth
in blood, or action or belief and seeks for words
let then my echoes rise
unbidden
in the tunnels of your mind.[252]

He does not always follow his injunction against propaganda.
Some of his lines are purely political statements as when he boasts of
his achievements:

that which they hold most dear
a prestige which they purchased with sweat
. . .
their sporting prowess and esteem
this I have attacked and
blasted
unforgettably.[253]

In later poems he becomes even more stridently militant, for instance
in 'Sharpeville' with its refrain of:

Remember Sharpeville
Remember bullet-in-the-back day.[254]

He is still standing too close to the event and can only proclaim. This
becomes evident when we compare this poem with that which gives
his first collection, *Sirens Knuckles Boots* its title. Here life in a
'Coloured' area is described, at first in quiet tones beginning: 'The
sound begin again', and, after talking of the almost silent response of
the people living there, he ends:

importunate as rain
the wraiths exhale their woe
over the sirens, knuckles, boots;
my sounds begin again.[255]

Such lines make it very clear what Brutus means when he says he is
aiming at a reverberation of his words.

Brutus's dedication to duty is the moving force in his life and work.
If, he says, 'this life is all we have', then surely 'we must fill each day
with living / and do each day as much as we can / of what seems to us
worthwhile':

all that is good, as we understand it
all that stirs us with a sense of joy.[256]

His commitment, however, is not just to a particular cause but to
humanity, 'sad, fumbling humanity', as he calls it in a resonant poem
in which his beloved is asked to 'forgive the world' and pledge her
commitment with him.[257]

Already while still in South Africa, Brutus saw himself as a wandering minstrel, challenging evil wherever he found it. In a well-known poem which begins his first collection, he compares himself with a troubadour, traversing all his land, exploring 'with zest' 'all the wide-flung parts' of his beloved country, making his views known and defying those who would stop him, even if he realises that often he is tilting at windmills. Although he enjoys the tussle he has no illusions. The end is inevitable, but he has no moral choice and wears his prison uniform—'the shadow of an arrow-brand'—with the pride with which the medieval knight wore his 'mistress-favour'.[258] His 'passion' does not allow him to consider an alternative to living dangerously and challenging the authorities, he tells us in another poem. Such 'parasitic ease disgusts' him and 'rich food' would knot 'to revolting clots / of guilt and anger' in his 'queasy guts / remembering the hungry comfortless'.[259]

With all he has done and suffered for his land, Brutus has no need to prove himself consciously black. 'What is the soul of Africa?' he asks,[260] and wonders whether it is perhaps 'simply that we have / contrived to be what humans are / while everywhere humanity / was being deformed?'. Quoting an expression used by Ebrahim Salahi at the first Pan African Cultural Festival in Algiers, he says that he will settle for being 'the non-totemistic "new" African artist . . . who will simply take his place in the whole world culture while always bearing certain distinctive features as a result of his origins and experience. And it may be that in some respects our experience is more humane, he continues, 'i.e. more considerate of human feeling, because we have, up to now, in some measure, escaped the dehumanizing process or events which have made a mark, or are marking other societies'.[261]

A wide compassion touches all of his poetry. His pity, like Nortje's, is rarely for himself. It is not an empty stance when he tells us of his mingled feelings on first being sent to Robben Island: relief, apprehension, a sense of challenge, 'vague heroism / mixed with self-pity' and:

> tempered by the knowledge of those
> who endure much more
> and endure . . .[262]

He is bitter about the older men who have grown too frightened to fight but he tries to show understanding:

> . . . I feel a measure of sadness
> —and no contempt—
> and have no wish to condemn
> or even grow impatient.[263]

Only rarely is there an outburst of hatred, yet he has understanding for the feeling of hatred for the enemy:

I have not, out of love, cursed you yet,
though anger and impatience often rock me;
. . .
but know that frenzies may yet come.[264]

His understanding of human failings embraces even the enemy and this he expresses in a poem which has led to much discussion, 'Their Behaviour, Blood River Day, 1965', which begins:

Their guilt
is not so very different from ours.[265]

In the interview at Texas University he explains the origin of the poem. 'I was writing,' he says, 'to a Welsh woman who said, "I wonder what it's like in South Africa?" I was just trying to help her, and I was replying on a particular day which seemed to catch the quality of South Africa . . . Blood River Day, a once-a-year tribal ritual when whites celebrate their historic victory over the Blacks in a battle which raged until the river ran with blood'.[266] In the poem he asserts that joy in an arbitrary exercise of power and the use of superior force is a temptation to which all can succumb. Wole Soyinka calls this 'negative compassion' and says:

It is an expression of the bleak intimations that must result from an uncompromising stare at the common denominators of humanity. Glared at in its turn from an uncompromising revolutionary stance it may appear to cross the edge of blasphemy, for it is possible to claim that the expression of such insights . . . is a palliative to the unrepentant conscience of criminal power possessed by the white social oppressor; or at the best, it could become a gratuitous *mea culpism* which enervates the revolutionary will. It is healthiest, however, to accept such insights fully and on their own terms, to regard them as a realistic and essential dimension of the moral equipment required for the reconstruction not merely of society but of man. It is hard and unsentimental, an inward-directed demand for self-cognition.[267]

A perceptive analysis; yet I feel that Brutus did not intend to make *excuses* for people who can drown 'the voice of conscience'; rather he sorrows for them and *warns* that such behaviour is human.

Similarly in another poem, 'the Mob', for which he was also taken to task, he refers to the white crowd who attacked protestors against the Sabotage Bill of the South African Government as 'my' people:

Oh my people
what have you done?[268]

Brutus still appears to envisage one South Africa for all. He is one of the few black writers and critics who include white South African authors in discussions on South African literature, and it is interesting to note that he refused the Mbari prize (second) offered to him by the University of Ibadan in 1962 because it was open only to black writers.

The prison experience is like no other in the life of a poet, especially where there has been solitary confinement. Contrary to what one would expect, it seems to soften the poet and make him less strident, more lyrical in expression. We have already seen this effect in the poetry of James Matthews. Brutus's poems become more simple and vivid. Often he achieves even a kind of repose amid the turbulence. In a poem written while under house arrest, 'For Daantjie—on a *New Coin* envelope', he finds hope '. . . in thinking that repose / can be wrung from these iron-hard rigidities',[269] just as Cézanne 'wrenched / new harmonies, the apple's equipoise / the immobility of deadlocked conflicts' from the 'screaming tensions' of his physical world. In the same way that Brutus finds Cézanne's work 'almost tactile on the eyeballs, / palpable on the fingertips', his poetry evokes a palpable reality in the mind of the reader. This happens for instance when he describes how nails, screws and other bits of metal are saved and sharpened:

and when these knives suddenly flash
—produced perhaps from some disciplined anus—
one grasps at once the steel-bright horror
in the morning air
and how soft and vulnerable is naked flesh.[270]

Many of the poems are written in a low key. All is grey: 'the grey silence of the empty afternoons', 'the greyness of isolated time'.[271] Yet interest never flags. He speaks of religion, fear of insanity, sodomy. The reader almost shares Brutus's cell with him. There is the longing, which blasts inside him with 'nuclear devastation', the 'whispers of horror' in 'this gibbering society'. The images are stark and clear.

The simplicity of style is deliberate. Solitary confinement, he told the Texas University interviewers, 'meant that you were in very great danger of going insane, and I came very close to it'. To keep himself busy he would organise his day in such a way 'that you could use up the whole day, because you saw no one, you spoke to no one, your food was just pushed under the door on the floor—a bowl of porridge three times a day'. So he said to himself, 'Well, I'll spend an hour thinking about literature and another hour thinking about movies,' and he stayed away from things like his family—'you didn't dare think of them'. And so, dissatisfied with what he had written in the past, he decided that he ought 'to write for the ordinary person: for the man who drives a bus, or the man who carries the baggage at the airport, and the woman who cleans the ashtrays in the restaurant. If you can write poetry which makes sense to those people, then there is some justification for writing poetry. Otherwise you have no business writing'.[272] The idea of presenting the poems as letters lent itself well to these ideals.

In his later poetry Brutus often comes back to his prison experience. It is almost as if the mind's eye had taken over at a time when normal sight revealed only bleakness or horror, and etched indelible impressions. In the 'Robben Island Sequence',[273] for example, he describes the background to a scene of torture:

The menace of that bright day was clear as the blade of a knife;
from the blade edges of the rocks,
from the piercing brilliance of the day,
the incisive thrust of the clear air into the lungs
the salt-stinging brightness of sky and light on the eyes,

and ends this section with the line:

the day was brilliant with the threat of death'.

By the time Heinemann published *Letters to Martha*, Brutus had left South Africa. The experiences he describes in his prison poems, and the events which led to his incarceration and departure, form the mental luggage of his travels. In a poem addressed to a friend who had also arrived from South Africa on a one-way exit permit, he describes how it feels:

To be thrown outward in a steel projectile
to hurtle outward in a quivering uncertainty
to a cold fragment of a continental ledge.

Anger is 'the self-conscious indignant pose' of the 'wounded "banneling",' [exile]

. . . holding off
the true deep wound that lies
like the dark bruised pulp at the heart of the fruit:
the agony the heart and mind hold in suspense.[274]

Brutus's agony is more for those left behind than for himself, men who

. . . lie on concrete
or fumble stones with torn hands
or sigh their cold breath
in the cold unlighted night.[275]

Much of his poetry written during the first few years abroad reads like the diary of an exiled wanderer and is often date-lined rather than titled. The nostalgia and the love for his country are unmistakable. One poem, entitled 'A South African in Algiers: Homesickness'[276] consists of two lines listing familiar flowers which he came across at

this other end of Africa; and in the poem which precedes it in the
volume *Poems from Algiers*, he glories in the similarity between an
Algerian scene and home:

> In the sunlight
> in the road along the sea
> they sell the pale-green streaked and patterned watermelon
> with its smooth and tepid skin;
> blue Algerian sky and blue Mediterranean sea:
> and by Clifton, Seapoint and the Cape.[277]

Any glimpse of Africa refreshes his spirit. 'This is my sustenance', he
says in a poem beginning 'Africa's jacaranda dusk'.[278] His 'recurring
hunger for the sun' is not homesickness, however, he tells us in 'Here,
of the things I mark',[279] because at home, under house-arrest, he felt
the same yearning. The yearning is therefore for a free and happy
South Africa, and not just for being back there. He is driftwood, he
says in one of his most beautiful poems, but although it appears that
he is at the mercy of the tides, in the unmarked waters he discerns:

> traceries of patterns like wisps of spume
> where I have gone
> and snailtrails in seasands on a hundred shores
> where I have dragged my sad unresting loins
> —tracks on a lunar landscape that suggest some sense.[280]

Thus he is constantly looking for purpose in the anguish of exile.
In his latest poetry the pain seems to be giving way to a feeling of
hopelessness, frustration and self-doubt. Hope has had to become
stubborn, as he 'plod[s] or shuffle[s] or amble[s] / wracked with
anguished frustrate hunger / and [goes] on'.[281] Others expect him to
continue his efforts but when he urges them to 'pursue the lines / that
brought me where I am', they 'shrink, or find excuse'.[282] What was
the good of it all when he was 'the tattooed lady of the prison':

> and warders would come to our section and get me to strip
> and stare and whistle in mingled pleasure and horror
> at the great purple bruise that ran from my neck down my back,
> from my neck to my thighs in a purple mass.

What was he then, he asks, 'heroic endurer' or 'submissive ass'?[283]
'Endurance', he says in the poem which gives the volume *Stubborn
Hope* its title, 'is a passive quality',

> transforms nothing, contests nothing
> can change no state to something better
> and is worthy of no high esteem.

and so he doubts whether there is any point in persistence. 'Yet', he
tries to reassure himself:

. . . somewhere there lingers the stubborn hope
thus to endure can be a kind of fight
preserve some value, assert some faith
and even have a kind of worth.[284]

Brutus's output is enormous. Poems pour out of him on every occasion. A list of journals in which his work has appeared reads like a library register of periodicals of African interest. Among them are *Black Orpheus, Transition, Breakthru, The New Africa, Africa Today, African Arts/Arts d'Afrique, Purple Renoster, African Freedom News, Okike, Gar, Journal of New African Writing, Présence Africaine, Mayibuyi, Sechaba, Ba Shiru, Benin Review, Blackprint, Granite, Mambo, Pearl, Research in African Literatures, Ufahamu.*

His first collection, *Sirens Knuckles Boots* was published by Mbari Publications in 1963, while he was in prison, and later in the same year by Northwestern University Press in Evanston, U.S.A. Then came *Martha and Other Poems*, written for his sister-in-law when her husband was sent to Robben Island. It was published by Heinemann in 1968. *Poems from Algiers* appeared in 1970 as an Occasional Publication of the African and Afro-American Research Institute of the University of Texas at Austin. Brutus had gone to Algiers to attend the first Pan African Cultural Festival and wrote the poems, as he tells us in a postscript, in an attempt to find an answer to the question of whether he could be called an 'African Voice'. His own Troubadour Press published *Thoughts Abroad* in 1970 under the pseudonym 'John Bruin', so that they could be circulated in South Africa. Then came the collection entitled *A Simple Lust* from Hill and Wang in 1973, with poems from most of the earlier volumes and some new ones. *China Poems*, in 1975, was another Occasional Publication from Texas University. These poems were written when Brutus was in China for the Friendship Invitational Table Tennis Tournament. Handwritten, and published in script in Chinese translations by Ko Ching Po, this visually most attractive volume was presented to his hosts as a mark of appreciation. Each set of short lines gives a brief pen picture of an aspect of Chinese life, such as a commune, an ivory carving factory. *Strains* was published by Troubadour Press in 1975. This volume was mainly retrospective, the poems having been written over the previous fourteen years. Finally, to date, there was *Stubborn Hope* in 1978, published by the Three Continents Press. It contains new poems as well as poems from other volumes, including some from another Occasional Publication of the University of Texas African and Afro-American Studies Center, *South African Black Voices* (1975), in which Brutus was one of the seven poets featured. Unfortunately we are not given dates for the new poems and have to guess from the contents which period of his life each individual poem is commenting on.

Naturally, with hundreds of his poems in print, one would not expect them all to be of an equally high standard. Later, perhaps, Brutus will bring out a carefully and personally selected volume of his best and most representative poems, those which he feels will continue to stand the test of time. At his best he is a lyrical poet of deep contemplation and a careful yet spontaneous craftsman. In his weaker moments he tends to proclaim, complain or hammer an image beyond its necessary function. In the early poems, the constant use of nouns and names as verbs and adjectives, effective and startling when first used in the troubadour poem (for example 'doomed by Saracened arrest' and 'quixoting'), begins to pall, as when he says 'Sharpevilled to spearpoint' 'stoic yourself' and 'andanted through my head'. Later poems with tortuous lines like 'to the consumer-merchants / who consume us',[285] should have been omitted. So, too, should some of the laboured metaphors which mar the beauty and effectiveness with which his work abounds.

In the earliest works the tone is sombre and the poems are complex, their meaning working on several levels and drawing references from his wide experience and reading. In the troubadour poem, for instance, together with the medieval references, there is a line from a very early Latin hymn written by Thomas Aquinas from which he took the phrase '. . . motion sweeter far than rest'. The 'unarmed thumb' in the same poem, standing simply 'when doomed by Saracened arrest' is code for the upraised thumb signal of the resistance movement in South Africa. The 'weathered strand' which is snapped off the captor's hand, is both cloth from a garment that is frayed and the strand—beach—of Robben Island to which he anticipated being sent. All this Brutus tells his University of Texas interviewers in some detail. He is right, I think, in feeling that in spite of the complexities it is a successful poem. Often in his work there is a strength in the imagery which illuminates the statement as, for instance, when the loveliness of Zoo Lake in Johannesburg:

> Light, green-yellow luminescent, tender
> seeps through these deep-foliaged weeping willows
> to filter streams and runnels of soft glow
> suffusing enclaves of green and sombre gloom,

distils in him 'a balm that eases and erases all my hurt'.[286]

Sexual images are often used for the purpose of stressing ravage, possession of the land:

> Dear my land—open for my possessing,
> ravaged and dumbly submissive to our will,
> in curves and uplands my sensual delight

mounts, and mixed with fury is amassing
torrents tumescent with love and pain.[287]

Brutus's style in these early poems is fairly conventional. The troubadour poem is roughly in sonnet form, and he devotes much care to construction, rhythm, rhyme, assonance, alliteration and the formation of stanzas.

In *Letters to Martha* the style becomes simpler. This, as we have seen, was due to a conscious effort to make his poetry more accessible to the ordinary person. These efforts come to fruition in *Poems from Algiers* in which he combines the simple statement of the *Martha* poems with vivid imagery, especially in the driftwood poem. Later, his pieces become shorter and more urgent, the effect of transience and movement as he circles the world. Many of his poems are written on planes, which he says, gives him a feeling of being freed from restraints.

Still later, in the new poems of *Stubborn Hope*, imagery recedes. Frustration and self-doubt are not inspiring . There are often only short stark statements and the whole lacks the cohesion of the earlier volumes. Sometimes, however, the increasing despair turns him inward, and in his honest self-assessment he becomes lyrical again. In a poem entitled 'Success cannot redeem despair', he says:

I who can, squirming, turn in the dark
and find some magnitude of stars
—pinpricks to bar the dark's enfolding tide—
still catch at the edge of vision a flicker,
life's fragile pulse in a shadowed hollow at my wrist.[288]

Usually Brutus is not an introspective poet in the sense that Nortje or Serote are. His poetry is personal but he stands away from himself. 'The mirror serves: / the viewer / sets the angle',[289] he says in *China Poems*. He is in the centre and agonises over what he must do, what he has done, but his search is for action and not identity.

Brutus has always been interested in poetic techniques, and is always exploring and experimenting. The China poems were a result of his exposure to *haikus* and their even earlier Chinese ancestors, the *Chueh chu*, as he tells us in a note in *Chinese Poems*. The trick, he says, is to say little, 'the nearer to nothing, the better', and to suggest 'as much as possible'. 'Non-emotive, near neutral sounds should generate unlimited resonance in the mind; the delight is in the tight-rope balance between nothing and everything possible.'[290] In the poems he puts these precepts into practice, sometimes successfully, sometimes a little pretentiously; sometimes the lines are whittled down to the point of banality.

Whereas modern African critics frown on analogy with Western literature, Brutus has no hesitation in drawing on his extensive and enthusiastic universal reading, and absorbing the writing of those he admires. He acknowledges his debt to Donne, Eliot, James Joyce, Browning, Ezra Pound, Patchen, Rexroth, Wallace Stevens, and describes himself as having been on a 'Hopkins kick' when he wrote 'So for the moment, Sweet, is peace', in *Sirens Knuckles Boots*. The new poets within South Africa he greets with delight as 'new voices, brave voices' and admires them for their 'controlled passion'.[291]

His own individual style is distinct, and however varied his output, at his best it is a mixture of lyricism with an underlying thrust of purpose, clothed in an imagery of sensuous scenic background and effective metaphor.

Cosmo Pieterse, who teaches in the English and Afro-American Departments of Ohio University, is better known as an anthologist and promoter of black literature than as a poet. He has edited several collections of drama, poetry and literary criticism, some of which we will discuss later. His poems appeared in black American publications and were included in two anthologies, *Poets to the People*[292] and *South African Voices*.[293] His individual collections are *Echoes and Choruses: Ballad of the Cells* and *Selected Shorter Poems*[294] followed by *Present Lives Future Becomings*.[295] The long work in *Echoes and Choruses*[296] is a mixture of poem and drama, and since Pieterse includes it in his collection of dramas we will discuss it later under that heading.

Pieterse is fascinated with words, their sound, their many meanings, even their physical appearance on the page, the typography often being carefully arranged. He probes them and extracts image and idea from their meaning and association. In the first poem in *Present Lives*, for instance, he recites the months of the year, evocative of a song which was popular among the choirs in the coloured townships, but March again reminds him of the other meaning of the word and he says:

> March until all may March right through
> the year of the land.[297]

In the same volume he introduces the poem 'Taste and Striation',[298] about the passage of time and hope for the future, as follows:

> There are buds on the tree
> There are buds on the tongue
> There are birds on the tree
> There are leaves on the trees which believe their earth
> Leaves on the trees which never entirely leave their rooted soil
> There are buds on the tongues of the tree
> The buds on the tongue of the ripe open mouth of the fig
> taste the kiss of the warm life breathing sun
> and reply with their shape and the form of their fruit.[299]

The sequence of ideas by which he tries to lead us to the point of his passages is not always easy to follow and the meaning of the poems is not easily accessible. His fascination with words often runs away with him. The final poem in *Present Lives*, for instance, plays on the African word for come back, *mayibuye*, with such unfelicitous lines as

Let it come back
To this   May we be you blue[300]

The shorter poems are often militant songs, with titles like 'Guerilla'[301] and lines like 'We sing our sons who have died red'.[302] *Present Lives Future Becomings* is a collage of narrative, poetry, a short play, a satirical dialogue, sketches, reminiscences and photographs by George Hallett and others. The different genres wander strangely through the work, but not at random. They run contrapuntally, contrasting in contents and execution, on a theme of exile and the expectation of return. The narrative concerns a miner on the Rand, Nkosi, and the nightmare of his daily hardships. This is underlined in one chapter by the bloody history of South Africa about which he is reading, and the present and past converge in nightmare. The poetry carries Pieterse's theme by a series of images such as that of cosmic creation in 'Earthwoman', of artistic creation in 'Painter, Maker, Musician', all working towards the final 'becoming', when both the narrative and poetry speak of the new dawn. Nkosi receives a letter from his wife in which she says:

The earth shall in time become its own sun. We shall not wait for the sun to rise, but shall turn the world into its own warm sun, a sun for you and me and everybody.[303]

The last poem, titled 'Inconclusion: For The Time Being[304] envisages the return of the exile.

With even greater impatience than Pieterse, Keorapetse Kgositsile looks to a release from bondage. He firmly believes in the coming of the new dawn, but is convinced that it can be arrived at only through direct action. He dedicates a poem entitled 'New Dawn'[305] to 'afrika, asia, south & afroamerica'. In the third-world-wide application of his ideas of freedom from servitude he differs from the other poets who have been discussed. He emphasises the universality of black revolt, for example by mixing African and American references, as in one entitled 'For Afroamerica',[306] in which he sees 'Patrice and Malcolm' in the step of a dancer nearing the sun, the symbol for the day of revolution.

Born in Johannesburg in 1938, Kgositsile was one of the earliest to leave South Africa. In 1961 he went to Dar es Salaam to work on a magazine, and after a few months arrived in the United States where he attended various Universities. For some time he was attached to the Columbia University writing programme in New York and since then has worked on various magazines. He is currently back in Dar es Salaam teaching literature at the University of Tanzania.

Paul Breman, who collected poems written by black writers from Africa, the West Indies and the United States in an anthology entitled *You Better Believe It*,[307] says in his notes on Kgositsile that he was welcomed by his contemporaries in black American letters, who at first seemed to use him as a mascot, 'at best as an ambassador from a motherland with which for many years it seemed almost impossible to establish tangible relations'.[308] The integration when it came was reciprocal. More than any other exile Kgositsile has become part of black American literature. He is almost totally unknown in his homeland. Mphahlele, reviewing his volume *The Present is a Dangerous Place to Live*[309] in *Okike*,[310] says: 'That is one way in which an exile may choose: the movement from native territory to near-integration into the new landscape', but he does not really feel that such integration is possible for a writer:

> Kgositsile does not, and I don't think can ever, acquire these resonances (that come from deep down the levels of ethnic consciousness), dreams, lore, belief, history that defy or modify stereotypes like Uncle Tom, the blackman's whiteness, white footprints, etc. He can only serve up the external trappings, the visual and therefore accessible dramatization of Afro-American Life, the visible heroes, cowards, buffoons, uncletoms, slaves, musicians, the behaviour of a people from decade to decade and so on.[311]

Kgositsile's appeal to his black American readers lies less in his making common cause than in the fact that he provides a link to their roots. The folk memory of an African ancestry becomes less contrived than it does in their own poetry in a poet whose roots were once firmly planted in African soil.

Kgositsile has published several collections. *Spirits Unchained*[312] was published by the Broadside Press in 1969, and won him the Conrad Kent Rivers Award given by *Black World* magazine in the United States. *For Melba*[313] (his wife) was published in 1970 by Third World Press, and *My Name is Afrika* followed in 1971. *The Present is a Dangerous Place*, published by Third World Press in 1974, contains poems from the earlier collections, from various journals and new poems. His poems, like those of Brutus and Pieterse, appeared in numerous black American journals. He has been much anthologised, his contributions appearing for instance in *Modern Poetry from Africa, Black Fire, Seven South African Poets, Yardbird Reader, Poems Now, Black Arts, Poets to the People, South African Voices, You Better Believe It, Contemporary African Literature* and in the anthology he edited himself, *The Word is Here*.

Kgositsile's poetry is an unequivocal call for action to bring about freedom for the black man. There is no doubt in his mind about the purpose of his poetry. 'Openly I tell you', he says in a poem entitled 'After Mongane':

> I am this eye
> when you hear guns
> my poem will be that sound
> hammered to heat of action
> in the sweetness of this pain.[314]

The 'unrelenting song' to which he and the other poets must listen, is 'the young talking drum', saying 'sift and shift', (the title of the poem)[315] for if they do not, like cowards they will

> bear sons without memory
> nor images to weave their song.[316]

Kgositsile is not a dreamer. Hope and nostalgia are not the metal of which his poetry is cast. Home is 'the bitter smell of Sophiatown winter',[317] Africa (with a 'c' as opposed to the new and more 'fragrant' future Afrika) is 'the stench of absence'[318] and any laughter remaining in his memory is 'stale as our glory'.[319] His emphasis is on the present. One must stop saying 'Some day soon, someday soon', while 'the pangs in fleshless ribs' of 'children swayed by hunger' 'clearer than glib verse or song ask now'.[320] Dreams, 'too / long deferred' explode 'Now'; truths 'defiant like volcanoes emerge / taller than shadows / from ghetto magicians / Now'. He can see that day, 'teasing like a whore, screaming, NOW.'[321] He therefore has little time for the black consciousness stance. 'It is fashionable', he says in 'Random Notes to my son'[322] to / scream of pride and beauty as though it were not / known that 'Slaves and dead people have no beauty,' and remonstrates more emphatically in 'To Mother':[323]

> We claim the soil of our home
> runs in our blood yet we run
> around the world, the shit of others
> drooling over our eyes . . .

'No more blues', he warns in 'No Celebration', 'the day is not here yet to sing'.[324]

As time passes a note of pessimism and despair creeps into his poetry as it has into that of most of the exiles. 'Where is the life we came to live,' he asks. In his last volume Kgositsile is no longer the 'Spirit Unchained', nor does he proclaim 'My name is Afrika'. 'The Present is a Dangerous Place to Live', he says.

Mazisi Kunene, banned like Brutus and Kgositsile, also left South Africa early, first for Britain where he studied at the School of African and Oriental Studies of London University, continuing his research into Zulu poetry for which he had gained a Master's degree. He became involved in politics and was the official United Nations representative of the African National Congress, and later its director of finance. His activities took him to Europe and the United States where he also lectured widely. He is now Assistant Professor of African Literature and Language at the University of California at Los Angeles.

The poems for Kunene's first volume in English, *Zulu Poems*,[325] were taken from a larger selection he had originally written in Zulu, and were translated by the poet himself. His subsequent work in epic poetry was also first written in Zulu, though there is little chance of its being published in South Africa today. Kunene's allegiance as a poet, however, is to an African world view rather than a particular African language. His purpose in translating, and therefore promulgating these poems among a larger audience, is to encourage a return to oral tradition in literature. This tradition, he explained at a symposium on Contemporary South African Literature and Inaugural Conference of the African Literary Association held at the university of Texas at Austin in 1975,[326] contains the following elements:

> it interprets, focuses, and analyzes the past as well as the present and then creates a perspective for the future. In African religion, the previous generation, the present generation, and the future generation are seen in terms of an integrated whole, and it is the function of literature to create this connection, this nexus, of the past, present and future.[327]

The poems are illustrative of these aims. Kunene rejects European culture and values. Once, he tells us in a poem entitled 'Europe', he was impressed by what the West had to offer:

> Once I believed the tales,
> Once I believed you had breasts
> Over-flowing with milk.
>
> I saw you rushing with books
> From which the oracles derive their prophesies.[328]

Now he has come to realise 'the hardness of your (Europe's) vision'. Instead, he embraces African culture, dedicating himself to the ideals handed down by the ancestors:

> So many are asleep under the ground,
> When we dance at the festival
> Embracing the earth with our feet.
> Maybe the place on which we stand
> Is where they also stood with their dreams.

They dreamed until they were tired
And handed us the tail with which we shall dance.

. . .

We too shall follow their path
Our dust shall arise at the gathering place.[329]

He glories in the concepts of life which he calls 'Triumph of Man' in a
poem of that title, man who 'alone created eternity'. This comes
about, he says because the dead come awake in those who follow
them.

The dead awake and frolic in a dance
Crushing the leaves that are daily scattered,
Because their faces have eyes,
And lips, and flesh, in the centuries.[330]

This he knows is the essence of art and creativity. Again, in 'Man's
Power Over Things' he stresses the function of man as the centre of
the world without whom all things are empty. This he is determined
to prove, until

No more will you hold your faith in things
But sing the greatness of your blood.[331]

Since he sees the function of literature 'not merely to entertain but
primarily to teach social values and serious philosophical concepts',[332] there is no question in Kunene's mind about the right of the
poet to make his protest, or, as he calls it, writing African resistance
poems. Like the oral poet in precolonial times, Kunene sees it as his
duty to uphold an unchanging set of values and attack those who
would destroy it.

Kunene goes back to the very foundation of African beliefs that
first brought about the clash with Europeans: the concept that the
land belongs to all and cannot be owned or divided:

Why should those at the end of the earth
Not drink from the same calabash
And build their homes in the valley of the earth
And together grow with our children?

he asks in 'Mother Earth, or the Folly of National Boundaries'.[333]

The importance of children in the continuity of life, and their
future role in the community, is often emphasised. It is interesting to
note that in his anthology *Poems of Black Africa* Wole Soyinka puts
Kunene's poem about a child which questions the inexplicable South
African world he lives in, next to Mtshali's poem 'Boy on a Swing'
followed by his 'The Face of Hunger', and we realise how much
South African protest poetry concerns children and the tragedy of
their lives.

There is little reference to exile in *Zulu Poems*. In a later poem—read to the conference at Texas University mentioned earlier—and published in *South African Voices*, the 'Dreams in Exile' of the title are nightmares of terror and violence, and especially the feeling of being sealed off by walls, 'inmate of an old shuttered house'.[334]

The African poet's main role, then, which Kunene demonstrates in his poems, is to express the consciousness of his people and to preserve their history and communal identity. Kunene succeeds in conveying the richness of oral poetry which becomes the vehicle for expressing contemporary ideas.

On the other hand his method also leads to obscurity. The Zulu poet Vilakazi, discussing the conception and development of poetry in Zulu, said that Zulu poets made use mainly of private and personal imagery which is incomprehensible to the general reader. One needs a key. This Kunene provides for some of the poems but not for all. One has to know, for instance, that proper names are often part of a system of ideas or personification, because the names bear meanings expressive of events. Thus the name Mpindelele means recurrent, which in the following lines is the name of a fountain and at the same time describes the action of the fountain and symbolises recurrent yearnings.

> May I when I awake
> Take from all men
> The yearnings of their souls
> And turn them into the fountain of Mpindelele
> which will explode into oceans.[335]

For another poem he explains a reference to the place of the setting sun as meaning distant places, and mythological regions and shade as a refuge, a place where gatherings were held and thinkers could meditate. A circular pot symbolises communal activity in the poem 'Repeat'[336]

> The substance of knowledge
> is a circular pot bursting with abundance
> On which many lips are feeding.[337]

All this Kunene explains in notes, but many symbols can easily be recognised in their context. An exploration of the meaning of symbols and thus of the poet's underlying ideas is the essence of the encounter.

In recent years Kunene has written few short works, as he was working on two long epics. His purpose, as he tells us in the introduction to *Zulu Poems*, in which an extract from one of them appears, is to capture the spirit and cosmology of the Zulu nation concerning the origin and purpose of life. *Anthem of Decades*[338] was published as a completed work after the period under consideration in this study, so we will speak only about the extract in *Zulu Poems*.[339]

The poem is told in the form of myths, but the narration of mythology of the past is not Kunene's purpose. He aims, instead, as he tells us in a note to the extract, at 'projecting the conception of life and the universe according to African (Zulu) belief and interpretation'.[340] *Anthem of Decades* is about the beliefs and systems defining the position and future of man in the universe.

Kunene's account of the first coming of life on earth, 'the ecstasy of heaven', is an imaginative one. To the existing myths he adds his own descriptions according, as he says 'to the dictates of Zulu culture'. Sodume, his voice 'round and powerful' shaking the heavens, and his wife Nodume with her high-pitched voice, who both cherish the lightning-bringing bluebird representing the wrath of the gods, are Kunene's invention, but they represent an undefined idea in Zulu mythology of male and female thunder. Nomkhubulwane is the daughter of the creator, 'the source of all life'. As the goddess of Plenty she does exist in Zulu mythology. In the epic she represents the force which wishes to give man his central position in the Universe:

> Saying: 'We have fulfilled the other tasks of creation
> But they are not complete without man,
> He who will bind all things of existence,
> A shepherd who excels with wisdom.'[341]

Opposed to her is Somazwi, who, 'dreaded by all', is known for his swift mind. He has his doubts about such a creature:

> When it realises the defects of its clan
> It will build dreams that will never be fulfilled
> And wander everywhere with painful doubts asking the question
> 'What is the earth, of what value is life?'[342]

Kunene is careful to explain that Nomkhubulwane and Somazwi must not be looked upon as the opposing forces of good and evil, since the triumph of good over evil does not exist in Zulu mythology. Somazwi must not be equated with the devil. Rather he is an opposing force with valid and reasonable arguments to give balance to the impending decision. Thus Sodume does not make up his mind between the forces lightly:

> He listened like all wise men
> Who do not rush without untying each knot.[343]

Then Nomkhbulwane explains that the creation of man is the inevitable outcome of the extension of creation: 'creation must always create. / Its essence is its change', Nomkhubulwane says, and Sodume adds:

> Whoever is the umbilical cord of life denies his existence
> If he disputes the oneness of which he is extension.
> It is not he alone who is, who is the reality of creation,
> But those who are and others who shall be
> Since the eye of life extends to the vastness of eternity.[344]

In answer to those who claim the uselessness of a creature that walks 'in ignorance, blind of his fate' the forces of creation reply that it is this 'very struggle of incomplete power' which will 'rouse his mind with the appetite for wisdom'. And so the moral force for the source of all life is triumphant: men are to 'stand supreme over the earth'. The rest of the extract describes the feasts and revels celebrating the achievement of the desirable goal.

Kunene's second epic, *Emperor Shaka the Great*,[345] was published in 1979, again written first in Zulu and then translated by the poet himself. Running to more than 17,000 lines, it is a monumental work. It is the story of the great warrior king who united several Nguni tribes to form the Zulu nation. Again this is not an academic or chauvinistic attempt at historical or heroic preservation, but an imaginative interpretation of African philosophy. Kunene tries to replace what black South Africa lost under conquest: the feeling for the continuity of history, not as an object lesson for modern times, not as stimulus to nostalgia and pride, but as part of one's own life. He demonstrates how we live in the past and present, and thus shape our future. Through the knowledge of Shaka's vision, Kunene tells us in the introduction, many may understand the dreams and realities that have shaped the destinies of the peoples of Africa. In this respect it may possibly stand beside some of the world's great epics. This is something time will decide and it is impossible to make decisive comments so soon after publication of a work of this kind. Many re-readings will be required, together with a thorough study of the historical, linguistic and philosophical background. Also a reading in the original language is probably essential, even though Kunene's translation into English, is, as always, impeccable.

Shaka has long stood in the centre of African literature and many Zulu praise poems have been written to him. It was in fact during Shaka's reign that this genre was perfected. Kunene incorporates the praise poem, which he describes rather as 'poems of excellence', elevating the highest desirable qualities in society, 'an ethical system beyond the circumstances of the individual'.

Kunene sees Shaka as a great and masterful African genius, a political visionary. At the same time he is representative of the community. His destiny is shaped both by his actions based on his character and by the great truths that rule all men. His downfall is caused not by empty prophecy or the casting of a spell but because he allows a personal relationship—that with his mother—to violate the nations' great ancestral heritage by forbidding all ploughing, reaping, milking and sexual relations between men and women for a year after his mother's death. Shaka has tried to pit himself against the community and must suffer the consequences.

Kunene builds up the story with loving care, and the narrative never flags in interest. Heroic scenes of war are balanced by domestic scenes and always at the centre is the destiny of man and his place in the continuity of life.

Our study of Mazisi's work must remain incomplete in a survey of this nature, so that this is only a pointer to his achievements in speaking poetically and imaginatively for the significance of African literature and thought in our time.

Some of the poets whom we have already discussed as writing most of their work at home continued to produce in exile. Mtshali's volume *Fire:Flames*,[346] of which a few poems had appeared in the anthology *South African Voices*, was written during the years he spent abroad; strangely, it was published in South Africa where it was inevitably and promptly banned.

Mtshali's long silence, or 'gestation period' as he calls it in his author's note to the volume and which took place during the period which saw the uprisings in Soweto and elsewhere, produced a considerable change in his outlook. He is no longer the poet of contemporary urban South Africa. Instead he takes a long hard look both backward and forward in history. Dedicating the volume to 'all our heroes, especially the brave school children of Soweto, who have died, been imprisoned and persecuted in the grim struggle for our freedom', he quotes Ibsen as saying that never did he see his homeland so fully and clearly as he did when he was far away from it. He now expresses a hope for a new order. His message is directed at 'the jaded soul of the forlorn', in whom he hopes 'to strike a responsive chord'[347] to rouse him to action in procuring the day of reckoning. In poems with titles like 'The Dawn of a new era', 'the raging generation', '16 June 1979' [the date of a commemoration in Harlem of the Soweto uprisings] and refrains of 'Be ready brother / be prepared sister'[348] and

> Amandla! Amandla! Amandla! Ngawethu!
> Power! Power! Power! To the People![349]

he exhorts the people[350] to

> gird your loincloth
> and bellow like a bull bristling with massive power,
> blow your nostrils to blur the sun,
> shake the earth to its rotten roots,

lick the gunpowder from the rusty cannons,
clash the shield against the spear,
let the bullet explode into a weeping droplet of sterile semen
let the assegai sing the sweet song of our victory,
let death despair and perish into the enslaver's dungeon of
    defeat.[351]

The first part of 'a song for South Africa',[352] which he read in a
slightly different version to the poetry reading associated with the
University of Texas conference mentioned earlier, is based on a chant
performed by young players from a musical called *Shanti*. The
courage of the players in glorifying the jailed and banned leaders in
performances in South Africa impressed him, and inspired him, too,
to speak out.

This poem, like several others, was first written in Zulu. A few are
translations of the work of other Zulu poets. Mtshali turned back to
an indigenous poetic expression, as he said he would before leaving
South Africa, and perhaps he also came under the inspiration of poets
like Mazisi Kunene and others whom he met in the States. His
concern in poems other than the straight-forward freedom songs is
now with abstract questions: what is a child, love, God? He often uses
the cosmic terms of oral literature as when he speaks of the depth,
abundance and profundity of the soul in the first poem of the
collection, 'The Richness of the Soul'.[353]

His style is generally more prosaic, though he often reverts to the
bold rhythms and ease of phrasing of his earlier work. In one poem
particularly, Mtshali goes back to his earlier style. 'Back to the
Bush'[354] is once again placed squarely within the South African
setting, and has Mtshali's sardonic touch. Commenting on the
double standards of Christianity as interpreted in Africa, the poet
says he heeded the priest's advice in abandoning his so-called
heathenism, but how did the Church welcome him?

You told me not to slaughter
the black ox for my ancestors
and not to wear its hide
which I tanned into a *beshu*

  Instead you taught me how to chop
  and pluck a Christmas turkey
  because all civilised people do that.

You told me that people
who wear *beshus* are barbarians
and those who smear their faces
with ochre are savages.

I heeded your fatherly advice
I exchanged my skins
for a Savile Row suit.

I wiped the ochre from my wife's face
and gave her Helena Rubenstein's cosmetics
then we went to where other people go,
and there we were turned away.

A group of exiles (or, to give them their official title, refugees) established themselves in Gaberone in Botswana and founded two cultural organisations, Pelandaba Cultural Effort (Pelculef), which later merged with a group known as Dashiki, and Medu Art Ensemble. Prominent members were Mongane Serote, Christine Douts, Lefifi Tladi, Mandlenkosi Langa and there were others, many of whom had taken part in the Black Consciousness organisations banned after the uprisings, such as BPC and SASO. The aims of these organisations in Botswana was to encourage the various arts in a manner relevant to the aspirations and goals of black people and thus, as stated in the editorial of the first issue of Medu's *Newsletter* to create 'a consciousness that will help awaken our people's thirst for freedom', to form the cultural—quoting Agostinho Neto—'people's army for the liberation of men'.[355]

The newsletters of both of these organisations, Medu and Pelculef, publish among other items poems which mostly grew out of readings. Pelculef organised two such reading programmes, 'Anthem of Liberation' and 'Shades of Change'. In Pelculef's first newsletter the poems featured are taken from the 'Anthem' programme, and are in the same vein as the freedom songs and protest poems produced earlier by the young members of the banned organisations, with titles like 'The Final Clenching' and 'Our Spears are Immersed in Blood'. Mandlenkosi Langa is one of the leading figures in the Pelculef venture. In the poem 'A City in South Africa'[356] he describes the unnamed place as 'cold, cold city' and its black inhabitants as 'unwilling and unconscious / members of a funeral procession'.[357] In 'The Final Clenching'[358] he ends a powerful dirge for the horrors perpetrated upon Africa:

. . . we began anew
the ultimate embracing of Africa
    in the clasp that death
in its hoary ugliness
    has no power to separate.[359]

Serote who, with Langa and others, is on the editorial board, contributes poems in similar style to that of the others, such as 'No More Strangers'[360] and 'Notes for a Fighter: For Dumile Feni'[361] and extracts from his then unpublished long poem 'Behold, Mama, Flowers'. The Medu Newsletter has a poetry section which includes poems by writers still in South Africa, among them James Matthews and Mafika Gwala.

These, then, are the main writers in exile, leaning consciously towards an African culture. They feel an optimistic faith in imminent return to the homeland; then despair, banned, silenced, attached to the country of their concern by a tenuous thread. In a poem entitled 'Hope for Your Return', addressed to exiled Lefifi Tladi, Matsemela Cain Manaka puts into words a life-line of hope for these poets:

> your poems and music lived on
> they never perished in the flames of your departure
> they never drooped when you visited your brotherland
> they never fell at the foot of your foe
> the flames of your fire reared and raged on
> your enemy could not douse only daze the blaze
> the spirit of your poetry and music lived on in your fatherland.[362]

The Novel

COMPARED WITH POEMS and short fiction few novels by black South Africans have appeared. The reason until recently lay partly in the lack of outlets for full-length books in South Africa. When the mission presses no longer satisfied the requirements of the writers they had to rely on publishers in England and later in America. There is also the financial factor. No semi-official patronage as in England or University support as in the United States is available, although recently the possibility of government aid to writers has been discussed. In the present political climate, however, it is hardly likely that black writers, producing their works in opposition to apartheid, will benefit. One government award for English writing was offered; it was never awarded because of an argument between the Government and the English Academy of Southern Africa, which had been asked to judge but refused to do so under the title of the Hendrik Verwoerd Prize. Another Government-sponsored prize, the Roy Campbell competition, was closed to black entrants in 1973.

The main reason for the paucity of novels, however, lies within the writers themselves. The short story, as we shall see, is a more suitable medium for expressing what they have to say. Moreover, since the novel as a *genre* becomes a personification of ideas, or, as E.M. Forster put it, has the power to make secret life visible, it is alien to African culture where the idea is embodied in a more abstract form. It is also interesting to note that orthodox Marxism, in its early days, regarded the novel as essentially bourgeois because of the emphasis on the individual.

Almost from the beginning of fiction writing in English by black South Africans, it was situation rather than individual characters and their interaction which interested authors.

R.R.R. Dhlomo's *African Tragedy*[1] was the tragedy of the black man in a changing society, and not the tragedy of one particular man. The plot of a black man coming to the city and succumbing to its evil ways has been repeated *ad nauseam* since then, but rarely by black South Africans writing in English because it was no longer a situation which interested them. Later writers were brought up in the city. What the city had to offer was no longer temptation to a Christian hero, but the amenities of a world of technology and culture which was closed to the black man. Fiction consequently took the form of protest against apartheid, a subject which lends itself to short fiction rather than to sustained writing, unless the writer follows the activities of a character from situation to situation. Since the situation was always one experienced by the writer himself, the longer works were autobiographical rather than fictitious.

Only in the last few years has the position changed. New publishing houses in South Africa now encourage novel writers by publication, and by offering awards and prizes like the Mofolo-Plomer prize founded by Nadine Gordimer, to which three publishing houses contribute (Ravan Press, Ad. Donker and Bateleur) and the Central News Agency Award. The English Academy offers the Olive Schreiner prize for full length works.

The early novels are mainly of historical interest. There is little point in discussing *African Tragedy* in detail. Dhlomo's novel is merely a collector's piece as the first novel in English by a black writer in South Africa. It is not of sufficient literary value to be regarded as a precursor to later novels on a theme which reached its climax with the publication of Alan Paton's *Cry, the Beloved Country*.

The innocent black man in the city is the subject of one other early work of fiction by a black writer in English, John J.B. Khafula. Published in 1946, it already deals mainly with the injustice of apartheid. *This Thing has Got to Stop*[2] is the title, a phrase most probably taken from a newspaper report of a court case as having been spoken by a judge when passing sentence. What is this thing that has got to stop, asks Khafula ironically. Did the judge mean the passing of a death sentence on an innocent man? Or was he perhaps referring to the hero's mother who knew nothing of the events until afterwards? There are only fourteen pages, but it is too complex to be classed as a short story. There is little interest in the characters or even the story, both of which are a social comment.

The theme of A.C. Mopeli-Paulus' novel *Blanket Boy's Moon*[3] is somewhat different. While Monare, the chief character, is also a country boy who comes to the wicked city and falls into evil hands, he does not become the innocent plaything of circumstances. Mopeli-Paulus, who was born in Lesotho—then Basutoland—in 1913 and was variously medical student, teacher, war-time soldier and lawyer's clerk in South Africa, saw Monare as the Pilgrim making Progress. Monare smokes dagga to forget his pain, he hesitates just too long before rescuing a friend from ritual murder so as to remain close to the chief who ordered it. His problems include homosexuality and extra-marital sex. Again it is man rather than a particular black man who faces conflict with the world around him.

Blanket Boy's Moon cannot, however, be considered entirely as a work by a black writer in English since it was written in collaboration with Peter Lanham. Collaboration is always disturbing to the reader who wishes to some extent to establish rapport with the author, even though ideally a work should be able to stand apart from its creator. The reader becomes confused if he cannot look upon a book as the product of one individual mind, and wonders constantly how much each author has contributed. *Blanket Boy's Moon* is sufficiently different in style from a later novel, *Turn to the Dark* (1956) 'by Mopeli-Paulus with Miriam Basner', to tip the balance of authorship towards the two white collaborators.

Mine Boy, by Peter Abrahams, is also about a country boy who comes to the city. I shall, however, deal with all the novels of this author later.

Whereas R.R.R. Dhlomo had tried his hand at a *genre* fairly new for the black writer, Sol Plaatje, by writing dramatically of historical events, in *Mhudi*, was continuing an African tradition which went well back to the days of oral tribal literature. The first printed version, published by Lovedale Press in 1930, differs considerably from the original manuscript discovered a few years ago, and published by Quagga Press in South Africa in 1975. This text subsequently appeared in the Heinemann African Writers' Series. In this version the story is told by 'Half-a-Crown', son of Mhudi and Ra-Thaga, thus giving the novel a framework of narration and an epic oral quality, which emphasises Plaatje's purpose of arousing the black man's interest in his past. There are differences in style between the two editions which, though slight, are also significant in that Plaatje's earlier version is less reliant on a romantic English style. The editors of the new edition, Tim Couzens and Stephen Gray, quote examples of the emasculation by the Lovedale version. For instance, where the original reads 'where our flocks increased—most of the ewes feeding two lambs each . . .' the Lovedale version became 'our cattle waxed fat along the green valleys and bred like so many wild animals, where our flocks with jocund lambs around their dams would frolic'.[4]

Throughout his varied career, and in his writings, Plaatje put his education, intelligence and humanity to the service of interpreting Western life to the black man and African life to the European. In *Mhudi*, however, he tries to combine both, and in this he is not entirely successful. The historical theme concerns the conflict between white and black at a time when the Boers were trekking north and confronted the Matabele under the leadership of King Mzilikazi. The Boers and the Barolong tribe formed a brief alliance against Mzilikazi and succeeded in driving him further north. But the alliance could not last and Mzilikazi's prophecy, which he formulated as a fable, was to come true. He told of one Zungu, who:

. . . caught a lion's whelp and thought that, if he fed it with the milk of his own cows, he would in due course possess a useful mastiff to help him in hunting valuable specimens of wild beasts. The cub grew up, apparently tame and meek just like an ordinary domestic puppy; but one day Zungu came home and found, what? It had eaten his children, chewed up two of his wives, and in destroying it, he himself narrowly escaped being mauled. So, if Tauana and his gang of brigands imagine that they shall have rain and plenty under the protection of these marauding wizards from the sea, they will gather some sense before long.[5]

When the battle was won the Boers kept the land and assigned the captured cattle to the Barolong, an absurd bargain to the tribesmen who wondered where their cattle were supposed to graze.

In his preface Plaatje says that it is his object to interpret to the reading public one phase of 'the back of the Native mind'. What he does, in effect and deliberately, is to demonstrate the historical background and origin of conflict between black and white, and to show how it was caused by the injustices of the white man.

Running parallel with the factual history is the story of friendship between two young men, Phil the Boer lad, and Ra-Thaga of the Barolong, the husband of the heroine of the title. Here, too, Plaatje shows how such a friendship must founder. The rest of the Boers look upon the 'fraternization' as a 'disgraceful spectacle' and they are relieved when they part. Phil's friendship for Ra-Thaga is genuine enough, but even he looks upon his black friend's future function as being his 'right hand man'. Phil's betrothed Annetje welcomes Mhudi and joins Phil in trying to persuade the couple to leave their own people and stay with them, but she in turn envisages Mhudi as a future 'ayah' to her children. Mhudi herself, although she has some liking for Phil and Annetje, rejects them as part of a community whose inhumanity and callousness towards black suffering she has witnessed.

Thus, by placing personal incident within the communal setting, Plaatje has combined fact and fiction to demonstrate the causes, motives and origins of black/white conflict. Where he has gone astray is in the different methods with which he handles the two themes. The historical scenes and narration are authentic and often stirring, and Plaatje seems at home in them. He tries to treat the romantic theme like a Western novel, but its events move inconsequentially in and out of the historical sections without making a coherent whole. The characters are neither the epic figures of tradition, nor are they psychologically motivated as in Western fiction. They barely touch us emotionally.

The mission presses published a few more works in English, but the appeal was limited and black South African literature in English seemed to have reached a dead end. There was no opportunity to publish and therefore no incentive to write, certainly not book-length material.

Perhaps more than one black child, battling to literacy in the adverse conditions of the townships, was discovering that books could provide a key to the understanding of his world. Such a discovery was made by Peter Abrahams, living in the township of Vrededorp in the Transvaal, when he first came across the writing of black Americans in the library of his nearest social centre. At St Peter's Secondary School which he later attended, he wrote a great deal of verse. He left school early, however, and wandered about South Africa, often jobless and homeless—in Natal he was befriended by H.I.E. Dhlomo—until he came to Cape Town. He wanted to write, but jobs on newspapers for non-whites were few. Although involved in Marxist politics, he always had reservations and was therefore not considered sufficiently sound to work for the Communist press. The more conservative black press, on the other hand, considered him a 'dangerous radical', as he tells us in his autobiographical work, *Return to Goli*.[6]

He signed on a ship as a stoker, and, 'charged with bitterness against the whites of that land in particular and all whites in general',[7] left South Africa. To be psychologically free of the colour bar had become an obsession. 'I had to escape or slip into that negative destructiveness that is the offspring of bitterness and frustration,'[8] he says. Only when he had built up the self-respect of which South Africa had deprived him, was he able to look back and write. He was therefore the first of the exiles, and the first to have novels published abroad.

The son of a man of Abyssinian origin, and a 'coloured' mother, he was also the first writer classed in South Africa as coloured to consider himself 'black'. In another of his autobiographical works, *Tell Freedom*, he relates how a coloured teacher complained that he 'met a Native fellow who said you belong to them more than to us', to which Abrahams replied: 'I'm glad he said so'. Much earlier, he tells the story of how a little black friend, Joseph, boasts of the black kings who lived in days before the white man. The next day, after consulting with his mother, Abrahams admits to Joseph: 'We didn't have Coloured kings before the white man. And he comforted me and said: "It is of no moment. You are my brother. Now my kings will be your kings".'[9]

Abrahams was the only writer of a historical novel in English besides Plaatje, since we are not considering works translated from the vernacular, like Thomas Mofolo's *Chaka*. His first major novel, *Mine Boy*[10] tells of a black man, Xuma, who comes to the city from a rural area and encounters the deprivations and inhumanities of the system.

In *Wild Conquest* Abrahams goes back to African history and, like Plaatje, to the origins of conflict between black and white. He chooses the same period and setting as *Mhudi* and in fact leans heavily on its background and part of its plot. Rather than a serious investigation, *Wild Conquest* becomes a vehicle for a message to South Africa to 'build hope instead of fear, to live with love instead of hate'.[11] Abrahams expresses the message through his chief characters in this work and repeats the theme throughout most of his novels. Paul van As, the young Voortrekker in *Wild Conquest*, is the prototype of the white man who embodies the message, and we find him re-embodied later in *A Night of their Own* as his descendant Karl van As, a rising young diplomat. In *Mine Boy* he is Paddy, the Irishman; he appears even in a story with a setting outside South Africa as the young Jewish businessman in *This Island Now*. This white man, in his various guises, is out of tune with, and despised by, his contemporaries: Paul van As hates killing, Karl van As loves across the colour line, Paddy invites blacks to his home. He always puts humanity before colour. Playing his part opposite the white man is the black man, Dabula, in *Wild Conquest*—and repeated as Richard Nkosi, alias Dube, in *A Night of their Own*, and as Xuma in *Mine Boy*—who is prepared to meet the white man without fear or hate. Dabula stands out from his associates by his voluntary monogamy, Richard Nkosi by his horror at murder as a means of gaining a radical political goal.

The minor characters fit into their allotted roles. There is, for example, the older man who communes with nature, the woman who complements the man, the vicious rival, representing evil in the form of sex. Abrahams was not slow in grasping the popular appeal of miscegenation as a subject for a novel. In *Path of Thunder* he weaves a melodramatic plot around a white girl and her coloured lover, with an unlikely *dénouement* in which everyone turns out to be related. Again the characters are stereotyped except perhaps for the woman, Fieta. She is the prototype of the shebeen queen whom we find in *Mine Boy*, and later in many short stories by other writers. Like them, she sparkles occasionally with a zest for life which is sadly lacking in his heroes and heroines, as well as in his villains. Swartz, Nkosi, Dabula, the two van As's and Udomo, indulge in endless political discussions at the most unlikely times. The effect in a story like *A Night of their Own*, about dramatic underground resistance and police action, is often quite absurd.

Abrahams found a formula that worked and exploited it thoroughly. His novels seem to lack the emotion and sincerity of his autobiographical writing, which I shall discuss later. In his appeal to a wide popular market—*Path of Thunder*, for example, had twelve printings in the Soviet Union and has been shown on the screen there and used as a ballet, and all the books have been translated into many languages—Abrahams stands outside the main stream of black English writing in South Africa.

The characters and plots of Abrahams's novels demonstrate a streamlined Marxism. Even if one cannot quarrel with Abrahams's promulgation of a common humanity, it is all too glib. It belongs to that school of political fiction popular before and during the Second World War, when readers yearned to have their liberal beliefs confirmed in story-book form by writers like Arthur Koestler and Upton Sinclair.

Young black readers fell readily under Abrahams's spell. Nat Nakasa said that when he first came across his writings he swallowed them up in rapid succession, permitting no criticism to take shape within him. 'Even the most glaringly naïve and parochial assertions went unopposed'.[12] Young white South African readers devoured the novels with equal voracity and were set by them upon a path of fervent liberalism.

Abrahams tried to copy the naturalistic technique of the black American writers—Richard Wright, William Gardner Smith and others—while at the same time operating within a conventional formula for popular fiction. The combination was not a happy one. Later, when Abrahams chose a West African subject in *A Wreath for Udomo*, he was criticised by African critics for failing to recognise the real forces at work. 'He succumbs', says a review in *Black Orpheus*, 'to the white man's myth of the "primitive Negro".' Udomo, a black man, is on the side of civilisation and progress, and on the opposing side is tradition representing evil. Similarly, Martha Lee in *This Island Now*, and again Mildred Scott in *A Night of their Own*, sees herself as 'a new breed, a kind of outpost of the future trapped here in the Twentieth century'. Udomo, like Abrahams in his novels, identifies himself with the West and as such has been rejected by his contemporary black readers.

Bessie Head chose the novel as a medium, she tells us in 'Some Notes on Novel Writing', because this form was 'like a large rag-bag into which one (could) stuff anything—all one's philosophical, social and romantic speculations'.[13] It was not, however, until she had left South Africa that she could marshal her thoughts and feelings into producing long fiction. In Botswana she found an environment where she derived a feeling of security from the people around her, who lived 'in a kind of social order, shaped from centuries past, by the ancestors of the tribe'.[14]

Bessie Head was born in Pietermaritzburg in 1937 of racially mixed parentage, and moved to Cape Town later where she worked as a teacher and journalist. She now lives in Francistown, Botswana, with her son, not, she insists, as an exile, but as one who has put down roots. Her first work was *When Rain Clouds Gather*.[15] As in all her work, she drew on her own experiences. Head, like the main character in the novel, Makhaya Maseko, left South Africa for

Botswana after anti-government political involvement. When she first arrived there, in 1964, she tells us, the major talking point was a terrible drought in which 300,000 cattle died, and another issue was the first general election for independence. These two features, independence and the physical hardships which must yet be faced, and the reaction to these of a black South African, form the focal point of this novel. In her other two novels, *Maru*[16] and *A Question of Power*,[17] the autobiographical element goes deeper. Margaret in *Maru*, like Bessie Head, belongs to a despised minority group, and, like Head, both she and Elizabeth in *A Question of Power* are teachers. Elizabeth, like Head, was involved in politics in South Africa and left that country. More important, however, than the factual parallels are the spiritual elements from her own life which she puts into the novels. Elizabeth's mental nightmare begins when the headmaster of her school tells the little girl that she is the child of a mother put away in an asylum because of her affair with Elizabeth's father, a black stableboy. Whether or not this was Bessie Head's own origin, *her* nightmare doubtlessly began as soon as she was old enough to perceive that the country that spawned her was insane.

In *Maru*, Margaret shows her friend Dikeledi her paintings. 'How did you do all this work?', her friend asks, and the author continues:

> Margaret turned round and smiled. There was no word to explain the torture of those days, but out of it she had learned. Something inside her was more powerful than her body could endure. It had to be brought under control, put on a leash and then be allowed to live in a manageable form.[18]

This must describe what happened to Bessie Head when she first began to write her novels.

In an article in *The New African*, before any novel had been published, Bessie Head said:

> If I had to write one day I would just like to say people is people and not damn white or damn black. Perhaps if I was a good enough writer I could still write damn black and still make people *live*. [italics the author's][19]

Let us see to what extent she achieves these aims in her novels. The 'hate-making ideologies', says Makhaya in *When Rain Clouds Gather*, 'gave rise to a whole new set of retrogressive ideas and retrogressive pride, and it was almost a mania to think that the whole world was against you. And how many pompous bombastic fools had not jumped on this bandwagon'.[20] Yet even for Makhaya bitterness is unavoidable. He asks an old woman who has befriended him, Ma-Millipede:

Do you understand who I am? I am Makhaya the Black Dog and as such I am tossed about by life. Life is only torture and torment to me and not something I care to understand.

He goes on to explain what a Black Dog is:

He is a sensation . . . He awakens only thrills in the rest of mankind. He is a child they scold in a shrill voice because they think he will never grow up. They don't want him to, either, because they've grown too used to his circus and his antics, and they liked the way he sat on a chair and shivered in fear while they lashed out with the whip. If Black Dog becomes human they won't have anyone to entertain them any more. Yet all the while they shrieked with laughter over his head, he slowly became a mad dog. Instead of becoming human, he has only become a mad dog, and this makes them laugh louder than ever.[21]

The author describes Ma-Millipede as one of those rare individuals with a distinct personality at birth who adopted Christianity to 'adorn and enrich her own originality of thought and expand the natural kindness of her heart'.[22] She still cannot understand what Makhaya means, since 'she has lived all her life inside this black skin with a quiet unruffled dignity'.[23]

She feels she must counter this violent torrent of hatred:

You are not a Black Dog . . . You must not be fooled by those who think they are laughing. I don't know these people but my search for a faith has taught me that life is a fire in which each burns until it is time to close the shop.

What is it that makes her see good in everything, Makhaya wants to know, and she quietly replies:

It is because of the great burden of life . . . You must learn only one thing. You must never, never put anyone away from you as not being your brother. Because of this great burden, no one can be put away from you.[24]

Head's feelings about the senselessness of hatred remained with her throughout her writing. In an analogy with another art-form, she speaks of the music of Miriam Makeba and marvels how, after having lived in South Africa, she can still sing a mother's lullaby about a canary. Head says: 'I believe in the contents of the human heart, especially when that heart was a silent and secret conspiracy against all the insanity and hatred in mankind'.[25] The separation of people is an evil she cannot tolerate, and she finds that it is not the prerogative of whites. It was there, she says in *Maru*, before the white man 'became universally disliked for his mental outlook'. It was just that the white man found only too many people who looked *different*, and:

. . . if the white man thought that Asians were a low, filthy nation, Asians could still smile with relief—at least, they were not Africans. And if the white man thought Africans were a low, filthy nation, Africans in Southern Africa could still smile—at least they were not Bushmen. They all have their monsters.[26]

Margaret, the main character in *Maru*, suffers under this mental outlook because as a Bushman (Masarwa) she is not accepted in Botswana. The principal of the Education department objects to having the children taught by a member of what he considers an inferior race. When the young chief Maru marries Margaret at the end of the novel, it is a mixed triumph. The people of Maru's village speak of him as if he has died. A 'Dilepe diseased prostitute' explains their attitude: ' "Fancy", she says, "He married a Masarwa. They have no standards".' The people of the Masarwa tribe, on the other hand, felt that a door had 'silently opened on a small, dark airless room in which their soul had been shut for a long time', and that the 'wind of freedom, which was blowing throughout the world for all people, turned and flowed into the room'. 'As they breathed in the fresh, clear air', the author continues, 'their humanity awakened'.[27]

Bessie Head feels that an ideal world can be brought about. Eventually, she says, the 'world wide awareness of struggle and suffering cannot help but lead to a sense of idealism in those who rule'.[28] A reviewer of *Rain Clouds*, Olive Warner of the *Spectator*, quoted by the publishers of *Maru* on the cover, speaks of her 'radiant optimism'. Yet in her more sober moments she is less naïve. 'It is preferable to change the world on the basis of love of mankind. But if that quality is too rare, then common sense seems the next best thing',[29] she says wryly in *Maru*, when speaking of Margaret Cadmore, wife of a missionary, who took in the young Masarwa girl and gave her her own name as well as a reliable grounding in life.

In *A Question of Power*, the optimism at first seems to falter. Again, Head's own experiences are relevant. She had not been granted citizenship in Botswana, her status still being that of a refugee under the protection of the United Nations. Her years in South Africa had made her feel dehumanised, and the vital human link to her new home was still tenuous. Elizabeth, like her namesake—Bessie usually being short for Elizabeth—learns that nowhere does the outside world embrace human beings for their own sake but, nevertheless, in order to survive it is necessary to belong. She lives through a series of nightmares and mental torture, weaving a precarious mental existence in and out of sanity. In her agony the dream figure Medusa appears to her and says:

Africa is troubled waters, you know. I'm a powerful swimmer in troubled waters. You'll only drown here. You're not linked up to the people. You don't know any African languages.[30]

Alienation means having no roots within the community. Without that, as Sello says at the beginning of *A Question of Power*, 'I am just anyone', a statement which Head describes as one of the most perfect, and a very African one. Belonging also means having one's roots firmly planted in the land. In her grasp of the significance of land in Africa, both as a symbol and a fact, Bessie Head is perhaps nearest to the Kenyan writer Ngugi wa Thiong'o. In the first novel, it is the land in the community of Golema Mmidi around which the action centres. The villagers, newly independent, try to cope with drought amid agricultural ignorance. Makhaya, the refugee who comes from a South African urban area and Gilbert, a British agriculturist, join forces in helping the community restore the land, hampered by reactionary chiefs and self-seeking politicians. Through their success the land provides their own peace of mind. In *Maru*, it is the antagonistic forces among the Botswana, rather than Margaret, who are alienated. Margaret has a prophetic dream, which she puts into three of her pictures. In them a pulsating glow of yellow light emanates from a field of daisies and dominates a pitch-black house. There is an embracing couple in the picture who do not want anyone near them. A strong wind, however, blows Margaret, the dreamer, in their direction; when she tries to grab hold of the daisies to save herself, she awakes. At the end of the story the couple in their black house will have to accept the dreamer whom the wind of freedom has blown into their midst. Elizabeth in *A Question of Power* finds her sense of belonging by joining a land project which, through its physical reality and international co-operation, keeps her nightmares at bay.

But the 'Question of Power' must still be resolved for Elizabeth. She and her author-creator come to realise that it is power in all its various guises that she has been fighting against in her struggle to make a new life for herself, and it is now Africa which is to teach her the answer. This question of power is not just a matter of one people making another suffer. That battle has almost been won in Africa. It is 'the arrogance of the soul', as Elizabeth and Tom, an American friend on the land-project, both come to learn, 'its wild flaring power, its overwhelming lust for dominance and prestige' which is the source of the evil of power. Elizabeth says to Tom:

> I was stunned, Tom . . . Africa isn't rising. It's up already. It depends on where one places the stress. I place it on the soul. If it's basically right there, then other things fall into place. That's my struggle, and that's black power, but it's a power that belongs to all of mankind and in which all mankind can share.[31]

Before she can find peace, she must go through another inferno of madness and horror in which she searches for a spiritual answer to man's destiny, a 'relegation of all things holy to some unseen Being in the sky'. The final solution comes to her in the guise of a poem her little boy has made up, an uncanny echo of her own thoughts. It ends:

> A fairy man and a fairy boy
> Can fly about the sky.[32]

That, says Elizabeth, is what she felt about people's souls and their powers, that 'there'd be a kind of liberation of these powers, and a new dawn and a new world'.[33] Power, therefore, need not be a force of evil. She had been seeking for a God detached from mankind, and in her experiences, thoughts and dreams had encountered every kind of religious belief. But now it came to her as a revelation. 'She said: There is only one God and his name is Man. And Elizabeth is his prophet'. The answer had been there, very simply, in Africa, all along. True, there was 'no direct push against those rigid, false social systems of class and caste,' but she had 'fallen from the very beginning into the warm embrace of the brotherhood of man, because when a people wanted everyone to be ordinary it was just another way of saying man loved man'. As Elizabeth falls asleep at the end of the novel she is released from the agony of her nightmares. 'She placed one soft hand over her land. It was a gesture of belonging.'[34]

Head's ideas and ideals are conveyed through her characters. The chief protagonist is usually her mouthpiece, and others stand as symbols for various themes. The novelist is not interested in exploring psychological depths for their own sake. However introspective Elizabeth may be, the sexual details of her nightmares do not form a psycho-analytical case-book but are a series of symbols for life's inferno. There is always an element of doubt as to whether Elizabeth's visions are entirely internal or verge on the metaphysical. There is already a hint of this in her previous two novels, as Arthur Ravenscroft has pointed out.[35] Are Maru and Moleka, friends who are both in love with Margaret, two separate characters, he asks, or are they symbolic extensions of contending character traits within the same man?

It is in these symbolic terms that Bessie Head conveys her themes in her later works. *A Question of Power* is of course her most ambitious effort, in which she spins a web of symbolism interwoven with scenes of realism to form a satisfying whole. At times the repeated descriptions of horror and nightmare tend to pall, possibly because the author's fund of knowledge of sexual perversities, through which she conveys the grip of power in which Elizabeth's husband holds her, is necessarily limited. The changes from the heightened emotion of her inner turmoil back to reality, are managed with great subtlety. In hospital Elizabeth has just formulated a definition of God and is floating slowly back to everyday reality on a 'huge tidal wave of peace':

Someone was touching her arm. It was the night-duty nurse. 'I've brought you some tea', she said, smiling. 'You must be hungry . . .'[36]

There is a change in the tone and rhythm of prose, from the mystical and mysterious complicated passages of the dreams, to simple short sentences with a quick staccato movement and straightforward dialogue, marking reality. The alternating scenes of mental torture and pursuit, with the poignant scenes featuring the small boy, are brilliantly achieved. Elizabeth awakens from a nightmare, in which the phantom figure of the man Sello who appears to her constantly in the first part of the novel claims to be an owl:

It was dawn. She sprang eagerly out of bed. It was an excuse to fetch some water and make tea or do anything, except suffocate. She picked up the empty water-bucket, walked to the door, opened it, then stood transfixed to the spot, her eyes wide with horror. An owl lay stone dead on the doorstep.

Now the small boy, as he is usually referred to, wakes quietly.

He clutched in one hand a toy car, took in the other a bowl of porridge and sat down on the mat. Then he totally disregarded the porridge and concentrated all his attention on circling the car round the bowl.

'Eat your porridge', she said, helplessly.

He looked up at her with a pair of unconcerned black eyes. He went on circling the car.

'I'm not going to take you shopping', she said.

'I'll follow you', he said, firmly.

She stood up and started to dress. He let out a loud wail: 'Why don't you dress me first? You want to go away and leave me.'

Her head was throbbing with pain from a sleepless and feverish night. She grabbed a pile of his clothing off a chair and said irritably: 'You'd like to be slaughtered, hey? Shut your mouth, you damn little nuisance.'

He took all his moods from hers and imitated her in every way. A day which started off like this could throw him off balance completely. Suddenly, he seemed to sense something funny in the air and mimicked in a shrill voice: 'You'd like to be slaughtered, hey? Shut your mouth, you damn little nuisance.'

'Put your car down,' she said. 'You can't dress holding a car in your hand.'

A wicked gleam shot into his eyes. He clutched the car in a vice-like grip: 'Put your car down,' he mimicked. 'You can't dress holding a car in your hand.'

'You're at death's door, my son', she said, murderously.

'You're at death's door, my son', he shrilled.

She sat down on the bed and burst into tears. He stood looking at her for a moment, his eyes turned big and solemn. Something's really wrong here, they seemed to say. How often had something not been wrong over the past months? There were only stormy seas in this house, and he was frequently tossed this way and that in the storm. His mother's concentration was riveted elsewhere. He straightened himself with a quaint, manly air:

'I can show you I know how to dress myself,' he said haughtily. 'I can put my own shoes on. I can eat my own porridge.'[37]

The boy has learnt to survive and he is her only thread to reality. At one time she plans to kill him and herself, but because of his trust in her and his faith that she loves him she continues the struggle, until, in the end, his poem which reflects her own thoughts brings her peace.

Dugmore Boetie, whose 'life story' *Familiarity is the Kingdom of the Lost*[38] appeared in the same year, 1969, as *When Rain Clouds Gather*, proceeds in the direction of dramatic realism. The chief character, as well as those in the supporting roles, have little overt inner life. Boetie never doubts that life is an external contest between man and his circumstances. That is his starting point, his term of reference, and thus he feels that there is no need to question the reason for any action. His sardonic attitude towards the morals under which he is expected to live in a sham-ethical society is illustrated in the following incident quoted on the dustcover of the book:

A European woman was sitting in the driver's seat. Lying negligently next to her was her handbag. The window beside the bag was open.

Sitting in the back seat and looking lost was the woman's African servant. I made a bee-line for the open window, while Tiny walked directly towards the servant. He shouted: 'Lies, lies, that's all you told me! I told you one day we'll meet and I'll mess you up. Come out of there!'

'What's the matter? What has he done to you? Leave my boy alone!' said the woman.

'I'm not talking to you, missus.'

'But I'm talking to you! What has my boy done to you?'

'I told him one day he'll get hurt'. Tiny made as if to open the door. Unseen, I lifted the bag . . .

As we walked back to the busrank Tiny said, 'Serves her right for not letting him sit next to her.'

Boetie does not accept the world he lives in, but he adapts it to his own purposes in order to survive:

The white man of South Africa suffers from a defect which can easily be termed limited intelligence. The cause of this mental handicap can be safely attributed to a frustrated background of poor beginnings.

I say this because no man, no matter how dense, will allow himself to be taken in twice by the same trick. They don't learn by mistakes, for the simple reason that they'd rather die than talk about their mistakes. Me, I learn by my mistakes because human beings make mistakes, and I'm a human being. Their pride is based on colour, and it's on this pride that we blacks feed ourselves. Call him 'Baas' and he'll break an arm to help you.

He takes advantage of his white skin, we take advantage of his crownless kingdom.[39]

The satire itself is never sharp and pointed. The clowning takes place almost behind the victim's back and when he turns round he finds that his foibles have been exposed.

Boetie tells the story of how a white clerk in his place of employment gives him her sandwiches because she is going out to lunch. But he has just eaten a large piece of ox-tongue and so, on his way, he in turn put the sandwiches on the desk of the company secretary. "Mr. Groenewald," I said, placing the packet of sandwiches on his desk. "Here's some sandwiches for you. I don't feel like anything today". With that, I went out.'[40] Taking him to task for such behaviour, the head of the department is infuriated by Dugmore's innocent replies to his attempt to explain why it was wrong for him to give his sandwiches to Mr Groenewald, when it was not wrong for the white clerk to give them to Dugmore. White men and women, the police, officialdom, all are fair game: 'If you want to get rich quick, take the road that leads to prison. There's a steel door at the end. As you go to it, don't go in, turn sharp right. Then you're on your way',[41] is his way of expressing it.

Yet his philosophy is by no means an amoral one. It is not the Hegelian law of universal order from which Boetie is estranged, but merely the absurd law of the land. The reader is asked to invert, not lose, his moral standards. Boetie, like his European contemporaries, has discovered the absurdity of existence, but not of existence *per se*, merely of existence as a member of a particular society to the principles of which he cannot subscribe. To the moral standards which he has set himself, Dugmore Boetie adheres strictly. The only time he feels ashamed is when he betrays and uses another black man in order to further his own aims:

A pet monkey once followed the aroma of frying peanuts into its master's kitchen. There strewn on the hot stove were the frying nuts. He looked around, to make sure that there was no one around. Then he reached out with his paw. As the tips of his fingers made contact with the hot plate, he screamed, somersaulted and sucked his scorched fingers. He tried again, with the same results. He was still sucking his poor fingers and trying to scratch out an idea from the crown of his head with the fingernails of his left hand, when the cat came in. At the sight of the cat the monkey grinned. In one swift move he snatched the cat up, and with it swiped the strewn nuts from the hot stove. The cat screamed and bolted through the door. Grinning, the monkey started picking up the nuts leisurely from the floor. I was sorry, but I was going to do to this man what the monkey did to the cat.[42]

What he did was to make fun of a black man in a pass office to the amusement of the officials, so that, when his turn came, he was issued with the coveted 'coloured' identity card instead of a 'Bantu' one:

Two passport photos. And I was a Coloured. Just like that. I limped out in a daze. My head was spinning, my heart was double-timing and my ears were going ping. I wanted to sing or dance or something. I wanted to fly. I needed my guitar. No more pass! No more pass! No more Influx Control! No more sit here, not there, no more shut up, take your hands out of your pockets . . . It was now somebody else's s--t—everybody else's—not mine! I wanted to start shaking hands, banging everybody on the back, buying booze for the whole bloody Joburg! I looked around wildly.

Standing forlornly at the building's entrance was the unfortunate black man.

My hand fished into my pocket and came out with a shilling. I went to him and placed the shilling in his hand, then quickly walked away. I was a few hundred yards from him, when something flew with terrific force past my head. It went *zinnng*, narrowly missing the tip of my ear. It clinked once and fell into the gutter. It was the shilling piece. I bent down, picked it up and walked on without looking back.[43]

Although the novel consists of an apparent chaos of incidents, the narrative progresses steadily. This is not the rambling autobiography for which it is frequently taken. As such there is very little truth in the story. Except for the last two years of his life, which are described in an epilogue written after his death, it is impossible to give any indisputable facts about Dugmore Boetie. For instance, he tells the story of how he came to lose a leg in North Africa, during the Second World War. His mother, who never 'fried and fried and fried' after being pushed into a fire-galley by her son as he would have us believe, said that it was quite untrue and that he was never out of the country. Even the origin of his name—if it was his name—is quite incredible. It is one of the incidents one is inclined to believe because it could not possibly have been invented. As a nameless youngster he was looking after an elephant in a circus. The elephant's name was Dugmore. When it was called, beast and boy both came forward, and so the name stuck. The 'Boetie' comes from 'Kafferboetie' which the boys called him during his first spell in a reformatory.

Why, we may ask, if it is a novel, did Boetie choose the method of making author and narrator one? He did this partly, perhaps, because the autobiographies of black writers already had a ready market. Possibly this is further evidence of his humour: an attempt—and a successful one—at a send-up of an autobiography. Unlike other writers who use narrative in the first person, Boetie had no intention of establishing a particular rapport with his reader. Boetie, the author, shrugs him off as a necessary prop in his life, like the people who sponsored him and towards whom he showed no gratitude—his co-author Barney Simon describes him as having the mentality of a confidence trickster—and as his fictional namesake shrugs off most of the people with whom he comes into contact.

Familiarity is the Kingdom of the Lost is the combined effort of a black and a white writer, and it is difficult to tell what contribution was made by each. Barney Simon, when interviewed, said that the writing was Dugmore Boetie's own. He saw himself in the position of a producer of a play, directing changes here and there but not altering the action or dialogue. Only when writing about genuine feeling did Boetie seem unable to express himself. The writing would deteriorate to sentimentality and thus once or twice Simon changed a paragraph. The title is the only place where an external contribution becomes obvious. 'Familiarity is the Kingdom of the Lost' seems to pre-suppose a conscious awareness of Boetie's condition over and above the narrative, and this contradicts the direct technique of the author/narrator.

Familiarity is the Kingdom of the Lost is the combined effort of a influence on writing that followed it, since it was directed at a white readership. Its interest lies rather in that it was symptomatic of the black urban viewpoint which was soon to be expressed in other literature. The absurdity of an existence in which the individual's chances depend on the colour of his skin, which Boetie demonstrates so well, points forward to later and more serious works.

Emergency by Richard Rive[44] was the first novel to be set against a background of the Sharpeville and Langa events in 1960, and was the first novel to be banned. The main action takes place in Cape Town between 28 and 30 March after the shootings had occurred and the Pan African Congress had called for a campaign against the Pass Laws. It ends with the declaration of a state of emergency which gave the authorities wide powers to arrest and hold people without trial.

The protagonist is Andrew Dreyer, who has worked his way out of the slum of District Six to become, like Rive, a graduate teacher at a 'coloured' high school. Andrew is torn between becoming involved in political action in the form of public speaking and the distribution of pamphlets on the one hand, and holding on to his hard-gained position in life on the other. In the end it becomes a matter of whether to escape into safety, and Andrew chooses to stay and face what awaits him.

The forces pulling Andrew in these directions are personified in his intellectual friend Abe Hanslo who cannot go along with the activism of the Pan African Congress, and believes rather in gradual political education, his friend Justin Bailey who joins in the fray and goes to jail for his beliefs, and his white girl-friend Ruth whom in the end he would only be able to protect from prosecution under the law forbidding black/white sexual relations by escape. Representing his slum background are his old friends in District Six who will never get out of the squalor and crime of their childhood, and his family whom slum conditions have coarsened and hardened in various ways. Andrew's new middle-class milieu is personified by his landlady and his quisling school principal on the debit side, and the idealistic young son of his landlady and his former teacher and later colleague on the other. Andrew's extrication from the slums is at great cost to his mental peace, and leaves him with a feeling of guilt which shapes his political ideals.

All the ingredients for a deep study of the options of a man under pressure in crisis have been assembled in *Emergency*, but Rive's novel is disappointing in that he fails to dramatise these ideas credibly. The events and characters remain flat on paper. The reader never really becomes involved in Andrew's dilemma and the only exciting passages, with the exception of a scene in which Andrew's distribution of pamphlets in Langa township leads to a riot, are the factual events such as the march on Cape Town's central police station by thousands of black protesters. Perhaps Rive wrote the novel too soon after the events to turn them into successful fiction. As a perceptive critic himself, Rive later became fully aware of the shortcomings of the novel and told an interviewer: 'Alas . . . I'm not very happy speaking about *Emergency* because I think it's dated and I'm hoping to have more stuff that will be far more relevant'. He realises that *Emergency* is not a satisfactory whole and says that 'it is basically a series of short stories with a particular character in common'. The reason for that, he continues 'is that I am essentially a short story writer, not a novelist. I haven't got the kind of view, the wide kind of vista that the novelist requires in terms of consistency'.[45]

Rive's forte in his other writing is the short witty dramatisation of incident, and short satiric character sketches and this occurs only once or twice in the novel. Braam de Vries, a white liberal and unconventional student embraced, we are told, 'the Movement with a "bear hug"', and when his type greets a black man, as Abe tells

Andrew 'they shove out their hands a little too soon'.[46] Elsewhere
Abe, who could pass as white, confronts a white railway ticket clerk
who refuses to serve him on the 'coloured' side of the booth. Abe will
not budge and there is a deadlock while commuters miss their trains.
A railway policeman intervenes and a whispered discussion takes place.

> Another ten minutes passed. The clerk looked up slowly, his eyes
> filled with hatred. Abe met his gaze unflinchingly. 'All right,' the
> clerk said at length. 'I'll serve you.' He slowly rose and left the
> office. Once outside he came to where Abe was standing. Andrew
> wondered what the hell he was up to. The clerk reached for the
> 'Non-Europeans Only' notice and withdrew it from its socket.
> The crowd watched expectantly. He reversed the sign, displaying
> the 'Europeans Only' printed on the other side. He glared at the
> crowd, then slipped it back into its socket.
> 'What a transformation!' Abe remarked, surveying the new
> sign. The clerk maintained a hostile silence as he went back into his
> office. Then he served Abe. He left his window for the second time
> and reversed the notice. The crowd roared with laughter.
> 'So we're back where we started', Abe remarked.
> 'How damn silly', said Andrew.
> 'Next!' the clerk ordered gruffly.
> 'One single first-class to Cape Town', said Andrew. 'It's quite
> safe, I'm not a European.'
> The clerk glared at him.[47]

The characters are all types rather than people, and their reactions
to events therefore predictable. The point which Rive wishes to make
in the story does not come through clearly, because he does not allow
for the fact that, by choosing the heroic way, Andrew seems to have
little regard for those close to him. By making the large gesture of
nonchalantly returning with Ruth to her flat where the police will
find them, he is choosing his options for her as well. He feels equally
entitled to choose his brother-in-law's and his landlady's options by
involving them in his actions. Their attempts to protect themselves
and their families are treated without sympathy by Andrew and his
creator. Rive does not attempt to answer, or even raise, the question
of whether a man's conscience may be assuaged at the expense of
others.

'Buke' Beukes, on the other hand, displays humanity and understanding towards those who feel that they must put their families,
jobs or possessions before the cause. 'Never mind,' he says
to a fellow conspirator who does not want to go on, 'I understand.
You don't have to worry, man. Each of us, we do what we can, isn't
it?' And he thought, who am I to judge him? How long will I last in
this?'[48] Beukes is the protagonist in *In the Fog of the Season's End* by

Alex La Guma. La Guma's characters do not indulge in soul-searching about the rightness of their cause. They know which way their path must lie and it is a matter of deciding whether one has the courage to follow it. In a later novel, *The Stone Country*,[49] George Adams does not have any regrets about his arrest on a political charge: 'You did what you decided was the right thing, and then accepted the consequences. He had gone to meetings and had listened to the speeches, had read a little, and had come to the conclusion that what had been said was right . . . There's a limit to being kicked in the backside . . .'.[50] In all of La Guma's fiction the characters are poised against the system. It is the interaction of system and individuals who have reached their limit of victimisation, that constitutes the narrative of the novels. But it is the battle of the individual to maintain his humanity under the system, which forms the underlying themes and raises La Guma's work above that of contemporary novelists using similar material.

La Guma's concept of the system needs some explanation. La Guma joined the South African Communist Party in his youth and has not abandoned Marxism. In his fiction the cause which his characters support is a Marxist one. But they are pitted against a regime of white victimisation of black, rather than one of capitalist domination over worker. Although La Guma does not believe in thinking in colour, he makes it clear in his fiction that the conflict is not identical with the class struggle. In his first longer piece of fiction, *A Walk in the Night*[51] the white drunken old former actor Doughty has been living in a 'coloured' area for many years. He tells his young neighbour Michael Adonis that their poverty unites them but Michael sees only his colour. In his own drunken and unhappy state he identifies Doughty with the white foreman who has just sacked him for going to the lavatory. He lashes out at him with a bottle, killing him. Even for a corpse there is still a distinction. 'There's going to be trouble', Michael says to himself. 'Didn't mean it. Better get out. The law don't like white people being finished off'.[52] In the next novel *And a Threefold Cord*[53] George Mostert, a white garage owner, is as much a victim of poverty as the brown and black people in the shanty-town around him. In his loneliness and misery he is tempted to accept an invitation to join them for a drink. But something holds him back until it is too late. In *The Stone Country* the black prisoners not only do not receive the same treatment as their white counterparts—their food is vastly inferior, for instance—but the very reason for their turning to crime lies in the hopelessness of their condition as black South Africans.

All the characters are living in a stone prison of their black skins, and nothing they can do, other than destroy white domination, can alter this. They are programmed by the system and this limits their free choice. Why did Michael Adonis have to be in the passage of his lodgings just as old Doughty was struggling to get to his room; why did Willieboy decide at that particular moment to visit Michael and why did a neighbour have to pass just then and see him near the dead man's room? Why was it that the trigger-happy Raalt, a policeman having trouble with his wife, should happen to be on patrol that night? ('I wish something would happen' he says to his partner, looking for an outlet for his murderous thoughts about his wife, 'I'd like to lay my hands on one of those bushman bastards and wring his bloody neck'.)[54] Was it fate that manoeuvred these events? Perhaps, but if the characters were not black in some instances and white in others, they would have been able to react differently to the circumstances. Wondering whether he should perhaps give himself up and explain what happened, Michael Adonis says to himself: 'You know what the law will do to you. They don't have any shit from us brown people. They'll hang you, as true as God. Christ, we all got hanged long ago'.[55]

Yet La Guma's viewpoint is not a pessimistic one even when the stories, based as they are on real situations, end in defeat. The individual still has his options in two respects. He can choose, as we have seen, whether or not to pit himself against the system and continue the fight. And he can choose to what extent he will allow his circumstances to deprive him of his humanity. Michael Adonis is a failure. Although he gets away with the killing, he deteriorates morally and joins a gang. Willieboy, who is mistakenly chased after the killing and mortally wounded by Raalt, was a moral failure before the story began. But Joe, a ragged boy without home or family, is the symbol for hope in the story. When his father walks out on the family and they are evicted from their home, his mother decides to take them back to the country. But Joe makes his stand and remains behind. It would have been like running away, he says. Joe advises Michael not to throw in his lot with the gangsters: 'Christ, I don't want to see you end up like that, Mike. Hell, a man'd rather starve'. Joe adheres to a philosophy of life which is as simple and as beautiful as the seashore which he loves. At the end of the story he makes his way towards the sea where he ekes out his existence, 'walking alone through the starlit darkness'.

> In the morning he would be close to the smell of the ocean and wade through the chill, comforting water, bending close to the purling green surface and see the dark undulating fronds of seaweed, writhing and swaying in the shallows, like beckoning hands. And in the rock pools he would examine the mysterious life of the sea things, the transparent beauty of starfish and anemone, and hear the relentless, consistent pounding of the creaming waves against the granite citadels of rocks.[56]

Similarly there is peace in the end for Franky Lorenzo, a man whom poverty threatens to force under, but who holds on to his love for his pregnant wife and family. For those like Michael, who fall moral victim to the circumstances, there is nothing but a void, but those whose humanity raises them above themselves can look forward with hope to a new life. The novel therefore ends:

> Franky Lorenzo slept on his back and snored peacefully. Beside him the woman, Grace, lay awake in the dark, restlessly waiting for the dawn and feeling the knot of life within her.[57]

In *And a Threefold Cord*, the effort to maintain even a thread of decency in the appalling conditions under which the people in it live requires almost superhuman qualities. When old man Pauls dies in a leaking hovel, after a long illness without medical attention because the doctor would no longer give him credit, his wife says of him:

> He was a good man to me and to his children, and he trusted in Our Lord. He just lived and worked and didn't do nothing that was wrong in the eyes of the Lord. He worked for his family and when he couldn't work no more, he lay down and waited for the Lord Jesus to take him away . . . Now the burden is taken from off his shoulders. . . .[58]

Those, like Uncle Ben, who do not have the faith to endure for the sake of others, take to drink. He says:

> Is an evil, Charlie, what makes a man drink himself to death with wine, an evil what make a poor old man shiver and shake himself to death in a leaking *pondok* without no warm soup and no medicine.[59]

Charlie Pauls cannot accept this force of evil as being outside oneself, nor can he, like his parents, simply hand over his responsibilities to the Lord. He feels accountable for the welfare of his mother, his young brother and his girl-friend, the young widow, Freda. At the end he is trying to comfort a hysterical Freda whose children have died in a ghastly fire in their shack. He says:

> 'Listen . . . There was this rooker I worked with when we was laying pipe up country. A *slim* burg, I reckon. A clever fellow. Always was saying funny things. He said something one time, about people most of the time takes trouble hardest when they alone. I don't know how it fit in here, hey. I don't understand it real right, you see. But this burg had a lot of good things in his head, I reckon.' He paused, and then stumbled on, his voice a little sad. 'Like he say, people can't stand up to the world alone, they got to be together. I reckon maybe he was right. A *slim juba*.'

He feels that perhaps this applies to his brother Ronald, who is awaiting trial for murder and who 'didn't ever want nobody to help him', and to his uncle Ben who had taken to drink.

Is not natural for people to be alone. Hell, I reckon people was just *made* to be together. I—[60]

Words fail him but the author supplies them from Ecclesiastes IV: 9–12, which provides the title for the novel:

Two are better than one; because they have a good reward for their labour.
For if they fall, the one will lift up his fellow: but woe to him that is alone when he falleth; for he hath not another to help him up.
Again, if two lie together, then they have heat, but how can one be warm alone?
And if one prevail against him, two shall withstand him; and a threefold cord is not quickly broken.[61]

Jobless, poverty-stricken and uneducated, there is little Charlie Pauls can do, but he makes a gesture of protest for his own satisfaction. During a raid for passes and marijuana, police have burst into his girl-friend Freda's shack and found them in bed together. Later Charlie stands and watches the victims of the raid. They are lined up, hand-cuffed, in the rain. When a policeman tells Charlie to 'Eff off' he argues with him: 'I'm just looking. Can't a man watch his own people being effed off to jail?'[62] The policeman calls him a Communist troublemaker. When the policeman turns to call for assistance Charlie hits him with a hard snapping blow on the jaw. Then he slips into the night:

. . . he sat in the mud in the rain and recovered his breath. He thought. That was a nice blow, never ever got one in like that. Then he began to laugh. He laughed silently, his body shaking under the yellow oilskin.[63]

In the other novels, too, the thread of contact with others is the all-important factor, just as it is in the novels of Bessie Head. Gus, in *The Stone Country*, fails in his attempt with two others to escape from jail and laughs hysterically at the irony of events which allow only Koppe, the frightened man whom they have to force to join them in their plan, to get away. Is this the blind and undiscriminating hand of fate? Gus strikes out for himself and yet fails. No, the author implies, Gus overlooks the fundamental factor in taking action. He ropes in his two companions because he needs them, but once over the wall he intends to abandon them while he boards the get-away car to freedom. George Adams, the political prisoner in the story, does not like this atmosphere of every-man-for-himself. His cell-mates are astonished when he offers his cigarettes round. 'Hey,' one of them says, 'what for you giving tobacco away? These baskets can find their own, *mos*, don't I say?' 'Hell,' George Adams tells him, 'we all in this —together'.[64] In *In the Fog of the Season's End* this theme is applied to active resistance against the regime. Elias suffers torture and death so that Beukes and his ring can continue their activities. In La Guma's last novel to date, *Time of the Butcherbird*,[65] Shilling Murile will probably die for the murder of the white farmer whom he kills to avenge the cruel murder of his brother, a gesture which, on its own, would be a useless one in La Guma's eyes, for it is merely a personal matter. At first he refuses to listen to Mma-Tau, the spirited sister of the local chief, to join in the passive resistance to the removal of the entire community from their ancestral home. This removal is ordered by the white authorities who find indications of mineral wealth in the area. But in the end Shilling joins the people in their resistance, bringing with him the shot-gun he has taken from the farmer he killed.

Hatred, then, La Guma wants us to understand, is a wasted emotion unless it is harnessed and put to the common good.

Like most black writers, whether they embrace Marxism or not, La Guma sees no conflict between politics and art. His art focuses on life; its quintessence is the relationship of individuals to the society in which they live.

The strength of La Guma's writing lies in the taut, streamlined, construction of the novels and the almost unflagging realism which involves the reader in the action and characters. The author never obtrudes. He tells the story by describing the action, words and thoughts of one or more of the characters. Sometimes, to make a point, he strangely describes minutely what a character *fails* to see or hear. For Michael Adonis, for instance, at the beginning of his symbolic walk through the night, the sights and sounds of the street which La Guma describes fade in and out of his consciousness as he concentrates on his rage at getting dismissed. It is as though his presence gradually materialises into a stage setting, rather than that he walks on to the scene. Always the author is behind the scenes, lighting the stage in matching or contrasting shades as required. In *A Walk in the Night* the township lies in almost unrelieved gloom, accentuated by a scrap of cloud struggling along the edge of Table Mountain. It 'clawed at the rocks for a foothold, was torn away by the breeze that came in from the south-east, and disappeared'. The people, 'in the hot tenements' feel the breeze 'through the chinks and cracks of loose boarding and broken windows' and they stir in their sleep.[66] Later, on the same day, 'Night crouched over the city':

> The glow of street lamps and electric signs formed a yellow haze, giving it a pale underbelly that did not reach far enough upwards to absorb the stars that spotted its purple hide. Under it the city was a patchwork of greys, whites and reds threaded with thick ropes of black where the darkness held the scattered pattern together. Along the sea front the tall shadows of masts and spars and cranes towered like tangled bones of prehistoric monsters.[67]

In *And a Threefold Cord*, the utter horror of existence is played out under a heavy threatening sky which opens periodically to fling water against inadequate roofs or drizzles miserably on the people in the streets. In *The Stone Country*, the monotony of prison life drags on, punctuated by the change of light against the prison wall. In *In the Fog of the Season's End*, a thin mist frosts the stars as the action opens, but the sky is flat blue and hazeless as the authorities in the interrogation room prepare to make the prisoner talk. In *The Time of the Butcherbird*, La Guma describes the backdrop to Shilling Murile's return to his homeland—he had left it to serve a prison sentence for attacking the foreman who had helped murder his brother and has come back for the purpose of taking bloody revenge:

> A red drop of sun lingered on the horizon, then spread, seeped over and was gone, and the sky was ablaze over the place where it had sunk and the dark crept over the sky from the eastern horizon to stain the land. The hills dropped slowly away to the karoo bushes, the camel thorn, the detritus of sandstone and basalt, so that the land took on the look of smoothness under the soft cloth of the night.[68]

There are several other scenes in this novel where the setting emphasizes meaning in this way.

There is no sentimentality in the narration. Charlie Pauls' gentle love for Freda, played out in the candle-lit room of her shack, her dressing-table next to them filled with assorted paraphernalia 'filched from madam's boudoir', could easily have become maudlin. La Guma handles it with skill.

> She smiled at him, but the candle was a stage light that cast shadows and picked up only the reflection of her eyes, so that he could not see the smile. But he could see the depth of her eyes and a softness there that took on a beauty he had not noticed before, and then she was struggling a little against his sudden brutality, quivering as he ground himself against her and his hands sang on her body.
>
> 'Charlie, Charlie. Charlie, man.'
> 'And you? You? You?'
> 'Charlie, you so *wild*, man.'
> Their bodies locked and he slid into the pleasure without thought like a stone into a pool, and was swallowed up in the fierce woman's smell of her armpits and breasts and the enveloping heat of her thighs.[69]

If there is melodrama in the novels, it is the melodrama available to every newspaper-reader in the land. Murder, violence, rape, children dying in shack-fires, are the order of the day. Even if you come from a middle-class background it frequently impinges on your life if you are

black. It touches George Adams for the first time when he goes to
prison for distributing political pamphlets. He finds it difficult to
believe the story his cell-mate, known as The Casbah Kid, tells him.
At first the Kid will not speak, but gradually he softens under the
friendship Adams offers, and he tells him how his father used to beat
him and his mother mercilessly. One day he was beaten almost
unconscious and his mother thought him dead. She kills herself with a
knife, placing the knife into the drunken father's hand to make it look
as if he had murdered his wife and child. The boy looks on and at the
trial refuses to exonerate his father, who goes to the gallows. Now it
is the Kid's turn: he is awaiting trial for a gang knifing and knows he
will hang. He is nineteen years old.

The dialogue is usually brief and to the point. The politically active
characters know what to think and what there is to do, so there is no
need for long drawn-out discussions. The ordinary people say what
has to be said, reaching out only rarely and briefly to touch each
other. Making up a quarrel about adding yet another mouth to feed
to the family, Grace Lorenzo in *A Walk in the Night* says, 'Franky
. . .'

> From the bed Franky Lorenzo's voice held a gentle quality:
> 'Awright. It's awright. I'm sorry I shouted.' He did not look at
> her, out of embarrassment.
> 'Really, Franky?'
> 'Ja. Really.' He coughed, as if something was obstructing his
> throat, and said again, 'It's awright, woman. It's okay. Yes.
> everything's okay.' Then with forced brusqueness: 'How about
> some tea, huh?'
> 'You . . . you hold the baby?'
> 'Of course. Why not?'[70]

The way various people speak is always in character and La Guma
shows great skill in reproducing the colloquial Afrikaans inflections
and racy idiom of the people he portrays.

It is by these means that La Guma lays the foundations of realism
for the stories. The sure hand of the author then manipulates theme,
plot, and character to present a slice of life as a cohesive piece of art.
The construction of the novels is by no means simple. La Guma's
earlier shorter fiction, which we will examine later, has developed
into novels by a complicated system of harmony and counterpoint.
La Guma the craftsman is always in control. *The Stone Country* is
probably the most successful in this respect. It works both for the
novel as a whole and for individual scenes. While the Casbah Kid is
telling George Adams the grim story of his parents, for instance,
three prisoners in the cell next door loudly sing hymns—allowed on
Sunday—to hide the sound of the tool as they hack their way to
freedom. Their sudden silence while a guard comes past coincides

with the climax of the Kid's story. Nothing occurs without the author's design. The court scene in the same novel—the 'smell of polished mahogany and the whirr of electric fans', 'the solemn white face of the Judge under the coat of arms', the 'neat suits and spotless shirts', the whole sterile atmosphere in contrast with the vibrant life in jail—give the Casbah Kid's trial a Kafkaesque air. We realise that it is the court which is alienated from the society of man, and not the prisoner. In *A Walk in the Night* several scenes develop in this way. A crowd looks on while Constable Raalt shoots down and wounds the cornered Willieboy:

> The crowd roared again, the sound breaking against the surrounding houses. They wavered for a while and then surged forward, then rolled back, muttering before the cold dark muzzle of the pistol. The muttering remained, the threatening sound of a storm-tossed ocean breaking against a rocky shoreline.

There are sporadic comments from the crowd—the 'mutter of dark water eroding the granite cliffs, sucking at the sand-filled cracks and dissolving the banks of clay'—followed by an altercation between the sullen Raalt and his driver who wants to do the right thing and call an ambulance. Their argument is interrupted by a scream of pain from Willieboy, the crowd surges forward again, Raalt holds them off with a pistol, the driver urges action. Eventually they drag the critically wounded man into the patrol car.

> They slammed the doors and came round to the driving cabin, Raalt still holding the gun, watching the sullen crowd.
> The driver was in the cabin first, fumbling with the ignition in his hurry and grinding the gears. Beside him Constable Raalt holstered his pistol and the van moved forward into the crowd. The driver was still scared and nervous and he caused the van to bounce and jerk, scattering the people around it and raising an uproar. Fists thumped on the metal bodywork and a shower of brickbats rained suddenly down on it, but the driver got the vehicle under control and ploughed slowly through the mob.[71]

Each novel moves steadily towards its inevitable end. The walk in the night reaches its destination. In *The Fog of the Season's End*, fog closes in and the season of revolt comes to an end with the death of Elias. But the fog will lift for yet another season because Elias's silence under torture has left others free to act. Like *Fog*, *Butcherbird* is constructed within a framework determined by the final act. We learn at the beginning that the authorities have been successful in removing a community to their desert-like new home. The story then moves through earlier events which demonstrate the toughness of a community that makes common cause, and in the end we know that they will survive.

But however stirring the action, and however skilful the hand manipulating the props, it is the players on life's stage that interest the author. These are not mere puppets. Some of them may serve as the narrative centre, but they are never merely mouthpieces for the author. All are figures of flesh and blood.

The same economy of expression, which etches the plots and the setting, depicts the characters. A simile can bring them to life. Joe, the ragged boy in *Walk in the Night*, with his passion for things that come from the sea, appeared in District Six like 'a cockroach emerging through the floorboard'.[72] The Casbah Kid is 'slap-happy. Like he'd been in a boxing ring all his life'.[73] Yusef the Turk, in the same novel, is 'long and lean and sleek and bright and dangerous as a knife-blade'.[74] The prison bully in *The Fog of the Season's End* who tries to attack Beukes, is 'dangerous and septic as a rusty blade'. The subtle difference here should be noted. Unlike the thug, Yusef is later to be shown as basically a good man. The eyes of policemen are always blue, sometimes like dirty water, at other times like a frozen sea or pebbles of glass. The policeman in *And A Threefold Cord* who barges into Freda's shack, has 'thick whitish eyebrows that writhed and wriggled when he spoke, like fat maggots curling and uncurling above his eyes'.[75] The guard in *A Stone Country* is 'heavy and paunchy and seemed to be constructed from a series of soft, smoothly joined sacks, and he had a plump, smooth, healthy pink face, like a Santa Claus with a blonde moustache instead of a snow-white beard'. But 'in the outwardly jolly face the eyes were pale and washed-out and silvery, much like imitation pearls, and cold as quicksilver'.[76]

There are fewer clearly defined characters, less attention to detail of place, in La Guma's later novels. There is more comment and discussion, the symbolism becomes heavier, the irony more pronounced. In *The Fog of the Season's End* a black nursemaid, sitting in the public gardens, looks towards a statue of Cecil Rhodes pointing north towards the segregated lavatories: 'Yonder lies your hinterland', the inscription reads. The geography becomes indefinite, and the realism becomes more diffuse. There is no longer the same emphasis on dilemmas of individuals. It is now, rather, one people confronting another. When Elias Tekwane in *The Fog of the Season's End* is tortured to death, La Guma is less interested in Elias's own moral salvation which comes from not giving away the other conspirators, than in the triumph of the movement for which he worked.

By the time La Guma wrote *Butcherbird* he had been away from South Africa for some twelve to thirteen years. *The Fog of the Season's End* still takes place in Cape Town, but in one where changes have occurred which La Guma knows only by hearsay. The District Six which he knew so intimately has been largely bulldozed, and he describes the ruins which he has never seen. He was banned in 1966, so he knows that he is no longer writing for a South African readership. His raw material has been cut off, and he must make do for as long as he can with what he remembers. He is falling victim to what Ezekiel Mphahlele calls the tyranny of place.

'A writer', Mphahlele says, 'wants to feel . . . that he is in touch with his cultural milieu, that he gets feedback. Well, how do you get feedback when you're writing abroad?'[77] Mphahlele tries to come to grips with this dilemma in his first novel, *The Wanderers*,[78] and he does so by making exile the theme of the novel. 'If *The Wanderers* . . . says anything at all, it should . . . be a personal record of [a] search for place', he wrote in a letter to the present author. It is therefore a highly autobiographical novel, and in fact there has been much discussion as to whether it is a novel at all. It is often so intensely personal as to give the impression of a revelation and a cleansing of the soul. It was written during one of the most unhappy periods of Mphahlele's life. He had left South Africa after much heart-searching. Banned from teaching for the part he played in fighting the Bantu Education Act, unhappy in his journalistic career and worried about the schooling of his children, who, he felt, were being educated to be slaves, he took this step in a desperate attempt at mental survival. But he was never happy in his self-imposed exile. Homesick, ridden with guilt about his departure, unhappy in the lack of cooperation in his work, disillusioned with Africa, he seized his pen and put it all down on paper. He had done so once before, as we shall see, when he wrote his autobiography *Down Second Avenue*. Perhaps this time, however, he felt too close to the events, the wounds were still too raw. Was it perhaps impossible for a man of his shy and retiring nature to reveal himself openly to this extent, and did he therefore hide behind the shadow of the narrator of the novel, Timi Tabane? Mphahlele insists that the work is fiction, that he intended it that way:

> It has an autobiographical framework and it has real-life people in it, but it is still more fiction than autobiography. I plotted it that way in the sense that I wanted to bring out the central character at different points. I then said to myself I want to find out in my own life what exile has led to. It has led to a disorientation in the children. It has led to a disorientation in my own self and it has led to discoveries in other territories and a realization of myself. Then I said I don't want to leave it as an open-ended thing in terms of a father-son relationship. Something has to happen to the son and that is a fictional plot. In that way I have a beginning and an ending, as distinct from *Down Second Avenue*. To that extent it is more fiction than autobiography.[79]

If it were merely a matter of a fictional beginning and ending to a personal account of search, then we would still have to look upon the work as an autobiography. There is, however, more to it than that, and Mphahlele points us in the right direction when he refers to the fictional plot regarding Felang, the son of his alter ego, Timi. Certainly there are autobiographical elements in the relationship between father and son, too; but Mphahlele's son did not return to South Africa to join an army of liberation, and he did not die in a heroic but foolish attempt to get involved in action as did Felang. Felang's story underlies what Mphahlele wants to say in this long creative work, and its significance reaches well beyond personal introspection.

The Wanderers begins with the news of Felang's death. Along with twenty-six other African nationalist guerillas he has been captured by a commando of white farmers on the borders of Zimbabwe and thrown to the crocodiles. We gather that this tragedy in the novel is an end as well as a beginning, not just the physical end of one of the characters, but the conclusion of the story which is to be built within its framework. It is indicated that there is an estrangement between Felang and his parents, and that the relationship between Felang and his father will provide the plot. The novel ends by recounting Felang's death and the events that lead to it.

Mphahlele's moving passion has been his career as a teacher. In his early days of teaching there was a rapport between him and his pupils which made his classes an unforgettable experience. The reason lay partly in his love for literature but even more in his concern for youth. This led to his conflict with the education authorities, was one of the factors—concern about his own children—in driving him out of South Africa and is undoubtedly the main reason for his return. His soul, he wrote in an article entitled 'Back Home',[80] hungered for the classroom. He wanted to be involved with the young, to understand, to share in the anguish, to help alleviate it. His own religious philosophy like Timi's is based on traditional African humanism, a philosophy that teaches its followers to 'seek harmony with other men, without letting anyone trample on you'. 'And so', Timi says, 'I try to light the way for the children. I try to help them understand the divine power that is in man—the power to create, to destroy, the urge to fulfil himself, to account for himself to that Supreme Force that seems to encompass us, to hold the balance of the Universe, the force waiting for man to touch it, to liberate its hidden energies'.[81]

Some of these ideas are expressed in the story of Felang, who is one of the wanderers. He goes astray in various ways, leaving his parents puzzled and hurt. His search for place is young Africa's search for identity, and his martyrdom is a vindication of its aspirations. We are given a further clue to the significance of the youth theme in Timi's recurring dream of terror. In it he is pursued, but the faces of his pursuers elude him. Only towards the end of the story does he recognise them. 'I did not know them individually, but I knew them to be black South Africans. Young men . . .'[82] Timi, as a mouthpiece for Mphahlele, is burdened with an overwhelming sense of responsibility for future generations.

The central theme, however, tends to get lost in the loosely woven and somewhat rambling account of real and imaginary characters. Within the confines of his own life story, Mphahlele uses the novel as a vehicle for many other themes which concerned him in his years of exile. Timi goes deeply into the meaning of exile, and tries to come to terms with his bitterness.

While still in South Africa, having left teaching to join the magazine *Bongo*, he is introduced one day to a young woman, Naledi, who believes that her husband has been shanghaied for slave labour on a farm. She asks Timi to investigate as a *Bongo* reporter. She and Timi journey to the place where the husband is rumoured to have been sent. Timi, with a false identity, obtains a job with a farmer and makes his enquiries. Eventually he discovers that the husband had indeed worked there, had been seriously injured by a savage beating, and then dismissed. Later, he finds proof of his death. During the period of investigation, Timi has been re-reading Richard Wright's *Uncle Tom's Children*, and wonders whether he too would continue to hate and curse and burn with the same anger, 'and all those feelings that had become reflexes among us blacks'.[83] He feels that exile is the solution. As a result of the farm prisoner *exposé* in *Bongo*, his passport application is refused and he has to escape over the border. His wanderings in Africa take him eventually to 'Iboyoru', where he has a teaching post. His initial elation at having reached freedom soon turns sour. He has not reckoned with the all-encompassing feeling of guilt which his departure from the scene of action engenders, the longing 'to be back in the fire, just so long as he would be suffering along with others of his kind'.[84] He also discovers that the real Africa is not the concept of his imagination. It is of no use to assume an immediate common heritage among black people everywhere, he says. 'You're an expatriate. Take your chances, tread softly, human cultures have stone walls'. But maybe, he continues, Africa has several enclaves with walls around them and several crevices in the walls. 'Take your chances. But what are we seeking when we enter through the crevices? How can we be sure? Maybe humanity must flow like water that cannot leave a crevice unflooded. Woe unto those whose crevices are few, or who don't have any'.[85] There is hope, but it is qualified, and in any case its fulfilment still lies in the future.

The personal search for a place in which to practise his simple humanity is also expressed in the intertwining lives of Timi, and Steven Cartwright, the white editor of *Bongo*. The white man must break out of his cruel heritage, and the black man, for whom self-fulfilment at present lies only in exile or physical confrontation, must bide his time. In Mphahlele's earlier works a will for humanitarian survival is the ruling force which moves his protagonists as it did those of the earlier La Guma, but this is no longer enough. Now Timi wants to 'answer that longing to do something about something that nags everybody else'.[86] The role of embodying this quality of control in shaping one's destiny is assigned to Naledi and she acquires it as a result of her suffering. Steven falls in love with her, they eventually marry and live in England. While he is in Iboyoru reporting for a news-magazine, Naledi goes to her parents in South Africa. Trouble flares up in the district when the people riot in protest against the carrying of passes by black women. Naledi's father is arrested, she is almost raped by a policeman, escapes and lays a charge. The constable is found guilty but given a suspended sentence and not dismissed from the force. Through her trials we see Naledi turn from a diffident country girl into a sophisticated woman, sufficiently human and individual to disregard racial barriers, prepared to endure but not passively. She is the only one in the end who comes to rest and finds her place. The others either continue to wander or fall by the wayside.

The Wanderers is thus about tragedy and hope for Africa, which Mphahlele has tried to symbolise in a story of his wanderings, and of the conflicts of those who will have to carry its heritage. Is this too ambitious a task? The novel fails to become a convincing work of art, because the themes are illustrated by the story rather arising out of it. The work is often interesting, often poignant, but there is little coherence. The plot about the relationship between Felang and his father begins far too late and is much too slight to carry the narrative. There are numerous characters in the novel held together tenuously by their association with Timi in his wanderings. They, and the events in which they feature, are seen through the eyes of three narrators, presumably to give three different points of view. There is little difference, however, in the tones or the attitudes of the narrators, so that no perspective is gained. The constant shifts in time and place destroy the continuity and hamper what little action there is. There is a singular lack of excitement about events that promise to be dramatic. We hear little about Timi's escape from South Africa, for instance. Action and adventure simply do not interest Mphahlele. The story of the rape attempt on Naledi reaches the reader third-hand. It is narrated by Steven, who heard it from Naledi's lawyer. The only events that happen before our eyes are those concerning Felang. We see him arguing with his parents, misbehaving at school and at home, running away and returning. Although Timi as narrator tells us about it, the anguish of all three people concerned makes its impact. Few of the characters, however, not even Naledi or Felang, come to life. It might be fun to spot the real characters behind the fictitious ones in this *roman à clef*—Don Peck of *Bongo* is Jim Bailey, owner of *Drum*; Steven Cartwright is

Sylvester Stein, one of its editors; Tom Hobson, Tom Hopkinson his successor; Lazy is Casey Motsisi, one of its journalists; Emil is Ulli Beier, and so forth. Mphahlele pays tribute to Kofi Awoonor by giving him his real name. Humour is provided by Timi's wife Karabo, an earthy woman who draws on a mixture of vernacular proverbs and modern colloquial images for her speech. She comes home after visiting a colleague of Timi's who has often been entertained by them. 'You can't believe it, Timi', she reports, 'We ate rice and milk. We had meat only once since we arrived—the first day. Mean people—ah! I hate mean people. What's food but decayed stuff in the teeth, as our people say. And the man carries such a large tripe in his belly. The next time he comes here, Timi, he's not going to touch this record player. I can feel *Carmen Jones* crawl up to my gullet right now.'[87] Another time, when she and Timi take some friends to a nightclub and the doorkeeper will not let one of the men enter because he is not wearing a tie, it is Karabo who demands to see the manager and tells him that he had better reconsider. 'Why all the fuss about ties anyhow?' she asks. 'We didn't go about dangling rags round our necks before you whites came to Africa.'[88] Mphahlele does not tell us much about his own wife. It is clear, however, that someone who supported him in all his wanderings, who stood by his side in adversity and success, who carried eight children of whom four survived and who, in one of their ports of call, managed to study and acquire a new profession herself, must be a woman of the same stamina, courage and forthrightness that he depicts in Karabo.

Timi's life story, actions, dialogue and thoughts are so close to Mphahlele's own that it is impossible to consider him as a separate character in a novel. We will hear more of Mphahlele when we speak of his short fiction, autobiography and essays.

His last published volume, however, is another novel. *Chirundu*[89] was completed some three years after *The Wanderers* but was not published until five years later, initially by Ravan Press. This was the first work since his very first volume, *Man Must Live* to be published in South Africa. The banning order, imposed on him in 1966 had recently been lifted, and the publishers immediately availed themselves of the opportunity to add the doyen of black South African literature to their list of authors. But why had *Chirundu* not been published abroad during these five years? The action takes place in an unnamed country thinly veiled as Zambia, and it is unflattering to the regimes of African countries in which British and American publishers with African lists sell their books. Yet other writers critical of their regimes, such as Ngugi wa Thiong'o, are prominent on the Heinemann list, for instance. Mphahlele himself says that the publishers, by their own admission, simply did not understand the novel. Although it takes place outside South Africa it is essentially a book with a black South African viewpoint.

Chirundu concerns the trial of cabinet minister Chimba Chirundu, whose wife accuses him of bigamy. Chirundu contends that Bemba marriage laws, according to which he married Tirenje, look upon a marriage as having ended if a wife leaves her husband, and her family take no steps to bring her back. Tirenje counters that the traditional marriage was subsequently registered under the old colonial ordinance, the divorce rules of which supersede the traditional ones. Since no divorce proceedings took place, Tirenje claims, her marriage still holds and Chirundu's marriage to Monde is bigamous. Chirundu does not expect to win the case but is 'out to fight a system'. He says that the ordinance should recognise traditional marriage as something that cannot be superseded. He tells his advocate that he does not want to plead guilty, he wants to 'speak up so that when the government gets around to marriage laws this inanity will not be repeated'.[90] Mphahlele sees the confrontation not as a clash between tradition and western values as would at first appear. Rather, he is investigating the effect of a foreign culture on an African one and how one should deal with the resulting conflicts. Should all Western culture be discarded, he asks. Chirundu tries to discuss polygamy with Tirenje before their marriage but Tirenje is too young and inexperienced to get her point across. She says:

'How can I share my man with another woman! . . . Am I not enough to care for, feed, clothe, love and give you children? Look at us all here, we are all poor, we have to scratch for dirt to eat like chickens.'
    'Suppose I earn enough to keep more than one?'
    'I'm not an illiterate woman.'
    'Why should an illiterate woman be able to handle one or two other wives of her man and you can't?'
    'It is not a matter of *cannot*, it is that I would not have it.'
    'Why? What is it that literacy has done that limits your capacity?'
    'Because I know more.'
    'Why?'
    'Because I am literate. I selected you among many men. I have pegged my piece of land. No woman but me is going to graze in that land. When you know more—when you're literate, I think—I think—how can I say?—I think you become aware that there are certain things that should belong to you alone—a man, for instance.'[91]

Chirundu makes fun of her hesitation, and they laugh the whole thing off. Her words, however, make Chirundu 'speculate a lot on the illiterate masses'.[92] The rival party, he says, often accuse his party of being an élite leadership. They say: 'Do not listen to these educated men! . . . They have learned the methods of the white man and they will trick you, they do not care about the sufferings of the common man.'[93] Chirundu calls this a wicked exaggeration but he admits that politicians like him had lost some 'native capacity' in their education. 'I knew it had happened. I knew there was something lost, but as to what it was exactly I was stumped for an answer'. Loss of tradition and what it meant is the theme of the book.

Mphahlele's ideal modern Africa, which he presents in much of his writing, both fiction and non-fiction, is a synthesis of tradition and the best of what Europe has brought it. In the novel, Tirenje and Chirundu's nephew Moyo represents this ideal. In her school days Tirenje falls under the influence of a young woman teacher, the first woman in her country to have obtained a B.A. degree and who tells her women students to wake up and fend for themselves.

Tirenje, described as firmly built, walking like a woman who knows where she is going, with an earthy tone to her voice and a steady look in her eyes, is contrasted with Monde who is modern in a superficial way. She has gained her veneer of Western sophistication by mimicry.

When he speaks of the young man, Moyo, Mphahlele goes back to his theme of youth as in *The Wanderers*. He represents the hope of a new dawn. He is innocent and carefree when he first comes to the city. His uncle finds him a job with the transport department of which he is Minister in charge. Soon Moyo becomes a prominent member of its trade union which strikes for better conditions. The strike coincides with a youth demonstration which gets out of hand, and there is rioting. Moyo, who has taken over the narration of the novel from Chirundu, says he feels as if he had been pushed out of a cocoon by these events. Chirundu's house is burnt down—literally by Tirenje and figuratively by his prison sentence for bigamy and his final parting from Tirenje. Moyo's house, however, has yet to be built. And its foundation will be solid, for unlike Chirundu, he has not lost touch with real tradition. Moyo is strongly aware of continuity in the community. He has brought his aged paternal grandfather to the city with him. Chirundu comments: 'Moyo would be seen [in Europe or America] as having towed behind him a wreckage for the scrapyard. To us, he would be walking beside a god'.[94] Even after the old man's death Moyo's faith in the power of continuity is strong. 'I've got Ambuye [his dead grandfather],' he says with confidence.

Against this background the interest of the novel lies in the question whether Chirundu is honest in the reasons he advances for his second marriage. The reader must decide whether Chirundu's protestation that he hopes his action will lead to a change in the marriage laws is genuine, or merely a stance. One suspects early that having a sophisticated town wife to entertain his guests, and another to fulfil the traditional functions of wife and mother in the country, suits him well. Years earlier, when he is sacked from his teaching job because he makes Tirenje pregnant while she is still his pupil, he makes a fine speech discarding Christian teachings, but he seems to show little feeling for the girl. He selects from both cultures what suits his purpose, and that purpose is power.

Chirundu is motivated entirely by a thirst for power, politically, personally, and sexually. His grandfather had told him that he was destined for great things, and this he believes firmly. Men like Chirundu wield a power they do not understand. It is a derivative power, based on a European legacy, says Pitso, a South African activist who has fled over the border. 'The white man spells power . . . Once he baptised us with his own urine, Europe's power was always going to fix us in a mind of stupor. Until . . .' he shrugs his shoulders and his companion asks 'Until?' 'Who knows? If we didn't hope for that day you and I wouldn't be here'.[95]

Chirundu is not unaware of the danger of such power. His teacher in the college makes him realise the hazards lying ahead for the new man of independent Africa. But Chirundu chooses power unequivocally. His wife compares him with a python in his sexual prowess, and the python, *nsato*, becomes the symbol of the novel. In 'Children's Playsong' which introduces it, the mother warns the children:

> If he comes at you, my child,
> To wrap you up in his coils,
> And flicks a tongue of fire
> And means you ill, my child,
> Go burn his house down,
> Burn down his house, my child,
> And let him wander, far and wild.[96]

The only way to tackle fear of *nsato* is to look him full in the face. Tirenje and Moyo both challenge Chirundu's power, and have nothing more to fear.

The South African significance of the novel is emphasised by a kind of chorus of comic relief in the form of dialogue between Pitso and his Zimbabwean companion Chieza, punctuated ironically by the prison guard's greetings of 'one nation! Kwacha, it's a bright new day.' Exile for these refugees, and for another South African, Dr Studs Letanka, has meant disillusionment. Studs, a brilliant mathematician, abandons his job at the University of Fort Hare when it falls under the Bantu Education system, and turns to African history. He drinks too much and dies in a car crash. Pitso decides to return to South Africa, though it is likely that he will be arrested as a terrorist.

The message for black South Africa is clear. Beware of the slogans and easy answers. Above all, beware of the abuse of power. As old Mutiso says, come face to face with *nsato*, or peep into its sleeping place: 'to know the size of *nsato* is to know the size of your fear the size of your liver the size of the stone you need to swallow for the strength you need.'[97]

As a novel, *Chirundu* is not entirely successful. In *Wanderers* and *Down Second Avenue*, there was no need to create a central character as the author put himself into that position. For the short stories and the minor characters in the novels, Mphahlele's fictional projection is sufficient to carry his ideas. But Chirundu as a person is not sufficiently clearly defined to hold the reader's interest, and he therefore does not provide a sufficiently strong vehicle for the theme.

At the time *Chirundu* was written, in the early nineteen-seventies, novelists, including those living in South Africa, still had to aim at overseas publication. The only novels, besides those of Peter Abrahams and La Guma, included in the prestigious Heinemann series of African writers, were *The Marabi Dance* by Modikwe Dikobe, *Robben Island* by D.M. Zwelonke and later *The Hill of Fools* by R.L. Peteni.

Marabi Dance[98] was published in 1973. One becomes a little suspicious when one reads the list of scholars who assisted in the revision of Dikobe's work. These included two editors and well known figures in non-black South African literature and social studies, Guy Butler, Monica Wilson, Don Maclennan and Lionel Abrahams. Their aim, we are told, was to 'make the author's intention clear'. It is possible that some literary and linguistic editing was necessary, since Dikobe did not complete his schooling, working instead as a newspaper vendor, clerk, book-keeper and nightwatch-man. However, he was by no means unsophisticated. As early as 1942, at the age of 29, he was secretary of an association in a bus dispute in Alexandra. Later he worked on various advisory boards, was active in trade union affairs and published a monthly journal, *Shopworker*. He is working on a history of blacks in Johannesburg. It therefore seems difficult to believe that Dikobe needed heavy revision to make his intention clear. It is just possible that something of the historical and political approach was destroyed in the process, to be replaced by overemphasis on scenes of traditional life, and that Dikobe's intention was obscured rather than made clear. This, however, is pure speculation; we must try to look at the work as coming from one writer.

The theme of *Marabi Dance* is the effect of township life on a people still partially rooted in tradition. By making gentle fun of the customs which have become distorted through contact with European city life, Dikobe points to the tragedy of this loss of roots. The protest against the evils of the South African system is not as overt as in the novels of La Guma, but emerges quietly in the story of people's lives. The characters have dignity which has its basis in the remnants of tradition. Disrespect, laziness, selfishness, are qualities associated with the white man who does not know any better and must be taught to realise 'we are all people'. Perhaps then, one of the characters says, 'they will learn to cook and wash for themselves and stop calling us boys and girls'.[99]

There is subtlety in the description of contrast between old and new. An old man, commenting on the hot dry day and seeing the signs of rain in the sky, remembers its blessings in the country and says:

> In the old days, men, women and children would go out amongst the graves and make supplication before the dead who lay buried there. After much praying and dancing and offerings, tjwala would be poured upon the burial place of the grandmothers and grandfathers. Then the supplicants would return to their homes without looking back from whence they had come. A heavy rain would follow and the maidens would dance for joy in the rain.[100]

Here in the township, however, the effect was very different:

> At nine o'clock, the sky became pitch black and the air felt damp and clammy. No thunder. No lightning. The sky remained as thick and pregnant as the Maluti Mountains. Then, suddenly, like a dam bursting, water poured from the heavens. The streets were flooded. The yards looked like dams and the water seeped into the houses. The men came out with shovels and opened furrows for the water to pass into the street.

The rains have flooded the yard of the old man's house and he says sardonically to his wife:

> The gods have answered our prayers and now we are engulfed in this yard.[101]

The air has been purified by the rain but it is polluted in this man-made slum by the stench from a broken lavatory which has overflowed so that the excrement and urine mix freely with the mud.

As in most fiction by black South Africans, white people exist on the periphery of their lives and touch them only as an authoritative force in the form of employers or officials. Success in obtaining an exemption pass which allows one to remain in a certain area, no matter by what means it was obtained, is a cause for celebration as though it were a wedding. A Northern Rhodesian, in South Africa as a contract farm labourer, changes his name when there is a pass raid to expel 'foreign Natives' and manages to convince the authorities that he is an ordained priest:

> Reverend Ndlovu walked out of the office of the Native Commissioner in ecstasy, waving the Exemption Certificate in the air, his white teeth in the photograph showing whiter than the paper on which it was printed. That night, the bells in the African quarters rang tumultuously, and a service was held attended by

thousands of people. Five sheep and several head of cattle lost their lives that weekend.[102]

The bogus priest and a child named Tiny provide much of the humour and earthy comments on township life in the story.

The action takes place in the nineteen-forties. It concerns Martha, whose father, July Mabongo, has arranged for her to marry her cousin to reconcile two sides of a divided family. The prospective bridegroom, Sephai, will go back to the country after a short spell in the kitchens of the whites. Martha, however, knows only city life. Both families realise there will be difficulties. Sephai's mother says:

> Location children don't know home work. They cannot go to the fields or chase birds away. They don't know how to smear the lapa with dung or keep it well. They can't balance a water can on their head.[103]

For Martha, however, the arrangement would be a solution to her problem, if she can keep her secret from the bridegrom and his family until after the wedding. She is pregnant, and the father is George, a young man she met at a wild Marabi party. At such parties, 'very popular but not favoured by respectable people',[104] illegal liquor is sold and there is singing and dancing. George is the pianist and Martha is sometimes engaged to sing. When she falls pregnant she has to leave school. George never speaks of marriage, and eventually escapes to a job in Durban. Martha, although she has been caught up in wild city ways, has been brought up to respect honesty and feels she cannot take the easy way out. She tells Sephai's relatives of her predicament when they come to make the final arrangements for the marriage.

It is war-time and Mabongo's employer becomes a recruiting officer in the Native Military Corps and has Mabongo enlisted. Both become prisoners of war. Martha lives with her mother who becomes ill and dies before she sees her grandchild. Martha gives birth to a boy and her father's employer's wife helps her find a house when the township in which she lives is razed to the ground. Martha works as a daily domestic servant and takes in washing at week-ends. When Sonnyboy, named after a song George used to play, is seven years old Martha receives a letter from George telling her that he wants to come back to her. The 'Marabi boy' has grown up. The bus company for which he works wants him to inform on the leaders of a newly formed drivers' trade union. He tells Martha he would rather walk the streets without work than sell out his own people: 'I want to come back to Johannesburg', he writes. 'I can always make a living without begging for work. I have done wrong to you, but I was still young and had not seen enough of life'.[105] When the little boy asks his mother why she is crying she replies:

My child, you are going to grow to be a man. George, your father, wants to leave work because he does not want to sell his people. I like him for that. Our people must talk without being heard by the white people. Some tell the white people what we have said and are given money. Last night the people talked about schools and high rent, and this morning some people were arrested.[106]

There are many other characters in the story faced with problems like the Mabongos'. These are people trying to maintain their traditional values within the foreign framework of the legal, economic and social set-up in the land. 'Martha, and many of her time,' the author says, 'hoped that the law would treat them as human beings because they had attained a certain measure of civilization. It was not to be.'[107]

At the end of the story she is still in tears. She says to her son: 'You, my child, must be a man.'[108] And we know that by the time Sonnyboy grows into a man things will not have changed.

Robben Island[109] by D.M. Zwelonke is based on the true experiences of the author on the prison island. In the introduction he says that it was 'Fiction but projecting a hard and bitter truth; fiction mirroring non-fiction, true incidents and episodes'. He says that the characters are all fiction, 'including in a sense, myself'.[110]

A thin narrative thread runs through the book. It concerns a Pan-African Congress leader, Bekimpi. The story is told in a complex way, in that he is in jail, his identity confused in his mind with that of the legendary hero Zweli. He is under duress and dreams that the events of earlier days are taking place now. At the end we learn that he is tortured to death.

But the story of Bekimpi forms only a small part of the novel. It is all the political prisoners on the island that are the heroes of the book and whose experiences Zwelonke relates. In the introduction he tells us of his original reluctance to speak about these experiences because of those left behind. This is something he has in common with all writers who have been on the island. It reminds one of the prison poems of Dennis Brutus, as does Zwelonke's resentment against those who ask him questions. Let them go there and find out, he says, they 'would be the first in the queue to pluck the fruits of freedom which they did not help to grow'.[111]

It would be futile to speak about the realism of a work dealing with a subject of this nature. It is not Zwelonke's aim to create a novel in the Western sense. He is telling his readers what happens on Robben Island, and expressing his pride, and that of others, as he tells us in the preface, in having fought without losing his convictions. He tells of torture, death and humiliation. 'Mind-drift', the grotesque effects of sparse diet on the mind, is described as being 'like a sea-ripple from sea to shore and from shore to sea'.[112] Of the mental disintegration taking place during solitary confinement, he says: 'I have seen a few men breaking, dismantling spiritually like a statue of sand when it gets dry, just crumbling'.[113]

The grim effects of homosexual experiences are described in detail. There is the harrowing story of Blacky, a young boy 'espoused' by one of the prison bosses. When the boss leaves, others fight over the boy. The chief warder laughs at his complaints because: 'the captain was a moffie too, before he was a captain . . . he won't help you'.[114] Blacky is desperate and knifes one of his assailants. He gets an additional two years for homicide.

Zwelonke's comments are often almost casual, as when he tells of the sadistic practices of some of the warders who indulge in torture for fun. This, the author says, is only to be expected in a place where ninety-nine percent of the inhabitants are men, separated from civilization by miles of sea, soldiers crowded together in barracks with raw convicts to chase around the whole day. 'Raw' is the pervading term for both prisoners and keepers. The warders inflicting the punishment of making prisoners run round the yard, beating them with batons if they slow down, are described as 'raw Boers determined to unleash their raw hatred' of the political militants.[115]

The author does not have to look for metaphor because the island provides its own without literary help. Its appearance is a reflection of its purpose. It is barren and dusty, a jumble of shrubs, its fields full of thorns, its soil made up mainly of crushed seashells. The shore is spread with yellow rocks and large dirty green sea-plants, with patches of stagnant water of a repulsive frog-green. Meticulous attention to detail provides its own comment in depicting the scenes of utter desolation and humiliation, as when the sea-gulls 'unloaded their bombs' into the dishes of the prisoners as they ate in the yard. The only garnishing it needs is the occasional repetition of a phrase, such as that describing men working on the quarries day after day, 'crushing the stones small, the small stones even smaller', which Zwelonke uses several times. Sound as well as sight is faithfully reproduced: the foghorn with its 'sickening low of a dying cow',[116] the growl of the sea-gulls, the yelling of the span-warders.

In this way Zwelonke's manipulations take the reader almost unawares and we gradually realise that the author is no mere compiler of experiences. He has a message, and it is important to him that his purpose is fully understood. His success lies in the control with which he guides the passions inherent in the book. He uses the account of his experiences to answer the question, the 'huge question-mark' which 'remained dangling like a seventy-pound steak in a butchery. What was to be the final fate of these doomed men on this devilish spookish island . . .'.[117] It could not be, he says, that the rubber stamp of South African courts declaring them guilty had settled their fate for all time. He finds the answer in a legend about a chameleon and lizard sent to the earth from the dwelling-place of the Lord. The first carries a message that the people must not die, the second that they must. The second messenger moves faster and therefore reached the earth first. Hope on the island rests in a little dwelling on the island. When the prisoners on their way to the quarry pass it 'our minds would be filled with visions' and they would catch a glimpse of 'the new Africa we so much yearned for and suffered so much for' as though it were just around the corner. 'All we needed was Noah's dove coming on its return flight to tell us that the waters had sunk and the land was now habitable'. All they needed was a 'peephole':

> . . . what we needed was hope. We felt revitalised and rededicated, because the man who occupied that house was none other than the one most loved by his followers, Robert Mangaliso Sobukwe.[118]

Zwelonke makes us aware of the irony of a situation in which the position of prison and outside have been reversed. A hardened criminal is mistakenly thought to be politically culpable and is sent to Robben Island:

> . . . I could not help exclaiming: worry no more, countryman, for there you will meet with men of integrity. No more shall you meet with incorrigibles, because political prisoners do not mix with them . . . Go well, fellow-African; the chances are you will come back a better man.[119]

Needless to say, the novel is banned in South Africa.

Hill of Fools, by R.L. Peteni,[120] was published in South Africa as well as in Britain. It is a novel about a community caught between the old order, which has lost much of its meaning to the people, and the new, which is totally devoid of meaning for them. Within the framework of a Romeo and Juliet romance the author demonstrates the futility of living in an unreasoning world, and pleads for tolerance, understanding and peace.

The romance between Zuziwe, a Hlubi girl, and Bhuqa, a Thembu boy, revives an age-old feud between these two communities in the Ciskei, the origin of which has long since been forgotten. Zuziwe's blood brother is killed in the battle which ensues, and a death must be reported to the local white authorities. Normally the villagers have as little to do with the authorities as they can. To go to law against an opponent is like grabbing a snake and setting it on an enemy to make it bite him, 'it might turn round and bite you', one of the characters says.[121] Bhuqa eloquently explains to the magistrate that a faction fight cannot be stopped any more than a drought or a swarm of locusts, but the magistrate cannot understand this and says that droughts and locust invasions are not against the law. The tragic ending of the story is caused just as much by the white man's rule as by the unbending older laws of the tribe. The unreasoning hatred of Bhuqa's father for the Hlubi girl who is bearing his son's child which makes him drive her away, is parallelled by the unreasoning law which prevents Zuziwe from following her lover to the city. Just because she belongs to a different race, the white authorities will not grant her a permit. Zuziwe has an abortion and dies of the consequences. A young orphan, Mlenzana, who had earlier refused to take part in the fighting, insists on Bhuqa's being allowed to attend her funeral. He reminds the mourners of Zuziwe's hatred of violence and argues with those who claim that one cannot break a tradition of feuding between two villages without betraying and provoking the ancestors who began the feud. Mlenzana says:

> What is it to you . . . if the Hlubis fought the Thembus in the past? Why do you trouble to remember the evils of the past? What merit is there in an evil tradition? It is not for you to boast about it and uphold it. It is for you to be ashamed of it. Go to the witchdoctors, if you believe in them, and ask them to exorcise the devil of hatred. Go down on your knees, if you are so minded, and ask almighty God to bring nearer the day when we can say the fight has ended.[122]

Although the mourners are unsympathetic they do not molest Bhuqa and he feels that Zuziwe has not lived in vain.

For the most part Peteni, a one-time school teacher, headmaster, lecturer and lay preacher, tells the story with the verve of a natural bard. At times a literary background of nineteenth century English reading betrays him into a clumsy turn of phrase, but mostly he relates the events simply, dramatically and effectively, and, above all, with enjoyment. Much as he abhors violence, he recounts the excitement of the battle between the young men of the two communities as though telling it to an enthusiastic live audience crowded around him. Peteni handles his plot, his characters, background and dialogue with steady confidence, and often with a wry humour. Dramatic incidents are seen to happen in swift sequence, interspersed with the tender yet passionate romance between the young couple. The characters are handled with compassion and insight, especially the women whose inner strength motivates much of the action. Of the men, the naïveté of Ntabeni, the Hlubi man whom the family want Zuziwe to marry, contrasts with the intellect and independence of her lover Bhuqa. The author describes the dilemma of Ntabeni who wonders whether the acquisition of a love potion from the witchdoctor will conflict with his standing in the church. Dialogue is always natural and often follows African idiom. Ntabeni does go and see the *sanuse* (witchdoctor/diviner) and says:

I have promised marriage to a sweet, young girl of the Bhele clan down at our village, a girl as bright and beautiful as the clear waters of the Xesi river, and as warm as sunshine in spring. She accepted me, and her family gave their consent to my family, all according to custom as you know. Suddenly I learnt that a Thembu boy has corrupted my girl when she visited her malume at the Thembu village. Then my girl rejected me. Can you believe it, wise one? My sweet Zuziwe jilted me for a wild, uncircumcised boy. The boy used a love-potion. I am sure of that. Please help me, Gabula-mehlo! Give me the strongest philtre in your stock so that I may win back my girl.[123]

The background is entirely authentic and filled-in with meticulous care and minute detail. Its tone fits the action, characters and mood.

While *Hill of Fools* does not probe into social, psychological and philosophic questions which it raises as deeply as does another novel of similar theme which it calls to mind, Ngugi wa Thiong'o's *The River Between*, it is an unpretentious, interesting and touching story told by a talented writer.

The Root is One by Sipho Sepamla was also published both in South Africa and Britain.[124] The novel takes place during a six-day period in Johnstown, a black township whose citizens are about to be forcibly removed, and its adjacent white town, Bergersdorp. Berger is a phonetic spelling of *burger*, Afrikaans for citizen. The story concerns Juda, a young man who is involved first in organising a strike and then in attempts to stop the removal. He is the son of a man known to be a 'sell-out' (someone who plays along with the authorities), and who is killed in the course of the story by a mob when he advises them not to fight against the removal. Juda is terrified of arrest and through the six days we watch his moral disintegration, ending in a betrayal of his friend Spiwo to the authorities and his own suicide.

The Root is One is a novel of unrelieved gloom and pain. It opens with the 'dim, dull dawning' of the first day and a dream of 'a terrible thing which is going to happen soon'.[125] It ends in a night of faint light cast by a horn-shaped moon which looked like a septic wound, on the sixth day. The deepening night swallows up 'the whole act and the people of Johnstown', and as they went away they 'unburdened their hearts of one's deeds; as they gesticulated in their talking, they hurled away the one root of their agony'.[126]

This is not the work of the confident, witty and satiric Sepamla who celebrated the purpose of living in his early poems, but still the poet of the 1977 volume *The Soweto I Love*, whose mood is one of total pessimism. Life is a nightmare. The brave who act against oppression, like the young man Spiwo, are arrested, tortured and perhaps killed, and those who succumb to fear and betray, like Juda, experience the same fate in their dreams. A crowd collects around the house in which Juda has hanged himself. As they wait for the arrival of the police to collect the corpse:

> . . . they began to chatter, to ask questions to discover the truth they lived but were unable to articulate . . . The dead were praised, the living were damned. In all they said, they hoped to reveal before their own eyes the meaning of their lives. But the mystery of it remained, only its particles were revealed in such events as the removals and the suicide of men.

Someone sums it up thus:

> Spiwo was in jail awaiting serious charges; Juda was dead after saying he had let down his friend. Then it was asked: how was survival? Each of these young men had sought survival. Each had been harassed by the moment and, in a desperate bid for survival, had dug his own grave. How ought people to behave in order to attain certain survival?[127]

Sepamla provides no answer to the question which he poses in the novel. For the moment endurance is all. The pain which the people must endure must be 'carried in the hearts of the living for days on end. The pain of suffering is like mist: it settles on every home,' as one of the crowd puts it.[128]

The Root is One makes painful reading. Sepamla provides no relief, not in the theme, in the story he wishes to tell or in the literary handling of the material. It is the work of a man in chains who has suffered so long that his vision of escape and freedom is dead. The novel is banned in South Africa.

In the mid-seventies the South African publishers Ravan Press began to produce novels by black South Africans. The aim was similar to that of their journal, *Staffrider*: to produce literature by South Africans for South Africans. Ravan Press aims at as wide a readership as possible and tries to keep prices low. They, and other publishers of works by black writers, face the financial loss brought by bannings with courage, and will make no concessions by exercising censorship themselves. One scene in the novel *Muriel at Metropolitan*[129] by M. (Miriam Masoli) Tlali, for instance, was bound to draw official disapproval. It speaks of a cleaner who hires out his rooms to lovers at night and charges a special fee to a police sergeant from Marshall Square and a black cover girl. *Muriel* was duly banned. Published by Ravan in 1975, it was subsequently included in Longman's Drumbeat series, and translations have begun to appear.

Muriel at Metropolitan is largely autobiographical, based on Tlali's experiences in a hire purchase firm in Johannesburg. Like

Mphahlele's *Wanderers*, however, it has a theme which goes beyond the beginning and end of the contents.

Metropolitan, the H.P. firm, is a microcosm of South African life, with its variety of people and their relationship to each other. Muriel is unhappy there, not so much because of the way she is treated by the white staff but because she has to become part of the system of charging unduly high interest rates to black purchasers who can ill afford it. She hates having to ask for their particulars and passes and thus becoming identified with the establishment. Muriel is never in doubt, of course, where her loyalty lies. She would not defraud the firm herself and refuses to cooperate with another black employee who is doing so, but she would not dream of giving him away. Muriel's inner tensions increase. While she 'knew the laws of this country' and did not want to 'stage a one-man protest against them', the constant insults also tell on her eventually. Since the white clerical workers will not sit in the same office with Muriel, a workshop in the attic is cleared for her. Later she is moved downstairs into a section of the general office, separated from her white colleagues by cabinets and steel mesh wires. When the white women object to her using the same toilet, the boss promises to repair an outside toilet for her, but this never happens so she takes a leisurely stroll to the nearest public convenience.

Muriel needs the money, so she resigns only when she finds another job. This is with a garage concern but ironically she later finds she cannot accept it after all, because the owner, an Italian immigrant, is less adept than her Jewish boss in bribing the authorities not to implement the apartheid laws governing the employment of blacks and therefore cannot obtain the necessary permission.

Irony is the moving force in the story. It sets the tone in which the absurd situations forming the action are told, and it underlies the description of the characters. It provides the humour with a sharp and serious undertone. The boss, Larry Bloch, is completely believable. Although we see only his business face, we can easily assume the rest to form a rounded picture. He is pleasant, he makes no bones about the fact that money is his god. Muriel looks on with amused tolerance. She accepts his brand of morality and never blames him for his system of doing business, only herself for being part of it. The three white women and the black characters also come to life. They are not an anonymous and interchangeable set of people identified by their colour only.

The tolerance with which Tlali views the outrageous set-up is a new note in black fiction; it contrasts with the bitterness of La Guma and Mphahlele, as well as with the devil-may-care attitude of Boetie and some of the short story writers. It coincides, however, with the note of new confidence we have found in black poetry during this period. It does not necessarily mean that the author is willing to

forgive. One day, for instance, Muriel goes with the driver to take
home one of the white employees and finds that she lives in the
suburb Triomf, built on top of the razed Sophiatown from which the
black community had been forcibly removed. Muriel's own home had
been there.

'This is where I stay, Muriel,' Mrs Stein says, but Muriel is not
listening.

> I was thinking. Just a few yards further up, I was led out of my
> uncle's home to the African Methodist Episcopal Church as a
> young bride, happy and full of hopes for the future.[130]

Tlali's tolerance for the situation at Metropolitan and for the
white characters is derived from strength. The black characters are
not afraid to answer back. Agrippa, who is willing to venture into the
townships to repossess goods, knows he cannot be replaced in the
firm. He drinks and disappears for days, then calmly turns up with a
lorryload full of repossessed goods. Mr Bloch rages and fumes but
does nothing. Mrs Stein addresses a black woman as 'Nanny' and the
woman says:

> 'I am not your Nanny. Your Nanny is looking after your kids at
> your house.'
> 'But I don't know your name.'
> 'You don't have to know my name in order to speak to me. I
> don't know yours either, but you can't allow me to call you
> Nanny, can you?'[131]

Muriel is at first disgusted when her boss scrutinises her desk and asks
her why she brings in such a big bag to work, but Adam, 'in his
wisdom' laughs and says:

> 'Please, Muriel, just ignore him. He is a sick man. Don't you see
> him always looking at me suspiciously or hear him asking me what
> I'm carrying every afternoon when I go home with a parcel? How
> long have I been here?' Adam answers himself emphatically: 'I have
> worked for him faithfully for twenty-six years but he still doesn't
> trust me for a second.'
> Adam shook his head.
> 'He even says he doesn't trust himself! What can you do about a
> man like that?'[132]

Muriel accepts the treatment meted out to her by her white
colleagues, up to a point. When Mrs Kuhn insults her, calling her
names, there is a confrontation.

'She thinks she's like us, you know,' Mrs Kuhn says to Mrs Stein,
and Muriel replies:

That's an insult, Mrs Kuhn . . . I don't think I'm like you. I don't *want* to be like you. I am very proud of what I am. I don't envy you. You're too small, too full of hatred. You are always occupied with issues that do not really matter![133]

This confidence with which Tlali fortifies her characters is a direct expression of black consciousness. It came to Tlali when she discovered her literary antecedents, and even found that her own ancestors, Tlale & Co., had run a printing press which had published a newspaper in Lesotho for decades. 'It was a revelation', she told an interviewer. But she was despondent because she was unable to read the books of her predecessors, authors like Mphahlele, Lewis Nkosi, La Guma and Brutus. She says:

Because I had no base, I had to change and find inspiration from within myself. I could not divorce myself from my peculiar status in an artificial society which refuses to recognise even my existence. It was while in this dilemma that I found myself: that I finally drew the line and retraced my steps. Only then could I come to terms with myself and walk upright again.[134]

These themes Tlali expresses most effectively in the tightly constructed novel. Almost the entire action is played out on the premises of Metropolitan, which establishes a unity of place within which to present the characters and action. Metropolitan is the centre from which we get a peep into the wider South African scene. We see Mrs Stein and Mrs Kuhn sniggering about letters they receive from customers. One man writes:

I will pay my account next week Saturday I have no money todayy because death took place I am going take Body out of Muntuary Yours faithfully Jonas.[135]

Another, acknowledging receipt of a letter with the heading LAST CHANCE, FINAL WARNING, points out that the collector failed to turn up. He says:

My name is an example to big firms, sir, like for example, John Orrs, Russels, etc, etc, from where I Possess Certificates of good customer.

I wish to keep my name up even to this your shop, to be able to buy from you even in any future sir or even to recommend my next friend or relative to you, sir.

Please do not hand over my acc. to any of your lawyers; I do agree with you, in saying: Handing over such, will just cause every thing uneasy to me and even unpleasant for me and my family sir.

Kindly send William to call for collecting at his earlier, Tell him, I am very unhappy because by not collecting his fairms money, he makes my name bad to you sir . . .[136]

The women continue to make fun of the letter-writers and one of the black employees says:

> They make me sick. Can't they find other ways of amusing themselves rather than by using the customers' letters? They can't even speak good English themselves but they see faults in others.'[137]

Muriel at Metropolitan is told in a number of vigorous and dramatic episodes. Business at Metropolitan is done with wild abandon. Mr Bloch has just made a sale and says to the customer through Muriel, in reply to his question when the bed will be delivered:

> 'Tell him I'll deliver it yesterday.'
> Everybody waiting, except Adam and myself, looked at the boss surprised.
> The customer asked:
> 'What? How can he deliver it yesterday?'
> 'That's right. Good-bye now!'
> Adam consoled the obviously disturbed customer by saying:
> 'No, you can go home my brother. The bed will be delivered in a day or two. He's only joking.'
> The customer left.[138]

The dialogue is faultless. Tlali has an ear for the intonation of the black characters, both the educated and those who know little English, for the Afrikaans-speaking women and for the Jewish boss. Her keen powers of observation are in evidence everywhere. Her skill in articulating people's thoughts led to her being asked to contribute a column to *Staffrider* magazine, 'Soweto Speaking', in which she tells the stories of various people on their behalf. She brings this genre, introduced in America by Studs Terkel, to South Africa, where it has been followed by such popular books as Carol Hermer's *Diary of Maria Tholo* and Elsa Joubert's *Die Swerfjare van Poppie Nongeni*.

Miriam Tlali's second novel, *Amandla*,[139] meaning 'Power', was published by Ravan Press in 1980. The censors probably did not go further than the title and the picture of the clenched fist on the cover, both symbols of the struggle for freedom, before banning it. *Amandla* is a very different novel from *Muriel at Metropolitan* in every respect. Gone is most of the easy humour, the ironic approach, the tolerance. As in Sepamla's *The Root is One* the bitterness of the earlier writers and the hope which was emerging from it has given way to rage, frustration and confrontation. The characters in *Amandla* and their creator have experienced the Soweto uprisings and it has altered their outlook. Muriel did not want to stage a one-man protest. In *Amandla* almost all the characters know that they must be part of a combined protest against the system. The struggle is a hard and ruthless one and it has transformed their lives. In one scene in the novel several men are ambushing two policemen who have been particularly harsh in acting against the people. One of the insurgents is giving instructions and adds:

> Remember that we are not going to destroy them. That would be too lenient. What we want to do is to deal with them so that they will remain a living example of what a spy, a traitor of the people should look like. Our two companions in the other Beetle will be waiting when we have finished making them 'sing'. They will take them, bound and gagged, to the ditches outside and there our 'experts' will work on them. After that they will be mere 'robots' for the rest of their miserable lives![140]

These words are spoken not by a hardened trained freedom fighter but by a 21-year-old youth, a high school student who, not long before, was described as 'a steady, astute head prefect'.

Tlali's method of telling the story is also very different from that of the other writers whom we have discussed. As narrator she is a 'witness to history'. Her authority 'rests on the fact that (she) was present at the critical moment when history took a new turn'. Yet she is not a historian or a reporter. 'Where the historian and the reporter are supposedly objective and concern themselves with bare facts and where the historian seeks to deal with events and their causes and effects' the work is 'creatively subjective. (It) deals with idea-forms, and subjective moulds in which events are first cast'. The novel is a 'vehicle for developing the collective wisdom or strength of the family, the clan or the nation'.

The above quotations come from the Foreword to *Ushaba*[141] by Jordan K. (Kush) Ngubane, and are his definition of an *umlando*, or narration, which, according to ancient Zulu practice, tells of ideas in action. While I am not suggesting that Tlali deliberately adopted the *umlando* genre as did Ngubane, his comments certainly fit *Amandla*. His own work he describes as concentrating on a limited area of South African life: the interplay of 'racial' ideas.

The racial ideas in *Amandla* concern the events in Soweto when schoolchildren rebelled against their inferior education, boycotted the schools, and were confronted by the police. The events are seen through the eyes of members of a family whom these events affect in various ways. Pholoso is a nineteen-year-old matriculation student. One of his friends is shot during a demonstration, which affects Pholoso enormously. He becomes a protest leader. Later he is arrested, tortured and put into solitary confinement. While being transferred he manages to escape; as he is wandering from place to place evading further arrest, he and others organise large-scale demonstrations in Soweto and elsewhere. Eventually, when arrest seems inevitable, he leaves the country in secret. Pholoso is the central character around whom the events in the novel are built, but there are many others, members of his extended family and their friends; all their lives are disrupted by the events in Soweto.

In the course of the narrative we learn about every aspect of life in black townships in a period of crisis: how the students organise demonstrations and strikes, meeting literally underground (in a bunker under a church) and swearing oaths of secrecy based on traditional initiation formulas. We see the mourners at the graveside of children killed in confrontation with the police. There is fear, but the dominant mood is one of defiance. The liberation of women, in the black South African context, means that women must play their part and this they do courageously. The melodrama of violence which we have experienced in La Guma's fiction now comes to a head, and again it is the melodrama of real events. For art and psychology, for anything extraneous to the events, Tlali can find no place in literature; there is no place for it in life at such a time. At the end of the novel Pholoso's girlfriend, Felleng, has come to say farewell, and they are waiting for his transport across the border. He is telling her of an incident during the crisis when he tried in vain to protect a white man who had been taken hostage. The young couple only have a short while left together and Pholoso tries to change the subject: 'Let us talk about more pleasant things, Felleng. Let us talk about ourselves'. The girl replies: 'But we are talking about ourselves, Pholoso. Talking about this land is talking about ourselves'.[142]

Ngubane's own work, published in the United States in 1974, does not have the unity of a limited and dramatic period in history as does *Amandla*, but tries to take in the whole sweep of black/white history in South Africa by pointing back to the battle of the Blood River which marked the defeat of King Dingane and his army by the Boers on December 16, 1838, and forward to the inevitable bloodbath of the future, with Sharpeville as the fulcrum of past and future. Like Tlali, Ngubane shows the causes of the events he describes, but goes further in that he looks for the underlying philosophies which have caused the clash between black and white. These he sees as irreconcilable spiritual values, a conflict between the Western concept of the human being as a creature, and of the African evaluation of him as a living ideal in the process of becoming. Ngubane puts the African idea into words through the *sangoma* or diviner, who says that a person, no matter who he is, 'has a creative potential, a power, which nobody can ever take away from him'. She continues:

There is locked in him all the forces in the cosmic order. He is invincible when he understands them and conquers when he controls them and gives them focus. This is the fortress of the soul handed down to us by our ancestors.[143]

Ngubane's African characters regard themselves as defeated rather than oppressed, and see the contemporary struggle as a continuation of the wars against conquest. Once the African recovers his own consciousness of the forces within him, the author feels, he will regain his power.

Ushaba moves backward and forward between history and the present in a demonstration of the traditional Zulu concept of timelessness. The author's attempt to 'recondition' a Zulu vehicle for publication in English, and therefore for a combined Western and African readership, is not a successful one. The work becomes too complicated and laboured, and the story, as well as the philosophical, historical and sociological theses, becomes lost in too much detail. Readability has been sacrificed to theory. *Ushaba* must be regarded as an experiment. It reveals the possibilities of adapting the novel so as to make it a vehicle for black South African protest.

Ngubane, who was an assistant editor of *Ilanga lase Natal* and *Bantu World* in the nineteen forties, went into exile and is now resident in the United States, where he has published several socio-historical works.

Readability goes to the other extreme, that of superseding both purpose and art, in novels about South Africa by other writers in exile in recent years. Their work has been sparse for the obvious reason that they have been cut off from the background. They must turn back to the ready-made plots of love, hatred and violence across the colour line and to the use of characters as symbols. In *A Dream Deferred* by Enver Carim[144] seventeen-year-old Noma-hlubi is raped by her employer and her impaled body, with the white man planted in her wound, symbolises the rape of Africa. Within their limited functions, Carim makes some of his characters fairly credible: the girl Noma-hlubi lonely in her little servant's room among white people, her boyfriend Lelinka, the wise Jewish lawyer and activist Lieberman who knows that all sympathy not born of suffering is necessarily meagre, and especially the sensitive white girl, Marie de Villiers, who, unlike other white women of her country, looks at black people and sees them. Marie must suffer for the sin of her father. When the story ends she is about to be raped by a black man. The story concerns a plot by black and white insurgents which eventually fails. Carim handles the narrative quite ably and succeeds in holding the tension, but, like the novels of Peter Abrahams, it is all too smooth. Realism gives way to popular appeal, with the added incentive to the reader of titillating sexual scenes. Again, such novels lie outside the stream of black South African writing, in spite of their relevance in the political field, as they are removed from the black South African actuality physically, psychologically and philosophically.

*

Turning back to South Africa, we find that the younger writers have now had an opportunity to read some of the works of the early writers, previously banned. Neil Alwin Williams, whose *Just a Little Stretch of Road*[145] shares a volume with Fhazel Johannesse's poems, *The Rainmaker*, has doubtlessly studied that other stretch of road, *Down Second Avenue*. He has brought Mphahlele's realistic account of township life up to date in an impressionist, often surrealist, style, as reality and dreams interweave. Williams's world, like Mphahlele's, pulsates and is vibrantly alive. Time and again it is swept up in ghastly scenes of violence and misfortune as, for instance, when the narrator's mother is raped and when his father dies in a fire. Like one of the characters in the narrative, who fills the wasteland of his existence with Bostik fumes, Williams is a 'child of the electronic cave age'.[146] Yet there are flashes of hope in human relationships where dreams and reality meet, which has prompted Williams to tell his publishers: 'I have sensed that time has been running out—that we are well past the midnight hour in South Africa. But I write in the hope that there still is time'.[147] There is much promise in Williams's writing, but he tends to get carried away by the rhythm and sound of words and there is little cohesion of theme or purpose.

At a first reading it would appear that Ahmed Essop's short novel, *The Visitation*,[148] does not belong into an account of specifically black South African writing. The moral satire about an avaricious wealthy merchant whose 'urban soul' meets its 'urban doom' at the hands of a protection racket gangster, applies anywhere. As we shall see however, Essop's theme goes a great deal deeper, and while universally applicable, has a particular relevance to the South African situation.

The conflict is between reality and illusion. Mr Sufi, the merchant, must learn that his comfortable world in which he apparently leads a quiet, dignified and unassuming life, is a world of illusion, and that the real world is very different. Essop creates the illusionary setting for the reader by weaving a mystical world of hallucination; landscapes move swiftly past the merchant as he sits in his stationary car, an island in the middle of Zoo Lake circles on its own axis. Mr Sufi, awakening after a particularly horrible dream, has to touch his face, his body and the floor in 'trying to establish his existence in a particular time and place';[149] a mysterious visit by a gangster boss becomes the 'Visitation' of the title. This technique of blurred reality is more like that of two leading non-black South African writers, John Coetzee and Etienne Le Roux, and Europeans dating back to Kafka, than to anything previously written by black South Africans. Essop's real world, however, is unmistakably South African, and seen from the black point of view. Essop's characters are South African Indians and their lives are played out within the confines of an Indian group area under the apartheid system. The story ends at the time of forced removal from the area which has been declared white. There are other indications of the nature of Essop's world: Mr Sufi thinks that he can get advice in his predicament from Yogi Krishnasiva because he feels the Yogi's 'theoretical insight into the instability of life had gained a practical dimension by his penal experience'[150]—he had gone to jail under the Immorality act for sleeping with a white woman—only to find that the Yogi had gone mad. Krishnasiva was a man who had declared that if one possessed inner liberty, political liberty was unnecessary. Clearly Essop does not feel that liberty is thus divisible. In the novel liberty is identified with compassion for mankind, and the lesson Mr Sufi has to learn is that living a quiet life, uninvolved with those dependent upon one, is not enough. No theme could be more relevant to its South African setting.

Essop tells his fascinating tale simply and steadily. Mr Sufi has inherited his wealth in the form of apartment blocks. Rent is paid by post but Mr Sufi calls personally on tenants who are in arrears. He has four daughters whose upbringing he leaves to his pleasant and submissive wife. In every apartment block he keeps a concubine. He owns several motorcars and changes them as new models come on the market. Besides women and cars he is fond of the cinema. Mr Sufi is well satisfied with his life. Every month Mr Sufi, like other merchants in the area, pays a retainer fee to Gool for 'protection'. Gool calls on the merchant and after a brief social ritual an envelope is handed to Gool and he leaves.

One day, however, Gool does not depart immediately. Instead, his assistants appear with huge crates containing thousands of lamps. Mr Sufi knows they are stolen goods but he is helpless. There are too many to hide or destroy and he cannot go to the police because they are in Gool's pay. Gool therefore has him in his power and his life becomes a nightmare. Gool makes inroads into his wealth so that he has to give up his concubines. Mr Sufi has to raise his rents which turns normal resentment of a landlord into open hatred among his tenants. His connection with Gool, though not its cause, becomes known and he loses respect in the community. He tries every possible way to extricate himself, including murder, but Gool foils all attempts.

Essop tells the story with a fine irony. The lamps which Gool has brought into the merchant's life have darkened instead of lighted his life. Mr Sufi was always too mean to light the stairways of his apartment houses. Now he has enough lamps, but his own life is suffused with gloom. Similarly, the name of the make of the lamps is Apollo but they have brought him no beauty.

The subtlety of the irony lies in Mr Sufi's firm belief that he is an innocent victim. He cannot understand why a man who has never actively harmed anyone should be punished to such an extent. Could

he, he wonders, have been a gangster in a previous existence? He has
no idea that his sins were committed in this life before he had become
embroiled with Gool. There was his harshness towards his tenants,
his cavalier treatment of his concubines, his exploitation of his wife,
his neglect of his daughters, in short his refusal to become involved,
and to pull his weight as a human being. He tries to find out the
derivation of the name of his tormentor. Did it mean ghoul or
goolam? It could in fact be both: Gool is his inner evil genius as well as
his tormentor.

Gradually he comes to realise his parallel relationship with Gool
and his mob and that the difference between them is only a matter of
degree:

> He and they lived parasitically off others, spending their lives with
> playthings—billiards, women, motor-cars—and eternally seeking
> entertainment in cinemas. He and they had never accomplished a
> day's work, work that contributed to the sum of man's creative
> labour. His money-minting properties had been acquired through
> inheritance; the income of the gangsters was a sort of inheritance
> received from those who were weak and fearful.[151]

Mr Sufi has to reach the lowest depths of degradation before self-
knowledge penetrates and there is a glimmer of light. When Gool
drags Mr Sufi to a party and makes him introduce his former
mistresses to the gangsters he has to witness an orgy in which they
indulge. His nausea and horror are due to a new insight into his own
actions. They seem 'to be enacting a brutalised gross parody of his
former erotic life'.[152] When his tenants are threatened and beaten up
by Gool's gangsters for not paying their rent he experiences a feeling
of pity for the first time in his life. He expresses it in the only way he
knows. The tenant, his face bruised, his eyes swollen and dark, pays
the rent. Mr Sufi:

> . . . took the money, counted it, then put some back into the
> envelope and handed it to Mr Rahim.
> 'You needn't pay the increased amount.'
> Mr Rahim, surprised by the magnanimity, left the building a
> bewildered man.[153]

When his daughter falls pregnant, for the first time he worries about
someone other than himself:

> Fawzia's agony and fate—who would marry her with an ille-
> gitimate child? Or even if the child were given away for
> adoption?—wrung the fibres of her father's being as nothing had
> ever done, not even his involvement with Gool . . . The sight of
> his daughter, doomed to an unhappy life by that mentally
> grotesque, sensual monster Faizel Adil (a monster who painfully

revealed to him something of his own sensual image) filled him with profound love which he was unable to express, for he had never found the time to become part of the lives of his children. And he was seized by fear for the safety of his other daughters: they too were vulnerable. Love and compassion for them filled him.[154]

When he meets one of his mistresses again she is no longer 'a physical body for his pleasure, but a complex being with a life of her own'.[155] He now sees her as a person 'whose worth transcended the pleasure she could give'.[156] He regrets his coolness towards his wife and is overcome with a longing to hold another being's hand. He craves to hold his children in his arms and kiss them. Most of all, when he sells his properties at a good profit to buy land in Elysia, the new group area for Indians, he feels somehow that the eventual destruction of the apartment houses, to make room for a new suburb for whites, 'was the result, not of a government order, but of a personal inability to protect it'.[157] He is still in the clutches of Gool, nothing has outwardly changed, but Mr Sufi has made contact with other human beings and feels responsibility. His final nightmare at the end of the story, when all the horrors of the past months pass before his eyes, is alleviated by the comfort of his wife and the sight of his beautiful children. He has woken up to reality.

Short Stories

'IT IS IMPOSSIBLE for a writer who lives in oppression to organise his whole personality into creating a novel', Ezekiel Mphahlele said in an essay entitled 'Black and White'.[1] 'The short story is used as a short cut (to get) some things off one's chest in quick time.' The themes which the writers wanted to express were so strong, as one of them, William ('Bloke') Modisane put it, that they could be contained only in a short story. 'Everything is always in a state of such violent change in human relationships—a man is not sure where he will be next month or next week or even for that matter next day—he wants to put all down in a short story. The situation is so vast and the best way to communicate is to pin-point the incidents.' Modisane told this to Philip Segal, who interviewed him on behalf of the magazine *Contact* on the purposes of the Conference of African Writers of English Expression held at Makerere University, Kampala, Uganda, under auspices of the Mbari Writers and Artists Club of Nigeria, in 1962. 'You think, in short,' Segal replied, 'that the dramatic nature of South African social and political life needs a certain explosive registry of moments to get it across'.[2]

Modisane and Mphahlele are typical of the black short story writers in English in South Africa during the flowering of that genre in the late nineteen fifties and early nineteen sixties in that both were leading contributors to or staff members of Drum magazine, both lived in Sophiatown where they formed part of a literary circle, both wrote autobiographies, both left South Africa, and both have been banned under the Amendment to the Suppression of Communism Act.

Mphahlele explains the difficulties of writing under the conditions in which they lived in his book of essays, *The African Image*.[3] Coming home after a day's work, which inevitably included clashes or near-clashes with police or with a white boss, or foreman or shop assistant or post office clerk,

> . . . you felt physically tired and spiritually flat. You tried to settle down to writing. Your whole being quivered with latent anger; words, words, words, spilled on to the pages and you found yourself caught up in the artistic difficulty of making a parochial experience available to the bigger world on terms that may very

well be impossible. For then you had to give an account of your bitterness. Blinded by it, in addition to other things, you had to grope for the truth. Somewhere in this dark alley, you felt it was a hopeless fight because so much of your energy went into the effort to adjust yourself to the conditions which threaten every moment to crush you . . .[4]

His confrontation with his bitterness was not the only difficulty which he had to face. The problems of daily living are explained in Mphahlele's autobiography *Down Second Avenue*.[5] He describes the period of his studies at St Peter's School where he had a nervous breakdown for fear that he might fail. If he had done so, his mother would not have been able to afford the fees for a further year: £15 out of her earnings of £3 a month as a domestic servant. Mphahlele passed easily, however, and continued his studies at Adams College in Natal where he qualified as a teacher. His first stories, published as a collection by the African Bookman in 1946, *Man Must Live*, were written while he was working as a clerk for an institute for the blind. During this time he was studying privately for the Matriculation certificate and teaching himself shorthand. He was earning £12 a month out of which he had to buy his books, send money to his mother—his brother and sister were now in high school—and clothe himself. When he first became a high school teacher in Orlando township, he earned £13 a month.

These almost insurmountable odds against producing literary works acted as a spur, as they often did for these writers. It is this drive which often gives vitality and power to their fiction. To be heard was an aim in itself.

Peter Abrahams, who preceded the *Drum* writers by some years in revealing black life in short fiction, was already abroad when his collection *Dark Testament*[6] was published in 1942. It consists of several sketches under the heading 'I Remember' and three longer stories. They were written between 1930 and 1938 and tell mainly about growing up poor and coloured in the township of Vrededorp. As a Marxist at the time, however, he made a point of introducing victims of oppression from other races, such as a Jewish refugee ('Jewish Brother'), who was shunned and ill-treated by the people around him. Unlike the writers of the *Drum* period, Abrahams rarely allows protest against conditions to arise naturally from the situations. Instead, he finds it necessary to make explicit statements such as in the sketch 'Jewish Sister':

My people said it was the will of God that the white man should be boss. They were not prepared to go against the will of God. They had no sympathy with me when I said it was all wrong . . . They said it had been so all the years and nothing could change it. I denied this.[7]

Only sometimes does he let the characters and background speak for themselves. The sketch 'Saturday Night', for example, foreshadows later writing such as Mphahlele's *Down Second Avenue* and the stories of Alex La Guma in its realistic description of township life.

For the most part, however, the stories and sketches are immature in their sentimentality, melodramatic plots and contrived situations. The collection already displays the ease and fluency of his novels, but Abrahams did not follow it up with further short fiction.

We have looked at Mphahlele's novels and we shall later consider his autobiography, essays and critical works. Many of his short stories are sketched from real life and thus form an extension of his autobiographical writing. Often the two are identical. An incident featuring a sweet-potato seller in the autobiography *Down Second Avenue* appeared originally as a short story, 'A Winter's Story', in the publication *Fighting Talk*. Conversely, a section of *Down Second Avenue* appeared as a short story in W.H. Whiteley's anthology, *A Selection of African Prose* (1959), as 'The Woman' in *The Living and Dead and Other Stories* and as 'The Woman Walks Out' in *The Purple Renoster*. As a result he is always at ease when describing the background to his stories. We meet familiar characters in fact and fiction. Sello in 'Out Brief Candle', for instance, is a messenger in an attorney's office like Mphahlele, and 'Tomorrow You Shall Reap' gives a good picture of the author's own youth in Pietersburg. 'The Leaves Were Falling' is based on a personal mental experience, and 'Grieg on a Stolen Piano' tells about his uncle.

'When Africans say a person "is there",' says Mphahlele, introducing a chapter about a character called Ma-Lebona in *Down Second Avenue*, 'they mean you cannot but feel she is alive; she allows you no room to forget she was born and is alive in flesh and spirit'.[8] Whether they really lived or not, Mphahlele's characters are certainly 'there', such as Ma-Lebona herself, for instance, who was so clean that she often had meat taken out of boiling water to be rewashed, and who used to play tennis and always spoke English when she talked about it later; or Uncle, a former school-inspector and musician whose gambling urge pushed him into grooming a country girl for a beauty competition.

In the article 'Black and White'[9] Mphahlele says that he has lived through three stages in the categories of African short-story writing, which he describes as follows: 'Between the outright protest of Richard Rive and James Matthews at the one end and the romantic escapism of Can Themba at the other, is a category in which rejection, revulsion and protest meet acceptance and conciliation'.[10] This third stage he defines in *Down Second Avenue* as 'something (I hope) of a higher order, which is the ironic meeting between protest and acceptance in their widest terms'.[11]

If his earliest stories, in the collection entitled *Man Must Live and*

Other Stories, represent escapism, then his brand of escapism is certainly not of the ivory-tower kind. The people in *Man Must Live* are deeply involved in living. 'The mad cruel world' drives a young foundling to homicide in 'Out, Brief Candle'. Zungu, in the title story, finds that the:

> world of love and plenty was a dream world . . . whose glories have vanished with the dawn of reality . . . The twinkle is gone. But there is something in that stolid blankness in those eyes, something of stubbornness. When he looks at you, you cannot help but read the stubborn words: What do you expect me to be—a magician or a superman, or a soft learned genteel animal? My Lord—I *must* live, man![12]

In 'The Leaves were Falling' he grasps the essence of man's struggle to be true to himself, not to be a leaf among falling leaves on a dry sapless twig destined to decay. In other words man must not follow in the wake of a crowd of religious or political opportunists. Unlike the Rev. Kumalo in *Cry, the Beloved Country* with his stereotyped naiveness, the Rev. Katsane Melato holds our sympathy as a shy and insecure human being who finds the inner strength to be himself. Strangely enough, although this was some ten years before Mphahlele left South Africa, he does so by removing himself from the conflict.

Mphahlele has virtually disowned his first collection and rarely lists it among his writings. Yet in its portrayal of the life and struggle of the black man to survive in his society it broke new ground for the South African reader. The African Bookman printed 700 copies and almost all of them were sold.

Soon after this one experiment with black fiction, The African Bookman closed down and there was no outlet for short stories by black writers in South Africa except for occasional fiction in the leftist newspapers, *The Guardian* (later *New Age* and *New Era*) and *Fighting Talk*.

In 1951 *African Drum* appeared on the scene. Although Mphahlele says that he developed 'in spite of *Drum*', it is doubtful whether the short story writers would have developed at all without it. In the article mentioned earlier, 'Black and White', Mphahlele takes *Drum* to task for failing to provide a workshop for experimentation, and for promoting a 'tough superficial prose'. In this respect Mphahlele developed in spite of being a contributor and one-time fiction editor of *Drum*. Some of his best writing appeared in this magazine between 1953 and 1959, sometimes under the pen name of Bruno Esekie and there is nothing brash or superficial about the prose. By now Mphahlele had had a University education and had read voraciously. Dickens, Dostoevsky, Chekhov, Gorky and Faulkner became his models.

Between December 1956 and April 1957 *Drum* published his series about a family in Newclare Township. It is surprising that no extracts have appeared in anthologies and that Mphahlele has not used it as a basis for a full-length book. Characters, situations and plots come pouring out. The humour is strong but although there is rollicking fun at times the stark grim realism of the life he depicts is clearly perceived. There is drama on Nadia Street, the 'Quiet Street' of the title. A deaf and dumb boy is abandoned by his parents and is choked to death by the strap that ties him to the bed:

> There were urine pools and stools all over the floor. The sooty walls told a murky story of degenerate backyard lives, a rickety cupboard lay on its side and life-size cockroaches glided merrily in and about as if nothing had happened. The window was shut. There was nothing else, except death.[13]

But usually it is not the highly dramatic incidents— the arrests, the raids and the brutality—that interest him at this stage. Rather, it is the weddings and funerals, a young man's first acquaintance with the city, poverty and illness, in short the ordinary events that go on while people try to survive. While the editors were describing the stories as being about 'that crazy mixed up family', the Lesanes, the readers must have been aware of the stark, sombre reality which always lay waiting in the background of their lives, ready to pounce. The 'bigger purpose of living' is often lost in the desperate day-to-day struggle against poverty. What hope is there for this huge family, housed in two rooms, which Ma-Lesane desperately but unsuccessfully tries to keep clean? The father, discharged from the mines because of ill health, is afraid of his wife and beats his teen-age daughter to prove his masculinity. The younger boys eat their supper secretly in turn, so that they need not feel obliged to invite their friends to share their meagre meal. Diketso herself realises that she is hurting her family and herself by defying her parents and going to her lover who lives in a squatters' camp, but this is the only way she can combat her frustration at having to leave school early because her parents can no longer afford to keep her there. This episode ends on a slightly more hopeful note. Diketso has not given up all hope and aspirations. There must be a future for her, she feels. And even the present has some happy moments. Unexpectedly, her lover gives her a birthday gift. Towards the end of the series there appears to be less and less hope. Diketso is in despair because she hates her work in a factory and sees no way out. The final episode is the tragic story of the neighbouring couple who abandon their child. But man must live, and so 'Nadia Street life went on as usual like a printing press'.[14]

The series ends on what seems a pessimistic note. It was certainly written at one of the most mentally devastating periods of Mphahlele's life, when he was considering exiling himself from his homeland. Throughout, however, there is a note of hope in the spirit of toughness of the individual people who refuse to submit to circumstances and continue to aspire to a better life.

A story in *Drum* in which the twist at the end supersedes character and circumstances is 'The Suitcase'. A situation is introduced, expectancy rises and leads to the climax. Timi, unemployed and desperate, is waiting 'for sheer naked chance', a desperate chance to find a way of bringing home something to his wife on Old Year's Eve. He finds it on a bus, when a woman passenger leaves a suitcase behind. Another passenger denounces him for taking it and at the police station he swears repeatedly that the case is his. But he has gambled with chance and lost. The case contains a dead baby.

This story also appeared in Mphahlele's second collection, *The Living and Dead and Other Stories*.[15] In most of the other stories in this volume racial conflict becomes the main theme. The *Drum* days were over now and Mphahlele was writing for a wider public. Man must live, it is true, but this is no longer sufficient. Man, the black man, has to shoulder his responsibilities. The characterisation and background of the early sketches and the plot and planning of 'The Suitcase' give way to social situations and conflict as the main interest. The characters, especially the whites, are no longer so important. A favourite plot is the one of the title story where the white man suddenly becomes aware of his servant as a human being, but decides that he had 'better continue treating him as a name, not as another human being'.[16]

The white 'do-gooder' has become a stock figure in South African fiction by black writers. In 'We'll Have Dinner at Eight' Miss Pringle is introduced in the story as making 'a conscious effort to win non-white friends, which she underlined with an eternal smile on her lips'.[17] Her protégé, Mzondi, kills her in the mistaken belief that she has invited him for dinner to get him drunk and reveal where he has hidden two thousand pounds which he has stolen. There is irony in the situation of the spinster who hides her unconscious sexual longings behind the cloak of a do-gooder, and the lack of comprehension of the cripple to whom anyone white represents an unjust law and therefore danger. Unfortunately there is neither tragedy nor pathos, however, partly because of the poorly motivated murder—if Mzondi was afraid Miss Pringle would make him drunk and drag his secret out of him all he had to do was to stay away from her dinner—but mainly because of the lack of sympathy for or even interest in the two protagonists.

In 'The Master of Doornvlei', which was probably written at the time of the Lesane series, we also have confrontation, but this time the labels are less distinct, the protagonists more complex. In the country the situation is different. The bond between white farmer and black labourer is a more vital one than between master and domestic servant or welfare worker and her charge. Miss Pringle sees only pity in her relationship, Stoffel in 'The Living and Dead' is aware only of his comforts, but Sarel Britz, the owner of the farm Doornvlei, knows that it is necessary to establish a workable relationship. Sarel's father thought of his black labourers as children, but Sarel has been to the city to study agriculture, and he knows that the father-child relationship is a white man's myth. He tries to treat his men justly because he needs them, but added to this is a new element, fear. They are no longer children, he assures his mother. How are they grown up, she wants to know? 'Yes, Ma,' he says, 'they're fully grown up, some of them cleverer and wiser than a lot of us whites. Their damned patience makes them all the more dangerous'.[18] The labourers are protesting against the actions of the Rhodesian black foreman, Mfukeri, who whips them in spite of Sarel's instructions to desist. Mfukeri drives the labourers beyond their physical endurance and the men ask for his dismissal. Sarel listens, but when the leader imposes an ultimatum on him he cannot tolerate this from a black man. He dismisses him, and keeps the foreman. The labourers are helpless as they cannot go from one farm to another without a 'trekpass', for the issue of which the former employer would have to give his consent. As time passes Sarel's fears increase. The more he grows afraid, the more dependent he becomes on his foreman. Yet he also fears the foreman and catches the nuances of diminishing deference in his attitude towards him.

The conflict culminates in a confrontation. Sarel becomes aware of the threat to his authority when Mfukeri's bull engages in battle with Sarel's pedigree stallion:

> Master and foreman watched, each feeling that he was entangled in this strife between their animals; more so than they dared to show outwardly. Sarel Britz bit his lower lip as he watched the rage of the bull. He seemed to see scalding fury in the very slime that came from the mouth of the bull to mix with the earth.[19]

When Mfukeri wins this symbolic confrontation—the bull gores the stallion—he feels overwhelming triumph. But it cannot be allowed to last. Sarel gives Mfukeri the choice of shooting his bull or leaving. The story ends:

> Mfukeri did not answer. They both knew the moment had come. He stood still and looked at Britz. Then he walked off, and coaxed his bull out of the premises.
> 'I gave him a choice,' Sarel said to his mother, telling her the whole story.
> 'You shouldn't have, Sarel. He has worked for us these fifteen years.'

Sarel knew he had been right. As he looked out of the window to the empty paddock, he was stricken with grief. And then he was glad. He had got rid of yet another threat to his authority. But the fear remained.[20]

The last story in this collection, 'He and the Cat', is an attempt at a different style. The reader is not told what the 'burden' is 'that would fall off' as soon as the narrator has seen and spoken to the lawyer. The story is merely a moment in time, which dissolves into recognition that the man closing envelope after envelope on a hot afternoon in a lawyer's waiting room and fixedly smiling at the lawyer's client is blind:

An invincible pair, he and the cat [a picture above him] . . . scorning our shames and hurts and the heat, seeming to hold the key to the immediate imperceptible and the most remote unforeseeable.[21]

As an impressionist reflection it is perceptively told, even if it lacks any inner significance.

Mphahlele's last collection of short stories to concern us, is *In Corner B*.[22] Some of these stories were written earlier ('Man Must Live', 'The Coffee Cart Girl'—which appeared as 'Across Down Stream' in *Drum* in 1957) and some go back to an earlier style such as, in parts, 'Grieg on a Stolen Piano' which is an autobiographical sketch like those in *Down Second Avenue*.

His writing in the new stories, however, has become more mature. There is an economy of words and a conciseness of imagery lacking before. Nature is used to a greater extent to create a symbolic atmosphere of menace as, for instance, when the narrator of 'Grieg on a Stolen Piano' is fleeing through the thick bush and remembers the stories of giant snakes which leaned over sleeping travellers. He feels that something is stalking him all the time, waiting for the proper moment to pounce on him. The title of this story brilliantly and ironically combines the elements of white culture and the enforced township way of life.

Stories like 'Mrs Plum' show a new sensitivity to human relationships which transcends the situation. This story fits into the category described in 'Black and White' 'where rejection, revulsion and protest meet acceptance and conciliation'. The bitterness is still there but underlying it is a new compassion which regrets the lack of understanding between man and man.

'Mrs Plum' is Mphahlele's most serious attempt to explore the relationship between white and black in South Africa. Once again two protagonists face each other. Mrs Plum, a widow living in the white suburb of Greenside in Johannesburg with her daughter Kate, her servants and her dogs, is concerned about the welfare of black people. She goes to meetings with others who think like her. They work towards including a few black people in the government of the country, electing their own representatives to rule the tribal villages, and obtaining higher wages and generally better treatment. She protests against the government in newspaper articles and demonstrations, she runs night classes for servants, helps her own servant with her English and asks her to sit at the table at meals.

All this we learn from the servant, Karabo, who is the narrator. Karabo is, or pretends to be, an *ingenue* who asks Mrs Plum's daughter all the wrong questions. 'My mother,' says Kate, 'goes to meetings many times'. Karabo asks 'What for?' and in response to Kate's reply, 'For your people' she says: 'My people are in Phokeng far away. They have got mouths . . . Why does she want to say something for them?' Kate explains patiently that she means all black people in the country. 'Oh,' says Karabo innocently, 'What do the black people want to say?'[23]

Karabo finds Mrs Plum's liberalism puzzling but accepts it at first as one of the eccentricities of the white race. This one, 'my madam . . . loved dogs and Africans and said that everyone must follow the law even if it hurt. These were three big things in Madam's life'.[24] Thus the story opens. It ends when Mrs Plum visits Karabo in her home village, after she has left her job, and begs her to return. She tells Karabo that her two pet dogs have died. Did this woman, Karabo wonders, come to ask her to return because she had lost two animals she loved? Mrs Plum says to her: 'You know, I like your people, Karabo, the Africans'. 'And Dick and me?' Karabo wonders.[25] In the course of the story we gradually realise that while Mrs Plum's liberalism is quite genuine, unlike that of Miss Pringle, it is completely impersonal, directed at ideas rather than at people. Mphahlele dislikes this type even more intensely, because it lacks the one characteristic that is his own ruling passion, a feeling of compassion for one's fellow men.

Bitterness, says Mphahlele, is not a healthy state of mind and feeling to revel in. Mphahlele's bitterness, says William Plomer,[26] is not the bitterness of despair or fanaticism, but the taste of the life he has known'. The taste of the life he has known is the substance of his writing. He does not revel in it. He uses it to create short fiction which, in this last volume, fulfilled the early promise, especially in the title story 'In Corner B' which is Mphahlele's own favourite. This story concerns Talita, whose husband has been stabbed to death. The description of the funeral preparations and wake is perhaps Mphahlele's most successful scene of township life. He is now completely confident in expressing himself. The story appeared in *The Classic* in 1964 and must have been written at that time since it would certainly have been published before if written earlier. By 1964, *Down Second Avenue* was about to go into a second edition, *African*

Image had appeared, Mphahlele had lived in Nigeria, France and Kenya. He was an established writer and a figure of consequence in the African literary world.

In the story, even death is an occasion for living fully. We see the people at the wake eating, drinking and laughing. Relatives and friends, 'and their relatives and friends' come from afar. There is 'singing, praying, singing, preaching',[27] women screaming in high-pitched voices, political discussions with acid comments that if a white man had been the victim the murderers would already have been caught. Women serve tea and sandwiches. Cousin Stoffel is the self-appointed and not altogether trusted collector of contributions for funeral expenses, which he enters in a school exercise book. The money helps to buy liquor from a shebeen. Talita sleeps where she sits and is disturbed only to be asked questions occasionally, like 'What will you eat now?' or 'Has your headache stopped today?' or 'Are your bowels moving properly?' or 'The burial society wants your marriage certificate, where do you keep it?'[28]

The plot of the story concerns the love between Talita and her husband. It is a simple and unembellished love story, tender without sentimentality. Talita, a lively and over-talkative, but affectionate woman, loves her gentle shy man. We see 'her man' through her eyes: he was, as she remembers now after his death, 'tall, not very handsome but lovable; an insurance agent who moved about in a car'. He was therefore more successful than most, since others in the business usually walked from house to house and used buses and trains between townships. Her man 'had soft gentle eyes and was not at all as vivacious as she'.[29]

They had been married for nineteen years and had three children when something occurred which darkened the brightness of their intense love for each other. A love letter from a woman to her husband fell into Talita's hands. Talita remembers the incident now, as she sits at the wake. 'No one was going to share her man with her, fullstop',[30] she said to herself in her forthright way. She walked in on the unsuspecting mistress. Her words to the woman's husband were outspoken. '"I am glad you are in, Morena—sir. I have just come to ask you to chain your bitch. That is my man and mine alone." She stood up to leave.'[31]

We now have one of Mphahlele's few sexual scenes, handled with great delicacy, between the shy husband and the woman who often blusters but is at heart as soft and timid as he is. Sex to Mphahlele is synonymous with love. The intensity of the scene makes it far more personal than anything Mphahlele has written about the women in his own life. This, one feels, is Mphahlele's idea of ideal love.

Often there were moments of deep silence as Talita and her man sat together or lay side by side. But he seldom stiffened up. He would take her into his arms and love her furiously and she would respond generously and tenderly because she loved him and the pathos in his eyes.

'You know, my man,' she ventured to say one evening in bed, 'if there is anything I can help you with, if there is anything you would like to tell me, you mustn't be afraid to tell me. There may be certain things a woman can do for her man which he never suspected she could do.'

'Oh, don't worry about me. There is nothing you need do for me.' And, like someone who had at last found a refuge after a rough and dangerous journey, her man would fold her in his arms and love her.[32]

Mphahlele completes his picture of a woman in love. 'Funny,' Talita, who is completely articulate, wonders to herself, 'that you saw your man's face every day almost and yet you couldn't look at it while he slept without the sensation of some guilt or something timid or tense or something held in suspension; so that if the man stirred, your heart gave a leap as you turned your face away. One thing she was sure of amidst all the wild and agonizing speculation: her man loved her and their children.'[33]

Mphahlele has learnt the effect of and necessity for comic relief after a tense and dramatic scene. He thus switches back to the wake and we have the relatives quarrelling over precedence. One outraged cousin begins a long harangue but is rebuked by 'uncle of the clan', who says that she has not got 'what the English call respection'. In another corner an elderly relative serves drinks to 'drown de sorry, as the Englishman says.'[34]

Finally the two themes of past and present, of drama and humour, are brought together in a highly climactic funeral scene. Marta, the mistress, appears at the cemetery seemingly out of nowhere, and flings herself on the grave. Talita is badly shaken, but she is led away to the car before she can act.

In his earlier fiction Mphahlele might have left the story on this note. Here, however, he provides us with relief from tension and at the same time with a perfect and touching ending to the love story between Talita and her husband. Out of his grave he declares his love for her, and he does so, gently as in his life time, through the barely literate medium of his mistress, Marta. Talita receives a letter from Marta which is well worth quoting in full:

Dear Missis Molamo, I am dropping this few lines for to hoping that you are living good now i want to teling you my hart is sore sore i hold myselfe bad on the day of youre mans funeral my hart was ful of pane too much i see myselfe already o Missis Molamo alreaddy doing mad doings i think the gods are beatting me now for holding myself as wyle animall forgeef forgeef i pray with all my hart child of the people.[35]

Talita, flushing with anger, wonders whether she should continue to read. 'These wild women,' she says to herself, 'who can't even write must needs try to do so in English'. But she continues:

now i must tel you something you must noe quik quik thees that i can see that when you come to my hause and then whenn you see me kriing neer the grafe i can see you think i am sweet chokolet of your man i can see you think in your hart my man love that wooman no no i want to tel you that he neva love me neva neva he livd same haus my femily rented in Fitas and i lovd him mad i tel you i loved him and i wanted him with red eyes he was nise leetl bit nise to me but i see he sham for me as i have got no big ejucashin he got too much book i make nise tea and cake for him and he like my muther and he is so nise i want to foss him to love me but he just nise i am shoor he come to meet me in toun even now we are 2 merryd peeple bicos he remember me and muther looked aftar him like bruther for me he was stil nise to me but al wooman can see whenn there is no loveness in a man and they can see lovfulness. now he is gonn i feel i want to rite with my al ten fingas becos i have too muche to say aboute your sorriness and my sorriness i will help you to kry you help me to kry and leev that man in peas with his gods. so i stop press here my deer i beg to pen off the gods look aftar us

i remain your sinserity
Missis Marta Shuping.[36]

How does Talita react to this revelation? She stands up and makes tea for herself. Her love has been restored to her. She feels 'like a foot traveller after a good refreshing bath'.[37]

The more one reads Mphahlele's stories of township life, the greater becomes one's understanding of the term 'acceptance' he uses to describe a phase in his fiction. This is not acceptance of township conditions or of life in South Africa; rather acceptance of the fact that human values of love, trust, and loyalty can continue even under impossible living conditions. In this story he calls it 'surrender' rather than acceptance, a poetic surrender to life and death, underlying which is 'the one long and huge irony of endurance'.[38]

Mphahlele had come to terms, not with the world in which he lived, but with his own attitude towards it. The other writers among his contemporaries also had to find a way of interpreting their world. Lewis Nkosi, speaking of the world of black writers in South Africa, describes the conditions under which they live as a 'gargantuan reality'; 'it impinges so strongly upon the imagination that the temptation is often compelling to use the ready-made plots of violence, chicanery and racial love tragedies as representing universal truth when, in fact, actual insight into human tragedy may lie beneath this social and political turbulence'. This world, he says, 'is a familiar one to those who have lived in race-torn areas: the ugly leer on the claustrophobic face of violence, the sweltering heat of talk about to simmer into social explosion, the senseless arbitrary death, the frenzied quest for emotional release in sex and drink. They are concerned with the phantasies evoked by a black and white world which, though divided, simultaneously seeks and is terrified by social fusion.'[39]

Unable to come to terms with their experience, the city dwelling black writers of the mid nineteen-fifties to the early nineteen-sixties either had to confront the situation or escape from it. But what form was the escape to take? Romantic literature for the popular magazines would have to be written—and some was—under an assumed European name to be acceptable and there was little outlet for such writing in the black press. Confrontation meant protest writing and most of the short fiction written during this period in *Drum*, and in other publications which became available as outlets in South Africa and abroad, falls into this category, although rarely is there the extreme revolutionary verve which looks upon literature as just another front in a battle for a cause.

'Conflict,' says Nadine Gordimer, 'can provide a deep and powerful stimulus but a culture as a whole cannot be made out of the groans and sparks that fly . . . The thirst that comes from the salt of conflict will need some quenching. Africa is a dry land in more ways than one.'[40] And: 'No artist will ever be content to substitute the noise of war for the music of the soul,' says Can Themba.[41] But the noise of war and the sparks that flew were the only raw material at the disposal of the writers.

We must remember that the writers, and the critics, were working at a time when the only fiction available to readers for comparison was European. The early fiction writers, Abrahams, Mphahlele right up to *The African Image* had been mainly addressing whites. Now, with the advent of *Drum*, there was a black readership. Instinctively the writers knew that to tell it as it was, was not enough. The reader had to be given some hope, and since hope lay only in change, the writer, in his stories, had to grapple with the forces of oppression.

Often the stories had to do little but demonstrate the situation by recounting an incident and allowing the protest to speak for itself. In Arthur Maimane's story 'A Manner of Speaking',[42] a black boy refuses to call a white woman 'Missus' and is eventually shot dead. This type of story usually provides exciting reading, the reader being carried along by the stark realism of the events. The medium in which such stories were now being published, journals, besides *Drum*, such as *Africa South*, *The New African* or *Transition*, guaranteed a sympathetic readership.

The events are often described with skill. In Webster Makaza's 'Wheels of Justice'[43] the scene is laid effectively:

> The judge was in his chair and old man van Dyk was in the dock, and outside, two banks of storm-clouds in the northern sky moved ominously towards each other.
>
> The court had grown quite dark as the black clouds massed across the sun, but it took the lightning to show how dark it really was.

Later, outside, the hostile mob turns over van Dyk's car because he has been unjustly found not guilty of kicking a black man. The car bursts into flames:

> A little trickle of liquid began to run from under the side of the car down the camber of the street. It did not run far, for as it flowed it evaporated. The young man had managed to wrench open the door above him and was pushing with his head. He still had that cigarette in his mouth and its smoke was getting into his eyes. His hands were busy with the door and he spat out the cigarette and it fell into the street and rolled in jerks down the camber towards the little pool of petrol.
>
> There was a flash, more vivid than lightning, then a shattering roar, then the tearing crackle of hungry flames, and, above all, the old man's screams.

The story ends as a black policeman guards the 'twisted heap of junk'—all that is left of the car—and 'a sodden mass of pulp that had once been two human beings'.

In Lewis Nkosi's story 'The Prisoner'[44] the protest writing is at its most direct even though it is clothed in terms of satire. A black man has a dream: He is the master and gaoler while George, the white man of the easy gesture, of the contemptuous voice and mocking eye, George who lost the last vestiges of humour whenever it came to social conventions like being called 'bwana' or 'baas', this same George becomes the prisoner. There are the 'false and unjustified reports in the newspapers', those 'garbage cans of rumour and scandal', about torture and unmentionable brutality, when all that ever happens to George is a bit of thumb-screwing and electric shock, and this only when he gets out of hand, for instance when he 'got terribly sozzled' on Christmas Eve and 'was reduced to a raving maniac':

> He was as you might say, in the clutches of a disgusting nostalgia for the old days when he was master and lord over the place. Completely beside himself with excitement, he marched up and down the place shouting and foaming at the mouth; his whole face

was beaded with sweat, the eyes bulged horribly and his emaciated legs clattered like sticks on the floorboard. Never have I seen such an exhibition. The man had quite forgotten the humble station to which he had been reduced by Fate in the latter years . . .

The story begins deceptively calmly: 'Like their jailers prisoners are the same basically' and works up gradually to the full horror of the imaginary situation in reverse, used to illustrate the real one.

Humour, even satire, is rare in the stories. One exception is the work of Casey Motsisi, a natural humorist, who used satire in his *Drum* column and later in *World*, subtly to expose the absurd state of the world he lived in. Some of his witty comments are put into the mouths of bugs who glory in the 'bloodmine' in which they have staked their claim, Sophiatown, where 'blood is just lying around for the picking'.[45] Motsisi often sets out with the idea of fulfilling a serious satirical purpose but his natural sense of humour takes over and runs wild. In the story 'A Very Important Appointment'[46] the action takes place through a haze of liquor. A party of blacks are setting out for a 'mixed' party, to meet some Cambridge students, but the driver is drunk and driving without lights. He overturns the car. One of the passengers comes out of a drunken stupor and suggests repeatedly that the car, lying on its side, should be put into second gear. 'That will make her go.' When they are finally rescued by a white couple, a woman passenger insists that they forgo the party and go home to her baby.

> As the car turned and sped in the direction of Sophiatown, Nat, who was not aware of what was going on, kept shouting:
> 'Hillbrow here we come.
> 'Hillbrow here we come.
> 'Meet us at the door with a glass of wine.
> 'Hillbrow here we come.
> 'Hillbrow, Hillbrow. Hillbrow—the white Sophiatown.'

This is the end of the story.

His short story 'Mita'[47] won a prize in a short story competition organised by the South African Centre of International PEN. Its beginning is a wry comment on township life summed up in a few deft strokes:

> It was Saturday morning. The sun peeped out slowly from the Easterly womb. Slowly, almost furtively as though it wanted to take Sophiatown by surprise. But Sophiatown cannot be taken by surprise. Sophiatown might go to sleep late in the night, drunk, violent and rowdy. But in the small hours of the morning she wakes up, yawns away her hangover and prepares herself for another uncertain day.
> It is a habit. A habit forced upon her by the machinations of the

law—the early morning beer raids, pass raids, permit raids. Raids, raids, raids. And yet a habit also nurtured by the very way of life typical in all other locations. A young man knocks at your door. You open it and recognise him as one of your relations. He has news—sometimes good, often bad. 'Father said I must come to let you know that Boikie is dead. The tsotsis stabbed him last night.' ... 'Uncle, Ma says I must come and find out if sister spent the night here.' Less often: 'Father says I must come and tell you that mother has given birth to twins. She wants auntie to come and spend the day with her.' It is a habit for Sophiatown to wake up early.

The story concerns the girl Mita, whose father throws her out when she becomes pregnant. She gives birth in her boyfriend's home. Even the pain and fear of the young girl in childbirth are converted into an unforgettably earthy scene by Motsisi's pen:

'Ma Tladi, one of the yard's shebeen queens, burst through the door. She was just in time to grab Mita and stop her from falling off the bed. The two women grappled like street brawlers on the bed. 'Ma Tladi began screaming too when she felt Mita's teeth slithering into the pudgy wrist, but she fought on gallantly. Her usual weekend clashes with her husband were standing her in good stead. Two other women darted into the room, saw what was happening and automatically gave a hand.

In a few moments it was all over. The fighting, biting, wrestling. All over. The three fleshy women were smiling—an almost holy radiance in their faces. Once more a miracle had come to pass. It was a baby boy.

By this time, however, Motsisi's writing had taken on a sombre note and the story ends with the young father's death when he is stabbed by gangsters after a night of drinking. Satire still appears in his columns but the stories are stark in their realism. A journalist of education and polish, one-time editor of *The Classic*, Motsisi alone of the Sophiatown literary coterie, remained in South Africa. Loved by his contemporaries, admired by the new writers of the seventies, his journalistic writing followed avidly by his fans, Motsisi's perch must yet have been a lonely one as he watched his friends go into exile and some to their death, and Sophiatown disappear and even grimmer townships take its place. He died in 1977.

William ('Bloke') Modisane also makes use of satire. In his stories 'The Dignity of Begging'[48] and 'The Respectable Pickpocket'[49] Modisane displays the same humour as does Dugmore Boetie, that of the man who follows his own values, and when he is punished under laws which bear no relationship to his own sense of values he shrugs his shoulders and feels that he has lost a round in a game.

In other stories, such as 'The Situation',[50] there is a more serious tone. It was published both in *The New African* and in *Black Orpheus*. The story was written while Modisane was still in South Africa and working for *Drum*. The 'situation' is that of a lonely man, Caiaphas Seduma. He is 'situated' (a word adapted to black use to mean social standing) above the average township-dweller because of his education—a master's degree in applied psychology—and his job with an advertising firm. At the beginning of the story he is at peace with himself, 'enjoying the emotional truce with South Africa'. But not for long. A group of Afrikaner farmers bait and threaten him. He grovels before them and before the police who arrive on the scene and he now feels that he has lost his manhood. He wants to lose himself among his own people but he has not the acumen of the shebeen queen Battleship, a former teacher, who has hidden her 'situation' from those around her. Once again Caiaphas is made to perform before a crowd. This time, too, his life seems threatened and he recites, at a gang leader's demand, the funeral oration of Mark Antony. The rival gang's *protégé*, however, 'wails the blues' and Caiaphas is unable to join in the joy uniting all the shebeen customers in their 'love-hate relationship with the colour black'. Caiaphas is alone, 'walking back to his little room alone'.

Here then we have a very early story with a theme of black awareness and its stress on the significance of the community in mental survival.

When the satirist can no longer escape from a reality too stark for portrayal, he adopts the hard facade of the cynic. Cynicism is evidence of defeat when it is turned inward, and if it is turned to face the outside world it can lead to successful writing only if expressed with sufficient wit. Can (Daniel Canadoise Dorsay) Themba, the most interesting personality and perhaps the most talented of the writers of the late fifties and early sixties, often turned cynic but he always expressed himself with vigour and wit.

Like that of most of his contemporaries, Themba's output was not large. A Fort Hare graduate with a B.A. with distinction, he taught for several years, then became a journalist. He was discovered as a creative writer as a result of his first published short story, 'Mob Passion',[51] which won a prize in the first short story contest held by *Drum*, in 1953.

Themba has been accused of throwing off cheap potboilers. It is true that his early *Drum* stories are not his best writing and often the style is lifted from American comic-magazine fiction. Yet they already foreshadow the excitement which he is capable of expressing, an excitement inherent not so much in what he has to say as in the vigour, the lack of self-consciousness and the whimsical wit with which he expresses it.

Mphahlele, who considered Themba's writing 'strictly escapist' and accused him of revelling 'in a verbal felicity' to 'protect himself against the "whips and scorns" of oppression',[52] yet included a story in each of his anthologies. *Modern African Stories* contains 'The Dube Train'[53] and *African Writing Today* 'The Urchin'. Both are the type of story—dealing with the eruption of township violence—upon which Mphahlele frowned. 'Dube Train' is written in the first person, yet Themba makes no protest that the narrator, a graduate High School teacher, must travel third class. The fact that the lateness of the trains, the shoving savagery of the crowds and the grey aspect around him—'Dube station with the prospect of congested trains filled with sour-smelling humanity'—gave him an 'impression of a hostile life directing its malevolence plumb at me', he ascribes to a 'rotten and shivering'[54] Monday morning feeling. The passengers of the train, who watch a man being stabbed and the culprit flung out of the window, 'were just greedily relishing the thrilling episode of the morning'.[55] Yet is it not a silent protest that this was 'just an incident in the morning Dube train' and that in this world in which he lived there was no room for sentiment?

The characters are described with startling realism:

> I was sitting opposite a hulk of a man. His hugeness was obtrusive to the sight when you saw him, and to the mind when you looked away. His head tilted to one side in a half-drowsy position, with flaring nostrils and trembling lips. He looked like a kind of genie, pretending to sleep but watching your every nefarious intention. His chin was stubbled with crisp, little black barbs. The neck was corded, and the enormous chest was a live barrel that heaved forth and back. The overall he wore was open almost down to the navel, and he seemed to have nothing else underneath. I stared, fascinated, at his large breasts with their winking, dark nipples.[56]

'The Urchin'[57] appeared earlier (1963) in *Drum*, accompanied by a photographic illustration showing the razing of Sophiatown. In both stories Themba writes about the people and the places he knew so well, not only because he lived there but because it was the raw material out of which he made his living as a *Drum* journalist. 'Requiem for Sophiatown',[58] his best known piece of writing, is not fiction but it comes alive with the same lusty style as the short stories.

By 1963 Themba had become a more accomplished and polished short story writer although his output was very limited. 'The Suit'[59] is a story about adultery and its gruesome punishment, told with mounting tension. The wife's lover leaves his suit behind, and the husband forces her to seat the suit at the table at every meal as an honoured guest. He insists on this even during a party for the members of a Cultural Club which she has joined, and thus drives her to suicide. The violence is no longer in the action, but contained within the characters. He describes the husband's reaction to the woman's death thus:

> Reeling drunk, late that sabbath, he crashed through his kitchen door, onwards to his bedroom. Then he saw her.
>
> They have a way of saying in the argot of Sophiatown: 'Cook out of the head!' signifying that someone was impacted with such violent shock that whatever whiffs of alcohol still wandered through his head were instantaneously evaporated and the man stood sober before stark reality.[60]

This story first appeared in *The Classic* Vol. 1, No. 1. Three years later, in Vol. 11, No. 1, Can Themba's tribute to Nathaniel Nakasa was torn out by hand from each copy because Themba had just been banned and it would have been a criminal offence to publish it. By then he had left South Africa and was teaching in Swaziland. He died there in 1968, and *The Classic* Vol. 11, No. 4, although not allowed to quote from his writing, published tributes to him. Stanley Motjuwadi writes:

> The official records have it that Can Themba died of thrombosis in Manzini, but Can Canza, Can Molimo Themba died the day the banning order was served on him. Those who saw the reckless way in which he lived after that regarded his death as a kind of prolonged suicide.[61]

Themba, perhaps, like his character in 'The Suit', finally stood sober before a reality he could no longer bear.

In a story entitled 'The Will to Die',[62] he explains an obsession with death allegorically, thus strangely prophesying his own end:

> I have also heard that certain snakes can hypnotize their victim, a rat, a frog or a rabbit, not only so that it cannot flee to safety in the overwhelming urge for survival, but so that it is even attracted towards its destroyer, and appears to enjoy dancing towards its doom. I have often wondered if there is not some mesmeric power that Fate employs to engage some men deliberately, with macabre relishment, to seek their destruction and to plunge into it.[63]

This story appears in a posthumous collection for which the above story was used as a title. *The Will to Die* includes several short stories, as well as reports and other non-fiction items under the heading of 'Endings'. Some of the stories, such as 'Crepuscule' and 'Kwashiorkor' are not acknowledged and were therefore possibly not published before. There is an introduction by Lewis Nkosi which had previously appeared in *Transition* (No. 34).

'Crepuscule'[64] is a bitter story of love across the colour line, possibly autobiographical in part, in which Themba describes the life of the township dweller, this time in a serious mood, as 'a crepuscular, shadow-life in which we wander as spectres seeking meaning for ourselves', having lost a culture to which 'the psyche could attach itself' and thus being 'caught in the characterless world of belonging nowhere'.[65]

Themba's most splendid moments were those which Nkosi, in the introduction, describes in Themba's own words as the celebration of '"the swarming, cacophonous, strutting, brawling, vibrating life" of the African township', because for him it 'represented the strength and the will to survive by ordinary masses of the African people'.[66] Nkosi writes from a personal knowledge of Themba and finds that his actual achievements fell far behind the man himself. He concludes:

> As it is, we mourn a talent largely misused or neglected; we mourn what might have been. But to have known Themba, to have heard him speak, is to have known a mind both vigorous and informed, shaped by the city as few other minds are in the rest of Africa.[67]

With the banning and subsequent departure of the leading members of the *Drum* generation of writers, the Fabulous Decade of short story writing came to an end. The writers in exile were published in African journals, *Black Orpheus* and *Transition*, or occasionally in British literary journals like *Encounter*, but they were cut off from their raw material and produced little new fiction. Anthologies included mainly stories published during the *Drum* decade. Those who continued to write short fiction in South Africa had to turn to the literary journals of the time, but the scope was limited and once again the readership was mainly white, unlike that of *Drum*. The exception was *The Classic* which continued to play a role in publishing those writers who were not banned, like Casey Motsisi and Webster Makaza.

Contrast and *Izwi* published prose pieces by Peter Clarke, an artist better known for his pictorial art than for his writing. His poems and prose pieces, however, had appeared in journals since the *Drum* days, some under the name of Peter Kumalo. Since then his work has been published in *Encounter*, *Gar* and, in conjunction with his art work, in a collection entitled *Soul Motion III*.[68]

His prose pieces in *Contrast* and *Izwi* are often sketches rather than stories; in them he combines his eye for colour and shape, and his ear for the rhythms of poetry, into poetic prose pictures. In 'Figures and Settings',[69] for example, he describes a leaf as he would capture it on canvas:

> . . . one marvelled at its colour structure, a network of veins in a leaf of red, vibrant red, the red of fire and rubies and blood.
> And further, a dry, hard leaf, of browns and ochres, bringing to mind the covers of leather-bound volumes of old stories.

And another leaf, green, reminding one of the freshness of the grain-country in spring with the first wheat-blades shooting up from the dark, damp earth.[70]

His locale is the pastoral country of his childhood, between Hermanus and Caledon in the Western Cape, to which he returns periodically from his present home near Cape Town. The pictures are not static but move with the activities of the workers whom we see ploughing and herding their sheep, with the change in colour of the landscape, or with movements in nature such as a caterpillar changing into a butterfly.

The changing face of nature is not so much idyllic as inevitable, and man must tune in to this inevitability as he has done for centuries. One can only hope for the best. The narrator comments about a young shepherd: 'One wonders. Because he is my friend I hope his way won't be too hard'.[71] 'Moving through a Rain Landscape',[72] a subtitled sketch in 'Pastorale', is a lesson in patience. 'And when you have the patience of a shepherd in the rain then you are a shepherd. The weather will improve later.'[73] Even when walking to a bottle-store in the middle of the slums of Kewtown, as in the piece entitled 'Blades of Grass',[74] the narrator becomes aware of beauty: in the growing grass and in the people themselves, all part of a whole. It is only when man loses touch with this totality that things go wrong. Then 'Brief Encounters', the subtitle of a section of 'Figures and Settings', cannot develop into friendships, there is suspicion between people, innocent bystanders are burdened with guilt for the wrong-doings of others and, finally, there is hatred, crime and violent death.

Among other contributors to *Contrast* and *Izwi* during this period were Ismail Choonara, who left South Africa in 1954, Sipho Sepamla, and Achmed Essop, Richard Rive, and Mbulelo Mzamane whose short fiction we shall look at presently. *Izwi* stopped publication in 1975 and *Contrast* continues as it did before. Meanwhile *New Classic* and *Staffrider* had begun publication and both gave a voice to black prose-writers as they did to poets. Other outlets were *The Voice* (a church publication), *Wietie*, published by a group of young writers, and an occasional story in popular magazines such as *Drum* and *New Dawn* and, provided they were sufficiently innocuous politically, in the journals published by the large government-supporting publishers Perskor and Nasionale Pers, *Bona* and *Bonanza*.

The prose contributors to *Staffrider*, *New Classic*, *Voice* and *Wietie* were those mentioned above as well as Bessie Head, Miriam Tlali and many newcomers. The stories naturally dealt with the same subjects as did those of the *Drum* period. It is still necessary to find a way of survival as a black person, and the problems of love, friendships and aspirations as well as conflict with the system continue. 'King Taylor'[75] by Sipho Sepamla, for instance, describes a situation similar to that of 'A Point of Identity' by Ezekiel Mphahlele in *In Corner B*. Both concern the attempt of a man to change his official identity from 'Bantu' to 'Coloured' for personal advantage, but in both cases, ironically, they lose more than they gain. Still the tone is often cynical, and satire is used as a weapon. In Mothobi Mutloatse's story 'The Truth . . . Mama',[76] for instance, a mother is questioned by her young children as to why their father is in jail. She has to define for them some of the terms she uses such as 'Politics is saying something the Government doesn't like'.

But there are some new trends. The white world is still shown as an outside controlling force, but the characters, in the few instances in which a white person appears, are seen as part of an impersonal machine rather than as symbols of white viciousness. The new confidence of the writers, conscious of their blackness, sometimes leads to a feeling almost of pity, mixed with contempt, for the white man, as in the story 'Thoughts in a Train',[77] by Mango Tshabangu, which speaks of the white man's fear. As in the poems, white culture is no longer something to emulate, and those who aspire to it are treated with contempt. Njabulo Ndebele, among the several poets who occasionally turn to the short story, in 'The Music of the Violin'[78] writes about a young boy, Vukani, who is a talented violinist and made to perform to the friends of his parents. Vukani's sister calls her mother 'a black white woman'. Her mother complains to a friend:

> She said I was a slave of the things I bought; that the white man had planned it that way. To give us a little of everything so that we can so prize the little we have that we completely forget about the most important things in life, like our freedom. I won't have that nonsense in my house.[79]

The mother has discarded all African values and finds relatives a nuisance:

> Once you have opened the door, they come trooping like ants. We cannot afford it these days. Not with the cost of living. These are different times. Whites saw this problem a long time ago. That is why they have very little time for relatives. The nuclear family! That's what matters. I believe in it. I've always maintained that. If relatives want to visit, they must help with the groceries. There I'm clear, my dear. Very clear.[80]

The boys at school ridicule and harass Vukani. They say 'Here's a fellow with a strange guitar,'[81] and ask him to play the latest township hits but he can only play music that is written down. He longs to be like the other children, to have relatives to visit, not to have to carry his violin through the streets or show off his parents' white culture at home. Finally he revolts and refuses to play any longer.

Stories with themes of general interest such as train rides, madam/ servant relationships, hardship in the mines, are still in evidence, but there is a widening of the spheres of interest. 'The Cane is Singing',[82] by Narain Aiyer, for instance, deals with the history of the Indian in South Africa, 'the bitter notes of this sad song, this soul-searing song that the cane is singing'. Political activity is the subject of a story by Miriam Tlali, 'The Point of No Return'.[83] It deals with conflict between the duty of a man to his family and to the community, and with the problem of women in modern African society. The girl in the story has to give up her University career because she is pregnant and feels the young man has abandoned his responsibilities towards her by participating in political activities. There are other women writers, Bessie Head, and Nokugcina Sigwili extracts from whose story 'My dear Madam . . .'[84] and several poems appeared in *Staffrider*. She says in a note:

It is very important for women to write what they feel. Really, we need more writing from women. I think women understand each other better when they are alone together than when there's a man around because then there is always the possibility of pretending and that's not communication. . . . So we should come together as women and try to do some creative writing—I mean writing that will help or encourage other people who might become our fellow-writers in the future.

We are very important to men . . . The point is that we need each other, for we depend on each other's strength. Men can be physically strong, but our strength as women is our motherhood: men are always women's children. And their manhood doesn't show if women aren't there.[85]

Many of the stories lend themselves to being read aloud. Some are in the first person, but even in the others one hears the voice of a narrator.

Soon there were volumes of short stories by individual writers. James Matthews began writing short stories during the *Drum* area. He stopped soon after the bannings and began to write poetry, but a collection, *The Park and Other Stories*,[86] appeared in 1974. It comprised the early stories and some previously unpublished. It is his only volume not to have been banned. Three of the stories, 'The Park', 'The Portable Radio' and 'Azikwelwa', together with another story entitled 'The Party', were first published in an anthology edited by Richard Rive, *Quartet*.[87] Stories appeared in the nineteen fifties and early sixties in *Drum*, *Flamingo* (a British publication for black readers) and, more recently, in *Wietie*. Stories were included in anthologies over the years, were translated, especially into German, and even today, according to Mothobi Mutloatse's notes on contributors to his anthology *Forced Landing*, 'any anthology without Matthews, be it prose or poetry, is inadequate because the man, though writing since the '50s, is still as fresh as the *Staffrider* generation of writers'.

The Park and Other Stories forms a cohesive collection in that the stories run through the entire gamut of life as it is lived by a coloured person in South Africa. The range is a wide one. We see the people in the city and in the country, they are members of gangs, old lags and earnest reformers, farm labourers, students and middle-class house-wives. At every turn they clash with the law and the ways of the white man. Some pit themselves against the system, some, usually older men, adhere to the security of submission, some are rudely awakened from their innocence. The story 'Whites Only' is an account of a man's anger at apartheid which he meets everywhere as he makes his way to the city by train, visits shops to make his purchases and attends to business. His raging anger increases to the point of explosion, and then fizzles out in futility. In one of the best stories, 'The Park', a child defiantly returns at night to a playground for whites only from which he was evicted during the day. He continues to swing even when the attendant goes to fetch the police. He is terribly afraid, 'wishing himself safe in his mother's kitchen, sitting next to the still-burning stove with a comic spread across his knees'. But such innocence of childhood is not to be for someone whom the apartheid system has forced to grow up before his time and act like a man. Still calling for his mother: 'Mama. Mama.' he continues to swing:

> His voice mounted, wrenched from his throat, keeping pace with the soaring swing as it climbed the sky. Voice and swing. Swing and voice. Higher. Higher. Higher. Until they were one.

The story, and the volume, ends:

> At the entrance of the park the notice board [which read *Whites Only*. and, in Afrikaans, *Blankes Alleen*.] stood tall, its shadow elongated, pointing towards him.[88]

In 'The Awakening' there is the dawning awareness of a farm labourer to the 'man-beast' conditions under which he lives. All his life Herman, and his father before him, has accepted the safety of his existence under the white *baas*. A pamphlet which students hand to him during a marketing trip to Cape Town makes him begin to think, and, after the farmer insists that Herman's older child attend the farm school instead of the village school, so as to have him available for farm-work, he decides to take the family to the city. One story, 'Caesar's Law', deals with the problems of a priest who is asked by a coloured girl to marry her to the white father of the child she is carrying, and thus receive her back into the fold as a Christian. The priest refuses because he is afraid to break the law.

In several stories, Matthews makes use of true incidents, such as the death in jail under suspicious circumstances of an Imam ('Tribute to a Humble Man') and of the boycott of the buses as a protest against increased fares ('Azikwelwa').

In the newer stories the characters tend to be stereotypes used to illustrate a particular aspect of coloured life, such as, for instance, two women in 'Colour Blind' who have been moved to an outlying district by the apartheid laws governing racial group areas, and despise their new neighbours. One is jealous of the other because she is richer, the other envies her friend her children who pass as white. Sometimes the stereotyping is done deliberately, as in 'Baby, that's the way it is', where Matthews shows how in South Africa everyone's path can lead to jail. 'Sit down,' one regular customer says to a newcomer, 'Tell us what yer in for?' And the man replies: 'I didn't commit a crime'.

> 'Dat's alright,' Jonas said. He waved a hand at the others. 'De ole toppies is in for drunk, an' so de two party boys. De lighty issa moffie mobster, an dey pick me up for gunston.'
>
> The newcomer looked at them ruminatively.
>
> 'You know why the law arrested me? I didn't rob anyone, neither was I drunk or caught with dagga. I'm here because I spoke the truth!'
>
> 'How's that?' Cyril asked.

He explains that he was arrested when he protested to a policeman who was throwing three small children in the van. 'Der Law is shit!' is Jonas's comment.[89]

The reversal in black South African literature of the normal roles of cops and robbers into baddies and goodies respectively is also emphasised in the story 'Tribute to a Humble Man'. The funeral of Imam Haron is seen through the eyes of an innocent young lad, Sarel, just come from a small village in which politics had been of little concern. On learning of the Imam's fate he says to himself:

> Imam Haron was detained under the Terrorist Act but surely the authorities must have been mistaken. . . . If all these people feel the same way about Imam Haron as the elderly man next to him then surely the Imam must have been a good man, a man Sarel's father would have welcomed to his mountain pasture, and in whose care he would have felt his sheep secure.[90]

After listening further to the people and watching the funeral procession of 30,000 on his very first day in town, he becomes aware of the true state of things and hopes that whatever his future, 'it would lead in the same direction Imam Haron had been going'.[91]

The newer stories are somewhat slight, both in plot and characterisation, but in older and much published stories Matthews draws his characters with care. There is Jonathan, in 'Azikwelwa', the young coloured man who makes common cause with the boycotting Africans in their long walks to work, so as to give his life some meaning, and then, in contrast, the youth in 'The Portable Radio' who has given up the fight for self-respect and finds solace in drink. There is subtlety in the character sketch of the coloured attendant in 'The Park' who is torn between making common cause with the little boy who wants to use the swings, and doing his duty for which he is paid. The dialogue in all the stories is earthy and true to life as Matthews catches the nuances of the different dialects in translation.

The newer stories sometimes tend towards melodrama such as the story of a modern Crucifixion in a story of that title but at his best—in 'The Park', 'The Portable Radio' and 'Azikwelwa'— Matthews shows great skill in building up drama and tension. In 'The Portable Radio', we follow the actions of the youth who looks longingly into the window of a furniture shop where the goods are far above his means. He finds a pouch full of money with which he buys a much coveted portable radio. But the rest of the money is spent on drink and eventually the batteries wear out and his aunt, with whom he lives, cuts off his electrical supply. The soothing music of the radio appears to him to have been transplanted inside his aunt where it has changed into her harsh laughter. He smashes the radio against the wall.

Richard Rive can almost be said to vie with James Matthews for the number of inclusions in anthologies. He too began writing a long while ago, in the early nineteen fifties, and was published in various journals. His first volume of stories, *African Songs*,[92] appeared in 1963. Then, in the same year, came *Quartet*,[93] his collection of stories by four writers, including himself. More recently he published his *Selected Writings*,[94] which included seven short stories.

Although Rive says that he is a short story writer rather than a novelist, he does bring some of the faults of the novel to his short fiction. There is a certain *naiveté* about his work which assumes that people will act in a certain way, and always do. The child-like character in 'African Song',[95] for example, comes to the city from the country without a pass and, as the police draw nearer to him at a meeting, has visions of love and joy while the people sing the Xhosa anthem. In 'The Bench',[96] Karlie is another innocent from the country who is so affected by hearing his first political speech about black being as good as white, that he refuses to get up from a bench marked 'whites only' and looks at the policeman who arrests him 'with the arrogance of one who dared to sit on a "European" bench'. Rive's early promise of realism shown in 'Willieboy'[97] did not come to fruition.

We often know what the outcome of a story will be, which leads to lack of tension and makes the story appear contrived. One knows, for instance, that 'No Room at Solitaire'[98] will be an illustration of a South African version of the biblical tale. The story concerns a hotel-keeper, Fanie van der Merwe, who discusses Christianity with a customer and they wonder how one would 'know Him when He comes again'.[99] A coloured couple arrive at the back door and ask for shelter because the woman is about to give birth and is ill. The hotel-keeper refuses but the servant puts them up in the stable. When Fanie and his customer hear of this the story inevitably ends:

> Fanie and Dawie slowly looked at each other and then, at the same time, timidly looked towards the sky to see whether there was a bright star.[100]

Satire of this kind, when used on a less obvious theme, is usually very effective in Rive's stories. 'Strike',[101] for instance, introduces the ironical situation in which a young man allows the police to find subversive literature in his brief-case rather than undergo the humiliation of showing the manager of a bookshop that he has not stolen a book. One of the assistants had accused him of doing so just because he was coloured, he felt.

As a satire 'Middle Passage'[102] is perhaps the most successful story, but as Rive has included the dramatised version, 'Make Like Slaves', in his own volume of selected works we will look at it when we talk of drama. The same applies to 'Resurrection'.[103] In fact Rive is at his best when writing dialogue, which he uses with skill both in furthering the stories and in delineating character, and one hopes he will continue to write drama.

For several of his stories Rive has chosen District Six, the former slum on the edge of the inner city of Cape Town, for his background. It forms an effective backdrop for his most anthologised story, 'Rain',[104] first published in the first issue of *Contrast* under the title 'North-Wester', which tells of an encounter between a country-girl, Siena, and a fish-and-chip shop-keeper, Solly. There is the contrast between the bleak grey mist and squelching pavements, with the inside of the shop 'stuffy with heat, hot bodies, steaming clothes, and the nauseating smell of stale fish oil',[105] and the contrast between the bleakness of the city slum to which Siena has followed her playboy lover, and her home-village with its beautiful church and balmy love-filled nights where she first met him. In the city there is only 'the roar of a thousand cars and a hundred thousand lights and a summer of carnival evenings'. 'Passion in a tiny room off District Six. Desire surrounded by four bare walls and a rickety chair and a mounted cardboard tract that murmured *Bless this House*.'[106]

'Rain' is a subtle story about two people reacting to each other. Solly, the Jew, is a gruff man who has little sympathy with his slum-dwelling customers and shouts and swears at each one as they enter to close the door against the rain. The pathetic young coloured girl touches a chord somewhere and he grudgingly allows her to wait in the shop for the cinema to come out. When he hears that the boyfriend has been arrested after a gang-brawl outside the cinema he makes the unprecedented gesture of offering her a free portion of fish and chips. As she leaves he swears at her again to shut the door, but this time with a grin. There is a similar subtle drawing-together in 'The Visits' between a lonely school-teacher and a derelict old woman.[107] It is a strange compulsive relationship on the part of the young man. No words pass between them. At first he tries to get rid of her, then tolerates her. But when his student flat-mate throws her out in his absence and she never comes again he is devastated. The story ends:

> He went into his study and slumped down at the desk. He felt like crying but couldn't. He heard the student banging the front-door, then the revving of the Honda engine. Long after the whine had faded away he sat at his desk just staring in the dark.[108]

When Rive was asked to comment on writing with a mission, in an interview with *Wietie*,[109] he advocated a marriage between committed writing and saying it well and meaningfully. His own commitment is to a breaking down of all colour discrimination, no matter where it is found. 'Streetcorner'[110] and 'Resurrection' express his hatred for those, coloured themselves, who discriminate against those darker than themselves. In 'Streetcorner', one such man is excluded from an elite sports club and in 'Resurrection', lighter members of a family pretend to be white and disown the darker members.

In his later years Rive has been turning his attention to critical writing and research, having gained a doctorate at Oxford University with a dissertation on Olive Schreiner. To his critical writing and lectures, which we will look at later, he brings an urbanity and sureness of touch which is often lacking in his fiction.

Alex La Guma's short stories were published mainly during the early nineteen-sixties in *Black Orpheus*, and the best of these, together with several previously unpublished stories and the novel *Walk in the Night*[111] appeared under the title of the novel (subtitled 'and other stories') in 1967. Because Rive and La Guma cover so much of the same area, both geographically and in their themes, one cannot help comparing their short stories. La Guma's stories tend to be more earthy and direct. Compare for instance, in Rive's 'Resurrection', Mavis's lengthy complaints to her mother about her play-white relatives with the narrator's description of the boxer in La Guma's 'The Gladiators':[112] 'He's a good juba awright,' he says, but he 'just miss being white which was what make him so full of crap'.[113] Like

Rive, La Guma despises those who look down on their darker brothers but 'The Gladiators' goes much deeper in its exploration of human nature. It is not just a matter of the near-white braggart meeting his just deserts by getting badly beaten in a boxing match. The narrator, by his speech clearly one of the boys of the slums, represents normality. The crowd are bloodthirsty spectators of a tournament:

> . . . the whole crowd is quiet like, waiting to see blood. I thought, Bastards, paying cash to see two other black boys knock themselves to hell. What you in this business for then? I don't know. Maybe just to see my boy don't get buggered too much.[114]

The boxing match is a symbol for a world gone mad with violence. The mob, which was supporting the whiter man, turn when they see blood:

> They all on their feet, screaming because they seen blood and they all gone mad with seeing it, because they seeing a man hit to a bloody mess. They don't give a damn about Kenny no more now, and they don't give a damn about nothing but seeing his blood.[115]

There is more subtlety in La Guma's story 'The Lemon Orchard'[116] than in Rive's 'The Bench', each about a man defying authority. In spite of knowing what lies in store for him, Karlie refuses to budge from the bench; but the teacher in 'The Lemon Orchard' who is going to be beaten up by the citizens of the little town in which he dared to take the school principal and *meester* of the church to court for hitting him, does accede to the men's demand to call them 'baas' eventually. But he says it with so much dignity and contempt that he shows them up for what they are. Both stories leave unsaid what happens to the men but the reader's imagination will find 'The Lemon Orchard''s outcome more frightening by virtue of what has gone before and through the symbolism of change in the natural surroundings:

> The blackness of the night crouched over the orchard and the leaves rustled with a harsh whispering that was inconsistent with the pleasant scent of the lemons. The chill in the air had increased, and far-off the creek-creek-creek of the crickets blended into solid strips of high-pitched sound. Then the moon came from behind the banks of cloud and its white light touched the leaves with wet silver, and the perfume of lemons seemed to grow strong, as if the juice was being crushed from them.[117]

La Guma's most successful stories are the sketches of the people in District Six whom he brings to life with a directness of approach, and a skill in construction of the plots in which they feature, unequalled by any of the other writers at that time. In 'Tattoo Mark and Nails'[118] he sets the scene without embellishment in the first short sentence, followed by a description of the heat in the cell. The first character is introduced in the second paragraph and at the same time La Guma expands on the theme of heat in the cell on a more forceful note as though the story, too, was warming up:

> The heat was solid. As Ahmed the Turk remarked, you could reach out before your face, grab a handful of heat, fling it at the wall and it would stick.[119]

Two themes are introduced. A gang leader known as 'The Creature' victimises a man in jail whom he suspects of having killed his brother, known as Nails, who had told him before his death that the killer carried a tattoo depicting a dragon. There is a trial-by-the-people in the cell of the man concerned. Meanwhile Ahmed the Turk tells the narrator about an incident in a prisoners' camp during the war, when water was rationed and the men sometimes gambled for the ration. One man cheated and the other men carved a tattoo on him which said PRIVATE SO-AND-SO A CHEAT AND A COWARD. For that reason, Ahmed says, he is trying to stop the trial. The narrator wants to know, what was the 'joker's' name. Ahmed replies 'I forget now.' The two themes come together when The Creature, his mind still on the tattoo of the dragon, turns on Ahmed and wonders why he never removes his shirt. The narrator continues:

> Ahmed the Turk licked moisture from his lips. He said, 'The hell with you.'
> 'Turk,' The Creature said, 'Turk, my boys can hold you while we pull off the shirt. Just as you like, ou Turk.'
> The gang edged nearer, surrounding us. Ahmed the Turk looked at The Creature and then looked at me. His face was moist.
> Then he laughed, and pulled himself up from his cramped position.
> 'Awright, all you baskets,' he sneered, and unbuttoned his shirt.[120]

And so the story ends.

Bessie Head, in a volume of short stories entitled *The Collector of Treasures*,[121] is concerned with ideas similar to those in her novels. This time she makes use of incidents that have been related to her, and of Botswana history, legend and myth, as the basis for her fiction. She explores the meaning and values of traditional life and as usual goes right to the heart of everything that she examines. What is it for instance, she wants to know, that prevents a city-reared girl, significantly named 'Life'[122] in the story that takes its name from the character, from finding her niche in the village community? Or rather, why is it that the rest of the people do not find the every-day round of village life deadly dull—'one big, gaping yawn'—in its unbroken monotony? The answer lies in contact between people:

. . . one day slipped easily into another, drawing water, stamping corn, cooking food. But within this there were enormous tugs and pulls between people. Custom demanded that people care about each other, and all day long there was this constant traffic of people in and out of each other's lives. Someone had to be buried; sympathy and help were demanded for this event—there were money loans, new-born babies, sorrow, trouble, gifts. Lesego had long been the king of this world; there was, every day, a long string of people, wanting something or wanting to give him something in gratitude for a past favour. It was the basic strength of village life. It created people whose sympathetic and emotional responses were always fully awakened, and it rewarded them by richly filling in a void . . .[123]

The help people give each other therefore brings meaning to a hard life. When Dikeledi, in the title story,[124] who has killed her husband, is befriended by another inmate in prison and thanks her for all her kindness, the woman replies, with 'her amused, cynical smile': 'We must help each other . . . This is a terrible world. There is only misery here'.[125] The treasures that are collected by Dikeledi in this story—one towards which the other stories lead, as the author tells us, 'in a carefully developed sequence'[126]—are 'deep loves that had joined her heart to the heart of others'.[127] Dikeledi (her name means 'tears') has had a hard life, her husband deserting her and her children and leaving her to support them by doing handicraft. After accusing her of infidelity with a neighbour, because he cannot understand friendship and compassion, and having led a debauched life himself, the husband returns to her. 'Garesego's obscene thought processes', the author writes, 'were his own undoing. He really believed that another man had a stake in his hen-pen and like any cock, his hair was up about it'.[128] Dikeledi prepares his meal and bath and when he is asleep she takes a knife, cuts off his genitals and watches him bleed to death. The tragic story ends on a faint note of brightness in the flashback account of why Dikeledi went to prison. There is still the help and compassion of the community to be relied on. Her neighbour enters the hut:

He took in every detail and then he turned and looked at Dikeledi with such a tortured expression that for a time words failed him. At last he said: 'You don't have to worry about the children, Mma-Banabothe. I'll take them as my own and give them all a secondary education.'[129]

Head subtitles the collection 'Tales' rather than stories and stresses the narrative note when she tells them. 'People say', is how she ends the story 'Jacob: The Story of a Faith-Healing Priest'[130] when she tells about the soul of a man sentenced to death for ritual murder returning from the grave.

The tales are firmly based on Botswana soil. We see the fertile areas where the 'people . . . are eating water-melon and fresh green mealies', and 'from their lands . . . are about to harvest bags and bags of corn',[131] and others in the grip of devastating drought. Head is well acquainted with Botswana life and history. The first story in the collection, 'The Deep River',[132] is subtitled 'A Story of Ancient Tribal Migration' and in a footnote the author tells us that it is a reconstruction in her own imagination of some historical data given to her by the old men of the tribe. Legend and myth, too, are worked into some of the stories. In the dialogue Head makes use of African proverbs and acknowledges an indebtedness to Professor C.L.S. Nyembezi's 'beautiful' interpretations of *Zulu Proverbs* (Witwatersrand University Press, 1954). For 'those graphic paragraphs on the harvest thanksgiving ceremony which appear in the first story' she acknowledges a Tswana school textbook in a footnote.[133]

With this background and within thirteen finely executed and gripping stories, Bessie Head once again explores the themes of good and evil, and the significance of religious belief, as she did in her novels. The outlines of right and wrong are still blurred. Can the girl Life be blamed for going back to promiscuity when she cannot fit into tribal life? Was her husband justified in killing her as his calmness seems to indicate and as even the judge seems to think when he gives him only five years? Dikeledi's murder of her husband and similar murders by her cell mates are accepted as inevitable by the other characters in the story, but is the husband entirely to blame for his evil ways? He too has suffered from a disorientation under the changing conditions in Botswana which Head describes. First there were the rigid and often uncompassionate traditional customs, then the evil system of the colonial days that separated families and kept them on the point of starvation, and then finally, the sudden huge increases in wages under independence. Head leaves these questions open for there is no ready answer.

Bessie Head has no time for the trappings and hypocrisies of religion, whether it is of the Christian or African kind. 'Heaven is not Closed'[134] is the title of one of the stories; it negates the words spoken by a missionary priest. "Heaven is closed to the unbeliever . . .', he says to a young girl, Galethebege, who tells him she wishes to get married but that the man she is to marry will do so only under Setswana custom. She is a devout member of the congregation but respects her man's devotion to his own religion. Her intention in approaching the missionary had been 'to acquire his blessing for the marriage, as though a compromise of tenderness could be made

between two traditions opposed to each other'.[135] Instead, he
excommunicates the girl.

Galethebege never gives up her belief in the Christian God. The
story is told by an old man, her husband's brother, after her death at
the age of ninety. 'Today,' he says to his grandchildren:

> . . . it is not a matter of debate because the young care neither way
> about religion. But in that day, the expulsion of Galethebege from
> the Church was a matter of debate. It made the people of
> our village think. There was great indignation because both
> Galethebege and Ralokae (the husband) were much respected in
> the community. People then wanted to know how it was that
> Ralokae, who was an unbeliever, could have heaven closed to him?
> A number of people, including all the relatives who officiated at
> the wedding ceremony, then decided that if heaven was closed to
> Galethebege and Ralokae it might as well be closed to them too, so
> they all no longer attended church.

When the old man finished his tale his listeners:

> . . . sighed the way people do when they have heard a particularly
> good story. As they stared at the fire they found themselves
> debating the matter in their minds, as their elders had done some
> forty or fifty years ago. Was heaven really closed to the unbeliever,
> Ralokae? Or had Christian custom been so intolerant of Setswana
> custom that it could not hear the holiness of Setswana custom?
> Wasn't there a place in heaven too for Setswana custom? Then the
> gust of astonished laughter shook them again. Galethebege had
> been very well-known in the village ward over the past five years
> for the supreme authority with which she had talked about God.
> Perhaps her simple and good heart had been terrified that the
> doors of heaven were indeed closed on Ralokae and she had been
> trying to open them.[136]

Religion, for Head, is significant only for the acts carried out in its
name. What kind of God is it, the people in the village of Makateng
want to know, who inflicts suffering on a good man like Jacob, the
faith-healing priest. Jacob answers the question by saying that every
time he hears the voice of God a great peace fills his heart. The people
cannot understand this but 'the way in which he expressed this
relationship in deeds arrested the attention. Everything about him
was very beautiful and simple and deeply sincere.'[137] 'Witchcraft', in a
story of that title,[138] is even more bitterly condemned as a disease and
'one of the most potent evils in the society'.[139] In 'Jacob . . .' and
'Looking for a Rain God'[140] Head expresses her horror at ritual
murder and infanticide.

Bessie Head is therefore completely independent in her beliefs and
will accept ideas only if she has tested them against her own values.

She feels free of the bonds of both the Western and the African world and will accept neither blindly. She refuses to romanticise the African world. She cannot accept the lack of individual freedom of the early days, when men lived by the 'traditions and taboos outlined by the forefathers of the tribe'[141] without the option of assessing whether they were compassionate or not.

One of the 'most bitter-making things' in the lack of the ancestors' 'attention to individual preferences and needs', the author says, was the way women were relegated to an inferior position in life, something from which they were still suffering today, in spite of the fact that with nothing to do during the dry season women often drifted to the church and acquired an education superior to that of the men. This Head tells us in the novel *Question of Power*, when she describes Mma-Millipede. In the same novel, we are told how Elizabeth's husband Dan exerts a mental stranglehold over her, the 'supreme pervert' 'thrusting his soul' into her 'living body'.[142] Head's ideal man is one like Makhaya, in the novel *When Rain Clouds Gather*, who asks his sisters to address him by his first name instead of the referential 'Buti' (Elder brother) and tells his mother when she protests: 'Why should men be brought up with a false sense of superiority over women? People can respect me if they wish, but only if I earn it'.[143] In the short story collection the treatment of women leads to tragedies such as that of Dikeledi in the title story. One of her cell-mates tells Dikeledi her own story:

> 'Our men do not think that we need tenderness and care. You know, my husband used to kick me between the legs when he wanted that. I once aborted with a child, due to this treatment. I could see that there was no way to appeal to him if I felt ill, so I once said to him that if he liked he could keep some other woman as well because I couldn't manage to satisfy all his needs. Well, he was an education-officer and each year he used to suspend about seventeen male teachers for making school girls pregnant, but he used to do the same. The last time it happened the parents of the girl were very angry and came to report the matter to me. I told them: 'You leave it to me. I have seen enough.' And so I killed him.'[144]

In the story 'Life', another reason, besides boredom, why the girl cannot become accustomed to village life is that she cannot accept her husband's claim of ownership over her. In 'The Special One', an elderly widowed school-teacher, Mrs Maleboge, loses a case against her brother-in-law who stole her inheritance because, as she tells everyone, 'women are dogs in this society'.[145] Her friend Gaenameltse, a lively young woman, loses her divorce case because the husband invokes an old tribal taboo against intercourse during menstruation to boost his image. 'She was trying to kill her husband,' a gossip tells the narrator. 'Many women have killed men by sleeping with them during that time. It's a dangerous thing and against our custom. The woman will remain alive and the man will die'.[146]

As a craftsman, Bessie Head is unrivalled in South African fiction. She builds up her tale carefully by setting out the scene or making a statement, and then progressing to the particular incident. She does this especially successfully in 'Jacob: The Story of a Faith-Healing Priest'. The setting is a quiet prosperous village. Once the reader is thoroughly acquainted with the scene he learns why the village is so important:

> Nor did the ordinary people of the country visit Makaleng because the people there were eating fresh green mealies in a drought year. Oh no, Makaleng village was famous in the hearts of ordinary people because it had two prophets.[147]

The author is always in control as she manipulates plot, incident, fact and character—and the smooth unlaboured prose in which she depicts them—to form a unified piece of art.

> Irrespective of nationality and time, the line at which light race meets dark is the line at which human sociality is found at the lowest ebb; and wherever that line comes into existence, there are found the darkest shadows which we humans have cast by our injustice and egoism across the earth.

These words, written by Olive Schreiner in *Thoughts on South Africa*, are quoted by Ahmed Essop in his acceptance speech of the Olive Schreiner Prize. This was awarded to him by the English Academy of Southern Africa in 1979 for a collection of short stories, *The Hajji and Other Stories*,[148] published in 1978, two years before his novel *The Visitation*. In his speech Essop points out how clearly Olive Schreiner perceived the great human rift and comments: 'I believe that literature can help us in closing the rift'.[149]

He confirms his belief in his own writing. Like Bessie Head, Essop puts humanitarian ideals above political and religious stances and goes right below the surface to search for motive in the human heart. Hatred of the apartheid system is implicit in many of the stories, and succinctly demonstrated in several, such as 'The Commandment'[150] in which a black man hangs himself after being evicted from his home. Apartheid also rules every phase of the lives of South African Indians and denies them a common humanity. It affects the lives of politicians, school-principals and respected businessmen as much as it does those of ordinary working men and women, all of whom are thrown together in the ghettoes under the law which defines where each racial group may live.

The lives of the people in Ahmed Essop's world are defined by apartheid from the outside and by Indian custom from the inside, with individuals squeezed between. How they react to these pressures forms the main theme in Essop's short stories.

Essop, a former teacher, has been writing short fiction since 1969 when his stories began to appear in *Purple Renoster*, *Contrast*, and later in *Staffrider*.

The story which the Academy chose from the prize-winning collection for publication in its *Annual Review*, 'Gerty's Brother',[151] is one in which the author describes how a flash of tenderness breaks down the barrier of black and white, and the even greater barrier of indifference. The narrator and his friend Hussein are interested in the white girl Gerty because 'she was easy and would not give much trouble in removing her undergarments to anyone',[152] and because the risk of sex across the colour line under the Immorality Act adds spice to an affair. Gerty and her little brother Riekie—they are orphans living with an alcoholic brother—move in with Hussein who is kind to them, but when he fears that the police have an eye on him he brings the affair to an end and leaves for Durban. One Sunday morning, the narrator's indifference is shattered when he finds little Riekie at Hussein's gate shouting for the man who had been kind to him. A neighbour chases him away: 'Goh way boy, goh way white boy. No Hussein here. Goh way'. The narrator suddenly remembers how he had held the little boy when he took him for a boat ride on Zoo Lake, while Hussein and Gerty had had their first encounter:

> A sensation of tenderness for the boy went through me. You must understand that this was the first time I had ever picked up a white child.[153]

Now, as he stands at the corner of the street he feels again, the narrator says, 'the child's body as I lifted him and put him into the boat many nights ago, a child's body in my arms embraced by the beauty of the night on the lake, and I returned to my landlady's with the hackles of revolt rising within me'.[154]

In the title story,[155] Essop makes it clearer still that even in an abnormal society politics may not be used as an excuse to absolve one from normal human values. 'The Hajji' is a very subtle story, in which the conflict is not between family feelings on the one hand and pride in race and religion on the other as would at first appear. The conflict in the Hajji's soul is between compassion and shallow pride.

Hajji Hassen's brother, Karim, had crossed the colour line, married a white woman and severed his family ties. 'By going over to the white Herrenvolk', the Hajji feels, 'his brother had trampled on something that was vitally part of him, his dignity and self-respect'.[156] But now Karim lies dying, and his final wish is to spend his last few days with his own people. Hajji Hassen refuses vehemently, but 'the rejection of his brother's plea involved a straining of the heartstrings and the Hajji did not feel happy'.[157] A visit from his white sister-in-law, who takes the blame for the breach upon herself, softens him and he visits his brother and agrees to take him to his home. But on the way down from his brother's apartment three white youths taunt him for using the 'white' lift, and the Hajji finds that he cannot forgive his brother after all. Hajji Hassen is not really concerned with the dignity of blackness or the pride of a Muslim. All that concerns him is what people think of him. When the congregation looks after Karim and puts him in a room behind the mosque Hassen is at a loss:

> He debated with himself. In what way should he conduct himself so that his dignity remained intact? How was he to face the congregation, the people in the streets, his neighbours? Everyone would soon know of Karim and smile at him half sadly, half ironically, for having placed himself in such a ridiculous position. Should he now forgive the dying man and transfer him to his home? People would laugh at him, snigger at his cowardice . . . Should he go away somewhere (on the pretext of a holiday) to Cape Town, to Durban? But no, there was the stigma of being called a renegade. And besides, Karim might take months to die, he might not die at all.[158]

He allows Karim to die without seeing him again. At the end, suddenly overwhelmed with memory and love for his brother, he rushes to his side for a last embrace of the dead man, but he is too late.

> The green hearse, with the crescent moon and stars emblem, passed by; then several cars with mourners followed, bearded men, men with white skull-caps on their heads, looking rigidly ahead, like a procession of puppets, indifferent to his fate. No one saw him.[159]

The title, the fact that Hassen is a Hajji, is significant. 'Hajji, can't you forgive him? You were recently in Mecca,' one of his neighbours asks him. His sin is against Allah and man.

A phenomenon of South African life, at least until the time of forcible removals to new and sterile areas, is the vibrancy of the communities which have been thrown together by the law. Outsiders find the nostalgia with which writers speak of the extinct slums of Sophiatown and District Six, with all their poverty and violence, difficult to understand. Essop, in a story entitled 'In Two Worlds',[160] describes why the narrator found the white suburb of a friend alien and chilling:

> It lacked the noise—the raucous voices of vendors, the eternal voices of children in streets and backyards—the variety of people, the spicy odours of Oriental foods, the bonhomie of communal life in Fordsburg.[161]

This is the rich world which we see in action in *The Hajji and Other Stories*. We meet a variety of characters, in the street and 'the yard', some of whom appear in several of the stories and even turn up again in Essop's novel, *The Visitation*. They are deeply involved with each other, all vociferous, articulate, fond of arguing their point of view, commenting on their neighbours, making decisions for them. There is the hypocritical Yogi Krishnasiva, in 'The Yogi',[162] considered by people to be the wisest and most learned man in Fordsburg until it becomes evident that his inscrutable deity-like silence is not due to a union with Brahman. As the shopkeeper Das Patel puts it and a court of law later confirms: 'I say he sleep wit wite women. One day you see me right. Dat all . . . He practise Yoga in bed.'[163] Then there is Mr Rijhumal Rajespery, in 'Gladiators'[164] principal of the Tagore Indian High School, who hates Indians, referring to them always as 'Yahoos' and explaining that he is 'a pure Dravidian'. There are politicians, gangsters, servants, shopkeepers, teachers and house-wives, each finely drawn by a few strokes of the pen. Hajji Musa, for instance, in 'Hajji Musa and the Hindu Fire-Walker'[165] comes to life instantly when we are told that in appearance he 'was a fat, pot-bellied, short, dark man, with glossy black wavy hair combed backwards with fastidious care'.

> His face was always clean shaven. For some reason he never shaved in the bathroom, and every morning one saw him in the yard, in vest and pyjama trousers, arranging (rather precariously) his mirror and shaving equipment on the window-sill outside the kitchen and going through the ritual of cleaning his face with the precision of a surgeon. His great passion was talking and while shaving he would be conducting conversations with various people in the yard: with the hawker packing his fruit and vegetables in the cart; with the two wives of the motor mechanic Soni; with the servants coming to work.[166]

The tone of the stories is adjusted to the contents. In his foreword, Lionel Abrahams compares the emotional richness as well as the vivacious variety of scenes with V.S. Naipaul. He continues:

> But among South African writers, it is hard to think of another, aside from Bosman, who is capable of bringing off, on the one hand, stories as lightheartedly funny as 'Hajji Musa and the Hindu Fire-Walker', as sweepingly satirical as 'Film' and, on the other, ones as astringently poignant as 'Gerty's Brother', as mysteriously disturbing as 'Mr Moonreddy', as poetically sombre as 'The Hajji'.[167]

Hypocrisy and sham come under Essop's axe, sometimes with anger—'That primitive ape is prostituting our religion with his hocus-pocus. He should be arrested for assault',[168] a spectator says of

Hajji Musa as he carries out meaningless rites over a terrified young girl to drive out her madness—and sometimes with good humour. In the same story, Hajji Musa meets his just deserts when he boasts that he can walk on fire. He ends up in hospital, unrepentant, 'as ebullient and resilient as always, with a bevy of young nurses eagerly attending to him'.[169]

'Film'[170] is a brilliant satire in which a group of dignified elderly members of the Muslim Council stage a quiet protest against the showing of the film 'The Prophet'. The demonstration eventually leads to a near-riot by a crowd that has collected, and police disperse the mob. No-one—neither the police nor the crowd nor the manager of the whites-only cinema—know who the protesters are or why they were standing outside the cinema. With final irony the manager takes them inside the cinema—'Gentlemen, come with me, please. I don't want you to be hurt.'[171]—and the shocked bewildered demonstrators see the hated film unrol before their eyes.

Mr Moonreddy in a story of that title[172] is 'a waiter of distinction' by his own definition:

> 'Gentlemen,' he said to the group of teachers over whisky and soda, 'you see me, Mr Moonreddy, a self-made man, not educated like you, not belonging to the intellectual class, but a waiter. Yet a waiter of distinction.'[173]

But the story turns dead serious, and Mr Moonreddy's life takes on an eerie note as he acquires a vicious Alsatian dog and takes on the dog's personality. Similarly the story about the ridiculously snobbish school principal, who treats his smart car with more respect than his fellow-men, becomes menacing, the laughter sinister as the man loses his mind. His hatred for his Indian neighbours narrows down to Mr Raja, the primary school principal. The final reckoning comes when a basin of dirty water has been emptied over Mr Rajespery's car. But the battle that ensues takes place by proxy, between the two men's women-servants. The next morning Mr Rajespery goes to sit in his car, refusing to come out, operating the automatic suspension:

> Many people came to see him; children milled around his car; and everybody laughed at the sight of Mr. Rajespery in his black Citroen, going up and down.[174]

In declaring Essop's collection the winner of the Olive Schreiner award the adjudicators called him 'an exciting new creative talent' and 'one which anatomizes its society . . . with precision, humour and sympathetic insight'. The adjudicators also remarked on the confident presentation of a wide range of characters, the mastery of dialogue and local idiom, the economy of style as well as the fine restraint the author exhibits in the portrayal of his human comedy:

Ahmed Essop neither points a moral nor directs our emotions; his stories are not made to end happily or tragically—often the plot is sketchy and the story implicit—yet character and situation are effectively conveyed and the reader is given a fascinating, at times frightening, glimpse into the complexities and ironies of life and human relationships.[175]

Among the most recent writing it is in the short stories by Mbulelo Vizikhungo Mzamane, winner of the Mofolo-Plomer prize, that we come closest to a direct line in black fiction. Mzamane's short stories appeared in journals such as *Izwi, New Classic, Contrast* and then in several anthologies. His collection *Mzala*[176] was published by Ravan Press in South Africa, and at the time of writing was to be published in Britain. The characters in the stories are direct descendants of those of the writers of the fifties—Mphahlele's uncle who played Grieg on a stolen piano, Dugmore Boetie and others. The new generation has become a little more worldly-wise, a little better educated, but they still have the same resourcefulness and the same verve for living in the midst of adversity. 'I've a very well developed survival instinct', says the narrator in 'My Other Cousin Sitha',[177] and in 'My Cousin and the Law'[178] the police sergeant says to the thief: 'Both our professions are arts of the expedient. We must live . . .',[179] echoing the title of one of Mphahlele's first stories.

Mzamane is aware of his debt to these writers. He was in the fortunate position of receiving his education in Swaziland and was therefore not only able to read their work but was acquainted with some of them personally. Can Themba gave him lessons in English and Jordan Mgubane's son was his friend. He acknowledges his debt to the writers with enthusiasm, and in fact calls one of his stories 'Dube Train Revisited',[180] dedicating it to Can Themba. We learn from it that gangsters are still free to terrorise township travellers on their way from work.

Mzamane's viewpoint, like that of many of the earlier writers, is a richly comic one with a serious undertone. His inventive humour and his purpose are well demonstrated in the story 'The Soweto Bride'.[181] Solomzi's bride is a black American girl named Norma, whom he brings back from the States and introduces to his family and friends. The satire is directed against black Americans, exploding the myth of the back-to-Africa call. The last thing Norma wants is to become part of this raucous down-to-earth Soweto community who greet her with shouts of 'Soul Sister' and 'Black is Beautiful' and 'other American slogans we knew'. Less harsh is the humour directed at the innocents as well as the self-styled sophisticates of the township in their reaction to Norma. The family shower the bored and disdainful girl with confetti improvised from discarded fahfee exercise books. First Solomzi's parents break down with tears of relief, to find that the girl is not white but 'as human as you and me', as Aunt Bessie put it. When one of the older women finds that Norma does not speak Zulu she switches to SeSotho. When the Methodist Mother's choir bursts into song, the narrator, Sol's friend Phambili, is torn between his instinct to join in and his sophisticated self-respect. He compromises by humming the tune with his mouth firmly shut.

The fun, like the wild welcome party which Norma insists on calling 'cocktail', comes to an end and the story gives serious attention to the problem of adjustment in a world in which artificial labels not only keep people apart but also try to force them together. Norma gets a job at the United States Information Service. Every night she drags Sol out of the township for parties with her white colleagues, and he takes refuge in drink. One night he smashes the car and subsequently dies in hospital. Norma, who is pregnant, goes back to the States.

The young man who sees himself as a man of the world is one of Mzamane's favourite objects of fun. He is the narrator in 'The Soweto Bride' and again in 'A Present for My Wife'.[182] 'Do not look a gift-horse in the mouth', he says to his wife, after resorting to various tricks to try and get her the coat she wants, and comments: 'It's a proverb I once read from one of her books. I'm not sure whether I've used it correctly. To cover up, I rise and kiss her fully on the mouth—you can't talk when you're being kissed'.[183] The would-be sophisticate maintains the reader's sympathy by being able to laugh at himself. 'We switch over to our white conduct', the narrator in 'My Cousin and His Pick-Up'[184] says, when the cousin brings home a white woman.

The first five stories in the collection all concern 'my cousin', a country boy 'as green and raw as a cabbage'[185] who has come to town and soon learns how to survive. The stories are based on fact. Mzala is a real person, Mzamane's own cousin, who was 'ignominiously repatriated to the Transkei for the umpteenth time only the other day', as the author tells us in the introduction, 'I Remember . . . .'.[186] The stories relate various incidents in his life and those of his friends. Mzamane sees the cousin of fact and fiction as 'a living testimony to all that's indestructible in my people: their resilience, resourceful-ness, vitality, humour and positive thinking'.[187]

A collection of short stories by Achmed Dangor, although it won the Mofolo-Plomer prize for 1980, bears a 1981 imprint. We will therefore concentrate on two extracts from one of the stories, both of which appeared earlier, one entitled, like the full version, 'Waiting for Leila'[188] in the anthology Forced Landing, the other being 'The Wedding'[189] in the first issue of Wietie.

Now, in the murky heart of District Six, in the netherworld of our lives, we snatch the fragile cloth from the corpses of our unused memories and clothe ourselves propitiously. We shall expire—*ons gaan vrek!*—and will be buried without the ceremonies of men. Without ash or prayer, we who slept to death behind our latticed minds.

Come, ghost of the twentieth century, open those darkened windows of grief, take the light that I, renegade, pagan from the skies, have to offer.[190]

So says Samad, the chief character in 'Waiting for Leila'. Dangor, who, in his poetry, had reached a state of despondency, finds fresh material for his pen when he writes his requiem for District Six. He brings to it the voice of the poet, while at the same time keeping a firm grip on reality. Immediately after the above passage he shatters the spell by showing that the world of the dying slum is still anchored among the living:

'Hey you *fokken dronklap*!' A man obviously disturbed by Samad's raving, stood at the railing of his balcony. His vest bore the stains of at least a week's honest sweat.

What grandeur in your broken backs!

'Go and do your *befokte* shouting somewhere else. A man can't even get a decent night's sleep here. Voertsek.'

A voice from within the hovel responded:

'I told you we have to get out of here, there's nothing decent left in this place.'

The man went indoors.

'Oh shut up. I told you—I'm not moving, this is my home!'[191]

Unwaveringly, Dangor distils the essences of both the real and the symbolic, turns them into metaphor, then makes his statement:

A dead rat somewhere, rotting. Thousands of dead rats here in District Six. One can hear their sorrowful souls rustle in the darkness, lamenting the death of their beloved city. City of a thousand nations, disgorge your stinking belly. No white man will ever build his home here. Our ghosts are ineradicable.[192]

For Samad, who is at times the narrator of the story, and who is one of the remnants of the dying township, it is peopled by the ghosts of his ancestors called up by old Suleiman the Dhukkum. Like Essop's characters, Samad and some of the other inhabitants of the area are Muslims. These, however, are not Indians, but the descendants of slaves from the Dutch East Indies, now intermingled in a melting-pot of the races to such an extent that even the South African authorities cannot group them as a separate race and therefore assign them to a 'coloured' group area. In a drink and drug-induced vision Samad sees

. . . shadowy, eyeless faces, some of which he vaguely remembered. They surged angrily towards him, then sniffing the wine, withdrew, howling like wounded children.

'And then, like an insolent skollie, came Benjamin the Malaccan, dispersing the hysterical spirits before him. Black as the earth his skin glistened. Thus he had probably arrived more than two hundred years ago, proud and unsmiling, at the Cape of Storms.

Manacled, hand and foot, he had dragged his lithe body to the Kasteel, where for three years he had watched the moon's progress across the walls of his cell. Then he saved the Governor's child with a 'magic' potion that arrested the illness which was wasting away her body. Many say it was just a laxative, but Benjamin was rewarded. The beautiful Amina, and freedom, after a fashion.

Now, with the same decisiveness with which he had embraced Amina and his freedom, he swooped down into the circle. The wine seemed to be absorbed from the street into his body, and bursting into gales of laughter, he soared into the sky, followed by the babble of shrieking spirits who beat him with flailing, insubstantial arms.[193]

Again the author brings us back to reality ungently:

Samad too was laughing, and thus incapacitated by the laughter of his ancestors rollicking in his throat, he did not notice Leiman sneak up behind him.

What a joyous gleam there was in the old man's eyes as he brought the empty bottle crashing down on Samad's head.[194]

Later we learn that Benjamin the Malaccan was strung up by his ankles, and whipped to death for his part in a slave revolt.

But the people of District Six, before the arrival of the jackhammer and bulldozer, are as vibrant as Essop's inhabitants of Fordsburg. The richness of life, and its innocence, is like the ripeness of a watermelon and is meant to be tasted to the full. Samad first meets Leila at a picnic on the beach.

WAT' LEMOOEN! FIVE BOB, NET FIVE BOB, SO ROOI SOOS DIE MOTCHIE SE LIPPE!'

You begged me to buy one, because of its swollen, ripe appearance. I tested the watermelon for ripeness by pressing it against the top of my head. It creaked, and then cracked.

A sudden, wild desire overcame me, as the sticky juice flowed into my hair. I raced towards the sea, gently cradling the fruit in my arms; the crack in its skin revealed itself to me, red and delicate, almost like the opening of your sex.[195]

Leila, however, is hesitant in becoming part of the boisterous world of her lover and finally withdraws to her family who live on the higher reaches of the city.

The second extract opens on her wedding day, the day after Samad's encounter with the dhukkum's ghosts. She is getting married to a prosperous young man, and Samad makes several attempts to attend the wedding. Every time poor drunk Samad, well-known as a derelict character, is beaten and evicted. Once again dream and reality merge, as he imagines he is the hero son of Ben Yusuf the Malaccan, who attempts to rescue his Leila, but is betrayed. When he wakes up he finds that he had been badly beaten and then rescued from the gutter by one of Auntie Minnie's girls, Calypso. He is forced to realise that no dreams of heroism or nostalgia will bring back Leila and the innocent days she represents.

'Waiting for Leila', and its sequel, is a wild and passionate story by a poet who can exploit every emotion from despondency to elation. The full story in the collection, published later than the period under consideration in this study, does not quite fulfil the promise of the two excerpts in that it is less tightly written, but the work as a whole introduces a strange and gripping variety of characters depicted with great originality and insight. The prize is well deserved.

One of the most original talents in the short fiction field is Mtutuzeli Matshoba. Encouraged from the beginning by *Staffrider* magazine, its publishers, Ravan Press, brought out his volume *Call Me Not a Man*[196] in 1979.

A product of Lovedale and Fort Hare, Matshoba began to write, he tells us, in 'An autobiographical note' prefacing the volume, when 'June 16, 1976 [the Soweto uprisings] exploded in my face', and 'life was so full that I knew that if I did not spill some of its contents out I would go berserk'.[197] Yet, he tells us, only a shell of him remains 'to tell you of the other man's plight, which is in fact my own',[198] and he gives the reason in the beginning to the title story:

> By dodging, lying, resisting where it is possible, bolting when I'm already cornered, parting with invaluable money, sometimes calling my sisters into the game to get amorous with my captors, allowing myself to be slapped on the mouth in front of my womenfolk and getting sworn at with my mother's private parts, that component of me which is man has died countless times in one lifetime.[199]

Hence, 'Call Me Not a Man'.

In powerful long stories—some of 50 and more pages—with titles like 'A Glimpse of Slavery', 'Three Days in the Land of the Dying Illusion' and that of the story after which the volume is named, Matshoba probes deeply into the evils of the society of his land. Sometimes he stops a little too long to break into preaching but usually social comment is worked unobtrusively, sometimes subtly, into the story. A pretty picture in 'A Pilgrimage to the Isle of

Makana'[200] of a city, 'bustling with mothers who reminded me of hens with newly hatched chickens', takes on a different hue as he continues the sentence: 'leading the little chicks all over the fowl-run, scratching up the dirt, pecking here and there as if showing the young crowd what to pick out of the rubbish, to subsist'.[201]

There is never any cant or use of slogans. Mere ideology, whether it be apartheid, socialism, communism, democracy, he calls 'hokum' by which some vainly 'attempt to assume a god-like stature'.[202] His honesty leads to his using unexpected targets for his satiric darts. The narrator and black friends in 'A Pilgrimage to the Isle of Makana' are discussing three white friends whom one calls 'good people'. Thandi, the narrator, comments:

> I nearly asked what did she mean, whites were good people. Okay, I agree: it is, in fact, my creed that judging people by their skins is an evil prejudice. But this is South Africa, and the whole world over knows that this is the in-thing here. To whites blacks are 'bad' and to blacks whites are 'bad'. The whites being the ones who started it, of course . . .[203]

And a little later, more seriously:

> So, normally, if I see a white I see a white and not another human being. I see an image of the man who plunders my humanity.[204]

The bitterness against whites and co-operating blacks in the soul of the narrator of this story when he begins his journey to Robben Island is somewhat modified after a party at which he is surprised to see black and white mix happily. But in his pilgrim's progress through the valleys and hills of his native land Thandi still has to meet many a slough of despond before he reaches his destination. The resignation in the eyes of an old sick man, a prisoner, as he is brought ashore from the island to a waiting ambulance fills his whole being with bitterness once again. Why, he asks, when they had already usurped his right to live, were they now denying him the right to die? 'I hated them! I hated God for condoning it!'[205] Thandi's journey, by van, train, and Kombi from his home in the north to the township of Langa in Cape Town is described in a sub-heading as 'A Journey through South African Life'. We meet a profusion of characters of all shades as the scene changes from the reposing giant of Soweto, sprawling to the horizon, to the high mountains of the Cape, shouldering the heavens. The section in which Thandi meets his new white friends is called 'The Enlightenment'.

For the last section simply 'The Island' suffices as a heading, because the author knows that the natural fortress prison, once confining the legendary hero Makana and subsequently enchaining leaders like Mandela and Sobukwe, will have meaning for every black reader. The significance for the pilgrim in the story lies in the unity of black people in this respect. Right at the beginning Thandi discovers that 'people bound for my destination, either as prisoners or visitors, carry with them the wishes and desires of many others'.[206] And when he tells people on the train of his destination, a hush falls over the compartment, and one of them says:

> So he's (Thandi's brother) there with *bo*Mandela le *bo*Sisulu le *bo*Mbeki? Tell him to say *bayethe* for us to all the great men there who have sacrificed themselves for us . . .[207]

The climax of the journey takes place in the cubicles in which the prisoners receive their visitors. Keeping to the metaphor of pilgrimage the author says:

> I walked slowly, like a sinner approaching the holiest of holies and, as I passed each cubicle, I saw a black son of the fatherland attired in the cloth of sin and shame . . . Their eyes were bright . . . and their faces were lit by brilliant smiles which shone right to the core of my soul . . .[208]

Matshoba completes the narrative with a terse meeting between Thandi and his brother, and his return to the mainland. The story is inspired by Matshoba's own experiences since he has a young brother who was imprisoned on Robben Island.

'Three Days in the Land of a Dying Illusion'[209] describes a different pilgrimage, this time into the depths of African history and the consciousness of the black mind. As the rattling train noses southwards on its way to the Transkei he sends 'a burning arrow searing backward through history':

> Every hillock, etched against a clear but moonless sky in which millions of stars formed part of the milky way, was to me like an historical cairn, which had stood there to mark the beginning of time, witnessing every form of life that ever passed over, below and around it; every event . . .[210]

He re-interprets the story of Nonqause, the girl instructed by voices that the people must slaughter all their cattle and destroy their crops, and that the enemy would then be driven back to the sea, as an inspiring legend instead of the fiasco of starvation and horror of the history books. In Matshoba's version, the sustenance is to be shared, not destroyed. The voices come from the depths of the young girl's mind and not from outside, and express a message of courage and hope for the future.

The journey ends in the Transkei, the illusorily independent state of the title, the society of which he submits to a searching and searing analysis.

The title story, 'A Glimpse of Slavery', 'My Friend the Outcast', and a story published later than the collection, in *Forced Landing*,

'To Kill a Man's Pride',[211] all deal with various pernicious aspects of the black man's life, like the evil practice of police reservists who extort money in exchange for freedom from arrest, farm labour for prisoners, bribery in the allocation of houses by which some who cannot pay are made homeless, and one which few writers have treated in such well-informed detail, the lives of men in the so-called 'bachelor quarters' which house mainly men separated from their families by the influx control laws.

Matshoba writes with a fine sense for the dramatic and the stories are highlighted by many brilliant scenes, such as the one about the elderly patient being brought from the island and the meeting of the brothers there which have already been mentioned, and one on the prison farm in which a white farmer tries to make the narrator put a dead but still wriggling snake around his neck. The narrator had found the snake and killed it, and the farmer, when he saw the disruption of work among the labourers, came galloping towards them.

'Who killed the snake?' he asked from the saddle.

'It was me,' I answered, thinking that there was nothing wrong with killing a poisonous snake where people were working.

He alighted slowly from the beautiful gelding, as if he wanted to take a closer look. A snake dies in a peculiar fashion. For hours after it has died its body keeps on moving slowly with ripples of muscles under its glossy skin. The sight is not at all pleasing to the eye or the nerves. Koos was unruffled. He sank to his haunches and turned the snake around studiously.

'Do you know that this snake eats these rats that destroy the maize?' he soliloquized, his eyes remaining on the dead snake. He took out a pocket knife and cut the snake where its thickness bulged out. Two wet, dead rats came out. 'You see? I told you; two dead rats that might have put away tons of grain and bred more rats. Did you think about this before you killed the snake?'

'I know that snakes eat rats. Someone might have been bitten,' I answered in unwavering Afrikaans.

'*Jy praat goeie Afrikaans—nê?*' was his answer to my explanation that I had killed the snake because the people were in danger of being bitten. No, that did not matter to Koos de Wet. What mattered more than the lives of the people who slaved for him was the grain. 'Have you been to school?'

'A little.'

'There is an English poem about a sailor who killed a bird he was not supposed to have killed and they hung the bird on his shoulders.' He meant Samuel Taylor Coleridge's *Rime of the Ancient Mariner*, and the implication of his example was clear to me.

He stood up with the snake held by the tip of its tail between his thick forefinger and thumb. 'I want you to wrap this around your neck like a scarf.'

Most people have a terrible phobia of anything that crawls, and more so of snakes because snakes can kill. I am no exception to other human beings. I might have been afraid of Koos de Wet, but I feared a dead snake more. I backed away, and this brought the smile I had seen at Modderbee to the wrestler's face. 'Here. Take it, it won't bite. It's dead.'

It was like someone coaxing a child to touch a toy made of fur that the child did not trust. I was not going to wrap a snake around my neck even if it meant that Koos de Wet was going to kill me if I did not. He threw it, but I ducked, having anticipated his move. The dead snake sailed over my head and landed behind me without touching me. For some reason missing me infuriated the ape. He rushed at me and, before I could turn, struck me down with his large hairy arm. I fell on my back. His oversized boot pinned me down on the side of my neck. The soil got into my mouth, nostrils and eyes. He unslung his rifle and I thought he was going to shoot me cold-bloodedly, a thing of which I knew him to be perfectly capable. I saw him turning his rifle in his hands and holding it by its barrel and I thought he was going to bash my skull in. He did neither, but pressed the butt into my ribs with slowly increasing pressure. I felt my ribs caving inward and prayed that I should pass out before they snapped. Crying out was impossible. The priority during those nasty moments was to get some air into my lungs without inhaling the dust as well. Just when I thought I heard the ribs cracking under my skin, he let go. I staggered and gasped and coughed to my feet.

'That'll teach you to do what I tell you, kaffer,' he said and went to his horse. 'Now, get on with the work!' he roared.[212]

Matshoba's humour is of the same sardonic kind that we have met often before, but he adds a touch of original flippancy, the throw-away line, which often startles in its context. This often happens when he uses township slang. 'Sell-out' is an often-used expression for a black man who co-operates with whites, but never more effectively than in the scene in 'Pilgrimage' where Thandi is called on by men from the Department of Prisons about his planned visit to his brother on Robben Island. 'There were two of them', he says. 'One white, and one sell-out, black and burly'.[213]
And again:

Another man boarded the train. A big man in a grey suit who might have aroused my wariness were his face not familiar. Sellouts seldom go around with familiar faces . . .[214]

Pictorial art had been Matshoba's first love as a youngster and perhaps cartoons would have been his forte. Here is a narrative cartoon of a railway inspector:

My ancestors! This penguin. Exactly! This seabird complete with white shirt, black epaulettes and ellipsoid shape. Good old penguin. His left paddle reached out for the ticket which he clipped and handed back. All the time sending down jets of hot wind out of his lungs, he scribbled on the list and grunted: *'Kompartement B,'* and stood there waiting for me to grab my baggage and light out to crowd the 'coloured' youths and an old man I had seen down the coach.

'Later. I'll go later. *Ek sit nog so 'n bietjie en gesels.'*

The last part got him where it counted. He melted like icecream on a hot day into a sweet fat Afrikaner boy: *'Ja. Jy kan maar sit en gesels, jong.'* (Yes. You may sit and talk).[215]

5

Autobiographical Writing

AT THE TIME when *Drum* ceased to be an outlet, and most of the writers had been banned, several of them felt that they were left with a great deal to say and no means of being heard. They therefore turned to the British and American book publishers who were ready to make use of the vogue for African literature. Since, as we have seen, the novel was not a suitable vehicle for these writers, and none except Mphahlele had sufficient publishable short stories for a collection, they put the incidents of their own lives into book form. Peter Abrahams, Ezekiel Mphahlele, Bloke Modisane and Todd Matshikiza published autobiographical works.

By this time the writers were in exile in Britain, most of them for a considerable time, and had adapted themselves as best they could to their new surroundings. They were addressing an exclusively European readership and felt that they had to put their case to them. What sort of a creature was the black man, their readers were asking, and the writers did their best to supply an answer. Many were torn between proving their equal status as men on the one hand, and, on the other, presenting the black man as the exotic being their readers were used to reading about, with strange, if interesting, customs. Nontandi (Noni) Jabavu, for instance, who also wrote about her experiences in a book entitled *Drawn in Colour*,[1] attempted to explain the apparently unconscious docility and humility of the African by describing the ritual concept of '*Akukhonto*, it is nothing' or 'such is life'. She recreates the atmosphere of African tribal life by using literal translations from the Xhosa and a liberal sprinkling of proverbs and metaphors. The following conversation takes place on a train journey, after her brother had been killed by *tsotsis* (thugs) in Johannesburg, the reason for her return to South Africa:

> 'And who may you be, young-ladies-of-ours?' . . .
> 'I am of Jili, *mama*,' I said.
> 'Then what about this "deprivation"? (euphemism for deaths being *de rigeur*!) 'How close is it to you?'
> 'It was my brother.'
> 'Your brother? *Brother* Truly, truly, in-the-house? (*Kanye*

kanye endlini?) Same mother same father?' (She had to be sure it was not an 'extended family' kind of brother.)

'Yes, mother, truly in the house. He followed-on-the-back of the sister-who-follows-on-my back.' She fell silent, looking at me, and her eyes suddenly filled with compassion. Then she made the little ritual speech and I was moved because this was happening so many hundreds of miles from my own home.

'It is nothing, my child, it is nothing; the Lord will bind you. Never are shoulders visited with a burden heavier than they can carry' quoting one of our proverbs, and finishing, 'Therefore He will give you the strength you need, Jili.' She went, leaving us to our Western style privacy.[2]

Noni Jabavu, as the British-educated daughter of Professor D.D.T. Jabavu and wife of a member of the prominent British Cadbury family, writes as a Westerner to the point of understanding the white man's attitude towards the black as 'fear of the unknown', a prejudice which she herself felt when visiting the more primitive Ghanda of the north. As a result she aroused the ire of her fellow black writers. A reviewer in *The New African* describes her as 'the new Un-African'.

In marked contrast to Noni Jabavu was Todd Matshikiza who, in *Chocolates for my Wife*,[3] portrays the new black man in South Africa, the sophisticated town-dweller. Born in Queenstown, Matshikiza was educated in Johannesburg and worked there variously as a musician, razor salesman and journalist. Like Motsisi, he wrote a regular column for *Drum*. He is best-known as the composer of the score for the popular musical *King Kong*.

Matshikiza's writing style—the Matshikize referred to by Can Themba—attempted to reproduce the language of the township jazz musicians who were his friends. He handled his typewriter, Tom Hopkinson tells us, 'as if it were a cross between a saxophone and a machine gun' and Bernard Levin describes his music as violent: 'Blaring brass, thudding drums, with the tunes weaving around the hypnotic volume of noise'. The same applies to his writing and often there is a deliberate syncopated rhythm to the words:

Then we saw white man loading bricks and making mud and fetching water and building his own house and sitting inside the house and looking through his window smoking a pipe and cleaning his own car on Sunday morning. Then we saw black man digging a trench and white man also digging. Some were digging back to back. Others head to head. But all were digging spade to spade and there was no foreman standing there smoking while the others were digging. The only thing they didn't do was singing while they were digging. Singing while you are digging digs the hole deep down.[4]

He continues the rhythm to a deliberate point of absurdity and the words keep pace in order to achieve a comic effect:

> White women stood around the notices reading Russian Borzoi. Their leashed pets lashed away at lights coloured conspectus and blue, at fellow Dalmatians, denims and aspirin reading, 'Don't be a dog. An ordinary dog. Come in and have shampoo an' be a poodle. An extraordinary dog. Did your dog shampoodle today?'[5]

The jazzy style tends to become self-conscious, forced and irritating as the book progresses, but as the contents become more serious so he switches from Matshikize to straight terse prose, for instance in a report of the trial of Ezekiel Dhlamini, otherwise known as King Kong:

> Eyes turned in the direction of the dock where the sound of pounding fists and stamping feet came. It was King, hands gripped tight against the handrails, feet stamping a violent vicious beat on the floor, body jumping up and down like a gorilla, an angered giant-sized ape trying to set itself free. Now and again his fists would pound against the rails. His teeth clenched tight to stop him from shrieking out aloud, but in the end he could not resist yelling out loud. 'It's a lie, you lie, you lie!'[6]

Most of the autobiographies succeeded in their attempt to appeal to the European in that they proved to be very popular. Noni Jabavu's *Drawn in Colour* was recommended by the Book Society and Mphahlele's *Down Second Avenue*[7] was translated into German, Hungarian, Czech, Serbo-Croat, Bulgarian, French, Swedish and Japanese, and extracts appeared in many anthologies.

The autobiographies were falling into the hands of liberal Europeans who provided an ideal readership for works dealing with conflict between black and white. Armchair revolutionaries eagerly sought books with titles like *Tell Freedom* (Peter Abrahams) or *Blame Me on History* (Bloke Modisane) or the escape story of a man held in a trial for treason (Alfred Hutchinson's *Road to Ghana*). Although the protest could now be made more directly, we find that it is usually more subtle than in the early fiction. Instead of the story being used to demonstrate the idea of unequal conflict, we now often find that the anecdote comes first and the reader is left to draw his own conclusions. In Abrahams' novel *Path of Thunder*, for example, we have the long and bitter story of Mad Sam who is almost beaten to death by whites for consorting with a coloured girl, and wanders through the rest of the book as a constant and living proof of the effect of evil. Far more effective in its condemnation of cruelty of white to black are three lines in the same author's reminiscences, *Tell Freedom*:[8] '"Ma worked for them," Maggie said. "She was washing

and the tin of boiling water fell on her. They made her come home by
herself . . .'''.[9]

Humour, which is absent in all but a few of the protest stories, is
used to advantage in underlining protest in the autobiographies.
Todd Matshikiza sardonically describes a visit to South Africa
House shortly after he comes to London. He finds himself wandering
through London streets down to Trafalgar Square, and suddenly
comes face to face with 'the sign of the Springbok, white South
Africa's national symbol':

> A naughty streak in me said:
> Eenie meenie mina mo,
> Catch a nigger by his toe.
> Go inside and then you'll see
> If Africa for you or me.

He is directed to the reading room.

> The chairs arranged all around the walls of the room were
> occupied by faces hidden behind newspapers. I went round the
> table looking like one searching for something to read. But there
> was nothing I could find an excuse to pick up and look at.
> Something inside of me said, lift up your head, and when I did I
> found numerous eyes, blue, green and fiery red, peering at me from
> all round the reading room. I left the table in the centre of the
> room and found myself crouching pressing against the wall as
> though someone was pushing me. I found myself in the silent mute
> company of the 'South African "Native" Bronze Heads' by a
> sculptor named van Wouw. They were to me grotesque. The first
> bore the title 'Native Awaiting Sentence'. The other was called
> 'Sleeping Kaffir'.
> I walked out of South Africa House . . .[10]

In another incident he tries to obtain seven pounds from his South
African superior, the chief reporter, to buy a gun for protection
against a gang who had objected to an article. The chief reporter says:

> 'I'll give you three pounds an' you can add what you like to that'.
> All the time it happens like that. The white man says, 'Tell me
> nothing 'bout the blacks. I know them. I've got ten of my own.'
> That's when life looked surrounded. You're one of ten of his
> own.[11]

We have seen in previous chapters how some fiction failed during
this period because imaginative writing could not arise out of an
impossible situation. When writing his own story the black author
could shed all pretence of using his imagination. He was no
longer forced to present 'journalistic fact parading outrageously as
imaginative literature'.[12] Yet all the elements which made the short

stories interesting and readable could be incorporated in the autobiography. I have shown how some of Mphahlele's best stories were taken from *Down Second Avenue.* Other incidents in the autobiography could be turned into effective short stories, for instance a story he heard from an old man in his youth, the Romeo-and-Juliet tale of a Christian man who falls in love with a Pagan girl. They flee from the girl's angry brothers but the girl is drowned as they cross the river. Mphahlele tells the story simply and with controlled emotion:

> I want to sit down, Thema said. You can cross and you must live. They will kill you if they find you here. And the young man said: It doesn't matter now. It matters, she replied. That put new blood into Thema. She got her hand round him and he felt her strength as he leant almost his whole weight on her. She kept saying, Come, my love, come, my love, as they crossed the river. And the wailing voices swept down to them and passed on, to be picked up by other people below them.[13]

Although Mphahlele himself describes the South African situation as 'a crushing cliché . . . as literary material', he can make a suspense story even out of obtaining a passport.

Noni Jabavu's two accounts of her return to South Africa, *Drawn in Colour* and *The Ochre People,*[14] often have the excitement of fiction, and Alfred Hutchinson's escape from South Africa[15] has all the ingredients of an adventure story.

Characters come to life far more vividly than in most of the fiction of the period. We need only compare, for instance, Peter Abrahams' Mabel in *Mine Boy,* who is characterised over and over again purely by speaking of the laughter in her eyes, with Aunt Liza who lives for us in a brief incident: Abrahams' foster parents are visited by a white man whose boy young Peter had beaten up:

> I looked at Aunt Liza and something in her lifelessness made me stubborn in spite of my fear.
> 'He insulted my father,' I said.
> The white man smiled.
> 'See Sam, your hiding couldn't have been good.'
> There was a flicker of life in Aunt Liza's eyes. For a brief moment she saw me, looked at me, warmly, lovingly, then her eyes went dead again.[16]

Gone, too, in the autobiographies is the wooden image of the white man. Jabavu makes us see him clearly through African eyes:

> 'My,' says an African woman and laughs, 'who would be a European? Folks, these people rise up angry at everything even from their sleep. First thing in the morning, angry, always angry, they were conceived on a twisted mat, those.'[17]

Together with the pretence of creating fiction, the auto-biographical writer could also shed some of his inhibitions. Abrahams tells us in *Return to Goli*[18] that in order to write fiction he had 'purged himself of hatred' because 'art and beauty come of love, not hate'. In his two memoirs, *Return to Goli* and *Tell Freedom*, Abrahams feels no need to put brakes on his real feelings. Nowhere in his novels do we find anything as simple and sincere as his account in *Tell Freedom* of his last days in Cape Town, or of his feelings on first coming across the works of black American poets in a public library. 'A man called Countee Cullen said that to me . . .'; 'Georgia Douglas Johnson stirred me to pride in the darkness of my mother and sister'; and 'Jean Toomer . . . stirred me to the verge of tears'.[19]

Abrahams' novels appear to take place in a vacuum. There is no feeling for the vast landscapes in *Wild Conquest* as there is in Plaatje's *Mhudi*, and neither the coloured people's village in *Path of Thunder* nor the Durban of *A Night of their Own* comes to life. Yet in *Tell Freedom* we live with the boy Abrahams in the slums surrounding Johannesburg.

> And from the streets and houses of Vrededrop, from the back-yards and muddy alleys, a loud babel of shouting, laughing, cursing, voices rise, are swallowed by the limitless sky and rise again in unending tumult. And through, and above, and under, all this is the deep throbbing hum of the city. It is everywhere at once. Without beginning, without end.[20]

Similarly Alfred Hutchinson, who wrote very little before *Road to Ghana* and only a couple of plays for the British Broadcasting Corporation before his death in Nigeria, often reveals himself in his autobiography as the most mature of the writers. Even Mphahlele, who has written valuable fiction, produced nothing more moving in his writing career than *Down Second Avenue*.

The writers welcome the opportunity to write what they feel about their homeland, to confess and purge their conscience of 'running away', and to express their dreams for the future. Although all these works are very personal stories of suffering, there is rarely any feeling of self-pity on the part of the author, or of embarrassing intrusion by the reader. The only one who writes an ungarnished personal account is Bloke Modisane in *Blame Me on History*,[21] which makes this work at times dull reading and is quite unlike his sardonic short stories. Modisane sees himself as the 'Invisible Man' of Ralph Ellison. In fact he describes himself as a 'hollow man' and his nickname, Bloke, was chosen for the same reason. In his somewhat breathless prose and hectic scenes of degradation, too, his debt to Ellison is unmistakable, but in the contents he emulates him only on a literary and not on a visionary level. Ellison uses his figurative invisibility as a symbolic means of working out his destiny as a black man. Bloke uses his anonymity merely in self-defence against the mental threat to himself. He developed what he called a bird-of-passage morality, and found it necessary to drug his conscience into insensibility in an orgy of reading Henry Miller, De Sade and Omar Khayyam.

In an article investigating the psychology of autobiography, Bruce Mazlish describes it as 'literary genre produced by romanticism, which offers us a picture from a specific present viewpoint of a coherent shaping of an individual past, reached by means of introspection and memory of a special sort, wherein the self is seen as a developing entity, changing at definable stages, and where knowledge of the external world, and both together provide us with a deep grasp of reality'.[22] In this sense, *Down Second Avenue* is a true autobiography. Just as Mphahlele spent the years of his exile in a search for human identity, or an identity 'of place', as he often called it, so he was occupied in this work in first establishing a personal identity. Towards the end of the book he speaks of his quest, in describing a visit to Basutoland:

> I went to Basutoland in search of something. What it was I didn't know. But it was there, where it wasn't, inside me. Perhaps it was hate, maybe love, or both; or sordidness; maybe it was beauty. As I say, I didn't know. Once I had landed on the soil of Moshoeshoe's country, the quest seemed never to come to an end. I'm not even sure it has, yet.[23]

He goes on to describe his feelings when he stood looking at the sky—'I tried to rip the dark with the razor edge of my desire'—and what he felt when standing on the top of a high mountain: 'There I felt the touch of the Ultimate, but only for a fleeting dizzy moment'. Then, 'for one brief moment of rich promise' he thought 'the secret was in the conical hat and the blanket of a Mosuto standing placidly on the edge of a summit at sunrise'. His longing search continued; his mind and heart stood still. It tormented him 'to feel so insufficient, and not to know the why and wherefore'. Many things became 'jumbled symbols' of his hope and yearning: 'the purple-pink sunsets; the wasting bleached earth; the rock hanging precariously on the cheek of a hill; the muddy grey waters of the Caledon; the eternal streak of cloud lying stretched out like one of heaven's drunken sots'. But alas, he concludes, the dreams 'had long since taken flight and now hung dry in shining cobwebs to which my fermenting furies clung crucified. . .'.[24]

The purple prose is a shield against exposing his feelings. Mphahlele is, in fact, surprisingly reticent about many aspects of his personal life. The love story of his youth with a girl named Rebone is one of the weakest chapters, for instance, and we never get close to his wife, Rebecca. The search for identity is the theme of the book, but the author as self obtrudes only in occasional deeply personal revelations. This reticence is due to his innate shyness and consequent aloofness, which often led to an inability to communicate verbally with those closest to him and set him apart as a lonely and often unhappy figure. 'I felt most bitter', he writes of his mother, 'over my inability to thank her substantially for all she had done for me and others. Her abundant love sometimes made me wish we could quarrel'.[25]

Yet, paradoxically, he succeeds in imparting the spirit of his experiences. The book was at first envisaged as a novel and is still sometimes regarded as such, in the same way as Camara Laye's *The African Child* and Herman Bosman's personal experiences in a South African prison, *Cold Stone Jug*, are catalogued under fiction. When asked in an interview at the London Transcription Centre by Cosmo Pieterse to what extent *Down Second Avenue* was true, Mphahlele replied that perhaps 'there is only autobiographical fiction or fictional autobiography in the final analysis'.[26]

Whether *Down Second Avenue* is strictly true is in fact of no importance. It is doubtlessly a true account in spirit of Mphahlele's life and that of the people around him. Even in his avowed fiction Mphahlele never compromises with the truth for the sake of dramatic effect or sentiment, as others are often tempted to do in their autobiographical writing. It seems very unlikely for instance, that anyone would remember how, at the age of two or three, he tried to lick a raindrop sliding down a windowpane, as does Peter Abrahams in *Tell Freedom*:

> I pushed my nose and lips against the pane and tried to lick a raindrop sliding down on the other side. As it slid past my eyes, I saw the many colours in the raindrop . . . It must be warm in there. Warm and dry. And perhaps the sun would be shining in there. The green must be the trees and the grass; and the brightness, the sun . . . I was inside the raindrop, away from the misery of the cold, inside my raindrop world.[27]

The incident makes a most effective introduction to the book, but one loses the sense of experience relived that Mphahlele succeeds in conveying to the reader. *Tell Freedom* is well organised and skilfully executed, the work of a storyteller. Only incidents likely to be of interest to the reader are selected. But as a personal document it does not have the impact of Mphahlele's often rambling story. While Abrahams opens his autobiography with a symbolic reminiscence of warmth and security inside a raindrop, Mphahlele, with no artifice, begins his story by admitting ignorance about parts of his early life: 'I have never known why we—my brother, sister and I—were taken to the country when I was five'.[28]

Each of the two writers has the same aim, to tell the reader how it feels to be black in South Africa, and how he wrestles with his bitterness and meets the challenge. Peter Abrahams never forgets his audience, whereas Mphahlele continues to look at the world around him and bring it into focus. Here, however, he is more personally involved than he is in his fiction. He describes himself as sitting on the veranda of a shop in Marabastad. 'If you were alone, you were in a position to view critically what you considered to be the whole world passing down Barber Street, half-detached, half-committed'.[29] Life is harsh, and it is here, on Second Avenue, that Mphahlele learns that man must live and make the best of his circumstances. To Ezekiel, even as a boy, living meant mental survival. With him, we watch his world deteriorate politically and socially, and his own tension mount. We follow him to school and college, watch him gain honour and distinction in education, followed by defeat and disillusionment and finally to the most bitter period of his life culminating in exile. It is to be hoped that it will not be long before there is a sequel. We learn about his subsequent activities in *The Wanderers*, as we have seen, but one would like to see his life both in exile and especially after his return to South Africa submitted to the same scrutiny as is his youth in *Down Second Avenue*.

Such a biography would be addressed to a readership different from that of *Down Second Avenue* and its contemporary works. The fashion for autobiographies at the time was short-lived. Having had their say, the writers felt no further need to explain themselves to the overseas reader. Black South African literature was turning inward, and the writers saw no point in writing the stories of their lives since everyone shared the same experiences. There was one more auto-biography, published as late as 1971, entitled *Autobiography of an Unknown South African*, by Naboth Mogkatle.[30] It is a long document in which the author describes faithfully, minutely and in measured tones his experiences in living and working in country and city, his involvement in Communist politics and trade union affairs, and finally his departure without passport for abroad and freedom. It is a political document, yet the story of his courageous battle against superior forces, and the almost matter-of-fact way in which he tells his own experiences and of his relationship with others, makes it a story of the human spirit and of human warmth.

Later writers, as we have seen, draw profusely on their personal experiences, but they transform it imaginatively and present it as fiction with a thematic purpose.

Drama

IN 1940, REPORTING to the Bulletin of the *British Drama League* about a visit to South Africa, Mary Kelly wrote that the whites had problems 'but these problems have not so much urgency as to force an expression through the drama, and so, for the most part, South Africans are content with secondhand entertainment of the bioscope'. She continues:

> If dramatic art among the Europeans lacks background and urgency, the same cannot be said of Bantu dramatic expression. The kraals can provide the white man with a living textbook on the origins of drama;—there one may see the unity and instinctive rhythm of the tribal dance and song, the emergence of the single actor, the echo and comment of chorus and audience, the improvisation and realistic acting of the mimes.

She tells how an improvised drama was put on for her by African interpreters and nurses of the hospital at Holy Cross:

> I was given a short synopsis, but it was hardly necessary, for the acting was so vigorous, the characterisation so clear, and the whole play so gripping that one quite forgot that one did not know the language in which it was played. The only thing that I regretted was that I could not follow the comic dialogue, which flashed from one to another at lightning speed, and obviously got home every time.[1]

She concludes: '. . . for the educated Native there is a very urgent need for expression in drama'.

Some twenty-five years later the white man was making use of this 'living text-book' by consciously drawing on all the features Mary Kelly mentions. The rhythm of dance and song, improvisation and audience participation were deliberately brought back to Western drama in the late nineteen-sixties, not so much in straight drama as in popular presentations such as *Hair*. However, the present century has also seen the beginning of a breaking down of the divergence between the highbrow and popular stage, as for example the influence of Charlie Chaplin on Samuel Beckett in *Waiting for Godot*. Such divergence did not exist in African drama.

In South Africa, one man was aware of the need to revive African drama for the westernised black man. In 1936 H.I.E. Dhlomo said that dramatic movements should be started to interest people in African history and tradition. 'Drama is the reconstruction, recreation and reproduction of the great experience of a people, and it helps them to live more abundantly.'

Writing on 'Drama and the African' in *South African Outlook*[2] Dhlomo begins:

> Action! Emotion! Rhythm! Gesture! Imitation! Desires! That is what drama was before it developed into an institution for propaganda, for the propagation of ideas, or for commercial entertainment.[3]

Action and rhythm and the other histrionic qualities, he says, are not foreign to the African and neither is drama. He explains that the origin of tribal dramatic representation was a combination of religious or magical ritual, rhythmic dances and song. Of audience participation he says that if the actors did not come up to standard, the rest would cease to join in. 'This was good for both sides—and would be good for many modern productions'.[4]

Contemporary critics who go back to the roots of African culture tend to forget that Western drama grew out of the same roots as traditional African drama: the basic and emotional urge of men and women to re-enact sacred and other stories illustrative or symbolic of their lives and the forces that rule them. Dhlomo reminds us of this when he says: 'Indeed, there is no race in the world which did not have some kind of tribal dramatic representation'.

Dhlomo recognised, however, that it is impossible to turn back the clock. African drama, he says, cannot be based purely on African roots:

> It must be grafted in Western drama . . . It must borrow from, be inspired by, shoot from European dramatic art forms, and be tainted by exotic influences . . . The African dramatist cannot delve into the past unless he has grasped the present. African art cannot grow and thrive by going back and digging up the bones of the past without dressing them with modern knowledge and craftmanship . . . We want African playwrights who will dramatise and expound a philosophy of our history. We want dramatic representation of African Oppression, Emancipation and Evolution. To do this the African dramatist must be an artist before being a propagandist, a philosopher before a reformer; a psychologist before a patriot.[5]

Significantly he says 'before' and not 'instead of'.

In another article, written for the same publication three years later,[6] Dhlomo discusses rhythm as the greatest gift of Africa to the artistic world. The marked sense and love of rhythm of the African he explains by the rigid rule of pattern under which the tribal African lived. 'There were rigid patterns of behaviour, rigid patterns even in architecture (the hut) and in the village of kraal planning'.[7] This element was marked in movement, dance, music and in tribal plastic art.

Yet Dhlomo does not claim rhythmic beauty as the sole property of the African:

> There is no doubt that Shakespeare, the Greek dramatists and the Hebrew writers used certain ingredients to produce rhythmic beauty in their works. There is a kind of law underlying all great literature, all beauty. One ingredient is poetic expression, but there are others. The very regular appearance of ghosts, clowns, fairies, kings, duels, lovers etc. in Shakespeare, the common use of the device of the chorus of suffering heroes and anthropomorphic gods in Greek writers, help to give rhythmic effect to these literatures. We too, can use archaic tribal forms to produce a form of poetry and rhythmic effect distinctly African.[8]

'Rhythm,' he says, 'is more than a physical sensation. It is inspired uniformity in motion, giving birth to thought and emotion and visions'.[9]

I have quoted from Dhlomo's essays on African drama at such length in order to show the direction which African literature in English could have taken in South Africa if a writer like Dhlomo had been given the attention he deserved. Only recently an effort has been made, as mentioned earlier, to revive interest in his work, but the interest has come from academics at the 'white' universities and not from black dramatists or students of drama.

The reason for Dhlomo's failure may have lain partly in the fact that in his own plays he failed to carry out his theories. He certainly did attempt to reconstruct, recreate and reproduce the great experiences of a people, but unfortunately his inexperience as a playwright prevented him from fulfilling his object successfully.

Recent research has revealed that he probably wrote some 24 plays. Only one of them, *The Girl Who Killed to Save*,[10] was published but some of the others were produced and manuscripts of these have been placed in the Library of the University of Natal by Dhlomo's family. *Dingana* was first performed by the Medical students Drama Group of the University of Natal on 28 May 1954, and about 50 copies were printed and bound at the University Library's Xerographic Photo Duplicating Bindery Department.

Dhlomo could not have chosen a better subject for dramatic treatment than the story of the prophetess Nonqause, 'The Girl Who Killed to Save', and the first scene of the eponymous play is full of dramatic promise. Dhlomo's aim is to bring out the historical meaning behind the story of the girl Nonqause, whom he describes in an introductory historical note as a 'prophesying *medium*' (italics his), daughter of the seer Umhlakaza, 'who in all likelihood exercised the powers of a ventriloquist'.[11] Nonqause declares that she has held converse with the spirits of the ancestors of the Xhosa tribe; they have promised to drive the European invader from their land. As a sign of faith, the people are to kill their cattle and destroy their crops.

Dhlomo treats the basic story on three different levels. There is a plot of realistic conflict and action between those who believe in the prophecy and 'the doubtful men'. In this, Dhlomo adheres to accepted history. There is also the beginning of a love-plot, never completed, in which Nonqause's suitor Mazwi, who refuses to believe the prophecy, asks Nonqause to flee with him. He loves Nonqause for herself alone and she returns his love and admires him because he is 'strong, wise, brave and will not kill cattle even to please us'.[12] Yet she will not flee with him.

Their conflict, however, leads to the second level which concerns Nonqause's psychological conflict: her very real doubts as to whether the sounds she heard near the river were, as her father and the Chief assure her, the voices of her ancestors. She becomes almost hysterical with fear for her people, in case she is wrong. She understands something the Old Woman who guards her has never considered—that the people will starve to death if she is mistaken. So conditioned is the Old Woman by the traditional ways of the tribe that it has never occurred to her to think independently of the consequences. Yet she is a woman of intelligence and psychological insight. When Nonqause becomes afraid she tells her that her fear is caused by 'the fact that since the day the Lion took up this matter you have been confined to your hut, supervised by an old thing like myself, guarded by the Chief's spies, and not allowed to roam about with your young friends'.[13]

Just before this dialogue, Nonqause has been asked by the Chief to tell the story of her vision to a number of 'doubtful men', and she immediately goes into what the stage directions describe as a 'hysteriomaniaclike trance' and re-enacts her vision. It is important to note that the stage directions describe her as *'feigning* to be seized'[14] (italics mine) with this trance. Yet it is a known fact of hypnotism that the subject sometimes thinks he is choosing to cooperate with the experimenter and yet is actually going into an involuntary trance. Dhlomo may have been aware of this, since there is no indication that Nonqause is merely a willing tool in the hands of political intrigue. Such intrigue is indeed hinted at, and remains one of the mysteries of history and of the play: did the chief and his seer deliberately hatch this plot, in order to drive the people to such a state of despair that they could be led into war against the Europeans? At any rate it is unlikely that Dhlomo intended to indicate that

Nonqause was knowingly part of such a plot. Rather, he wanted to give the impression that although she was torn between belief and disbelief she felt it her duty to cooperate. In this way the psychological tension of the drama is created and held.

After she has expressed doubts to her guardian, her lover asks her to flee and Nonqause, this time without feigning, falls to her knees 'rapt in pain' and cries: 'The People! The Truth!'.[15] This brings us to the end of Scene 1 and ends the psychological drama of Nonqause, *The Girl Who Killed to Save*. Neither Nonqause nor her lover appear again in the remaining four scenes and she is barely mentioned.

On the third and deepest level Dhlomo attempts to bring out the historical meaning of the story of Nonqause. The theme is stated with the introduction of an Old Man in Scene 1. Nonqause's guardian is shocked by his arrival in the hut, since the chief has decreed that men may not visit it. The Old Man explains that this does not apply to him, since age has made him a 'helpless babe'. He then continues:

> Age, by bringing us near our grave, brings us near our re-generation. Near death shines life. The crumbling dry bones of our autumn herald the spring of our new life. No, woman, I am no man—I am man in the making. My wrinkles show that Life is softening this old human clay in order to remodel it into new forms. Man never dies although men do.[16]

The Old Man has explained the basis of African belief in the continuity of life. He now asks Nonqause whether, as a result of the killing of the cattle, *lobola* (bride price) is to cease. Nonqause says to him: 'Nothing will be destroyed. Life is only being organised on a higher scale. Like you, the country is near a new birth, a greater day, a happier life'.[17]

Dhlomo has introduced his theme, and in order to preserve artistic unity he must carry it through to the end. Yet historically the movement ended in complete failure. The cattle and grain were destroyed, and the people starved to death except for those rescued by the Europeans. How did Dhlomo attempt to reconcile historical truth with the theme of his play? The answer seems surprising. It comes first from the Native Commissioner's brother-in-law, Hugh, who, like Nonqause, sees the events as a great metamorphosis—an 'agony of birth' leading to an acceptance of the European way of life; and then from the mouth of a character introduced in the last ten minutes of the play. Daba, a victim of the famine, reveals a deathbed vision to his wife:

> Ah! This is the host of those who perished in the Great Famine. Do you see these people, surrounding, thanking and laughing with Nonqause. They tell her that hunger and destitution drove them

into the paths of life, led them to the missionary and his divine message: put them into the hands of God. So there is triumph in death: there is finding in death; there is beauty in death. Nonqause laughs as she tells them that she was really in earnest but was ignorant. They laugh and sing. They call her their Liberator from Superstition and from the rule of Ignorance. These people are dressed, not in karosses and blankets as we are, but in Light . . .[18]

One must draw the sad conclusion that Dhlomo, with the mission-presses and mission-controlled schools as the only outlet, succumbed to the temptation of expediency and turned the theme of African continuity of life, with its promise of hope for the future, into one of triumph for Christianity and Western culture. The betrayal looms so large in the eyes of black critics that the rest of Dhlomo's work is ignored. Forgotten, for instance, are the lines in *Valley of a Thousand Hills* quoted earlier, in which he sees a vision of the ancestors arisen, the black man enthroned and the foreign yoke thrown off, in fact the real prophesy of Nonqause come true.

In *Dingana* there is no pandering to a mission-orientated public. Here he attempts to carry out the rules he laid down in his essays. The play is introduced by a narrator. The actors then proceed to illustrate what he tells, and Dhlomo thus tries to recreate the atmosphere of a tribal drama.

Among the unpublished manuscripts are a few more historical plays, *Cetewayo*, *Moshesh*, *Ntsikana*, as well as a number of modern plays, in which the dialogue is often almost embarrassingly stilted.

In spite of all evidence throughout most of these plays to the contrary, Dhlomo is essentially a poet, and often he discards all attempt at drama for a lyrical passage. In *Dingana* the servant of Shaka is asked to tell about his master and he says:

Shaka the man who set the world on fire! It is right that I should spend my last moments speaking in his praise. O countryside, o hills, o cattle paths and winding streams—how much he loved these things, Shaka, King of Man, the Black One. In the listening hours of night we sought the path, he and I, to the inner mystery of life, the soul of watching mountains and the pregnant darkness. For beauty of bird or woman or evening strangely stabbed him, and in all his wildest acts I believe he sought the blood of beauty, and the heart of it.[19]

Such passages are partly explained by the same character: 'In Zululand we run to eloquence; we are all orators and bards', and partly by the fact that once again Dhlomo is demonstrating a theory, that the praise poem, which was often included in tribal drama, forms the basis of the modern monologue. *In The Girl Who Killed To Save* there is also a simple and effective praise song by the Bard, announcing the arrival of the Chief.

The only other play published during this period was an interesting collector's piece entitled *Shaka* by one S. Goro-X.[20] Unfortunately its origin and the identity of its author seem to be lost. It is presumed that Goro-X is a black man by the English usage and by the fact that he portrays Shaka as a tragic hero. Unlike Dhlomo's historical characters, however, there is little that is African about Goro-X's Shaka. In fact the author more or less adapts Macbeth to the story.

A number of black drama groups have existed since the nineteen-thirties, but they did not often have an opportunity to perform works by black dramatists. A Natal medical students' group, as we have seen, performed a Dhlomo play and also an authorised adaptation of Peter Abrahams' *Mine Boy*. A drama group at Adams College, before the dissolution of the school, was very active, and there were Church and school groups in the Rand townships as well as in other centres.

In Queenstown, Sunny Ray Matshikiza, nephew of Todd Matshikiza, wrote and produced a musical play entitled *Scintilla* which dealt with the Matshikiza clan. It was presented in Queenstown as well as in East London. He attempted to combine tribal and modern themes in the text as well as in the music. In the music he uses African folk tunes as well as Beethoven themes, the latter being in connection with a Beethoven festival at the time of composition.

In the nineteen-fifties organisations like the Transvaal Association of Girls Clubs and Youth Clubs tried to encourage indigenous drama, but it was something foisted on the players from outside. This, too, was the criticism of drama-groups, workshops and theatre-schools which were now coming into existence in several centres. Admirable as was the leadership of men and women like Barney Simon, Ian Bernhardt, Bess Finney, Des and Dawn Lindberg and Rob McLaren (who called himself 'Mshengu'), the fact that white sponsorship was deemed necessary was resented. Also, there were few suitable plays. Those of Wole Soyinka's were popular, and in fact later one group, in Diepkloof, called itself 'Soyikwa' after the Nigerian playwright. Plays by white South Africans with an African theme were produced, as well as Shakespeare, Greek classical drama, Camus and Brecht.

In 1959 one such group, Union Artists of Southern Africa, produced the musical *King Kong*, with Miriam Makeba, the score for which was written by Todd Matshikiza. It took South Africa, and later London, by storm. Sipho Sepamla, writing about the drama of the time in *S'ketsh*, a theatre journal he edited, says that the success of King Kong gave 'us a sense of achievement, a sense of pride and the will to work for the bright lights that gave many of our brothers and sisters a taste of the larger work'. He continues:

> KK gave us back the material for later productions, e.g. the idea that we could satirize those aspects of our life which we didn't approve of; the use of gangsters and their molls; the gumboot-dance and the current dance routines; the shebeen queen and her exploits; the policeman and the S.A. ways. These were the ingredients KK revealed to us.[21]

And indeed these were the themes that were to be used in innumerable plays that followed, written and produced by blacks though often still with the cooperation of whites. When *King Kong* finished its run, the group staged *Back In Your Own Backyard*, written and produced by Ben 'Satch' Masinga, and *Manana the Jazz Prophet*, by Gibson Kente. These plays had long runs in the townships. Kente used the *King Kong* formula and others followed him. Also associated with Union Artists was Bob Leshoai, one time school headmaster who had resigned at the time of the Bantu Education Act. He was manager of Union Artists from 1960–1961, before leaving South Africa to travel widely and pursue his studies, with special reference to African Theatre.

The groups began to take theatre to schools, and encouraged students to form drama groups. A music and drama school was formed, and plays were improvised in workshops. There were now groups all over the Reef around Johannesburg, in Cape Town, Port Elizabeth, East London, Durban, Grahamstown, Alice and elsewhere. Phoenix Players, headed by Ian Bernhardt, also helped to launch the promising young dramatist Gibson Kente. One of the best known groups was Experimental Theatre Workshop 71 founded by Rob McLaren. Other successful groups were Ikhwezi Players, Sechaba, Cape Flats Theatre (with Adam Small as director) and Stable Theatre Workshop.

The plays which were put on by these groups for black audiences were in many ways a continuation of oral African drama. Some were in English, some in the vernacular and often a mixture of several languages was used. The main difference between African and Western drama, as H.I.E. Dhlomo already indicated, lies in the fact that the former integrates various art forms. It is always a mixture of music, drama, dance and mime, and there is no clear division between tragedy and comedy. There is always a degree of spontaneity, and as many ingredients as are necessary for a particular occasion may be fed into it. Real names are often used. The plays are put together in workshops and do not follow a rigid script. As a result, the scripts which are compiled afterwards, some published in magazines, anthologies, collections or as separate volumes, are often dull, whereas the play in performance was full of vitality.

During the nineteen-sixties and early seventies the groups spread. Performances took place all over the country in church, school and municipal halls and outdoors. 'We were going right out to places like Nylstroom, places where people had probably never seen drama before. And we would just ask people to vacate the grounds, football grounds, and start doing our thing,'[22] James Mthoba said in a discussion with Joe Rahube and Matsemela Manaka about experimental theatre.

Serpent Players was a black drama group in Port Elizabeth which began to experiment with improvisation under the directorship of Athol Fugard, a dramatist already well known for more conventional plays. Fugard felt the need to use the stage for a much more immediate and direct relationship with the audience than had been possible with the ready-made plays which the group had been performing. Fugard, under the influence of Grolowski, came to see the actor as not merely an interpretative artist. Out of the idea of releasing the creative potential of the actor grew the complex collaboration between Fugard and the two actors John Kani and Winston Ntshona in the two plays *Sizwe Bansi is Dead* and *The Island*. They were both first performed at the Space Theatre in Cape Town in 1972. In the introduction to the volume *Statements*, in which the two plays, plus a third, were published, Fugard says:

> . . . I would just like to make one point clear: we did not jettison the writer. It was never a question of coming together with the actors on a 'let's make a play' basis. The starting-point to our work was always at least an image, sometimes an already structured complex of images about which I, as a writer, was obsessional. In all three of these plays the writer provided us with a mandate in terms of which the actors then went on to work. In the case of *Sizwe Bansi* our starting point was my fascination with a studio photograph I had once seen of a man with a cigarette in one hand and a pipe in the other; *The Island* began with the notes and ideas I had accumulated over many years relating to Robben Island . . .
>
> The initial mandates from the writer were also not his final contribution. He kept pace with us as fast as we discovered and explored . . . sometimes as no more than a scribe, but at other times in a much more decisive way. The final dramatic structure of each play, for example, was his responsibility. Looking back on the three experiences now, it was as if instead of first putting words on paper in order to arrive eventually at the stage and a live performance, I was able to write *directly* into its space and silence via the actor.[23]

Here is John Kani's version of how 'Sizwe Bansi' was born:

Athol Fugard, Winston Ntshona and myself found an old photo

of an African man with a lit cigarette in one hand and a lit pipe in the other. This looked very funny, of course, but then we started musing about this man and why this picture was taken. He looked like a man from the country who had just bought some new city clothes. They didn't fit. On his face was an expression of absolute joy as if the most exciting thing in the world had just happened to him. We asked ourselves what would excite a Black man in South Africa to this extent, what dream had come true? Only one thing—he must have solved his pass problem enabling him to stay in the city. He was going to send the photo to his family at home to show them what a success he had been in the city.

That was the germ of the play. Then the three of us worked on some more ideas and formulated a general theme and a rough sequence of events. But we did not write anything down, except for the letter which Sizwe Bansi sends his wife. The rest is in my mind. I know what I want to say.[24]

To convey to the audience that what they are about to hear and see was devised for them here and now and would be relevant to their lives, Kani, as Styles, the photographer who takes the pictures of Sizwe Bansi, starts the action by reading the headlines of that day's newspaper and then comments on it.

The marriage between the experienced playwright who manipulated the timing, tone and shape of the play and the actors who interpreted, not from his script, but straight from the lives of black men, was a happy one. The scenes are forceful and often brilliant such as one near the beginning, for instance, in which Styles explains why he left his job with the Ford Motor company by acting out what happened at work. It is the day on which 'Henry Ford Junior Number two or whatever the hell he is'[25] is visiting the factories in South Africa. The factory and the men are spruce. Styles is to act as interpreter and this is the scene that ensues:

> (*Styles pulls out chair. Mr 'Baas' Bradley speaks on one side, Styles translates on the other.*)
> 'Tell the boys in your language, that this is a very big day in their lives.'
> 'Gentlemen, this old fool says this is a hell of a big day in our lives.'
> The men laughed.
> 'They are very happy to hear that, sir.'
> 'Tell the boys that Mr Henry Ford the Second, the owner of this place, is going to visit us. Tell them Mr Ford is the big Baas. He owns the plant and everything in it.'
> 'Gentlemen, old Bradley says this Ford is a big bastard. He owns everything in this building, which means you as well.'
> A voice came out of the crowd:

'Is he a bigger fool than Bradley?'

'They're asking, sir, is he bigger than you?'

'Certainly . . . (blustering) . . . certainly. He is a very big baas. He's a . . . (groping for words) . . . he's a Makulu Baas.'

I loved that one!

'Mr "Baas" Bradley says most certainly Mr Ford is bigger than him. In fact Mr Ford is the grandmother baas of them all . . . that's what he said to me.'

'Styles, tell the boys that when Mr Henry Ford comes into the plant I want them all to look happy. We will slow down the speed of the line so that they can sing and smile while they are working.'

'Gentlemen, he says that when the door opens and his grandmother walks in you must see to it that you are wearing a mask of smiles. Hide your true feelings, brothers. You must sing. The joyous songs of the days of old before we had fools like this one next to me to worry about.' (To Bradley) 'Yes, Sir!'

'Say to them Styles, that they must try to impress Mr Henry Ford that they are better than those monkeys in his own country, those niggers in Harlem who know nothing but strike, strike.'

Yo! I liked that one too.

'Gentlemen, he says we must remember, when Mr Ford walks in, that we are South African monkeys, not American monkeys. South African monkeys are much better trained . . .'[26]

Satire of this kind, gentler humour when Styles tells of his customers in the photographic studio, drama and tragedy, alternate as the two actors, by dialogue and mime, create their illusions for the audience and involve them in the play.

(A man *walks nervously into the studio. Dressed in an ill-fitting new double-breasted suit. He is carrying a plastic bag with a hat in it. His manner is hesitant and shy. Styles takes one look at him and breaks into an enormous smile.*)[27]

This is our first introduction to Ntshona as Sizwe Bansi. Styles in an aside to the audience says 'A Dream!' The audience knows what he means. Styles has already explained how he creates a dream for his customers:

This is a strong-room of dreams. The dreamer? My people. The simple people, who you never find mentioned in the history books, who never get statues erected to them, or monuments commemorating their great deeds. People who would be forgotten, and their dreams with them, if it wasn't for Styles. That's what I do, friends. Put down, in any way, on paper the dreams and hopes of my people so that even their children's children will remember a man . . . 'This was our Grandfather' . . . and say his name . . .[28]

The story concerns one Sizwe Bansi who has been endorsed out of Port Elizabeth and must return to his home near Kingwilliamstown where there is no work. He acquires a new identity when he takes up a dead man's passbook. At first he is hesitant but when he asks: 'How do I live as another man's ghost?' his friend Buntu (also played by Kani) replies: 'Wasn't Sizwe Bansi a ghost?'[29] and explains:

> When the white man looked at you at the Labour Bureau what did he see? A man with dignity or a bloody passbook with an N.I. number? Isn't that a ghost? When the white man sees you walk down the street and calls out, 'Hey, John! Come here'. . . to you, *Sizwe Bansi* . . . isn't that a ghost? Or when his little child calls you 'Boy' . . . you a man, circumcised with a wife and four children . . . isn't that a ghost? Stop fooling yourself. All I am saying is to be a real ghost, if that is what they want, what they've turned us into. Spook them into hell, man![30]

Sizwe Bansi agrees to the exchange, and we return to the photographic studio where 'Robert Zwelinzima' is having his picture taken.

The Island, which, like *Sizwe Bansi* is presented as 'devised by Athol Fugard, John Kani and Winston Ntshona', is a powerful political statement encapsulated in the play within a play, as the prisoners on Robben Island put on a performance of *Antigone*. Winston Ntshona, playing himself, 'Winston', takes the part of Antigone who defied the authorities to bury her dead. The reference to the people of Sharpeville and later Soweto, who did the same, is obvious. The following dialogue takes place between Winston and John, as Creon:

> John: Antigone, you have pleaded guilty. Is there anything you wish to say in mitigation? This is your last chance. Speak.
> Winston: Who made the law forbidding the burial of my brother?
> John: The State.
> Winston: Who is the State?
> John: As King I am its manifest symnbol.
> Winston: So you make the law.
> John: Yes, for the State.
> Winston: Are you God?
> John: Watch your words, little girl!
> Winston: You said it was my chance to speak.
> John: But not to ridicule.
> Winston: I've got no time to waste on that. Your sentence on my life hangs waiting on your lips.
> John: Then speak on.
> Winston: When Polynices died in battle, all that remained was the empty husk of his body. He could neither harm nor help any man again. What lay on the battlefield waiting for Hodoshe to turn rotten, belonged to God. You are only a man, Creon. Even as

there are laws made by men, so too there are others that come from God. He watched my soul for a transgression even as your spies hide in the bush at night to see who is transgressing your laws. Guilty against God I will not be for any man on this earth. Even without your law, Creon, and the threat of death to whoever defied it, I know I must die. Because of your law and my defiance, that fate is now very near. So much the better. Your threat is nothing to me, Creon. But if I had let my mother's son, a Son of the Land, lie there as food for the carrion fly, Hodoshe, my soul would never have known peace.[31]

The reference to Hodoshe, the carrion fly, again emphasises the relevance because it is the name of the warder in charge of the work party to which the two prisoners belong. The performance of *Antigone*, and of *The Island*, comes to an end with Winston's last words, for which he removes his wig, confronting the audience as Winston:

Gods of our Fathers! My land! My Home!
Time waits no longer. I go now to my living death,
because I honoured those things to which honour belongs.[32]

The play therefore ends with a mimed scene, as effective as the mimed beginning when for some ten minutes the two actors present *an image of back-breaking and grotesquely futile labour as each in turn fills a wheelbarrow and then, with great effort pushes it to where the other man is digging, and empties it. As a result the piles of sand never diminish. The labour is interminable. The only sounds are their grunts as they dig, the squeal of the wheel-barrows as they circle the cell, and the hum of Hodoshe, the green carrion fly.*[33]

In the final scene the stage directions read:

The two men take off their costumes and then strike their 'set'. They come together and, as in the beginning, their hands come together to suggest handcuffs, and their right and left legs to suggest ankle-chains. They start running . . . John mumbling a prayer, and Winston a rhythm for their three-legged run.
The siren wails.
Fade to blackout.[34]

As in *Sizwe Bansi*, it is the spontaneous fun and humour—as when Winston protests against donning of women's clothes for the part of Antigone—and anger and despair as when Winston, joyful at hearing about John's remission of sentence, is faced with the bare pain of his own life-sentence—which gives body to the play.

The success of the two plays in South Africa and later in Britain and the United States, always with Kani and Ntshona as the performers, was enormous. It took black audiences by storm, as

Sipho Sepamla told the readers of *S'ketsh* in an article about theatre in the cities.[35] He continued:

> We had been diluted by the many musicals around us and now we were being uplifted almost literally out of the gutter. We did not know until then that we could have theatre define our new self as this play *Sizwe Bansi* did. As those who saw the play will recall it told of the black man straight from the shoulder.[36]

Several plays followed in a similar mould with often a loose script, an existential theme and the thrashing out of life's problems between two characters against a stark background. Such a play was *Job Mava*, a workshop production by the Ikwezi Players, and *The Train* by Zakes Mofokeng and Corney Mabaso, the latter about a coloured man and a Sotho in a *Waiting-for-Godot* situation of united and divided pain as they wait for the train that does not come.

Uhlanga [the Reed] 'devised' by Mshengu and James Mthoba, is a play produced as a deliberate experiment in improvisation and teamwork by the Experimental Theatre Workshop 71 in 1975. With only one actor and a simple set, subtle lighting changes, tribal and modern music, taped voices and the use of poetry by Serote, the play runs through the entire gamut of black experience from the primeval to the modern township, and explores what is this gift that God has given man. The living reed, Uhlang, above the water, is a symbol of a culture which cannot be destroyed, however hard external forces try to eradicate it.

But to what audiences were these plays being addressed? John Kani, interviewed by *The Johannesburg Sunday Times*, felt that the meaning for theatre in South Africa was the breaking down of the 'total communication block': 'Whites must be made to see that we are all men, and theatre is one of the few means left to us in South Africa of getting this across'.[37] Similarly Bob Leshoai, in the introduction to an extract from his play *Lines Draw Monsters*[38] says that he is not 'preaching hatred and death, but I am saying to the White South African, listen to me tell you about the aspirations and frustrations of my father, mother, brother and sister'.[39] The lines of the title are those along which the regime expects people to develop, each along his or her own and the monster is what one of the characters turns into as a result, when at the end of the extract, in an outburst of hate, she says:

> . . . when I'm old enough, when the revolution comes, I'll pluck their eyes out! I'll tear their flesh with my teeth and nails! I'll maul them like an angry tigress![40]

In Cape Town, Fatima (Fats) Dike, interviewed by Stephen Gray for *Contrast* says that she is trying 'to bridge . . . the cultural gap for those who come to the theatre'.[41] Adam Small's play, 'The Orange

Earth', performed at the Baxter Theatre in 1978, is an indictment of
the regime and its moral and religious attitudes, but at the same time
Small is still hopeful for a humanity that transcends colour and race.
Neither the coloured man who joins the South African forces nor his
brother who works with the insurgents has the answer. For Small it
lies somewhere between, and Johnny Adams who plants a bomb in a
supermarket, shows the prison warder that they are essentially the
same people.

Opposed to these efforts of the black man to stretch out a hand to
a white audience was a growing black consciousness which distinguished between drama by blacks and black drama, the latter being
for blacks on themes of black awareness and liberation. Members of
groups saw no point in playing to white audiences, and white
sponsorship came to be resented more and more, culminating in
angry criticism of the popular play *Ipi Tombi* as having been written
and produced by whites for white audiences while exploiting a black
theme and black players.

The new movement was also not happy with the type of play being
produced for black audiences in which entertainment was the only
aim. These plays were following the formula of the early Kente plays
with their mixture of music, dance and drama, melodrama and farce,
and their stock situations and characters of the shebeen queens,
tsotsis, brutal but ridiculous policemen. The formula also spilled
over into radio plays, films and even closed circuit television beamed
at the 400,000 men in the mines.

It was only to be expected that a man of Gibson Kente's talents
should be one of the first to realise that the formula was beginning to
grow stale. Beginning with *How Long*, followed by *Too Late*, he
began to introduce relevant dialogue, songs with a message and a
theme of political awareness and black pride. Soyikwa Black Theatre
produced Matsemela Manaka's *Egoli* [The City of Gold—Johannes-
burg] of which its author, in a note in *Staffrider* accompanying
pictures of scenes from the play says:

Through our eyes we have seen the sufferings of our people. We
have seen them being moved from fertile lands to barren areas,
we have seen them starve in squatter camps. Through our eyes we
have seen the life of our people assume various shapes of
humiliation and suffering. Thus the continual struggle to create
'Egoli' was for us unavoidable . . . We felt committed to focus our
creative thoughts on the plight of the workers, more especially the
mine migrants . . . The group believes in positive art, theatre of
purpose, communal theatre, theatre of survival and liberation,
original and relevant indigenous African theatre and, of course,
creative theatre. We hope our theatre will not be mistaken for
mere public entertainment.[42]

Uhlanga expresses pride in Africa's culture. Fatima Dike shows in her first play, *The Sacrifice of Kreli*,[43] that her aim is less to reconcile the races than to proclaim pride in the black man's past. It was performed by the Sechaba Players in Cape Town and Johannesburg in 1976. She told Stephen Gray why she chose a part of history as her theme:

> Now, what made me write this play is that one day I realised there were eighteen million black people in this country who had no past, because whatever past we had as a nation was oral history, and it was wiped out by the history which the white people in South Africa had written against what we had to say. Here was part of my history, my past. From then onwards I felt that if I had a past and a present, I could also have a future.[44]

She chose the story of the fate of the Gcalekas after the Ninth Frontier War. Kreli the King led an army of 12,000 men against the British army. At the end of the war 500 men were left but still they refused to surrender and decided to go into exile in a natural fortress called The Hole. The play takes place seven years after the end of the war. The women and children are elsewhere and the men feel they cannot continue to live under such conditions. The ancestors are to be propitiated by a sacrifice. During the ceremony a white reporter arrives and Kreli interrupts the sacrifice to receive him, because otherwise 'They will think we are pagans'.[45] The sacrifice fails through his subservience to the possible opinion of an outsider. The men blame their diviner, Mlanjeni, and condemn him to death by being sewed up in the skin of a bull slaughtered that morning for the sacrifice, and then put out in the open for three days. Through the heat of the sun the skin shrinks and crushes him. Mlanjeni, however, lives long enough after the skin is opened to give a message to his people from the ancestors. 'They say there is a way.' Kreli sends his warriors to spread the message of hope and survival among his people:

> . . . go and tell our people that our sun is rising . . . go and tell our people to plough their burnt fields and build their fallen walls . . . go and tell our people we will work and grow.

'And now,' he says to the last one, 'my son, go and tell our people we will defend the honour of what we are'.[46] Dike first wrote the play in Xhosa and then translated it herself, keeping to the idiom for authenticity in dialogue.

In her second play, *The First South African*, written in 1977 and produced at the Space Theatre in Cape Town in that year, Dike turned to a modern theme. It is about a young man, Ruben Zwelinzima Jama, known as Rooi, whose mother was black and his father white. Dike says of the play that it is based on a true story. 'Through some fate of the genes he was born white physically, blonde hair and blue eyes. He grew up in Langa, spoke Xhosa fluently and was classified as coloured when he was old enough. Here was a man who looked like a white, who had the heart of a black, and was coloured. My question was: what is that man?'.[47] His friend Max, a man who lives by his wits, is asked by Rooi's stepfather to answer that question. He says:

> Well . . . I mean . . . I . . . I've never really thought of him as anything else but a person . . . well . . . in the beginning . . . I saw him as white . . . but when I got used to him . . . really I don't put any name on him now . . . well . . . I don't say he is white, and I don't say he is a Xhosa . . . he's just himself . . . but I do feel that he is a Xhosa especially when other people say that he is white.[48]

Dike makes use of improvisation in the play to some extent when Rooi is accepted into manhood, a most effectively dramatic scene. We see Rooi sitting still wrapped in a blanket. Only his light hair shows. Slowly he brings out his white arm to accept the symbolic gifts that the men have brought. The men are in their every-day clothes, one in a business suit, one in the uniform of a watchman, another of a garage attendant. Dike says it was fortunate that in Cape townships the circumcision ceremony was still performed and the men were able to improvise the accompanying dialogue. The play ends tragically. Dike shows that there is no room in South Africa for a man who does not carry a recognisable racial stamp. Rooi is eventually accepted by no-one and becomes insane.

In her last play to date, *Glass House*, Dike goes back to exploring the possibilities of bridging the gap between the races. Her theme is a doubly ironical one. Linda's father is killed by a rioting mob while trying to rescue Phumla, the daughter of his black employees. Phumla knows who are the people that killed him but will not speak. The man's will, in what his daughter calls a 'sick joke', leaves his house to the two girls who have grown up together. Under the group areas act it would only be possible for them both to live in it, as they wish to do, if Phumla pretends to be Linda's servant, but this both girls refuse to do. *The Glasshouse* is a microcosm of South African life in which two young people try to find a way of living together. Rambling, discursive, and far too long, this is the least successful of Dike's plays. Since it fails to grip the audience, it cannot make its point. It was performed in 1979 at the Space, where Dike was its resident playwright.

Not His Pride was produced by a group called The People and first performed at the University of the Witwatersrand in 1973. There followed performances in Soweto, Mamelodi and Pretoria, and in other English-speaking campuses. The author is Makwedini Julius Mtsaka, who studied speech and drama under the direction of Trinity College in London. The play is about a legal dilemma caused by the pernicious laws which prevent families without the right papers from living together. Meko's father had two women, Nogqwashu who is legally married to him but cannot get a permit to join him in the city, and Meko's mother who lives with him in the city. The question arises as to who will get compensation for a house which Meko and his stepmother have to vacate under the group areas act. The play is designed to work on two levels, as the author tells us, one in which the characters Meko, Nogqwashu and her brother-in-law Palamente are recognisable individuals, and one where Nogqwashu and Meko appear as 'Man' and 'Woman' and symbolise different forces at work in South African society. The house that has to be vacated is also a metaphor for the emptiness, lack of security, hope and peace of the black people's lives. The play is witty and satirical, with a zany brittle humour that involves the audience. Most of the humour is supplied by Palamente, an old scoundrel who pretends to save souls. His spirit is 'resting on something like a Sealy Posturepedic, happily waiting for the big Day' and when pressed by Meko to tell 'how many sheep have you brought home safe?', He replies: 'Son, do you think they'll accept my excuse if I say I had no transport?'.[49] The humour changes subtly in tone until the reverse side of laughter, its bitter side, explodes in Meko's account of 'the funniest incident of death in my life' that he has witnessed:

A friend of mine insisted that he carry his portable radio transistor while we were walking down the street to a gumba gumba session. I couldn't stop him. He wanted to listen to a 7.30 p.m. boxing commentary. The announcer was saying 'King Marshall was knocked out of the ring and literally flew, to land safely on the table of the judges', when a big stone from the darkness struck my friend here (hits the back of his neck). Vido lay sprawling on the ground. The radio continued to say that this was a dramatic end to the fight, and just then the advertisement came: 'Going -ng-ng. Gold Cross' . . . Laughter came to my lips but I didn't wait for it—I ran when I saw four guys come rushing towards me. I stopped somewhere to give myself a rest, then I started laughing. Then I went to report to the police station. When we got there at 12.10 a.m. in the police van, Vido was cold. Back at home I laughed again, and laughed and laughed until the tears ran down my cheeks. I know King Marshall, he is quite a character. I know the radio announcer, he is very naughty. I thought of Vido the great boxing fan and this machine which could not stop talking even when the owner was in trouble.[50]

Khayalethu Mqayisa's play *Confused Mhlaba* is about the return of a prisoner from Robben Island, who finds that the spirit of militancy which put him on the island no longer exists. Written in 1973, it was performed at various places in Johannesburg and Soweto in 1974. *Dark Voices Ring* by Zanemvula (Zakes) Mda deals with a former 'boss-boy' on a potato farm who is beaten up by three farm labourers so badly that he is paralysed and does not speak. His hut and baby girl have been burnt. The play consists of dialogue between the old man's wife and the man who would eventually have become the daughter's husband. The young man tells the woman that he can no longer fetch their pension because he is going to join the war of freedom. The old man breaks out of his paralytic state for the first time to smile when he hears of this.

The Shah Theatre Academy produces plays of relevance for a black, largely Indian, audience, like *Lahnee's Pleasure* directed by Ronnie Govender. *Working Class Hero*, by Kessie Govender, was performed in Durban by the Stable Theatre Workshop in 1978. *Lindiwe*, by Shimane Solly Mekgoe, who was a member of the Workshop 71 group but formed his own group, Super Afro Players, to produce *Lindiwe*, is about the clash between tribal and modern. It rejects a blind acceptance of both old and new without testing their moral value.

These are some typical examples of the type of play being produced, with strong traditional elements and treating social issues searchingly and dramatically. One of the most militant is *Give us This Day* by the Rev. Mzwandile Maqina, about the assassination of black consciousness student leader Abraham Tiro, who died in Botswana when a letter-bomb exploded in his hands. It was performed in Port Elizabeth and Johannesburg in 1975.

It was not long before the government took cognisance of plays with political themes and, as with written works, bannings and harassment followed. The directors and cast members of a play called *Shanti* were arrested and the equipment confiscated. Both Maquina's and Mqayisa's plays were banned. Mqayisa was himself banned for five years in 1976, and he and Maqina were detained in 1978. Kente's play *Too Late* was banned, but the author challenged the banning and it was later released with cuts. Apart from the usual bannings the authorities, in the shape of Administration control boards to whom scripts had to be submitted, could also prevent plays from being performed by refusing permits for production in public halls. This left only church halls or clubs, and University venues in white areas.

Not many of these plays have been published. *S'ketsh* published reviews of plays, full scripts and extracts from them, including Kente's *Too Late*[51] and Leshoai's *The Rendezvous*[52] as well as many others mentioned above. Another periodical, *Speak*, which catered for all the arts but was especially strong on theatre, published reviews of black plays among others, and *Snarl* had among its aims to 'disturb the prevailing torpor reigning over the relationship between artist and audience by providing honest, informed criticism'.[53] *Staffrider* published the script of *Job Mava*[54] in its December 1980/January

1981 issue, and its publishers, Ravan Press, brought out a series of Playscripts in 1978, which included *Lindiwe* (1978), *Not his Pride* (1978) and *The First South African* (1979). Earlier Ravan had published *Confused Mhlaba* (1974). *Statements*, containing *Sizwe Bansi is Dead* and *The Island*, together with Fugard's *Arrest Under the Immorality Act* was published by the Oxford University Press in 1974. An anthology of 'New South African Drama', *Theatre One*, edited by Stephen Gray and published by Ad. Donker in 1978, included Fatima Dike's *The Sacrifice of Kreli*. *Contemporary South African Plays*, edited and introduced by Ernest Pereira and published by Ravan Press in 1977, included the first act of Benjamin (Bob) Leshoai's *Lines Draw Monsters*.

A collection of Leshoai's plays was published in Kenya in 1972 under the title *Wrath of the Ancestors and other Plays*.[55] *Lines Draw Monsters*, as we have seen was written to make the white man listen. Leshoai now asks his audience to have a good laugh at themselves, 'at people who speak like ourselves and not imitators of foreign culture'. (Prologue). Leshoai is a skilful dramatist and can turn incident into effective satire. In *The Rendezvous* he makes use of a humorous situation which recurs in black South African literature, the camouflage of a funeral with a coffin to transport liquor to a shebeen. The 'mourners' in the play are a collection of rogues from all walks of life. The other two plays, *Revolution* and *Wrath of the Ancestors* are more serious and somewhat oversimplified in their themes. The character around which the short play *Revolution* is built is a cleaner, Sebetsa, who exposes the hypocrisy of a white priest who will not allow him to pray in a white church. Sebetsa makes his own revolution by killing the priest in a frenzy. *Wrath of the Ancestors* deals with the revolt of the simple people against oppression, in this case the foisting on them of a chief who is the white man's choice.

Leshoai's plays were performed mainly abroad before his recent return to South Africa. Richard Rive's plays, too, were mainly performed in Britain and published in collections of African plays in the Heinemann African Writers Series, *Resurrection*[56] in *Short African Plays* edited by Cosmo Pieterse in 1972, and *Make Like Slaves*[57] in *African Theatre*, as well as in *Eight Prize Winning Plays for Radio* edited by Gwyneth Henderson in 1973. The latter won the BBC African Theatre Competition Prize in 1971, chosen from 600 entries, and was broadcast in the BBC African Theatre service in 1972. Wole Soyinka, Martin Esslin and Lewis Nkosi were the judges.

Make Like Slaves is a dialogue between two South Africans, a coloured man, 'He', whom 'She', a white woman, asks for advice about her production of a play with an all-black cast. Soyinka characteristically appreciated Rive's grasp of the relationship not only between the two characters of opposing colour, but 'between each character and the social reality each thought He or She understood'.[58] He and She are not puppets, dressed figuratively in black and white to represent good and bad. She is a do-gooder, it is true, but she is genuinely struggling to understand. She is producing a play about the Middle Passage, but is baffled by the lack of cooperation of her actors. She appeals for help to a young man of education whom she has met aboard a ship. As a person of mixed blood he should, she feels, be able to bridge the gap of communication between black and white.

Her efforts to be tactful in her approach to him are pathetic and constitute the satire of the play. The harder she tries, the less she succeeds. He accepts her efforts as genuine, and tries to be patient with her blunders, but the harder he tries, the more impossible it becomes. When he goes too far in his cutting responses, he draws back. He, like the audience, realises immediately why the black cast balk at the play. In his short story, 'Middle Passage' from which Rive adapted the play, the punch-line 'make like slaves' comes at the end. In the play, the title and an earlier explanation tell us that the white producer is quite unaware of the irony for South Africa of the plot of the play she is producing.

The first act, she tells the young man is set in Africa. 'The throb of the primitive. Dancing and rhythm. Palm-fronds and jungle drums. Africa.'[59] The only comment he allows himself on this white view of blackest Africa, as portrayed by a company of black city dwellers—clerks, teachers, factory workers, no doubt—is 'continue'. We picture him stony-faced as she describes Act II, the Middle Passage, which she has based on Robert Hayden's epic. But when she describes the finale: 'They make like slaves', an exclamation of shocked surprise escapes him: 'What?'. 'Oh,' she explains, 'It's a bit of drama school slang I picked up when I was studying in London'.[60]

There are only the two characters in the play. We do not hear the players speak. We feel them strongly, however, at the end, after the producer has given her injunction: 'I want you to . . . make like slaves'.[61] If there is tragi-comedy in the characterisation of the woman, there is deeper pathos in that of the man. Just as she is totally ignorant of the feelings of black people about their situation, she misunderstands the position of the man of mixed blood. Far from serving as a go-between, he lives in a no man's land, and his only defence is to remain uninvolved. He surprises the woman with his announcement that he has hardly ever been inside an African location and has no African friends. He attempts to explain this but admits his confusion: 'I dare not have too intimate friendships (with blacks) until I am absolutely convinced, of what I do not know'.[62] As for white friendships: 'I can't say. There are many factors'.[63] Her unintentionally offensive remarks find their mark more easily because of his own confusion about his identity. This is brought out in just a few words of dialogue:

SHE: . . . I'm sorry about dragging you away. I am sure you were
  working on something big. One day you'll prove a
  credit . . .
HE: To what?
SHE: To . . . Oh, I know it sounds dripping wet and sugary—
  sometimes I feel ashamed of being white, of sounding
  patronizing. But you will prove a credit to . . .
HE: To my people?
SHE: There now, you said it, not me. Yes, if you put it that way,
  to your people.
HE: To the coloured people. To two million brown South
  Africans. And maybe to a few million blacks thrown in.
SHE: That's not what I mean.
HE: That's what I mean.[64]

The young man tries to avoid contact with the woman by
conveniently forgetting their appointment. She cannot reach him
because the telephone is off the hook. But when forced to
communicate with her, he takes refuge in confusion. Why had he
agreed to come with her and try to help her? He says that he does not
really know. 'I will probably be even more confused after than what I
was before.'[65] Are the black actors taking similar refuge from
confrontation by turning up late, or not at all, 'Or,' as He says, 'if
they had phones . . . they'd take them off the hook'.[66] She hopes that
He and She will have an interesting discussion after the rehearsal. 'I
wonder whether it will be necessary,' he replies.

Both Esslin and the third judge Lewis Nkosi, commented on the
rich texture and vivacious dialogue of which the above extracts give
some idea.

In South Africa *Make Like Slaves* was first performed in St
George's Cathedral in Cape Town in 1975 and in 1976 it was a star
item in the Shakespeare festival in Grahamstown, organised by the
1820 Settlers National Monument Foundation.

Rive's earlier play, *Resurrection*,[67] was written while he was a
student at Columbia University and it was produced there and later
off Broadway. It is less accomplished than *Make Like Slaves* in that
the dialogue is more stilted, the dramatic possibilities of the situation
are not sufficiently explored and the characters are too simple in their
single-mindedness. In the play, as in the short story version, which
has already been discussed, the lighter members of Mavis's family
disown Mavis and her mother—with the mother's connivance—
because they cannot pass as white. The play takes place after Ma's
death. Prayers are being led by a white priest whom the play-white
children have called in although Ma had asked to be buried by her
black mission priest. Most of the action takes place in Mavis's mind as
she speaks to a vision of the mother who materialises for the

audience. The somewhat too obvious irony of the situation is brought out at the end, when the priest intones a prayer of blessing for the children for heeding the Lord's commandment of honouring their father and their mother. At this point Mavis jumps to her feet and shouts hysterically, in the voice she believes to be her mother's

> Misbelievers! Liars!
> You killed me. You murdered me!
> Hypocrites!
> Don't you know your God![68]

Later Rive attended a course in drama writing and won a play-writing competition at Oxford University in 1973 for a dramatisation of Olive Schreiner's *Story of an African Farm*. This was the year in which Rive received his doctorate at Oxford University for a dissertation on Olive Schreiner.

The BBC African Service was a useful outlet for writers in exile. The British Broadcasting Corporation had been encouraging African theatre since 1962 when it introduced drama on its African Service in order to provide an outlet for black writers and actors in England. As well as Rive, Alfred Hutchinson, Bloke Modisane, Arthur Maimane, Cosmo Pieterse and others had plays broadcast.

Alfred Hutchinson introduces his play *Fusane's Trial* in *The New African* as follows: 'Today I like to think that my education, (he was a Fort Hare graduate) far from removing me from my people, has made me more aware of their permanent valuableness. For as the Swazi saying goes "A person is only a person because of other people".' The play, about a girl who kills the man to whom she is betrothed by tribal custom, was produced on the African service of the BBC in London on 25 November 1964.

Another play by Hutchinson, a full-length drama entitled *The Rain-Killers* was published in an American collection 1968, *Plays from Black Africa*.[69] It takes place in a country area where the women and children are starving but the women are not permitted to join the men in the cities to look for work. The people are waiting for rain, some putting their faith in a Christian God, some in the witchdoctor. As one of the women, Ma-Nkosi, says:

> There's Mfundisi praying for rain. And now Maziya may be sacrificing for rain. Which one is God to listen to? These are the rain-killers. All of us.[70]

In the end the Mfundisi, who has sinned, hangs himself, and the witchdoctor, after a ritual killing, goes mad. The rain comes down. Although the play has considerable interest, it is too stretched out and repetitive.

Fusane's Trial as well as Arthur Maimane's *The Opportunity*, was published in Cosmo Pieterse's anthology *Ten One Act Plays* in

1968. Maimane, who is a current affairs commentator for the BBC, has also had several other plays broadcast. *The Opportunity* concerns an African politician who has been asked to divorce his uneducated wife so that he can become a credit to his country as ambassador to the United Nations Organisation. The pace of both these plays is slow, the plots contrived, the characters wooden, and one wonders why they were included among much better fare.

The plot of Lewis Nkosi's *Rhythm of Violence*[71] also fails to convince, and it is difficult to conceive how a man of his critical faculties and sophistication could have produced a work of this nature. Even if he had an eye on the box-office, as Anne Tibble in an introduction to her anthology[72] suggests—with apologies for criticising a work 'on so agonising a subject'—the play could only have been carried by the popularity of the subject matter.

The play concerns an attempt by a racially mixed group of students to blow up Cape Town City Hall. A newcomer to the group is an Afrikaner girl, Sarie Marais, who is attracted to the African leader's young brother, Tula. When Tula finds that Sarie's father is attending a National Party meeting in the City Hall in order to hand in his resignation, he rushes in to save him, getting killed in the attempt when the bomb explodes.

Neither the events recorded, the interaction of the stereotyped characters, nor the artificial theatrical devices, succeed in creating any dramatic tension. The symbolism of 'curiously nervous' jazz rhythms, which later become wild and blend with the detonation of the bomb, and finally, after we have heard 'a few bars of soft fragile melody' as Sarie and Tula fall in love, mount 'into a harsh violent, discordant melody' as Sarie is arrested, is naively transparent. The dialogue drags and at times becomes ludicrous, as when one of the characters says: 'I feel now a sombre darkness upon life itself'.[73] Nkosi becomes guilty of the transgression of which he once accused other black fiction writers: using 'the ready-made plots of violence, chicanery and racial love tragedies as representing universal truth when, in fact, actual insight into human tragedy may lie beneath this social and political turbulence'.[74] There is neither insight into individual human tragedy in the play, nor a social vision in the African sense.

Rhythm of Violence was produced in London in 1963, at the Ife Festival of Arts in Nigeria, 1971, at the Commonwealth Institute in London and on tour including Brighton and Cardiff in 1975, and off Broadway in New York in 1979. Other plays by Nkosi were *Malcolm*, a television script commissioned by Swedish Television in 1967 and performed in London in 1972 and 1973, *Come Back Africa*, a screenplay for film produced by Lionel Rogosin in 1959, *The Red Rooster* commissioned by a Dutch organisation in 1976, and *We Can't All Be Martin Luther King* broadcast by the BBC in 1971.

Alex La Guma's radio play *The Man in the Tree*[75] was published in a special South African edition of *The Literary Review* in 1971. It concerns a coloured man who hangs himself when he is removed from his home under the group areas act to make room for whites, and comes back each year to haunt the new owners. As in so many of these radio plays, the dialogue is stilted and the plot so obvious that it lacks all tension.

Cosmo Pieterse's own play, *Ballad of the Cells*,[76] was published in his collection *Short African Plays*. It is a dramatised poem which he describes as 'A physiology in 27 pulses and a choral elegy'.[77] The main setting is a police interrogation cell in which Looksmart Ngudle is being questioned. It is based on a true incident in the early nineteen-sixties when a prisoner's death was attributed to heart-failure. Between questioning Looksmart recalls various scenes from his life. He is being held under a law which allows suspects with adverse political knowledge to be held for ninety days without trial. The various 'pulses', or retrospect scenes, are enacted in different measures. There are satiric jingles, for instance, such as one in which Looksmart replies to the interrogator's 'We give you votes, government, land' by saying:

> Yes, Bah! bah! Black man
> Will you get a vote?
> In 'Yes Baas'—Baahntunstan
> of Sheep in sheep's coat
> Chief-Caesar-Headman
> Foot-man-fool
> Of the brand-new ethnican-
> Niballistic school!

A play on words implies association of ideas in the thought-destroying atmosphere of the prison:

> Forms, farms, times! fames
> Notions, names, nations
> (Amandhla! Isawandhla
> Assagai's impi
> Shield, axe and kierie
> Drums of our feet
> And the arms of our mind.[79]

Looksmart repeats the names of his heroes in politics as well as those of the enemy and its stooges in order to retain his sanity, as the 'voices' bombard him with questions and ask him to make a statement. There is the same manipulation of words in rhythm, rhyme and sound to explore meaning as there is in Pieterse's poetry, used here sometimes with success, but more often with the effect of obscuring meaning or sounding contrived.

*

Since the BBC African Service is not beamed to South Africa, and the dramatists we have discussed are in any case either banned or dead, drama in exile is totally divorced from the South African scene today. Plays are still being produced in London and Botswana by exiles for exiles but they are not published and therefore not available for this study.

Critical Writing

APART FROM H.I.E. Dhlomo's comments on drama and poetry which have already been discussed there was little writing in South Africa about black literature in English before the late nineteen-fifties. The leading black scholars of African literature, such as D.D.T. Jabavu, S.M. Guma, Daniel P. Kunene, C.L.S. Nyembezi and B.W. Vilakazi had produced studies written in English of African literature, but their concern was only with writers in the vernacular and is therefore not part of this study. Yet Vilakazi was explicit in his ideas of what the African writer in any language—in fact the writer anywhere—should do. He felt that Dhlomo's 'Valley of a Thousand Hills' did not rise to the heights which poetry should reach, because it failed to pass from the region of the sensuous to the higher realm of interpretation of life. Dhlomo's shorter poems, Vilakazi said prophetically, might yet win greater fame, 'for through them penetrates the light of a spiritual lament, a pleading fraught with constancy and hope. His imagination in these poems becomes an instrument of intuitive insight and therefore the most authentic guide to ultimate truth'.[1] Mazisi Kunene's Master of Arts thesis, used later for the introduction to his *Zulu Poems*, is relevant to the understanding of his poetry and has been discussed in that context.

A.C. Jordan's articles on the history of Xhosa literature in South Africa in *Africa South*, 'Towards an African Literature',[2] are considered one of his greatest contributions to the writing of his country. His simple love for the literature he describes shines through the pages of a sophisticated crusading journal like *Africa South*. The dramatically told folk tales with which he intersperses the history 'have survived through the ages' he says, 'because of their artistic value, each one of them symbolising something of permanent meaning to Man as Man'. After his death, the tales which Jordan had gathered were collected and published as *Tales from Southern Africa*.[3] In these tales he does for prose what Mazisi Kunene did for poetry. He stresses their communal aspect and their didactic purpose in conveying social values. In an analysis of each story, he demonstrates its symbolic significance. The meaning of custom, and the senseless-ness of adhering to customs without meaning, are some of his favourite themes.

Earlier, Bob Leshoai had published a collection of tales as *Masilo's Adventures and other Stories*.[4] He, too, stresses their moral value, and points out that such stories constituted the education of children by their elders in tribal life. Both Jordan and Leshoai prove, however, that another function of the tales was to entertain, with plenty of interest, suspense, drama and humour as well as the more serious content.

When the black writers of the nineteen-fifties began to comment in reviews and critical essays on black writing, they were mainly concerned with the response of the writer to his environment. This does not mean that their yardstick was the writer's sociological or political achievement, rather that they attempted to evaluate literary content according to certain tenets which they saw as fundamental truths. For Ezekiel Mphahlele, who claimed that he was a 'simple practising writer' and not 'a non-African Africanist who is looking for categories and theories for a doctorate thesis', it was the artist's search for his collective personality, his 'African Image' which was important. This process Mphahlele saw as a search for the truth about the writer himself. If a writer's tone was healthy, he said, he was bound to express the African in him. Unlike Vilakazi, he described Dhlomo's 'Valley of a Thousand Hills' as a soul-searching journey, and found Dhlomo a romanticist who could 'pray for a world without pain, where life is not sacrifice—in a scheme of things where life is always pain'.[5] This romanticism, Mphahlele said, pervaded African character:

> To this, and to the African's fatalism which enables him to face and carry the tragic moment, add Christianity, and you get a personality that is at once submissive and violent, accommodating and uncompromising, full of laughter and tears—no, we can't define it: we can only search for the African personality.[6]

Africa he saw as 'an ambivalent continent searching for equilibrium' to form a synthesis of Europe and Africa. In spite of this emphasis on a search for the African personality, Mphahlele saw no need for a writer to turn this into a slogan and felt that if he thought of it as a 'battle cry it's bound to throw him into a stance, an attitude, and his art will suffer'. This was the difference between Mphahlele and the exponents of the movement of going back to one's African roots, which began in the West Indies and French-speaking Africa. The Negritude writer, Mphahlele felt, made a cult of wanting to recapture the past. It interfered with the real business of being a black man and a black writer today, he said. Only the educated African from abroad could afford to walk about 'with his mouth open, startled by the beauty of African women, by the black man's "heightened sensitivity"'. 'It is all so embarrassing', Mphahlele comments.[7] In South Africa, the black man was occupied with a very real fight against government efforts to legislate him back to his tribe, to force him to accept the fabricated concept of 'Bantu Culture'. 'We daren't look back', he concludes.

Mphahlele expresses these ideas in the original version of *African Image*[8] published in 1962, which incorporated his Master of Arts thesis, written in 1956, 'The Non-European character in South African Fiction',[9] and some previously published papers. A doctorate was awarded to him in the United States for his novel *The Wanderers*.

In a revised edition of *African Image*,[10] Mphahlele heads the chapter on the theme of the black man reaching back to his roots 'Negritude revisited'. He is no more enchanted with the formal concept of Negritude than he was during his first encounter. Negritude, he says, can have meaning only if one regards it as a social force, never static, a tension, a continuing movement that asserts the value of African culture and its institutions of learning. If that is its function, he says 'let it shake its rhetoric-saturated, lyric-larded backside and get to work. If it does not, let it shut up'.[11]

Here Mphahlele shows his disillusionment, not with Negritude, to which he never subscribed, but with the achievements under its banner for which he had had some hope. He feels that most of the originators did not really understand what they were up against: that the white world might be quite willing to concede the black man his culture and would even ask to be invited to his arts festivals, but would continue to manipulate him politically and economically. Negritude as an artistic programme, he insists, has proved itself unworkable for modern Africa. He remains the realist who entreats the exponents of Negritude to 'stop telling the masses how beautiful they are while they are starving'.[12]

There was a definite shift in the readership at which he aimed between the old and the new version of *African Image*. In the second edition he seemed to be addressing the black Americans among whom he was living rather than the white man to whom he previously felt he had to explain himself. He had little time for the Afro-American who 'almost literally grovels on his stomach so as to rub Africa's earth into his skin as a symbol of edification'.[13] He gives a brief survey of survivals of Africa in black American culture such as spontaneous dancing, folk tales based on African legends and certain rituals in religious worship, and then investigates the role of Africa in black America. He tests writers like Claude McKay, Countee Cullen, Arna Bontemps and others, against a yardstick of genuine emotional attachment to the continent. He comes to the conclusion that black Americans must still get to know Africa as it is, and not as a mere grand idea, if black people of the world are to have something to give one another. At the moment, he says, 'we are playing games'.[14]

Mphahlele's rejection of the Negritude stance does not mean that he rejected his African roots. His repudiation of the Christian faith, and his feeling of affinity for African religion, have become firmly established. His ancestors, he feels, can help the African 'snap out of the trance into which we were thrown by Western education'. The significance is not that the black man can go back to ancestor worship, but that the ancestors have historical and spiritual relevance, and thus help to free him mentally. *'Why now should we be fed on the history, the folklore, the allegory and poetry of the Hebrews (however beautiful) who had no functional connection with Africa? Why be tied to the shackles of Christ's and Muhammed's ideas when we have our own ancient liberal wisdom?'*[15] he asks, with the emphasis of italics.

In *Voices in the Whirlwind and Other Essays*,[16] Mphahlele turns to the question of commitment to a political purpose. He finds Jean-Paul Sartre's insistence on social and political programmes in literature too rigid. While he feels that every writer 'is committed to something beyond his art', to a statement of value not purely aesthetic, to a 'criticism of life',[17] he finds this functional meaning a dangerous tendency, since it can limit the author's vision. 'Can Sartre's kind of discipline and aims for literature become inviolable rules for a craft that is always breaking rules, breaking down myths?'[18] he asks in an essay entitled 'Writers and Commitment'. Mphahlele then demonstrates various forms of commitment in African literature, without as he says, attempting 'to be categorical about whether propaganda should or should not enter a work of art'.[19] He quotes Tolstoi's remarks in *Literature and Revolution* about the necessity of the Russian proletariat to express in art the new spiritual point of view. Then he says he would like to think that Negritude propaganda has prompted, similarly, the need to search for a new spiritual point of view; not a black pride that drugs the black man into a condition of stupor or inertia, but one which continues to see the African hero in an integrated communal world, as opposed to the Western literary hero of a Kafka or a Camus, stricken with *angst* and dashing about like a trapped fly.

He makes it clear, in *African Image*, that he does not consider it the function of creative writers to foist their ideas on society. 'They are but mere craftsmen, mere recorders, mere observers, who must take the cue from what the mass of society do, think, say and hear and dream',[20] he says. Yet he feels that it is the creative writer's duty to involve himself in the black man's present and future. The white man must understand the black man and the black man must understand himself. Consequently, it is necessary for the leading black writers to become better known, especially among black readers. Mphahlele was one of the first to work towards the acceptance of black writers in university and school syllabuses in black countries. He also encouraged conferences and workshops.

His research into the early history of black South African writing, forming the basis of his academic thesis, is thorough and original. He traces black South African literature from early religious writing published by the mission presses, to the present day. He discusses most of the leading works, often skilfully distilling the essence of their meaning. Mhudi, main character in a novel of that name (by Sol Plaatje), for example, comes alive for him, in spite of the author's historic detachment and use of stilted dialogue, because 'his love for human beings is profound'.[21] He realizes that the kind of protest Peter Abrahams expresses in the novel *Path of Thunder*, where the black hero turns his wrath on a society that forbids his marriage with a white girl, limits the emotional and intellectual range of characterisation.

Although Mphahlele was closely involved with other writers of the nineteen-fifties who were his colleagues on *Drum* magazine, their writing often did not appeal to him. Can Themba, the most talented of the *Drum* story contributors, he felt, cynically turned his back on life. Todd Matshikiza, sending up, as we would say today, American fiction with impish humour, he finds slickly American. He seems to miss the irony in their fiction, by concentrating on the unlikely plots. In the new version of *African Image* he adds an appreciation of Themba, but it is an appreciation of the man rather than his writing.

Summing-up the state of black South African fiction at the time of writing *The African Image*, Mphahlele agrees with his compatriot, Lewis Nkosi, that the gargantuan reality that is South Africa makes it unexploitable as literary material. He wonders, however, whether the reality is equally inaccessible through the imagination of the poet. Poetry, after all, he says, 'rushes soonest into situations that call for urgent self-expression and interpretation'.[22] When considering the individual poets at the time of writing, he finds Oswald Mtshali possibly, 'too young to want to take a cold look at power and evaluate the pain'.[23] He concedes that Mtshali is trying to understand life in his own ghetto in the conflict of social chaos, but finds his poetry too full of rhetoric and 'custom-made images'.[24] He finds that Mtshali 'sneaks in' his good and telling lines. At the time of his writing, Mtshali's *Sounds of a Cowhide Drum* had just been published in South Africa. Mphahlele finds himself more in sympathy with the poets in exile such as Arthur Nortje and Dennis Brutus.

Voices in the Whirlwind and Other Essays derives its title from a poem by Gwendolyn Brooks, who, Mphahlele feels, has a lot to teach the black man. The whirlwind, Brooks says, 'is our commonwealth', and Mphahlele explains that strife is there and must be acknowledged. Nevertheless, he explains, 'people must live', and thus, as Brooks says 'Live and go out/Define and/medicate the whirlwind', and 'conduct your blooming in the noise and whip of the whirlwind'.[25]

'Voices in the Whirlwind' is the title of the first essay in this collection and was specially written for the collection. All but one of the other essays were previously published in periodicals, and they continue the themes raised in *African Image*. In the first essay, Mphahlele explains his concept of poetry as a balance of personal experience and communal voice, and at the same time an ironic tension between what a poem has to express and the urge to communicate.

In the second essay he asks specifically (in the title) 'African Literature: What Tradition?' and proceeds to answer the question. The third essay examines African culture in more detail, while the fourth looks at Pan-Africanism from the viewpoint of colour rather than culture. The fifth essay turns to protest writing, examining, as we have seen, the writer and his commitment, and the last one deals with censorship in South Africa.

Mphahlele shows increased confidence in the treatment of his subjects matter. The contents hold together more coherently, though still presented with deliberate subjectivity, and he develops his themes methodically and brings them to logical conclusions. His arguments are often crystallized into images and metaphors. In 'The Fabric of African Cultures', for instance, the image of the African aesthete devoid of a synthesis of Europe and Africa, glorifying only his ancestors and celebrating African purity and innocence, is one of a continent lying in state. The difference between a writer of the Negritude school—in this case Senghor—and a South African writer, he symbolises in *African Literature: What Tradition* by their different attitudes towards night. Senghor's 'night of Africa' is a night teeming with suns and rainbows—'yes, there are poets who are in love with the night', says Mphahlele—whereas for him night spells violence, police raids, screams. 'The South African writer is always searching for daytime.'[26]

Mphahlele's love for literature as a motivating force in his critical writing comes through clearly. Tradition in Africa, for instance, is not an academic subject for him, but a living theme in literature. His lengthy quotations often seem selected not just to prove a point, but also to share with the reader a piece of writing worthy of being chosen. With an economy of words he succeeds in presenting the core of a literary work—for instance the poems of Gwendolyn Brooks—and at the same time expresses the deep effect it had on him.

In Mphahlele's uncollected essays, and in his lectures, the same themes are raised as in the collections. Many of the important journals of three continents have asked him to contribute, and his presence as a speaker at conferences and as a visiting lecturer at universities is much sought after. His comments are always distinguished by their honesty and integrity. For him, the greatest crime a writer can commit is false posturing, striking a pose, peddling in dogma, sloganising, and indulging in intellectual snobbery, while his highest praise is for a writer who maintains a balance between artistic integrity and commitment. His aim as a critic is always to bring us closer to the writer's intentions. Throughout, however, runs his search for literature that fulfils what he considers its highest aim, the search for 'truth that lives in an historical context,' that seeks 'beauty in man, that thing in man which has permanence and stands the test of political change'.[27]

His love for literature, and joy in teaching it, comes through again and again. In an essay entitled 'Black Literature at the University of Denver' he tells us how, in a course in African literature, he changed the prescribed works from time to time 'for one's own edification and interest as a lecturer'.[28] 'Teaching is my vocation', he declares in 'Why I teach my Discipline'. 'On my own terms I do nothing else as successfully.'[29] Even in his novel *The Wanderers*, his counterpart enjoys teaching and is always innovating, exploring, finding reasons for poor performance. It was mainly Timi/Mphahlele's frustration as a teacher that drove him out of Iboyoru/Nigeria. He had suggestions for improvements in adult education, but could not get his superiors to discuss them.

And yet, sometimes, even in Nigeria, he yearned for the response, the lack of complacency, of his South African students:

> In the south the boys and I were caught up in a violent situation. We both carried a pass and we could be stopped and searched or arrested the moment we stepped out of the school grounds. We were both hungering for many things and getting little, which in turn sharpened the edge of our longings. I responded to every throb of pain and restlessness in them, and I think they responded to my yearnings.[30]

Towards the end of his stay in the United States, Mphahlele seemed to become defensive about his principles. Sometimes it was almost as though he had been driven against a wall and had to defend himself against the onslaught of those among whom he was exiled. We feel that he is confused by the new political developments in independent Africa and by the strivings of Black Power in America, with which he would like to identify yet finds it impossible to do so. A note of uncertainty creeps into his style, and as a result there is the acknowledged loss of place, perhaps even loss of foothold. His critical, like his creative writing, began to show a lack of vitality.

In August 1978, Mphahlele returned to South Africa:

> The inner compulsion to return (for himself and his wife he says) began in 1972 with the feeling that we should work in a culture we can identify with because we know its terms of reference for our people. Nostalgia and the distance from meaningful involvement, from relevance, began to gnaw at one's vitals.[31]

Although the banning imposed on him in 1966 was lifted soon after arrival, he found that fundamentally little had changed. Some of his books were still banned. The Council of The University of the North voted unanimously to appoint him as head of its English department, but the Government vetoed the decision on the grounds that it was against their educational policy to make a black man head of an English department. He became inspector of education in charge of English teaching in Lebowa. But his soul hungered for the classroom, and when the University of the Witwatersrand offered him a senior research fellowship at the Institute of African Studies, he accepted it, even thought it meant he was teaching mainly white students. 'For me it is a living in the same way that millions of other blacks work for whites to earn a living', he told Gavin Shreeve of the Guardian (May 7, 1979). 'Teaching at Wits is the best I can do. I am doing research most of the time and so I have the basis for a lot of extra-mural activity'. He helped with the running of writing workshops under auspices of the PEN Club. 'In this way I can do a lot to teach young blacks outside the formal schooling situation.'[32] Some of the workshop talks were published in *Staffrider*. He also began to travel through the northern Transvaal recording oral literature which has become his main interest. More and more he is finding his place in the continuity among the people of Africa. 'We still identify strongly with our ancestors', he says. Writing as 'Es'kia' Mphahlele—the closest he could come to Africanising his given name—he now feels he can identify with at least some of Senghor's Negritude ideas, with his longing to return to the ancient shrines.[33] His projects in oral literature will no doubt see publication in due course. A paper on the 'Voice of Prophecy in African Poetry'[34] appeared in *English in Africa* in March 1979, in which he relates the work of modern black poets in their role as poet-priest-oracle to their traditional function. Going deeply into the meaning of the voice of prophecy in African oral poetry he says:

> In so much of African oral poetry one hears that prophetic voice coming across through the resonances of an intensive sense of absolute organic unity in the universe: man, not alone in the universe but unique in the rhythm of being and in harmony with other men, with animals, natural phenomena and so on.
>
> The prophetic vision implied in the poetry cannot be interpreted as simply 'prediction' or 'foreknowledge'. It is rather an expression of a sense of the flux of life extending from a past that is reckoned in relation to one's ancestral heritage and actual events experienced by a community, through the present to some infinite time that cannot simply be equated with the western concept of 'future'. The reason I choose to call it 'prophetic' is that it has implications beyond a man's consciousness of the past and the present.[35]

He finds the apocalyptic voice subdued or altogether absent in much black South African poetry of the late sixties and seventies based on its native soil, but says that these poets—Sipho Sepamla, Wally Serote, Oswald Mtshali, Mafika Gwala, Zulu Molefe, Njabulo Ndebele, and the *Staffrider* poets for example—still give a poetic expression to an experience that is communally felt. The public voice in poetry, he says, is the one point of contact between literature and social needs. He concludes the essay with an interpretation of the function of literature as a force of renewal, revitalising experience and language:

> There is a constant interplay between the historical and the transcendental in literature. Literature is a product of history and may move us today, but two or three decades later only interest us. It moves with the consciousness of a people at a given time in history. Simultaneously it aspires to move beyond the image of the now that captures a moment of moments. We expect it, as an individual work or a body of imaginative writings, to increase our capacity to feel, a capacity that often eludes the yardstick of history, a capacity that moves towards the transcendental.
>
> We are always hungry for emotional experience, and so if it is adequate for us only now, trashy stuff aside, it is still an act of language we must not dismiss. Language is meaning; there is no shame in being moved by it. We still respond pleasurably to those art forms that are a repetition of emotional reality; for example, oral literature, blues, folk songs, which have become ritual, in the best and broadest sense of the word.[36]

Mphahlele's return to South Africa was inevitable. 'If it should mean nothing less than reaffirmation of life on our part, we are contented', he says.[37] 'Man must live.' Mphahlele has come if not in a full circle, in an open-ended one.

Lewis Nkosi is another leading critic of black English writing in South Africa. As a one-time journalist on *Ilanga Lase Natal* and the *Golden City Post*, literary editor of *The New African*, and, contributor since his sojourn in Britain to publications like the *New Statesman*, *Guardian* and *Observer*, Nkosi is well qualified to comment. He saw African writing south of the Sahara as the product of a culture conflict, an encounter, not a synthesis, between Europe and Africa, in which Africa was 'emerging from the violence done to it'.[38] This, he said brought about a certain ambivalence in the African writers' relation to Western culture:

> . . . for the anguish and the torments which have laid hold of the African intelleculals, the need for the black writer to reach within

himself and into his past, arises out of this peculiar, really ironic, and terribly dangerous relation in which the black man stands to the unyieldingly arrogant white world.[39]

It was the lack of imagination in making use of their tradition in creating new African art forms that he deplored. His emphasis was always on the future, since he felt that nothing had as yet been achieved. 'What we would like to see in Africa,' he said, was 'whether our artists can point out an alternative direction from the one provided by a civilisation which has culminated quite ignobly in a heap of broken images'.[40]

Writing in the mid-sixties, Nkosi measured writing by Black South Africans of the *Drum* period by European literary standards, and found their fiction lacking in 'any significant and complex talent'. Their 'mere concern with *telling* [italics his] a story . . . this lack of self-consciousness . . . could be supposed to allow for a certain freshness and originative power in the writing; yet these are virtues which would be very difficult to find in fiction by black South Africans'.[41]

At the same time, Nkosi demanded that writing by black South Africans should respond to the problems posed by conditions there, and found that in fiction this was not the case. The writers, he said, have neither 'the vigour of the imagination' nor 'sufficient technical resources' for this. Black writing, as opposed to music, 'showed the cracks and tension of language working under severe strain'.[42]

Nkosi was blunt to the point of critical incivility. He left no doubt about his opinion of Richard Rive as a novelist, when he found that to read *Emergency* 'is to gain a minute glimpse into a literary situation which seems to me quite desperate'.[43]

He did make some allowances and praised Rive for some of his shorter fiction. Some of the comments above come from his collection of essays, *Home and Exile*, and in these he appeared genuinely angry about a state of affairs in his former homeland where 'mediocre writing by black writers is painlessly endured'. The only writer in whom he saw any promise, judging as he did from the one extract of *Familiarity is the Kingdom of the Lost*, which had appeared at that time, was Dugmore Boetie.[44]

Another target of Nkosi's was the 'European critics who now find it such profitable enterprise to preside over the rebirth of African art and literature'.[45]

Yet Nkosi was never merely vituperative. He substantiated his attacks and arguments clearly and logically. He has the ability to extract the essential elements when reviewing a new work, as for instance in the article entitled 'White on Black' (parodying the title of an article by Mphahlele, 'Black and White') about Mphahlele's *The African Image*.

This book reveals, ironically and sometimes painfully, the bottomless confusion which now attends the efforts by African intellectuals to re-create an image of themselves from the disparate elements of their cultures as well as from the debris of their shattered pre-colonial past. For if anything emerges it is not a single coherent image of Africans or a clear projection of who Africans really are; rather is it an affirmation by the author— sometimes too joyous an affirmation it seems to me—that such an image has been fragmented almost beyond recognition.[46]

His pen-sketches of the *Drum* writers and his description of the background against which they—and he—moved showed sharp powers of observation. His skill in summing-up meaning was shown repeatedly by apt phrases like his description of Negritude in French-speaking Africa as a 'spurious synthetic form of anguish imported from the cafes of Paris through cellophane-wrapped paperbacks'.[47] He was, however, sometimes on the verge of breaking into slick journalese and using the felicitous phrase for its own sake, as when he spoke of 'the ugly leer on the claustrophobic face of violence'.

In spite of his occasional excesses Nkosi performed a necessary function in bringing common sense and clear judgment into criticism of black writing in a period of exuberance. In Britain he has been studying for postgraduate degrees and still today writes regularly for the British press on literary subjects. A new edition of *Home and Exile*, incorporating literary pieces and reviews which appeared previously in *The Transplanted Heart*,[48] appeared after the period under discussion.

As time passes, Nkosi's attitude has tended to soften and become tinged with nostalgia. In a review of *The World of Nat Nakasa*,[49] for example, Nkosi reminisces about the *Drum* days and remembers best the 'sheer gusto of living'[50] of the writers, their humour and exuberant protest. He describes their style as oblique and allusive, 'as incisive as it was sometimes tendentious, schooled in laughter and mockery, while remaining "purified" of the polemical extremities of radical politics'.[51]

Nkosi is a skilled interviewer, often acting in that capacity for radio, television and educational films. His interviews with Chinua Achebe, J.P. Clark, Cyprian Ekwensi, Mazisi Kunene, John Nagenda, Christopher Okigbo and Richard Rive for broadcasting to African countries, were recorded at the Transcription Centre in London and published with other such interviews in *African Writers Talking*.[52] He knew how to draw pertinent information and comments from these writers because of his thorough knowledge and comprehension of their work. He hosted a series entitled 'African Writers of Today' which was filmed by National Educational Television in New York in collaboration with the London Transcription Centre.

It is worth noting that Alex La Guma and Cosmo Pieterse have also taken part in recorded interviewing for broadcasting from London.

Richard Rive, who has a D.Phil from Oxford University, an M.A. from Columbia, and a B.A. (Hons) and B.Ed from the University of Cape Town, is the most sought-after commentator on black South African writing living in South Africa today. In a paper on 'Senghor and Negritude', read to a Conference of the South African Indian Teachers' Assocation in Durban and published in both *New Classic* and his *Selected Writings*, Rive, like Mphahlele, shows that he is opposed to repudiating the present for the past. 'It is from the present into the future,' he says, 'that the poetic imagination must direct itself, not into an orphic descent so that it may wallow in its past. The past is only valid in its usefulness in interpreting the present and future'. And he quotes Frantz Fanon as saying 'correctly':

> The man of today, and particularly the black man must not appeal to a culture for the right to live. A culture is acquired in the present, not with the past. No extinct culture can serve as the basis of a new culture.[53]

Strongly independent in his views, Rive went further than Mphahlele when he discussed the question raised at a conference in Kampala in 1962, 'What is African literature'. He did not consider the 'so-called clash of cultures, African and European' as a 'valid thesis':

> I am certainly not the product of a clash of cultures, rather a synthesis of all experience, and the boundaries are more comprehensive than Africa and Europe. A writer creating in his own small corner, must of necessity have an approach differing from another in another small corner, depending on who he is, where he is, and what he is writing. Different stimuli must produce different responses.[54]

Although this conference took place twenty years ago, Rive confirms his stand by including the report, 'No Common Factor'[55] in his *Selected Writings* published recently.

On black consciousness writing, which he defines as 'writing by blacks for blacks defining their position as blacks', and on the direction it will take, he is not prepared to commit himself. It is sufficient, he says, 'to see the role of meaningful literature as one to align itself on the side of forces determined to overthrow prejudice, racialism and cant'.[56]

In an essay entitled 'The Black Man and White Literature',[57] in which he explores the history of literature in South Africa in relation to the role of the black man, Rive speaks of the literary scramble for

Africa. In a satiric tone, of which he is an unequalled master, he compares the rush by foreign publishers to find African writing with the white man's march into Africa, 'armed with gun, bible, topee, brandy and righteousness . . . bringing his version of civilization to the local Black inhabitants'. The details were changed, he says, but 'the methods remained the same':

> This time the explorer came armed with a fistful of Ph.Ds in Black literature, passed Through Africa's Doors, and taught the Black to understand Soyinka and Achebe, and discuss Negritude, if not meaningfully then at least soulfully.
>
> The Professional Africanist created the professional African. The former must have beamed when he saw his protégé don his beads, fuz his hair, beat his cowhide drum, and tell whites what they in any case already knew.[58]

He ends the essay:

> If poetry is to last, indeed if any form of creativity is to last and be meaningful, it must go deeper and beyond any special pleading at any particular time. And there are poets in South Africa, very fortunately, who are making this type of contribution. The enduring poems will emerge whatever the situation and make their claims on time.[59]

The first issue of *English in Africa*, published in 1974 by the Institute for the Study of English in Africa at Rhodes University, Grahamstown, was devoted to a fragmentary manuscript by Olive Schreiner, with introduction, notes and selected bibliography by Rive. He had discovered the manuscript in the course of his studies of this writer, the subject of his doctoral dissertation. In an article in *Contrast* 'New Light on Olive Schreiner',[60] he tells about his work. He obtained access to papers not studied previously and these led him to an unpublished novel and to alternative endings to the incomplete novel *From Man to Man*. He calls Schreiner 'the greatest of the early South African writers'. 'An infinite Compassion'[61] is the title of another comment on his work on Olive Schreiner. It was this quality of the writer which attracted Rive. One looks forward to the publication of his thesis.

In a tribute to Arthur Nortje,[62] Rive tells of his meeting with the young poet. Nortje introduced his landlord and family to Rive at some length, and then, turning to Rive 'with a deliberateness . . . all he said was 'Richard Rive—writer'.[63] Hence the title of the article, 'Arthur Nortje: Poet'. Rive's account of the death of Nortje, preceded by the death of Ingrid Jonker and Nat Nakasa, and his tribute to Nortje, is more poignant than any of his fiction. It ends:

> When I went up to Oxford I asked others about him. Some said he was depressed and was an introvert, others said he sat in a pub and

wouldn't speak, but read Dickens. And others were even more vague. Then a friend of his came up to read poetry at Ruskin, and before he read he told us about Arthur, and I learnt that he had severed his ties, that his passport had expired, that he took drugs, that he faced deportation. Then I knew what he meant when he wrote:

> Night after night I lie and wait
> for sleep's return, but she, but she,
> is gripped in spastic fits of fear,
> trembling at noises made by me.

There is no more to say. So little remains, so little to tell. Maybe it's best to stop, sufficient to know that he still is, Arthur Nortje—poet.[64]

This is what literature means to Rive, a poem by Nortje that touches the heart, the compassion to find in Olive Schreiner, the deference of a 17-year old Richard for Langston Hughes who wrote to him and asked him to go on writing and send all his stuff. 'And I did,' Rive tells us:[65]

> . . . nervously tying up the fledgling manuscripts and sending them over the seas. And long after a book came back, smelling sweet and fresh-paged, and there was my name on the cover, and that book was me.[66]

In his essays Rive is always lucid, sophisticated, knowledgeable and highly readable. The accent is always on objectivity and perspective. At conferences he likes to see a divergence of opinion, the presence of elements from different camps to give a balance to discussions. Fresh assessments, further analyses, is what he demands in literary ideas.

Mbulelo Vizikhungo Mzamane, formerly lecturer in English at the University College of Botswana, is currently engaged in a study of contemporary black poetry for a doctoral degree at the University of Sheffield. His *forte* lies in clearly and meticulously assessing black writing and placing it within its historical context. For him, the answer to the question of whether writing which communicates urgent political messages or records facts about oppression has a right to regard itself as creative and imaginary, expressed in an article entitled 'The 50s and Beyond: An Evaluation',[67] is simple:

> F.R. Leavis' way, even in English literature, is not the only critical method. A category for African committed literature must be made to which we may not apply purely western standards, just as we may not apply these to, say, an assessment of Chinese literature, just as the West itself, needs a separate set of standards to assess existentialist literature or the stream-of-consciousness writing. The critic must bear in mind that the African artist has

consciously concerned himself with his world, his people and their destiny. He's divorced himself from the concept of 'art for art's sake' and sees his art as being for 'life's' sake. He intends his art to be functional, to enable him to cope with his urgent problems, which often range from personal problems of identity to continental problems of a political nature.[68]

This is not to say, he continues, that 'what's being said is not as important as how it's being said—we have our share of poor literature with very little claim to being anything else but blatant pamphleteering, like Peter Abrahams' *A Night of their Own*'. 'Commitment to relevance is not enough', he says.[69] Literature for Mzamane is about people, 'a whole people, and issues of great import to humanity'.[70]

Mzamane made these comments at a conference on 'Black Writing: Problems and Prospects of a Tradition', sponsored by *New Classic* and *S'ketsh* magazines in 1976. In the following issue of *New Classic*, in an article entitled 'Literature and Politics Among Blacks in South Africa'[71] he emphasises the socio-political aspect of black South African writing because 'Art and politics in South Africa, as in many parts of Africa, have become inseparable for the simple reason that politics pervade all aspects of a Blackman's existence'.[72] The paper deals with political themes in poetry, fiction and drama.

Like Mphahlele, Mzamane pleads for the inclusion of black writing in school and university syllabuses, in which recently some little progress has been made.

It seems, then, that on the whole black South African critics writing in South Africa, while wholeheartedly supporting writing which is socially and politically relevant to the black man's life, are cautious in their attitude towards a black aesthetic which they feel still needs definition and must grow out of the literature itself.

An adjunct to critical writing is the anthology, which can be a practical and perhaps most valuable demonstration of the critic's assessment of a particular form of writing. Thus Mphahlele's two collections, *Modern African Stories*,[73] which he co-edited with Ellis Ayitey Komey, and *African Writing Today*,[74] emphasise the major universal concerns in literature, interpreted in African terms, as he tells us in the introduction to the latter work. We do not know whether the authors of *Modern African Stories* worked independently, each making his own choice, but it is likely that Mphahlele was largely responsible for the South African stories. The publishers insisted that the editors include their own stories, and Mphahlele chose one of his best, 'Greig on a Stolen Piano'. Most of the leading South African fiction writers of the time are represented: Alex La Guma with 'Coffee for the Road', James Matthews with 'The Second Coming', Richard Rive with 'Rain', and Can Themba with 'The Dube Train'.

Although the title indicates that it is a collection of stories, an extract from Alfred Hutchinson's *Road to Ghana*, under the title 'Machado' and a sketch from Casey Motsisi's *Drum* series 'On the Beat' are included.

There is no professed theme in the two anthologies other than to reflect Africa's awareness of itself. In *African Writing Today*, Mphahlele includes as many important writers as possible, explaining omissions, which he lists, as economy. In his introduction he also explains that, rather than include works easily available elsewhere, he has chosen several new authors and less well-known works of established writers. He divides the work into areas. There is more emphasis in this work on the authors themselves. At the end are biographical notes on the writers, giving their careers, publications and present places of residence. Of his own works, Mphahlele includes two essays, one entitled 'Remarks on Negritude', which he presented as a paper at a conference on African Literature in French at the Universities, held at the University of Dakar in 1963, and which voices his usual stand on this issue, and an extract from an article published in *Encounter*, entitled 'An African Autobiography', about his stay in Nigeria. The South African section contains one of Alex La Guma's stories, 'Blankets', Richard Rive's 'Dagga-Smoker's Dream', and Can Themba's 'The Urchin'. The latter is the violent and melodramatic type of story of Themba's that Mphahlele disliked, but felt necessary to include, especially as it had won a contest organised by the South African Centre of the International Pen Club. There are poems by Dennis Brutus and Mazisi Kunene, Lewis Nkosi's searingly satiric story 'The Prisoner', and an extract from Todd Matshikiza's *Chocolates for my Wife*.

Richard Rive's collection, *Quartet*,[75] is subtitled 'New Voices from South Africa'. The four are Alex La Guma ('Out of Darkness', 'Slipper Satin', 'A Glass of Wine', 'Nocturne') Rive himself ('Strike', 'Resurrection', 'No Room at Solitaire', 'Rain') James Matthews ('Azikwelwa', 'The Portable Radio', 'The Party', 'The Park') and Alf Wannenburgh ('Awendgesang', 'Echoes', 'The Snake Pit' and 'Debut'). There are four sections, each with one story by each writer, headed 'Without Justice', 'The Dispossessed', 'The Possessed', and 'The Outsider'. There is no introduction.

His anthology, *Modern African Prose*,[76] contains eight items by South African writers such as Abrahams, Matthews, Peter Clarke, Hutchinson, Mphahlele and Rive himself, and contributions by the leading writers in other parts of the continent: Achebe, Laye, Ngugi, Honwana and others. The work was intended mainly for schools. In the introduction, Rive explains that by African prose he means literature produced by Africans regardless of colour, language or national distinction which deals with situations and experiences happening in Africa. He therefore includes two contributions by white South Africans who, he feels, must not be denied a place in the body of South African literature.

We have already discussed Cosmo Pieterse's collections of radio plays. His collection of poetry, *Seven South African Poets*, was published by Heinemann in 1971. It is subtitled 'Poems of Exile' and includes contributions by Dollar Brand, Dennis Brutus, I. Choonara, C.J. Driver, Timothy Holmes, Keorapetse Kgositsile and Arthur Nortje. These poets and their work, Pieterse says in the introduction, 'focus attention on, and perhaps encourage the reader to reassess two central facts of the South African language writer's existence', that they write 'not, as many earlier South African poets did, with a sense of spiritual exile from a European home, but out of a conviction that something is rotten under the Southern Cross',[77] and second, that much of the poetry 'is charged with protest'. While it is not the intention of the volume, Pieterse says, to answer the questions it brings to mind, such as whether South African poetry becomes 'shrill, hysterical, thinly disguised political propaganda' and how exile affects a poet's vision, he hopes that the reader who is interested in such questions 'will be stimulated and helped by this collection'.[77]

Pieterse, with Donald Munro, has also collected a number of essays under the title *Protest and Conflict in African Literature*[78] to which some of the subcontinent's leading writers contributed essays on the subject of committed writing in South Africa. Pieterse himself writes the introduction and about William Plomer and Vilakazi. Among other contributors are Dennis Brutus and Ngugi wa Thiong'o.

Also abroad, Alex La Guma helped to select items for a German collection, *Das Schwarze Wort, Südafrikanische Erzählungen*[79] [The Black Word, South African tales] which included the works of authors such as Bessie Head, Mafika Gwala, Jolobe, Matthews, Motsisi, Serote, La Guma himself and others. Keorapetse Kgositsile collected 'Poetry from Modern Africa' in *The Word is Here*.[80] Poetry, he says in the introduction, 'the word at its most expressive, can be a prayer, an appeal, condemnation, encouragement, affirmation—the list of endeavors is endless. And if it is authentic, as anything else expressive of a people's spirit, it is always social'.[81] He divides the anthology into geographical areas and includes examples of the work of most of the better-known African poets such as David Diop, Gabriel Okara, David Rubadiri, Antonio Agostinho Neto, Christopher Okigbo, Wole Soyinka and others. From South Africa, he includes only poets in exile, among others Dennis Brutus, Mazisi Kunene and himself. He has tried, he says, to gather poetry from all over Africa 'not to reflect my preferences but to reflect the pulse of Africa today'.[82]

Forced Landing[83] is the most recent anthology in this period, collected by Mothobi Mutloatse. It consists mainly of short stories, and a few columns and 'messages' by Toivo Herman ja Toivo, imprisoned leader of the South West African People's Organisation (SWAPO) and Bishop Desmond Tutu. In the introduction, Mutloatse explains the purpose of the collection:

> The black community is hungry, and hungrier since 16 June 1976: ever-ready-and-willing to lay its hands on 'relevant' writing, writing by blacks about blacks. The overwhelming response to poetry recitals held in the townships is proof of this bond between the writers and their audience.[84]

The anthology covers 'about two and a half decades in the black man's history, ranging from the early '50s with James Matthews's still-as-fresh "Azikwelwa", through Mongane Serote's Sharpeville to Mtutuzeli Matshoba's 1976'.[85] The stories are arranged alphabetically to avoid, as Mutloatse says jokingly, 'lining up contributors as if they were participating in a beauty contest'.[86] Some of the contributions had not been published previously, including the remarkable stories 'Waiting for Leila' by Achmed Dangor (extract), 'To Kill a Man's Pride' by Mtutuzeli Matshoba, and the story which gives the anthology its significant title, 'Forced Landing' by Mathatha Tsedu. The latter is a satiric story of the future, the year 2561, when a cruising missile from Mars on its way to Salumus is forced to make an emergency landing on Jupiter because of food shortages aboard. Unfortunately for the strangers 'of colour', led by Captain Teargas, the black people of Anazia on Jupiter had recently found a book dealing with the planet Earth, and a country called Safrika in particular, which told how a handful of settlers 'had conned the local population into allowing them to settle for time to plant vegetables and fruit'. The settlers, the author continues,

> . . . however, on realising that Azania—as it was then called—was very fertile, annexed the land by using sophisticated weapons combined with subtle diplomacy and religion. The settlers then declared themselves rulers over the local population and outlawed their culture as barbaric. They passed legislation curbing the natives' movement and their political aspirations and also exploiting their labour. The next generation in that country cursed the older generation for selling their birthrights. They resolved to win their country back—come what may.[87]

It was explained to the strangers that the Anazian people believed 'the book was a warning to them not to extend their hospitality to strangers of colour'.[88] Captain Teargas is overheard, by means of a bug, discussing with his men how they had in fact planned to repeat 'that Jan van Riebeeck story'. They are sentenced to death.

Notes

INTRODUCTION

1. Segal, Philip. 'Taking Stock with *The Classic*' (*Contrast*, II,2, 1963, p 9).
2. Jahn, Janheinz. *History of Neo-African Literature* (London, Faber & Faber, 1966, p 24).
3. Mphahlele, Ezekiel. Report on Conference of African Writers at Makerere University, Kampala, 1963 (*Transition*, III,10 [misprinted as IV] p 175).
4. Ullyat, A.G. 'Dilemma in Black Poetry' (*Contrast*, XI,4, 1977, p 51–62).
5. Mphahlele, Ezekiel. His reply in *Blackworld*, January 1974 to Addison Gayle Jr's review of *Voices in the Whirlwind* in *Blackworld*, July, 1973.

CHAPTER 1: Black Writing in English

1. Shepherd, Rev. R.H.W. *Bantu Literature and Life* (Alice, Lovedale Press, 1955, p 173–175).
2. Shepherd. *Lovedale and Literature for the Bantu* (Alice, Lovedale Press, 1945, p 89).
3. *ibid*, p 75.
4. Shepherd, 'Recent Trends in South African Vernacular Literature' (*African World*, March 1955, p 7).
5. Bokwe, John Knox. *Ntsikana, The Story of an African Convert* (Alice, Lovedale Press, 1914).
6. Dhlomo, H.I.E. 'Three Famous African Authors I Knew' (*Inkundla ya Banto*, August 1946, first fortnight p 4, second fortnight p 4).
7. Comaroff, John L. ed. *The Boer War Diary of Sol T. Plaatje* (London, Macmillan, 1973).
8. Couzens, Tim, and Willan, Brian, ed. *English in Africa*: Plaatje Centenary Issue (III,2, 1976).
9. Dhlomo, H.I.E. 'Drama and the African' (*South African Outlook*, Oct. 1, 1936, p 232–235).
10. Dhlomo, H.I.E. 'Why Study Tribal Dramatic Forms?' (Transvaal Native Education Quarterly, March 1939, p 20).

11 Makiwane, T.W. Letter to editor (*South African Outlook*, Dec. 2, 1935, p 265).

12 Nhlapo, Jacob. *Bantu Babel* (Cape Town, The African Bookman, 1944, p 5).

13 Vilakazi, Benedict Wallet. Letter to the Editor (*South African Outlook*, July 1, 1939, p 166–167).

14 Conference report, Committee on Christian Literature at Florida, Transvaal (*South African Outlook*, November 2, 1936, p 256).

15 Matthews, Professor Z.K. 'Ethnic Universities' (*Africa South*, July–Sept. 1957, p 44).

16 Mphahlele, Ezekiel. 'Black and White' (*New Statesman*, Sept. 10, 1960, p 346).

17 Nakasa, Nathaniel (Nat). 'Writing in South Africa' (*The Classic*, I,1, 1963, p 57).

18 Nkosi, Lewis. *Home and Exile* (London, Longman, Green & Co., 1965).

19 Hopkinson, Tom. *In the Fiery Continent* (London, Victor Gollancz Ltd, 1962, p 10).

20 Sampson, Anthony. *Drum* (London, Collins, 1956).

21 *ibid*, p 15.

22 *ibid*, p 15–16.

23 Pitso, Randolph Ben. 'Nomoya of the Winds' (*Drum*, April 1951, p 14–15).

24 *ibid*, p 15.

25 Sampson, *op cit*, p 28.

26 Nkosi, *op cit*, p 12.

27 'Bethal Today' (*Drum*, March 1952, p 4–9,33,40).

28 'Mr. Drum Goes to Jail' (*Drum*, March 1954, p 10–16).

29 Hopkinson, *op cit*, p 364.

30 *ibid*, p 357.

31 Mphahlele, Es'kia (Ezekiel). 'South African Writers Talking' (*English in Africa*, VI,2, 1979, p 3).

32 Cope, Jack. 'The World of Contrast' (*English in Africa*, VII,2, 1980, p 11).

33 Serote, Wally (Mongane). 'What's this black S---' (*Ophir*, No 9, 1969, p 16).

34 Kirkwood, Mike. 'The Colonizer: A Critique of the English South African Culture Theory' (*Poetry South Africa, Selected Papers from Poetry 1974*, ed. Wilhelm, Peter and Polley, James, Ad.Donker, Johannesburg, 1976).

35 Matthews, James. 'Azikwelwa' (*The Park and Other Stories*, Athlone, Blac Publishing House, 1974, p 80).

36 Recorded at Transcription Centre, London, 1963 (pub. *African Writers Talking*, ed. Duerden, Dennis and Pieterse, Cosmo, London, Heinemann, 1972).

37 Rive, Richard. 'No Common Factor' (*Selected Writings*, Johannesburg, Ad. Donker, 1972, p 70).

38 Rive, Interview with *Wietie* (No 2, p 11).

39 Povey, John. 'Conference on South African Writing' (*Research in African Literatures*, I,1, 1970, p 76–77).

40 Manganyi, N. (Noel) Chabani. 'Mashangu's Reverie' (*Mashangu's Reverie and other essays*, Johannesburg, Ravan Press, 1977, p 21).

41 Nakasa, Nat. 'Castles in the Air' (*The World of Nat Nakasa*, ed. Patel, Essop, Johannesburg, Ravan Press, 1975, p 111).

42 Nortje, Arthur. *Dead Roots* (London, Heinemann, 1973, p 146).

43 Nortje, 'Native's Letter' (*op cit*, p 118).

44 Mphahlele, Ezekiel. *The Wanderers* (New York, Macmillan, 1970, p 53).

45 Mphahlele, *Down Second Avenue* (London, Faber & Faber, 1959, p 210).

46 'South African Writers Talking' (*English in Africa*, September 1979, p 18).

47 Mphahlele, 'The Voice of Prophecy in African Poetry' (*English in Africa*, March 1979, p 39).

48 Sartre, Jean Paul. *Black Orpheus* (Translated by Allen, S.W., Paris, Présence Africaine, 1963).

49 Kunene, Mazisi. Introduction to Cesaire, Aimé. *Return to my Native Land* (Harmondworth, Penguin, 1969).

50 Manganyi, N.C. (Noel Chabani). *Being-Black-in-the-World* (Johannesburg, Spro-Cas/Ravan Press, 1973).

51 Manganyi, *Mashangu's Reverie and Other Essays*.

52 *ibid*, p 55.

53 *ibid*, p 55.

54 Tshabangu, Mango, 'Thoughts in a Train' (*Forced Landing* ed. Mutloatse, Mothobi, Johannesburg, Ravan Press, 1980, p 156–158).

55 Mphahlele, *African Image* (London, Faber & Faber, 1962).

56 Ngubane, Jordan K. (Kush). *Ushaba* (Washington D.C., Three Continents Press, 1974).

57 Mtshali, Oswald (Mbuyiseni). *Sounds of a Cowhide Drum* (Johannesburg, Renoster Books, 1971 and London, Oxford University Press, 1972).

58 Mtshali, *ibid*, p 43 (References are to O.U.P. edition).

59 *ibid*, p 43.

60 Barnett, Ursula A. Interview with Oswald Joseph (Mbuyiseni) Mtshali (*World Literature Written in English*, XII,1, 1973, p 26–35).

61 *ibid*, p 29.

62 *ibid*, p 29–30.

63 *ibid*, p 35.
64 Mzamane, Mbulelo. 'The Short Story Tradition in South Africa' (*Donga*, September 1979, p 1-8).
65 Gray, Stephen. 'The Struggle', interview with Sipho Sepamla on 21 June 1977 (*Contrast*, XI,3, 1977, p 92).
66 Mphahlele, *English in Africa*, VI,2, p 21.
67 Sepamla, Sipho. 'A Note on *New Classic* and *S'ketsh*' (*English in Africa*, VII,2, p 83).
68 Gordimer, Nadine, 'Note for 20th anniversary of *Contrast*' (*Contrast*, XIII,2, 1980, p 26).
69 Dangor, Achmed. 'The Voices that are Dead' (*Wietie*, 1, p 17).

CHAPTER 2: Poetry

1 Kunene, Mazisi. *Zulu Poems* (London, André Deutsch, 1970, p 11).
2 Mtshali, Oswald Joseph. *Sounds of a Cowhide Drum* Johannesburg, Renoster Books, 1971 and London, O.U.P, 1972).
3 *ibid*, p 55.
4 Vilakazi, Benedict Wallet. 'The Oral and Written Literature in Nguni' (Doctor of Philosophy Thesis in Bantu Studies presented at the University of the Witwatersrand, October 1945).
5 Vilakazi, 'In the Goldmines', originally published in Bantu Treasury Series No VIII, translated by A.C. Jordan, *Africa South*, January-March 1957 and in *Zulu Horizons* translated by D. McK. Malcolm and Florence Louie Friedman (Cape Town, Howard Timmins, 1962).
6 'Life is "Bitter Sweet"', written to welcome Noel Coward to Bantu Social Centre (*Ilanga Lase Natal*, April 1 1944, p 10).
7 *Ilanga Lase Natal*, May 19 1945, p 15.
8 Kunene, Mazisi. 'The Proud' (*Modern Poetry from Africa* ed. Gerald Moore and Ulli Beier, Harmondsworth, Penguin Books, 1963).
9 Kunene, 'A Poem' (*Zulu Poems*, André Deutsch, 1970).
10 Ndebele, Njabulo S. 'Five Letters to M.M.M.' (*Izwi*, II,10, 1973, p 16-19).
11 Ndebele, 'Little Dudu' (*To Whom it May Concern*, ed. Robert Royston, Johannesburg, Ad. Donker, 1973, p 37-39).
12 Kgositsile, Keorapetse. *My Name is Afrika* (New York, Doubleday, 1971).
13 Jolobe, James J.R. 'Thuthula' (*Poems of an African*, Alice, Lovedale, 1946, p 9-31).
14 *ibid*, p 24.
15 *ibid*, p 25.
16 *ibid*, p 25.
17 *ibid*, p 30.
18 *ibid*, p 30.

19 *ibid*, p 1–4.
20 *ibid*, p 4–9.
21 *ibid*, p 4.
22 *ibid*, p 4.
23 Mahlasela, B.E.N. Working Paper No 3, Department of African Languages, Rhodes University, Grahamstown, 1973.
24 *ibid*, p 20.
25 Jolobe, *op cit*, p 4.
26 Dhlomo, H.I.E. 'African Drama and Poetry' (*South African Outlook*, April 1 1939, p 90).
27 Dhlomo, H.I.E. *Valley of a Thousand Hills* (Durban, Knox Publishing Company, 1941, p 4).
28 *ibid*, p 4.
29 *ibid*, p 7.
30 *ibid*, p 10.
31 *ibid*, p 10.
32 *ibid*, p 12.
33 *ibid*, p 12.
34 *ibid*, p 18.
35 *ibid*, p 21.
36 *ibid*, p 35.
37 *ibid*, p 41.
38 *ibid*, p 37.
39 *ibid*, p 41.
40 *ibid*, p 21.
41 *ibid*, p 34.
42 Dhlomo, H.I.E. 'Masses and the Artist' ('H.I.E. Dhlomo, Literary Theory and Criticism', ed. N.W. Visser, *English in Africa*, IV,2, 1977, p 61–62, originally published in *Ilanga Lase Natal*, April 10 1943).
43 *ibid*, p 62. The line quoted as attributed to *Valley of a Thousand Hills* but does not appear in the poem. Perhaps Dhlomo was quoting from a manuscript version of his poem. Was the line censored by his publishers?
44 Visser, N.W. 'Towards an Edition of Literary Works of H.I.E. Dhlomo' (*Research in African Literatures*, VII,2, 1976, p 233–235).
45 Dhlomo, H.I.E. 'The Nile' Typescript by an anonymous collector in the Killie Campbell Library, Durban, probably Trevor Cope or Killie Campbell herself.
46 Abrahams, Peter. *A Blackman Speaks of Freedom* (Durban, Universal Printing Works, undated).
47 Mtshali, Oswald Mbuyiseni. 'Black Poetry in South Africa, What it Means, Its Direction and Dimension' (Typescript, International Writers' Program, University of Iowa, January 9, 1975).

48 Barnett, Ursula A. Interview with Oswald Mtshali (*World Literature Written in English*, April 1973, p 34).
49 Mtshali. *Sounds of a Cowhide Drum*, p 3.
50 Mzamane, Mbulelo Vizikhungo. 'The 50s and Beyond' (*New Classic*, No 4, 1977, p 23–32).
51 *Sounds of a Cowhide Drum*, p 11.
52 *ibid*, p 23.
53 *ibid*, p 20.
54 *ibid*, p 1.
55 *ibid*, p 18.
56 *ibid*, p 8.
57 *ibid*, p 16.
58 *ibid*, p 57.
59 *Bolt* No 5, 1971, p 3–6 and in *Sounds of a Cowhide Drum*, p 67–70 (not included in original Renoster Books edition).
60 *Sounds of a Cowhide Drum*, p 5.
61 *ibid*, p 63.
62 Serote, Mongane Wally. *Yakhal'inkomo* (Johannesburg, Renoster Books, 1972, p 4–5).
63 *ibid*, p 48–51.
64 Serote, *No Baby Must Weep* (Johannesburg, Ad. Donker, 1975, p 28).
65 *Tsetlo* (Johannesburg, Ad. Donker, 1974, p 41).
66 *Yakhal'inkomo*, p 27.
67 *Tsetlo*, p 11.
68 *Bolt*, August, 1973, p 7.
69 *Yakhal'inkomo*, p 22–23.
70 *ibid*, p 22.
71 *ibid*, p 23.
72 *ibid*, p 16.
73 *ibid*, p 44.
74 *ibid*, p 36.
75 *Tsetlo*, Preface.
76 *ibid*, p 14.
77 *ibid*, p 10.
78 *ibid*, p 47–48.
79 *ibid*, p 50.
80 *ibid*, p 34.
81 *ibid*, p 58.
82 *ibid*, p 57.
83 *ibid*, p 62.
84 *ibid*, p 24.
85 Serote, *No Baby Must Weep*.
86 Serote, *Behold Mama Flowers* (Johannesburg, Ad. Donker, 1978).
87 *ibid*, p 16.

88 *ibid*, p 21.
89 *No Baby Must Weep*, p 54.
90 *ibid*, p 59.
91 *Behold Mama Flowers*, p 44.
92 *ibid*, p 61.
93 Sepamla, (Sydney) Sipho. *Hurry Up to It* (Johannesburg, Ad. Donker, 1975).
94 Sepamla, *The Blues is You in Me* (Johannesburg, Ad. Donker, 1976).
95 *ibid*, p 69.
96 *ibid*, p 27.
97 Sepamla, 'The Black Writer in South Africa Today: Problems and Dilemmas' (*New Classic*, No 3, 1976, p 19).
98 *The Blues is You in Me*, p 34–35.
99 *ibid*, p 35.
100 *Hurry Up to It*, p 16–17.
101 *ibid*, p 17.
102 *ibid*, p 26–27.
103 *ibid*, p 27.
104 *ibid*, p 23.
105 *The Blues is You in Me*, p 17–19.
106 Royston, Robert, ed. *To Whom it May Concern* (Johannesburg, Ad. Donker, 1973).
107 Sepamla, 'To Whom It May Concern', *Hurry Up to It*, p 9; *To Whom It May Concern*, p 96.
108 *Hurry Up to It*, p 69–70.
109 *ibid*, p 69.
110 *The Blues is You in Me*, p 52.
111 *ibid*, 'To Makana and Nonqause', p 23.
112 Proceedings of the Conference of the 1820 Settlers National Monument Foundation published under the title *English-Speaking South Africa Today*, ed. André de Villiers (published for the 1820 Settlers National Monument Foundation by Oxford University Press, Cape Town. Reference on p 377).
113 *The Blues is You in Me*, p 70–71.
114 *ibid*, p 70.
115 Sepamla, *The Soweto I Love* (London, Rex Collings with Cape Town, David Philip, 1977).
116 *ibid*, p 1.
117 *ibid*, p 6–9.
118 *ibid*, p 6–7.
119 *ibid*, p 10–11.
120 *ibid*, p 11.
121 *ibid*, 'On Judgment Day', p 25.
122 *ibid*, 'Civilisation Aha', p 27.

123 Gwala, Mafika Pascal. *Jol'iinkomo* (Johannesburg, Ad. Donker, 1977).
124 *ibid*, p 70–71.
125 *ibid*, p 71.
126 *ibid*, 'Since Yesterday', p 36.
127 *ibid*, p 64.
128 *ibid*, p 60–68.
129 *ibid*, p 64.
130 *ibid*, p 66.
131 *ibid*, p 67–68.
132 *ibid*, p 14.
133 *ibid*, p 14–15.
134 *ibid*, p 10–11.
135 *ibid*, p 57–59.
136 *ibid*, p 42.
137 *ibid*, p 42–43.
138 *ibid*, p 57–59.
139 *ibid*, p 37–39.
140 *ibid*, p 37.
141 *ibid*, p 36.
142 *Staffrider* Workshop (*Staffrider* II,3, 1979, p 56).
143 *Jol'iinkomo*, p 33.
144 Matthews, James, *Black Voices Shout*, p 64 (Athlone, Blac Publishing House, 1974).
145 *ibid*, p 7.
146 Matthews, 'For Nina Simone' (*Black Voices Shout*, p 14).
147 Matthews, James and Thomas, Gladys. *Cry Rage* (Johannesburg, Spro-Cas Publications, 1972).
148 Matthews, *Pass Me the Meatballs, Jones*, p 2 (Athlone, Blac Publishing House, 1977 and *Cape Times*, March 23, 1977).
149 *Pass Me the Meatballs Jones* (Blac), p 28.
150 Nadine Gordimer. 'Writers in South Africa: The New Black Poets' (*Dalhousie Review*, LIII,4, 1973/74, p 663).
151 *Meatballs*, p 15.
152 *ibid*, p 34.
153 *ibid*, p 40.
154 Douts, Christine. 'To You' (*Black Voices Shout*, p 2).
155 Douts, 'Dear God', *ibid*, p 55.
156 Mackay, Ilva, '. . . and liberty' *Black Voices Shout*, p 6.
157 Mackay, 'Beware', *ibid*, p 34.
158 Mackay, 'The Call', *ibid*, p 65.
159 Tladi, Lefifi (*Ophir*, July 1975, p 27).
160 Ndebele, N. (Njabulo). 'Be Gentle' (*Contrast*, VII,3, 1971, p 27).
161 Mutloatse, Andrew Mothobi. 'Sir' (*New Nation*, January 1973, p 16).

162 *ibid*, p 16.
163 Ndebele, 'Portrait of a Love' (*Purple Renoster*, No 11, 1972, p 16).
164 Mutloatse, 'On Marriage' (*New Nation, op cit*, p 16).
165 Nkondo, (Zinjva) Winston. (*New Classic*, No 1, 1975, p 6).
166 Ndebele, 'I Hid My Love' (*To Whom It May Concern, op cit*, p 45–46).
167 *ibid*, p 46.
168 Ndebele, 'Little Dudu', p 37–39.
169 *ibid*, p 39.
170 Mutloatse, 'When Love is Banned' (*New Classic*, No 1, 1975, p 30–34).
171 Mutloatse, 'Train Roof Jive' (*New Classic*, No 1, 1975, p 52).
172 Mutloatse, 'Don't Lock Up Our Sweethearts' (Gray, Stephen, ed., *On the Edge of the World*, Johannesburg, Ad. Donker, 1974, p 107–111).
173 *ibid*, p 108–109.
174 Madingoane, Ingoapele. *Africa My Beginning* (Johannesburg, Ravan Press, 1979).
175 *ibid*, p 26.
176 Ndlazi, Mandla. 'The Battle of Isandhlwana' (*Staffrider*, I,3, 1978, p 47.)
177 Monare, Morena King. 'A Gossip' (*Staffrider*, III,3, 1980, p 31).
178 Motaung, Bonisile Joshua. 'So Well Tomorrow' (*Staffrider* I,2, 1978, p 23).
179 Ruddin, Muhammed Omar. 'Tokologo' (*Staffrider*, I,2, 1978, p 37).
180 Nicol, Mike. 'At the Window' (*Staffrider*, I,1, 1978, p 25).
181 Mthimkulu, Oupa Thando. 'Nineteen Seventysix' (*Staffrider*, I,1, 1978, p 21).
182 Shikwambane, Hanyane Nelson, 'Stray Bullet' (*Staffrider*, I,1, 1978, p 33).
183 Buthelezi, Bafana 'Tribute to Mapetha' (*Staffrider* II,1, 1979, p 49).
184 Makama, Timothy Motimeloa. 'For Existence Sake' (*Staffrider*, II,1, 1979, p 43).
185 Setuke, Peter. 'The Marathon Runner' (*Staffrider*, II,4, 1979, p 11).
186 a'Motana, Nape. (*Staffrider*, I,3, 1978, p 28).
187 waLedwaba, Makhulu. 'Freedom' (*Staffrider* II,2, 1979, p 32).
188 King, Melissa. 'One Teaching Day' (*Staffrider*, II,4, 1979, p 37).
189 Johannesse, Fhazel. *The Rainmaker* (Johannesburg, Ravan Press, 1979).
190 *ibid*, p 107.
191 *ibid*, p 106.

192   Banoobhai, Shabbir. *Echoes of My Other Self* (Johannesburg, Ravan Press, 1980, p 1).
193   *ibid*, p 3.
194   *ibid*, p 6.
195   *ibid*, p 42–43.
196   *ibid*, p 51.
197   Asvat, Farouk. 'Weapons of Words' (*Wietie, No 1, p 17*).
198   Dangor, Achmed. (*Wietie*, No 1, p 17).
199   Patel, Essop. *they came at dawn* (Athlone, Blac Publishing House, 1980).
200   *ibid*, p 9.
201   *ibid*, p 23.
202   *ibid*, p 29.
203   *ibid*, p 7.
204   van Wyk, Christopher. *It is Time to Go Home* (Johannesburg, Ad. Donker, 1979).
205   van Wyk, 'Twenty Years of Experience' (*Heresy*, No 1, 1979, p 7–12).
206   van Wyk, 'Aunt Molly and the Girls' (*Wietie*, No 1, p 27–30).
207   *It is Time to Go Home*, p 27.
208   *ibid*, p 44.
209   *ibid*, p 12.
210   *ibid*, p 34–35.
211   *ibid*, p 35.
212   Davids, Jennifer. *Searching for Words* (Cape Town, David Philip, 1974).
213   *ibid*, p iii.
214   *ibid*, p iv.
215   *ibid*, p 12.
216   *ibid*, p 25.
217   *ibid*, p 8–9.
218   *ibid*, p 18.
219   *ibid*, p 16–17.
220   *ibid*, p 2.
221   *ibid*, p 2.
222   Small, Adam. 'There's Somethin'' (Cope, Jack and Krige, Uys, ed. *The Penguin Book of South African Verse*, Harmondsworth, Penguin Books, 1968, p 241).
223   Small, *Black Bronze Beautiful* (Johannesburg, Ad. Donker, 1975).
224   *ibid*, p 25.
225   Pieterse, Cosmo, ed. *Seven South African Poets* (London, Heinemann, 1971).
226   Nortje, Arthur. *Dead Roots* (London, Heinemann, 1973, p 102).
227   *ibid*, p 90–91.

228   *ibid*, p 91.
229   Nortje, 'In Exile' (*New Coin*, IX,3/4, 1973, p 35).
230   *Dead Roots*, p 51.
231   Brutus, Dennis. 'In Memoriam, Arthur Nortje 1942–1970' (*Research in African Literatures*, II,1, 1971, p 26–27).
232   *Roots*, p 108.
233   *ibid*, p 52.
234   *ibid*, p 52–54.
235   *ibid*, p 128.
236   *ibid*, p 75.
237   *ibid*, p 104–105.
238   *ibid*, p 138–141.
239   *ibid*, p 62.
240   *ibid*, p 217–218.
241   *ibid*, p 40–41.
242   *ibid*, p 88–89.
243   *ibid*, p 51.
244   *ibid*, p 112–114.
245   Nortje, Diary entry in *New Coin* (IX,3/4, 1973).
246   Brutus, 'In memoriam', *op cit*.
247   Brutus, Dennis, *Strains* (Austin, Troubadour Press, 1975, p 24).
248   *ibid*, p 16.
249   Brutus, *A Simple Lust*, p 176 (New York, Hill & Wang, 1973).
250   Lindfors, Bernth et al. *Palaver* (Occasional Publication of the African and Afro-American Research Institute, The University of Texas at Austin, 1972).
251   *ibid*, p 32.
252   Brutus, *Stubborn Hope* (Washington, D.C. Three Continents Press, 1978, p 24).
253   Brutus, *Letters to Martha* (London, Heinemann, 1968, p 51).
254   *Strains*, p 38–39.
255   *A Simple Lust*, p 19.
256   *Stubborn Hope*, p 26–27.
257   *Strains*, p 27.
258   *A Simple Lust*, p 2.
259   *ibid*, p 22.
260   *Stubborn Hope*, p 36.
261   Brutus, author's note, *Poems from Algiers* (Occasional Publication of the African and Afro-American Research Institute, The University of Texas at Austin, 1970, p 26–27).
262   *Letters to Martha*, p 2.
263   *ibid*, p 24.
264   *Stubborn Hope*, p 5.
265   *Letters to Martha*, p 28.
266   *Palaver*, *op cit*, p 33.

267 Soyinka, Wole. *Myths Literature and the African World* (Cambridge, C.U.P., 1976, p 75).

268 *A Simple Lust*, p 48.

269 *Letters to Martha*, p 30.

270 *ibid*, p 3.

271 *ibid*, p 6.

272 *Palaver*, p 28–29.

273 *Stubborn Hope*, p 58–60.

274 *A Simple Lust*, p 112–113.

275 *ibid*, p 111.

276 *Poems from Algiers*, p 13.

277 *ibid*, p 12.

278 *Strains*, p 23.

279 *Stubborn Hope*, p 25.

280 *Poems from Algiers*, p 5–9.

281 *Stubborn Hope*, p 25.

282 *ibid*, p 11.

283 *ibid*, p 29.

284 *ibid*, p 22.

285 *Strains*, p 21.

286 *A Simple Lust*, p 39.

287 *ibid*, p 16.

288 *A Stubborn Hope*, p 49–50.

289 Brutus, *China Poems* (Occasional Publication of the African and Afro-American Research Institute, The University of Texas at Austin, 1975, p 34).

290 *ibid*, p 35.

291 *Strains*, p 43.

292 Feinberg, Barry, ed. *Poets to the People* (London, Heinemann, 1980).

293 Lindfors, Bernth, ed. *South African Voices* (Occasional Publication of the African and Afro-American Research Institute, The University of Texas at Austin, 1975).

294 Pieterse, Cosmo. *Echoes and Choruses: Ballad of the Cells* and *Selected Shorter Poems* (Athens, Ohio, Ohio University Centre for International Studies, African Program, 1974).

295 Pieterse, *Present Lives Future Becomings* (Richmond, Hickey Press, 1974).

296 Pieterse, *Echoes and Choruses*, and Pieterse, Cosmo, ed. *Short African Plays* (London, Heinemann, 1972, p 129–159).

297 *Present Lives Future Becomings*, p 1.

298 *ibid*, p 62–63.

299 *ibid*, p 62.

300 *ibid*, p 88.

301 *Poets to the People*, *op cit*, p 159.

302 *South African Voices*, *op cit*, p 158.

303   *Present Lives*, p 87.
304   *ibid*, p 88.
305   Kgositsile, Keorapetse. *My Name is Afrika* (New York, Doubleday, 1971, p 47).
306   *ibid*, p 55–56.
307   Breman, Paul. *You Better Believe It* (Harmondsworth, Penguin Books, 1973).
308   *ibid*, p 405.
309   Kgositsile, *The Present is a Dangerous Place to Live* (Chicago, Third World Press, 1974).
310   Mphahlele, Ezekiel. Review of *The Present is a Dangerous Place to Live* (*Okike*, December 9, 1975, p 119–122).
311   *ibid*, p 121.
312   Kgositsile, *Spirits Unchained* (Detroit, Broadside Press, 1969).
313   Kgositsile, *For Melba* (Chicago, Third World Press, 1970).
314   Kgositsile, 'After Mongane' (*Yardbird Reader* Vol. 4, 1975, p 48).
315   *My Name is Afrika*, p 39–40.
316   *ibid*, p 316.
317   *ibid*, p 53.
318   *ibid*, p 50.
319   *ibid*, p 28–29.
320   *ibid*, p 41.
321   *ibid*, p 55–56.
322   *ibid*, p 26–27.
323   *ibid*, p 28–29.
324   *ibid*, p 57.
325   Kunene, Mazisi. *Zulu Poems* (New York, Africana Publishing Corporation, 1970).
326   Proceedings of the Symposium on Contemporary African Literature and First African Literature Association Conference (*Issue*, VI,1, 1976).
327   *Zulu Poems*, p 5.
328   'Europe' (*ibid*, p 76–77).
329   'Cycle' (*ibid*, p 40).
330   'Triumph of Man' (*ibid*, p 79).
331   'Man's Power Over Things' (*ibid*, p 36).
332   Kunene, Review of Isidore Okpewho, *The Epic in Africa: Towards a Poetics of the Oral Performance* (*Research in African Literatures*, XI,4, 1980, p 552–558).
333   'Mother Earth, or the Folly of National Boundaries' (*Zulu Poems*, p 45).
334   Kunene, 'Dreams in Exile' (*South African Voices*, p 22).
335   *Zulu Poems*, p 47.
336   'Repeat' (*ibid*, p 63.)
337   *ibid*, p 63.

338 Kunene, 'To the Proud' (Moore, Gerald and Beier, Ulli, ed., *Modern Poetry from Africa*, Harmondsworth, Penguin Books, 1963, p 151).

339 Kunene, 'Anthem of the Decades' (*Zulu Poems*, p 89–95).

340 *Zulu Poems*, p 26.

341 *ibid*, p 91.

342 *ibid*, p 92.

343 *ibid*, p 93.

344 *ibid*, p 94.

345 Kunene, *Emperor Shaka the Great* (London, Heinemann, 1979).

346 Mtshali, Oswald Mbuyiseni. *Fire Flames* (Pietermaritzburg, Shuter & Shooter, 1980).

347 *ibid*, p 63.

348 *ibid*, p 20.

349 *ibid*, p 33.

350 *ibid*, p 19–21.

351 *ibid*, p 21.

352 *ibid*, p 27–28.

353 *ibid*, p 1–2.

354 *ibid*, p 47–49.

355 Editorial, *Medu Newsletter*, I,1, p 3–4.

356 Langa, Mandlenkosi. 'A City in South Africa' (*Peculef*, I,1, p 12–13).

357 *ibid*, p 13.

358 *ibid*, p 14–15.

359 *ibid*, p 15.

360 *ibid*, p 17–18.

361 *ibid*, p 19–21.

362 Manaka, Matsemela Cain, 'Hope for Your Return' (*Staffrider*, I,1, 1978, p 32).

CHAPTER 3: The Novel

1 Dhlomo, R.R.R., *An African Tragedy* (Alice, Lovedale Press, undated).

2 Khafula, John J. *This Thing has got to Stop* (Cape Town, African Bookman, 1946).

3 Mopeli-Paulus, A.S. (with Peter Lanham). *Blanket Boy's Moon* (London, Collins, 1953).

4 Plaatje, Sol., *Mhudi* (Alice, Lovedale Press, 1957, p 19. London, Heinemann, 1978, p 39).

5 *ibid*, Lovedale edition p 208, Heinemann edition, p 175.

6 Abrahams, Peter, *Return to Goli* (Faber & Faber, 1953).

7 *ibid*, p 14.

8 *ibid*, p 14–15.

9 Abrahams, *Tell Freedom* (London, Faber & Faber, 1954, p 45).

10 Abrahams, *Mine Boy* (London, Faber & Faber, 1946, Heinemann, 1963).

11 Abrahams, *Wild Conquest*, dedication page (London, Faber & Faber, 1951).

12 Patel, Essop, ed. *The World of Nat Nakasa* (Johannesburg, Ravan Press/Bateleur, 1975, p 81).

13 Head, Bessie. 'Some Notes on Novel Writing' (*New Classic*, No 5, 1978, p 3).

14 *ibid*, p 30.

15 Head, *When Rain Clouds Gather* (London, Gollancz, 1969).

16 Head, *Maru* (London, Gollancz, 1971).

17 Head, *A Question of Power* (London, Davis-Poynter, 1973).

18 *Maru*, p 102.

19 Head, 'Let Me Tell a Story Now ...' (*New African*, September 1962, p 8).

20 *When Rain Clouds Gather*, p 81.

21 *ibid*, p 129–130.

22 *ibid*, p 69.

23 *ibid*, p 130.

24 *ibid*, p 130.

25 Head, 'MAKEBA Muse' (*Donga*, February 1977, p 6).

26 *Maru*, p 11.

27 *ibid*, p 126.

28 Head, letter to *Transition* (IV,17, 1964, p 6).

29 *Maru*, p 12–13.

30 *A Question of Power*, p 44.

31 *ibid*, p 134.

32 *ibid*, p 205.

33 *ibid*, p 205.

34 *ibid*, p 206.

35 Ravenscroft, Arthur. 'The Novels of Bessie Head' (*Aspects of South African Literature*, ed. Christopher Heywood, London, Heinemann, 1976).

36 *A Question of Power*, p 54.

37 *ibid*, p 49.

38 Boetie, Dugmore, with Simon, Barney. *Familiarity is the Kingdom of the Lost* (London, Barrie and Rockliff, The Cresset Press, 1969).

39 *ibid*, p 62.

40 *ibid*, p 93.

41 *ibid*, p 17.

42 *ibid*, p 175–176.

43 *ibid*, p 178.

44 Rive, Richard. *Emergency* (London, Faber & Faber, 1964; also London, Collier Macmillan, 1970).

45 Interview with Richard Rive (*Wietie*, No 2, p 10).

46 Rive, *Emergency*, p 11.
47 *ibid*, p 127.
48 La Guma, Alex. *In the Fog of the Season's End* (London, Heinemann, 1972, p 138).
49 La Guma, *The Stone Country* (London, Heinemann, 1967).
50 *ibid*, p 74.
51 La Guma, *A Walk in the Night and Other Stories* (London, Heinemann, 1967).
52 *ibid*, p 52.
53 La Guma, *And a Threefold Cord* (Berlin, Seven Seas Publishers, 1964).
54 *A Walk in the Night*, p 39.
55 *ibid*, p 43–44.
56 *ibid*, p 96.
57 *ibid*, p 96.
58 *And a Threefold Cord*, p 107.
59 *ibid*, p 81.
60 *ibid*, p 168.
61 *ibid*, opposite p 9.
62 *ibid*, p 141.
63 *ibid*, p 142.
64 *The Stone Country*, p 39.
65 La Guma, *Time of the Butcherbird* (London, Heinemann, 1979).
66 *A Walk in the Night*, p 48.
67 *ibid*, p 71.
68 *ibid*, p 66.
69 *ibid*, p 95.
70 *ibid*, p 37.
71 *ibid*, p 89.
72 *ibid*, p 9.
73 *The Stone Country*, p 129.
74 *ibid*, p 38.
75 *And a Threefold Cord*, p 135.
76 *The Stone Country*, p 61.
77 Mphahlele, Es'kia (Ezekiel). *English in Africa*, V,12, 1979, p 18.
78 Mphahlele, *The Wanderers* (New York, Macmillan, 1970).
79 Lindfors, Bernth, et al. Interview with Ezekiel Mphahlele (*Palaver*, Austin, African and Afro-American Research Institute, Austin, Texas, 1972, p 41).
80 Interview with Ezekiel Mphahlele (*Weekend Argus*, April 7, 1979).
81 *The Wanderers*, p 308.
82 *ibid*, p 301.
83 *ibid*, p 107.
84 *ibid*, p 174.
85 *ibid*, p 264.

86   *ibid*, p 204.
87   *ibid*, p 245.
88   *ibid*, p 302.
89   Mphahlele, *Chirundu* (Johannesburg, Ravan Press, 1979).
90   *ibid*, p 9.
91   *ibid*, p 45.
92   *ibid*, p 46.
93   *ibid*, p 45-46.
94   *ibid*, p 53.
95   *ibid*, p 73.
96   *ibid*, p vii.
97   *ibid*, p 116.
98   Dikobe, Modikwe. *The Marabi Dance* (London, Heinemann, 1973).
99   *ibid*, p 40.
100 *ibid*, p 30.
101 *ibid*, p 31.
102 *ibid*, p 13.
103 *ibid*, p 84.
104 *ibid*, p 2.
105 *ibid*, p 115.
106 *ibid*, p 115.
107 *ibid*, p 79.
108 *ibid*, p 115.
109 Zwelonke, D.M. *Robben Island* (London, Heinemann, 1973).
110 *ibid*, p 3.
111 *ibid*, p 1.
112 *ibid*, p 30.
113 *ibid*, p 78.
114 *ibid*, p 22.
115 *ibid*, p 33.
116 *ibid*, p 42.
117 *ibid*, p 13.
118 *ibid*, p 39.
119 *ibid*, p 29.
120 Peteni, R.L. *Hill of Fools* (Cape Town, David Philip, 1976 and London, Heinemann, 1976—page numbering identical).
121 *ibid*, p 43.
122 *ibid*, p 149.
123 *ibid*, p 74.
124 Sepamla, Sipho. *The Root is One* (London, Rex Collings in association with David Philip, 1979).
125 *ibid*, p 2.
126 *ibid*, p 131.
127 *ibid*, p 129-130.
128 *ibid*, p 130.

129 Tlali, M. (Miriam Masoli). *Muriel at Metropolitan* (Johannesburg, Ravan Press, 1975).
130 *ibid*, p 71.
131 *ibid*, p 76.
132 *ibid*, p 15–16.
133 *ibid*, p 43.
134 Interview with Miriam Tlali (*Argus*, July 17, 1980, p 10).
135 *Muriel at Metropolitan*, p 46.
136 *ibid*, p 47.
137 *ibid*, p 48.
138 *ibid*, p 27.
139 Tlali, *Amandla* (Johannesburg, Ravan Press, 1980).
140 *ibid*, p 139.
141 Ngubane, Jordan K. (Kush). *Ushaba* (Washington D.C., Three Continents Press, 1974).
142 *Amandla*, p 288–289.
143 *Ushaba* p 58.
144 Carim, Enver. *A Dream Deferred* (London, Allen Lane, 1973).
145 Williams, Neil Alwin. *Just a Little Stretch of Road* (Johannesburg, Ravan Press, 1979).
146 *ibid*, p 63.
147 *ibid*, back cover.
148 Essop, Ahmed. *The Visitation* (Johannesburg, Ravan Press, 1980).
149 *ibid*, p 53.
150 *ibid*, p 38.
151 *ibid*, p 49.
152 *ibid*, p 53.
153 *ibid*, p 45.
154 *ibid*, p 72.
155 *ibid*, p 80.
156 *ibid*, p 81.
157 *ibid*, p 97.

CHAPTER 4: Short Stories

1 Mphahlele, Ezekiel (Es'kia). 'Black and White' (*New Statesman*, September 10 1960, p 343).
2 Philip Segal's personal notes of the conference shown to the author.
3 Mphahlele, *The African Image* (London, Faber & Faber, 1962).
4 *ibid*, p 37.
5 Mphahlele, *Down Second Avenue* (London, Faber & Faber, 1959).
6 Abrahams, Peter. *Dark Testament* (London, Allen & Unwin, 1942).
7 *ibid*, p 27.

8   *Down Second Avenue*, p 59.
9   Mphahlele, 'Black and White', p 342–346.
10 *ibid*, p 343.
11 *Down Second Avenue*, p 217.
12 Mphahlele, *Man Must Live and Other Stories* (Cape Town, The African Bookman, 1947, p 9).
13 *Drum*, April 1957, p 47.
14 Mphahlele, 'Lesane' (*Drum* April, 1957, p 47).
15 Mphahlele, *The Living and Dead and Other Stories* (Ibadan, Ministry of Education, 1961).
16 *ibid*, p 17.
17 *ibid*, p 19.
18 *ibid*, p 30.
19 *ibid*, p 36.
20 *ibid*, p 36.
21 *ibid*, p 66.
22 Mphahlele, *In Corner B* (Nairobi, East African Publishing House, 1967).
23 *ibid*, p 44.
24 *ibid*, p 164.
25 *ibid*, p 208.
26 Plomer, William. Review of *Down Second Avenue* (*New Statesman*, April 25 1959, p 582–583).
27 *In Corner B*, p 111.
28 *ibid*, p 109.
29 *ibid*, p 110.
30 *ibid*, p 115.
31 *ibid*, p 116.
32 *ibid*, p 116–117.
33 *ibid*, p 117.
34 *ibid*, p 118.
35 *ibid*, p 124–125.
36 *ibid*, p 125–126.
37 *ibid*, p 126.
38 *ibid*, p 123.
39 Nkosi, Lewis. 'African Fiction: South Africa: Protest' (*Africa Report*, October 1962, p 3).
40 Gordimer, Nadine. 'The Novel and the Nation' (*Times Literary Supplement*, September 1961, p 520).
41 Themba, Can. Review of *Darkness and Light*, Rutherfoord, Peggy, ed. (*Drum*, May 1959, p 15).
42 Maimane, Arthur. 'A Manner of Speaking' (*Africa South in Exile*, IV,4, 1960, p 113–118).
43 Makaza, Webster. 'Wheels of Justice' (*The New African* ('The Mob') July 13, 1963, p 116–118, and Drum short story contest 1962–1963).

44 Nkosi, Lewis. 'The Prisoner' (*African Writing Today*, ed. Mphahlele, Ezekiel, Harmondsworth, Penguin Books, 1967).

45 Motsisi, Casey (Kid). *Casey & Company*, Selected Writings of Casey Motsisi, ed. Mutloatse, Mothobi. (Johannesburg, Ravan Press, 1978, p 6).

46 Motsisi, 'A Very Important Appointment' (*The Classic*, I,1, 1963, p 41–50).

47 Motsisi, 'Mita' (*Drum*, March 1963, and *Casey & Company*, p 72–77).

48 Modisane, William 'Bloke'. 'The Dignity of Begging' (*Drum*, September 1951, p 4–5).

49 Modisane, 'The Respectable Pickpocket' (*Drum*, January 1954, p 22–23).

50 Modisane, 'The Situation' (*Black Orpheus*, No. 12, p 10–16).

51 Themba, Can (Daniel Canadoise Dorsay). 'Mob Passion' (*Drum* Short story Competition, 1953 also p 38–45 in *Darkness and Light*.)

52 Mphahlele, *The Africa Image*, p 187.

53 Themba, 'Dube Train' (*The Will to Die* ed. Stuart, Donald and Holland, Roy, London, Heinemann, 1972, p 57–62).

54 *ibid*, p 57.

55 *ibid*, p 62.

56 *ibid*, p 58.

57 Themba, 'The Urchin' (*The Will to Die*, p 26–36).

58 Themba, 'Requiem for Sophiatown' (*ibid*, p 102–108).

59 'The Suit' (*ibid*, p 36–46).

60 *ibid*, p 46.

61 Motjuwadi, Stanley. 'Can Themba Remembered' (*The Classic*, II,4, 1968, p 14).

62 'The Will to Die' (*op cit*, p 62–66).

63 *ibid*, p 62.

64 'Crepuscule'. *ibid*, p 2–11.

65 *ibid*, p 8.

66 *ibid*, p viii.

67 *ibid*, p xi.

68 Clarke, Peter. *Soul Motion III* (Nashville, Division of Cultural Research, The Department of Art, Fisk University, Nashville, Tennessee, 1973).

69 Clarke, 'Figures and Settings' (*Contrast* VI,4, 1970, p 80–90).

70 *ibid*, p 82.

71 Clarke, 'Winter Shepherding' (*Contrast*, III,2, 1964, p 44).

72 Clarke, 'Pastorale' (Gray, Stephen, ed., *On the Edge of the World*, Johannesburg, Ad. Donker, 1974, p 34–38).

73 *ibid*, p 38.

74 Clarke, 'Figures and Settings', p 88-90.
75 Sepamla, Sipho. 'King Taylor' (*New Classic*, No 1, 1975, p 8-18).
76 Mutloatse, Mothobi. 'The Truth . . . Mama' (*The Voice*, December 17, 1977, p 6-7).
77 Tshabangu, Mango. 'Thoughts in a Train' (*Staffrider*, I,2, 1978, p 27 and *Forced Landing* ed. Mutloatse, Mothobi, p 156-158).
78 Ndebele, Njabulo. 'The Music of the Violin' (*Staffrider*, III,3, p 7-11,40-41).
79 *ibid*, p 40.
80 *ibid*, p 41.
81 *ibid*, p 9.
82 Aiyer, Narain. 'The Cane is Singing' (*Staffrider*, III,4, 1980/1981, p 5-6).
83 Tlali, Miriam. 'The Point of No Return' (*Staffrider*, I,2, 1978, p 29-32).
84 Sigwili, Nokugcina. 'My dear Madam . . .' (*Staffrider*, III,3, 1980/1981, p 11-12,14).
85 *Staffrider*, III,1, 1980, p 44.
86 Matthews, James. *The Park and Other Stories* (Athlone, Blac Publishing House, 1974).
87 Rive, Richard, ed. *Quartet* (London, Heinemann, 1963).
88 Matthews, *The Park and Other Stories*, p 102.
89 *ibid*, p 43-44.
90 *ibid*, p 48.
91 *ibid*, p 50.
92 Rive, *African Songs* (Berlin, Seven Seas Publishers, 1963).
93 Rive, *Quartet*.
94 Rive, *Selected Writings* (Johannesburg, Ad. Donker, 1977).
95 Rive, 'African Song' (*ibid*, p 38-46).
96 Rive, 'The Bench' (*African Songs*, p 93-102).
97 Rive, 'Willieboy' (*African Songs*, p 44-49).
98 Rive, 'No Room at Solitaire' (*Selected Writings*, p 20-28).
99 *ibid*, p 23.
100 *ibid*, p 28.
101 Rive, 'Strike' (*African Songs*, p 53-67).
102 Rive, 'Middle Passage' (*Contrast*, VI,1, 1969, p 37-44).
103 Rive, 'Resurrection' (*Quartet*, p 41-51).
104 Rive, 'Rain' (*Selected Writings*, p 11-19).
105 *ibid*, p 11.
106 *ibid*, p 14.
107 Rive, 'The Visits' (*Selected Writings*, p 51-58).
108 *ibid*, p 109.
109 Interview with Richard Rive (*Wietie*, No 2, p 10-13).
110 Rive, 'Streetcorner' (*Selected Writings*, p 29-37).

111 La Guma, Alex. *A Walk in the Night and Other Stories* (Ibadan, Mbari Publications, 1967 and London, Heinemann, 1968).

112 La Guma, 'The Gladiators' (*Walk in the Night*, p 114–120).

113 *ibid*, p 114.

114 *ibid*, p 114.

115 *ibid*, p 120.

116 La Guma, 'The Lemon Orchard' (*op cit*, p 131–136).

117 *ibid*, p 135.

118 La Guma, 'Tattoo Mark and Nails' (*op cit*, p 97–107).

119 *ibid*, p 97.

120 *ibid*, p 106–107.

121 Head, Bessie. *The Collector of Treasures and Other Botswana Village Tales* (Cape Town, David Philip, 1977).

122 Head, 'Life' (*The Collector of Treasures*, p 37–46).

123 *ibid*, p 43.

124 *ibid*, p 97–103.

125 *ibid*, p 91.

126 *ibid*, inside front cover.

127 *ibid*, p 91.

128 *ibid*, p 101.

129 *ibid*, p 103.

130 *ibid*, p 19–36.

131 *ibid*, p 19.

132 *ibid*, p 1–6.

133 *ibid*, acknowledgement page.

134 *ibid*, p 7–12.

135 *ibid*, p 10–11.

136 *ibid*, p 10.

137 *ibid*, p 25.

138 *ibid*, p 47–56.

139 *ibid*, p 47.

140 *ibid*, p 57–60.

141 *ibid*, p 9.

142 Head, *A Question of Power* (London, Heinemann, 1974, p 138).

143 Head, *When Rain Clouds Gather* (London, Victor Gollancz, 1969, p 16).

144 Head, *Collector*, p 89–90.

145 *ibid*, p 81.

146 *ibid*, p 84.

147 *ibid*, p 20.

148 Essop, Ahmed. *The Hajji and Other Stories* (Johannesburg, Ravan Press, 1978).

149 Essop, Olive Schreiner Prize acceptance speech (*The English Academy Review*, 1980, p 19–20).

150 Essop, 'The Commandment' (*The Hajji*, p 70–72).

151 Essop, 'Gerty's Brother' (*English Academy Annual Review*, 1979, p 11–15 and *The Hajji* p 89–93).
152 'Gerty's Brother' (*The Hajji*, p 89).
153 *ibid*, p 92.
154 *ibid*, p 93.
155 *ibid*, p 1–13.
156 *ibid*, p 2.
157 *ibid*, p 2.
158 *ibid*, p 9.
159 *ibid*, p 13.
160 *ibid*, p 98–102.
161 *ibid*, p 99.
162 *ibid*, p 20–26.
163 *ibid*, p 22.
164 *ibid*, p 61–65.
165 *ibid*, p 40–49.
166 *ibid*, p 43.
167 *ibid*, p x.
168 *ibid*, p 46.
169 *ibid*, p 49.
170 *ibid*, p 77–84.
171 *ibid*, p 84.
172 *ibid*, p 116–120.
173 *ibid*, p 117.
174 *ibid*, p 65.
175 *The English Academy of Southern Africa Annual Review*, 1979, p 8.
176 Mzamane, Mbulelo. *Mzala* (Johannesburg, Ravan Press, 1980).
177 *ibid*, p 49.
178 *ibid*, p 29–40.
179 *ibid*, p 38.
180 *ibid*, p 146–152.
181 *ibid*, p 125–145.
182 *ibid*, p 77–95.
183 *ibid*, p 85.
184 *ibid*, p 14–27.
185 *ibid*, p 3.
186 *ibid*, p xi.
187 *ibid*, p xi.
188 Dangor, Achmed. 'Waiting for Leila' (*Forced Landing*, ed. Mutloatse, Mothobi, p 159–169).
189 Dangor, Achmed, 'The Wedding' (*Wietie* No 1, p 3–6).
190 'Waiting for Leila', p 164–165.
191 *ibid*, p 165.
192 *ibid*, p 160.
193 *ibid*, p 168.

194 *ibid*, p 168.
195 *ibid*, p 161.
196 Matshoba, Mtutuzeli, *Call me not a man* (Johannesburg, Ravan Press, 1979).
197 *ibid*, p x.
198 *ibid*, p 18.
199 *ibid*, p 18.
200 *ibid*, p 92–142.
201 *ibid*, p 97.
202 *ibid*, p 46.
203 *ibid*, p 118.
204 *ibid*, p 119–120.
205 *ibid*, p 133.
206 *ibid*, p 94.
207 *ibid*, p 108.
208 *ibid*, p 138.
209 *ibid*, p 143–187.
210 *ibid*, p 147.
211 Matshoba, 'To Kill a Man's Pride' (*Forced Landing*, p 103–127).
212 *Call Me Not a Man*, p 58–59.
213 *ibid*, p 93.
214 *ibid*, p 99.
215 *ibid*, p 101.

CHAPTER 5: Autobiographical Writing
1 Jabavu, Nontandi (Noni). *Drawn in Colour* (London, John Murray, 1960).
2 *ibid*, p 67–68.
3 Matshikiza, Todd. *Chocolates for my Wife* (London, Hodder and Stoughton, 1961).
4 *ibid*, p 66–67.
5 *ibid*, p 34.
6 *ibid*, p 111.
7 Mphahlele, Ezekiel. *Down Second Avenue* (London, Faber & Faber, 1959).
8 Abrahams, Peter. *Tell Freedom* (London, Faber & Faber, 1954).
9 *ibid*, p 64.
10 Matshikiza, *Chocolates for my wife*, p 19.
11 *ibid*, p 115.
12 Nkosi, Lewis. 'Fiction by Black South Africans' (*Home and Exile*, London, Longman Green & Co. 1965, p 126).
13 Mphahlele, *Down Second Avenue*, p 17.
14 Jabavu, *The Ochre People* (London, John Murray, 1963).
15 Hutchinson, Alfred. *Road to Ghana* (London, Victor Gollancz, 1960).

16 Abrahams, *Tell Freedom*, p 39.
17 Jabavu, *Drawn in Colour*, p 21.
18 Abrahams, *Return to Goli* (London, Faber & Faber, 1953).
19 Abrahams, *Tell Freedom*, p 196–197.
20 *ibid*, p 58.
21 Modisane, William (Bloke). *Blame Me on History* (London, Thames and Hudson, 1964).
22 Mazlish, 'Autobiography and Psychoanalysis' (*Encounter*, October 1970, p 28).
23 Mphahlele, *Down Second Avenue*, p 184.
24 *ibid*, p 185.
25 *ibid*, p 153.
26 Pieterse, Cosmo. Interview with Ezekiel Mphahlele, Transcription Centre, London, 1969 (Duerden, Dennis, ed. *African Writers Talking*, Heinemann, London, 1972).
27 Abrahams, *Tell Freedom*, p 9.
28 Mphahlele, *Down Second Avenue*, p 11.
29 *ibid*, p 111.
30 Mogkatle, Naboth. *Autobiography of an Unknown South African* (Berkeley and Los Angeles, University of California Press, 1971).

CHAPTER 6: Drama
 1 Kelly, Mary. *Bulletin of the British Drama League*, 1940 (as published in *South African Outlook*, July 1, 1940, p 26).
 2 Dhlomo, H.I.E. 'Drama and the African' (*South African Outlook*, October 1, 1936, p 232–235).
 3 *ibid*, p 232.
 4 *ibid*, p 233.
 5 *ibid*, p 234–235.
 6 Dhlomo, 'African Drama and Poetry' (*South African Outlook*, April 1, 1939, p 88–90).
 7 *ibid*, p 90.
 8 *ibid*, p 90.
 9 *ibid*, p 90.
10 Dhlomo, *The Girl Who Killed to Save* (Alice, Lovedale Press, 1935).
11 *ibid*, historical note, first page.
12 *ibid*, p 12.
13 *ibid*, p 10.
14 *ibid*, p 6.
15 *ibid*, p 12.
16 *ibid*, p 3.
17 *ibid*, p 5.
18 *ibid*, p 40–41.

19 Dhlomo, *Dingana* (play in manuscript, Library, University of Natal, Durban).

20 Goro-X, S. *Shaka.* (Johannesburg, Juta, 1940).

21 Sepamla, Sipho. In *S'ketsh*, Winter 1979, p 18.

22 Manaka, Matsemela. 'Theatre of the Dispossessed' (*Staffrider*, III,3, 1980, p 28).

23 Fugard, Athol, Kani, John and Ntshona, Winston. *Statements. Three Plays* (London, Oxford, Cape Town, O.U.P., 1974, introduction—page unnumbered).

24 Charad, Linda. 'Kani the actor without a script' (*Sunday Times Colour Magazine*, July 29, 1973, p 19–21).

25 Fugard et al, *Statements*, p 4.

26 *ibid*, p 7.

27 *ibid*, p 17.

28 *ibid*, p 13.

29 *ibid*, p 38.

30 *ibid*, p 38.

31 *ibid*, p 75–76.

32 *ibid*, p 77.

33 *ibid*, p 47.

34 *ibid*, p 77.

35 Sepamla, 'The Urban Cultural Scene—Theatre' (*S'ketsh*, Winter 1979, p 17–19).

36 *ibid*, p 19.

37 Charad, *op cit*, p 19.

38 Leshoai, Benjamin (B.L., Bob.) *Lines Draw Monsters* (Pereira, Ernest, ed., *Contemporary South African Plays*, p 251–266).

39 *ibid*, p 254.

40 *ibid*, p 266.

41 Gray, Stephen, interview with Fatima Dike (*Contrast*, XII,1, 1978, p 82).

42 Manaka, Matsemela. Note on *Egoli* (*Staffrider*, I,1, 1978, p 49).

43 Dike, Fatima. *The Sacrifice of Kreli* (Gray, Stephen, ed., *Theatre One*, p 33–79).

44 Gray, interview with Fatima Dike, p 79.

45 Dike, *The Sacrifice of Kreli*, p 52.

46 *ibid*, p 79.

47 Gray, interview with Fatima Dike, p 81.

48 Dike, Fatima. *The First South African* (Ravan Playscript No 4, Johannesburg, Ravan Press, 1979, p 15).

49 Mtsaka, Makwedini Julius. *Not His Pride* (Ravan Playscript No 1. Johannesburg, Ravan Press, 1978, p 27).

50 *ibid*, p 3.

51 Kente, Gibson. 'Too Late' (*S'ketsh*, Winter 1975, p 17–22).

52 Leshoai, Bob (Benjamin, B.L.) 'The Rendezvous' (*S'ketsh*, Summer, 1975, p 35–38).

53 *Snarl* No 1, August 1974, p 1.

54 Mofokeng, Zakes, and Mabaso, Corney. 'Job Mava' (*Staffrider*, III,4, 1980/81, p 21–23,26–29).

55 Leshoai, *Wrath of the Ancestors and Other Plays* (Nairobi, East African Publishing Company, 1972).

56 Rive, Richard. *Resurrection* (Pieterse, Cosmo, ed., *Short African Plays*, London, Heinemann, 1972, p 75–92).

57 Rive, *Make Like Slaves* (Henderson, Gwyneth, ed., *African Theatre: Eight Prize-Winning Plays for Radio*, London, Heinemann, 1973, p 1–18).

58 *ibid*, p 2.

59 *ibid*, p 4.

60 *ibid*, p 5.

61 *ibid*, p 4.

62 *ibid*, p 14.

63 *ibid*, p 14.

64 *ibid*, p 9.

65 *ibid*, p 15.

66 *ibid*, p 17.

67 *ibid*, pp 75–92.

68 *ibid*, p 92.

69 Hutchinson, Alfred, *The Rain-Killers* (Litto, Fredric, ed., *Plays from Black Africa*, New York, Hill & Wang, 1968, p 129–207.

70 *ibid*, p 133.

71 Nkosi, Lewis. *Rhythm of Violence* (London, O.U.P., 1964).

72 Tibble, Anne, ed. *African/English Literature* (London, Peter Owen, 1965).

73 Nkosi, *Rhythm of Violence*, p 7.

74 Nkosi, 'African Fiction: Protest' (Africa Report, October 1962, p 3).

75 La Guma, Alex. 'The Man in the Tree' (*The Literary Review*, XV,1, 1971, p 19–30).

76 Pieterse, Cosmo. 'Ballad of the Cells' (Pieterse, Cosmo, ed., *Short African Plays*, London, Heinemann, 1972).

77 *ibid*, p 129.

78 *ibid*, p 139–140.

79 *ibid*, p 141.

CHAPTER 7: Critical Writing

1 Vilakazi, B. (Benedict Wallet). 'The Oral and Written Literature in Nguni' (D. Litt. Thesis in Bantu Studies, Johannesburg, Witwatersrand University, October 1945,).

2 Jordan, A.C. 'Towards an African Literature' (*Africa South*, 1958-1960. Subsequently published as *Towards an African Literature: The Emergence of Literary Form in Xhosa*, Berkeley,

Los Angeles, London, University of California Press, 1973).

3   Jordan, *Tales from South Africa* (Berkeley and London, University of California Press, 1973).

4   Leshoai, B. (Benjamin, Bob.) *Masilo's Adventures and Other Stories* (London, Longman, 1968).

5   Mphahlele, Ezekiel (Es'kia). *The African Image* (London, Faber & Faber, 1962, p 186).

6   *ibid*, p 186.

7   *ibid*, p 23.

8   *ibid*, p 23.

9   Mphahlele, 'The Non-European Character in South African Fiction' (M.A. Thesis in English Literature, Pretoria, University of South Africa, 1956).

10   Mphahalele, *The African Image* (Revised edition, London, Faber & Faber, 1973).

11   *ibid*, p 88.

12   *ibid*, p 89.

13   *ibid*, p 102.

14   *ibid*, p 122.

15   *ibid*, p 49.

16   Mphahlele, *Voices in the Whirlwind and Other Essays* (New York, Hill & Wang, 1972).

17   *ibid*, p 187.

18   *ibid*, p 188.

19   *ibid*, p 194.

20   *African Image*, revised, p 22.

21   *ibid*, p 106.

22   *ibid*, p 176.

23   *ibid*, p 237.

24   *ibid*, p 239.

25   *Voices in the Whirlwind*, p 31, quotes Gwendolyn Brooks 'In the Mecca' (acknowledged to New York, Harper & Row, 1964).

26   *Voices in the Whirlwind*, p 36.

27   Mphahlele, 'The Real Africa' (*Commonwealth Challenge*, VII,4, p 54).

28   Mphahlele, 'Black Literature at the University of Denver' (*Research in African Literatures*, III,1, p 72).

29   Mphahlele, 'Why I Teach my Discipline' (*Denver Quarterly*, VIII,1, p 32).

30   Mphahlele, *Down Second Avenue* (London, Faber & Faber, 1959, p 221).

31   *Weekend Argus*, April 7, 1979, p 11.

32   *ibid*, p 11.

33   Mphahlele, 'Exile, the Tyranny of Place and the Literary Compromise' (*UNISA English Studies*, XVII,1, 1979, p 37–44).

34 Mphahlele, 'The Voice of Prophecy in African Poetry' (*English in Africa*, VI,1, 1979, p 33–34).
35 *ibid*, p 34–35.
36 *ibid*, p 45.
37 *Weekend Argus*, *op cit*.
38 Segal, Philip, personal notes quoting Lewis Nkosi at Conference of African Writers of English Expression, June 1962, at Makerere University College, Uganda.
39 Nkosi, Lewis, 'White on Black' (*Observer*, April 1, 1962, p 46).
40 Nkosi, 'A Question of Identity' (*Home and Exile*, London, Longmans, 1965, p 42–51).
41 *ibid*, p 126.
42 *ibid*, p 125.
43 *ibid*, p 126.
44 *ibid*, p 132.
45 *ibid*, p 45.
46 Nkosi, 'White on Black', *op cit*, p 46.
47 Nkosi, 'A Question of Identity', p 51.
48 Nkosi, *The Transplanted Heart* (Benin City, Nigeria, Ethiope Publishing Co., 1975).
49 Nkosi, Review of *The World of Nat Nakasa* (*Research in African Literatures*, IX,3, 1978, p 475–479).
50 *ibid*, p 477.
51 *ibid*, p 479.
52 Nkosi, interviews with writers (*African Writers Talking*, ed. Duerden, Dennis and Pieterse, Cosmo, London, Heinemann, 1972).
53 Rive, Richard. 'Senghor and Negritude' (*Selected Writings*, Johannesburg, Ad. Donker, 1977, p 139).
54 Rive, 'No Common Factor' (*Selected Writings*, p 72.)
55 Rive, *ibid*, p 69–73.
56 Rive, 'Writing and the New Society' (*Contrast*, XII,3, 1979, p 67).
57 Rive, 'The Black Man and White Literature' (*New Classic*, No 4, 1977, p 61–70).
58 *ibid*, p 61.
59 *ibid*, p 70.
60 Rive, 'New Light on Olive Schreiner' (*Contrast*, VIII,4, 1973, p 40–47).
61 Rive, 'An Infinite Compassion' (*Contrast*, VIII,1, 1972, p 25–43).
62 Rive, 'Arthur Nortje: Poet' (*Selected Writings*, p 107–109).
63 *ibid*, p 108.
64 *ibid*, p 109.
65 Rive, 'Taos in Harlem: An Interview with Langston Hughes' (*Selected Writings*, p 110–118).

66 *ibid*, p 116.
67 Mzamane, Mbulelo Vizikhungo. 'The 50s and Beyond: An Evaluation' (*New Classic*, No 4, 1977, p 23–32).
68 *ibid*, p 25.
69 *ibid*, p 26.
70 *ibid*, p 26.
71 Mzamane, 'Literature and Politics Among Blacks in South Africa' (*New Classic*, No 5, 1978, p 42–57).
72 *ibid*, p 42.
73 Mphahlele, Ezekiel (Es'kia) and Komey, Ellis, eds. *Modern African Stories* (London, Faber & Faber, 1964).
74 Mphahlele, ed. *African Writing Today* (Harmondsworth, Penguin, 1967).
75 Rive, Richard, ed. *Quartet, New Voices from South Africa* (London, Heinemann, 1963).
76 Rive, ed. *Modern African Prose* (London, Heinemann, 1964).
77 Pieterse, Cosmo, ed. *Seven South African Poets* (London, Heinemann, 1971, p xi).
78 Pieterse, Cosmo, and Munro, Donald, eds. *Protest and Conflict* (London, Heinemann, 1969).
79 Ripken, Peter. *Das Schwarze Wort, Südafrikanische Erzählungen* (Wuppertal, Peter Hammer Verlag, 1974).
80 Kgositsile, Keorapetse. *The Word is Here* (New York, Anchor Book Doubleday, 1973).
81 *ibid*, p xv.
82 *ibid*, p xvii.
83 Mutloatse, Mothobi, ed. *Forced Landing* (Johannesburg, Ravan Press, 1980).
84 *ibid*, p 1.
85 *ibid*, p 5.
86 *ibid*, p 6.
87 *ibid*, p 71.
88 *ibid*, p 71.

Selected Bibliography

PRIMARY WORKS

POETRY

'a Motana, Nape. Another Black Boy, Exile, The Pick-Pocket, Mahlalela, Growing, Night Dies for My Rebirth, Hunger Dies a Calabash Death (*Staffrider*, I,3, 1978); (for Thembeka) (*Staffrider*, II,1, 1979); from Elder Afrikaner (*New Classic*, 4, 1977).

Abrahams, Peter. *A Blackman Speaks of Freedom* (Durban, Universal Printing Works, 1944); Me, Colored, Lonely Road (Hughes, ed. *Poems from Black Africa*; *vide* anthologies).

Asvat, Farouk. Possibilities for a man hunted by SB's, The Journey of a Slave (*Staffrider*, II,3, 1979); Part of Africa, Whiteflower, An Act of Immorality, The Barrier (*Wietie*, I).

Banoobhai, Shabbir. *Echoes of my Other Self* (Johannesburg, Ravan Press, 1980); The Flames (*New Coin*, VIII,3/4, 1972); Country Girls, At my Soul's Last Spring Cleaning (*New Coin*, X,1/2, 1974); The Rising and the Falling (*New Coin*, XI,1/2, 1975); St Michaels-on-Sea prostitute (*Ophir*, 22, 1975); poem (*Ophir*, 23, 1976); i have known god (*UNISA English Studies*, XIV, 1976); i have rooted myself . . . , within your womb . . . , a fear induced . . . (*New Classic*, 3, 1976.)

Brutus, Dennis. *Letters to Martha and Other Poems from a South African Prison* (London, Heinemann, 1968); *Poems from Algiers* (Austin, Texas, Occasional Publication of the Afro-American Research Institute, University of Texas, 1970); *A Simple Lust*, Selected Poems [includes *Sirens, Knuckles, Boots* (Evanston, Northwestern University Press/Ibadan, Mbari Publications, 1963), *Letters to Martha* (*q.v.*), *Thoughts Abroad* (John Bruin, pseud., Del Valle, Texas, Troubadour Press, 1970), *Poems from Algiers* (*q.v.*)] (New York, Hill and Wang, 1973); *China Poems* (Austin, Texas, Occasional Publication of the Afro-American Research Institute, University of Texas, 1975); *Strains* (Austin, Texas, Troubadour Press, 1975); *Stubborn Hope* (Washington, D.C., Three Continents Press, 1978).

Buthelezi, Bafana. Tribute to Mapetha (*Staffrider*, II,1, 1979).

Cassim, M.F. Autumn in Ladysmith, A Circular Track, Waggons (*UNISA English Studies*, XII,2, 1974).

Choonara, Ismail. A Lament for my Step-Mother Country (*The Literary Review*, XV,1, 1971).

Clarke, Peter (pseud. Kumalo, Peter). *Soul Motion II* (Nashville, Tennessee, Division of Cultural Research, Department of Art, Fisk University, 1973); Play Song, In Air, Young Shepherd Bathing his Feet (Hughes, ed. *Poems from Black Africa, vide* anthologies); Party Conscience (*New Nation*, May 1973); The Looking Glass (*Contrast*, I,4, 1960); A Winter's Night (Ba Shiru, IX,1/2, 1978); At Effity Mounds National Monument, Iowa (*Contrast*, X,4, 1976).

Cloete, Austin. House Arrest, Bachelor Flats, Dimbaza, Removed, A Land Forsaken (Matthews, ed. *Black Voices Shout! vide* anthologies).

Dangor, Achmed. Accolades (*New Nation*, June 1972); poems (*Staffrider*, II,3, 1979); Piety (*Staffrider*, III,4, 1980); The Voices that are Dead, The Silence of the Rocks, Once there was a Poem (*Wietie*, I). [undated]

Davids, Jennifer. *Searching for Words* (Cape Town, David Philip, 1974); I know (*Contrast*, IV,2, 1966); Songs for an Autumn Morning (*Wurm*, 8, 1968); Birds in the Sky, Flowers in a Vase (*New Nation*, August 1969); Locus (*New Coin*, VI,2, 1970); Javanese Marionette, Air, Rock (*Contrast*, VI,4, 1970); Conversation (*Contrast*, VIII,1, 1972).

Dhlomo, H.I.E. *Valley of a Thousand Hills* (Durban, Knox Publishing Company, 1941; extract in Macnab, ed. *Poets in South Africa* and in Wake and Reed, eds. *Book of African Verse, vide* anthologies); Benedict Wallet Vilakazi, M.A. (*Ilanga Lase*, Jan. 15, 1944); Life is 'Bitter Sweet' (*Ilanga Lase*, April 1, 1944); Not for Me (*Ilanga Lase*, May 19, 1945; Zulu (Traditional) Conception of the Universe (*Ilanga Lase*, July 21, 1945); The Nile (Filed without source in collection 'Izibongo', Killie Campbell Africana Library, Durban); Fired, Harvest Time, The Question (Beasts or Brothers), Because I'm Black (*English in Africa*, I,2, 1974).

Dike, Fatima. For a Black Woman, Malaina (*New Classic*, 3,1976).

Douts, Christine. To You, Come! my brave warrior . . . , Sounds of the Night, They jumped on him . . . , Evening is sweeping . . . , My Township, Dear God! . . , Uhuru Day (Matthews, ed. *Black Voices Shout! vide* anthologies).

Dues, Mike. Hunger wrote this Epitaph (*Staffrider*, II,1, 1979); Timol, The Raid, My fishing village is . . . , you want . . . , (Matthews, ed. *Black Voices Shout! vide* anthologies).

Gwala, Mafika (Pascal). *Jol'iinkomo* (Johannesburg, Ad. Donker, 1977); An Attempt at Communication, Food for the Couple, Promise (*Ophir*, 11, 1970); Back to Mama (*New Classic*, 4, 1977); Words for a Mother, Bonk'Ababjahile, In Defence of Poetry, Circles with Eyes (*Staffrider*, I,2, 1978); A Poem, Blue Bluessing In (*New Classic*, 3, 1976); There is . . . (*Staffrider*, I,3, 1978); Story of the Tractor, Time of the Hero (*Staffrider*, II,2, 1979); So it be said, After the Rainstorm (*Staffrider*, II,4, 1979); A Reminder (*Staffrider*, III,2, 1980); Africa at Peace (*Staffrider*, III, 3, 1980); Beyond Dreams, From the outside (Matthews, ed. *Black Voices Shout! vide* anthologies); Promise (*Ophir*, 11, 1970).

House, Amelia Blossom. Truant, Melanie . . . , Exile . . . , White Reply . . . , Burials (*The Gar*, Jan. 20, 1977).

Johannesse, Fhazel. The Rainmaker (with Williams, Neil Alwin, *Just a little Stretch of Road* (Johannesburg, Ravan Press, 1975); *The Four Lives of a South African* (Quarry, 1978-9).

Jolobe, J.J.R. *Poems of an African* (Alice, Lovedale Press, 1946).

Ka Mnyayiza, Nkathazo. Kneel and Pray, The Durban Indian Market Fire (*Ophir*, 18, 1973); Do they Deserve It, Bad Friday 1972 (*Ophir*, 19, 1974); Poem for Myself, Fear (*Ophir*, 20, 1974); Keep your City Clean (*Ophir*, 22, 1975); A Day in Our Life (*Ophir*, 23, 1976); The Question, Window of the World, Petty Stuff (*New Classic*, 3, 1976).

Kgositsile, Keorapetse (William). *Spirit Unchained* (Detroit, Broadside Press, 1969); *For Melba* (New York, Third World Press, 1969); *My Name is Afrika* (New York, Doubleday, 1971); *The Present is a Dangerous Place to Live* (New York, Third World Press, 1974); Shotgun (*Transition*, 27,4, 1966).

Koza, Leonard. Salaam Abdol (*Izwi*, II,7, 1972); Cynthia (*New Classic*, 3, 1975); Robbed, The Street Lamp (*Ophir*, 22, 1975); Under the Bridge (*Staffrider*, III,4, 1980); Winnie (*Staffrider*, II,4, 1979); The Border (*Wietie*, I).

Kumalo, Peter (pseud.) *vide* Clarke, Peter.

Kunene, Mazisi. *Zulu Poems* (London, André Deutsch, 1970); *Emperor Shaka the Great* (London, Heinemann, 1979); To the Proud, Echoes, Farewell, As Long As I Live (Moore and Beier, eds. *Modern Poetry from Africa, vide* anthologies); Universal Love (Mphahlele, ed. *African Writing Today, vide* anthologies).

Kunene, Obed. *The Happy Bantu* (*S'ketsh*, Summer 1975); Apartheid Falling (*New Classic*, 2, 1975).

Langa, Ben I. For my Brothers (*Staffrider*, III,1, 1980).

Langa, Mandlalenkosi. They no longer Speak to Us in Song (*Staffrider*, II,4, 1979); The Moulting of a Flea, Ritual on a Saturday Afternoon (*Ophir*, 16, 1972).

Mackay, Ilva. To All Black People, . . . and liberty, Powerful Thoughts for All, Hate is Negative, No More, Beware, Free Yourself, The Call (Matthews, ed. *Black Voices Shout! vide* anthologies).

Madingoane, Ingoapele. *Africa my Beginning* (Johannesburg, Ravan Press, 1979); Behold My Son (*Staffrider*, II,4, 1979).

Makama, Timothy Motimeloa, for Existence Sake, Everything is Justified (*Staffrider*, II,1, 1979).

Manaka, Matsemela (Cain). Hope for your Return (*Staffrider*, I,1, 1978); We have heard the Blues (*Staffrider*, III,2, 1980).

Mandela, Zindzi. *Black as I am* (Los Angeles, The Guild of Tutors Press, 1978).

Maseko, Bicca. King Mzilikazi Revisited, Mate, Lifemare, Bloodstream (*New Classic*, 3, 1976).

Mattera, Don. For a Cent (*Izwi*, October 1971); Friday Night (*Izwi*, 1,5, 1972).

Matthews, James. *Cry Rage* (with Thomas, Gladys) (Johannesburg, Spro-Cas Publications, 1972); *Pass me the Meatballs, Jones* (Athlone, Blac Publishing House, 1977); *Images* (with Hallett, George) (Athlone, Blac Publishing House, 1979); 18 poems in *Black Voices Shout!* (Matthews, ed. *vide* anthologies); Trip to Botswana (*Staffrider*, III,4, 1980); Poem (*Cape Times*, March 23, 1977); Poems of Prison and Release (*The Gar*, 32, 1978).

Modisane, William (Bloke). One Thought for my Lady, blue black, black blues, Lonely (Hughes, ed. *Poems from Black Africa*, *vide* anthologies).

Mojapelo, Jimmy. New Love, Is it the Drinker or the Drink, Too Much of This, Too Little of That (*New Classic*, 2, 1975).

Monare, Morena King. A Gossip (*Staffrider*, III,3, 1980).

Molefe, Zulu (Zuluboy). Children of Technology, Jerusha's Dance (*New Coin*, April 1970); Dear Miss South Africa (*Contrast*, VII,2, 1971); The River (*Contrast*, VIII,1, 1972); To Paint a Black Woman (*Contrast*, IX,3, 1974).

Motaung, Bonisile Joshua. Poem (*Donga*, April 1977); At the Sugar Cane Fields, So Well Tomorrow (*Staffrider*, I,2, 1978); Black Woman (*Staffrider*, II,1, 1979).

Motjuwadi, Stanley. White Lies, Taken for a Ride (*The Classic*, III,1, 1968).

Motsisi, Casey. The Efficacy of Prayer (*The Classic*, I,1, 1963).

Mphahlele, Ezekiel (Es'kia). The Immigrant (*Black Orpheus*, 6, 1959); Exile in Nigeria (Hughes, ed. *Poems from Black Africa, vide* anthologies); Death, Somewhere, Homeward Bound (Okpaku, ed. *New African Literature, vide* anthologies).

Mtshali, Oswald (Joseph Mbuyiseni). *Sounds of a Cowhide Drum* (Johannesburg, Renoster Books, 1971; London, O.U.P., 1972); *Fire Flames* (Pietermaritzbung, Shuter & Shooter, 1980); God and Me (*Wurm*, 2, 1969); Doubt, The Crossbearer, Nibbling (UNISA English Studies, XII, 1974); A Burning Chimney, Effigies are Falling (*Okike*, II, 1976).

Mutloatse, Mothobi. Lofty University, Legalised Killers (*Izwi*, I,4, 1972); Sir, Wa'reng, On Marriage, Mamellang (*New Nation*, January 1973); Don't Lock Up Our Sweethearts (*Izwi*, III,14, 1974); Train Roof Jive (*New Classic*, 1, 1975).

Mzamene, Mbulelo Vizikhungo. South of the Border (*Izwi*, IV,19/20, 1974).

Ndebele, Njabulo Simakahle. Looking at the Girl I love (*The Classic*, III,2, 1969); Birth, Be Gentle, An Argument (*The Classic*, VII,3, 1971); Portrait of Love (*Purple Renoster*, 11, 1972); Five Letters to M.M.M. (*Izwi*, II,10, 1973); The Man of Smoke, Little Dudu, A Child's Delirium, A Carol, I Hid My Love, Invention (Royston, Robert, ed. *To Whom it May Concern, vide* anthologies).

Ndlazi, Mandla. The Battle of Isandhlwana (*Staffrider*, I,3, 1978).

Nhlapo, Walter M.B. To H.I.E. Dhlomo (*Ilanga Lase*, March 30, 1946); Dr B.W. Vilakazi (*Ilanga Lase*, Nov. 22, 1947); Mahatma Gandhi (*Ilanga Lase*, Feb. 21, 1948).

Nicol, Mike. At the Window (*Staffrider*, I,1, 1978); After Cavafy, Rhodes on the Matopos (*Quarry*, 1977).

Nkosi, Lewis. Spanish Roses, Jealousy (*Black Orpheus*, 17, 1965).

Nortje, Arthur. *Dead Roots* (London, Heinemann, 1973); Poems (*New Coin*, special edition, IX, 1973).

Ntshodi, Motshile. Leshoboro-Umsogwabo, Ghosts (*Ophir*, 21, 1975).

Patel, Essop. *They Came at Dawn* (Athlone, Blac Publishing House, 1980); All but gone (*Literary Review*, XV,1, 1971); Between her Pendulous Breasts . . . (*Ophir*, 21, 1975); Afrika (*New Classic*, 4, 1977); The Me Nobody Cares (*Donga*, Sept. 1977; The Truth, for Sipho and Benjy (*New Classic*, 5, 1978); Note to Khatija, Note to my Son, Notes on the Steps (*Staffrider*, II,1, 1979); On a Trip at Samantha (*Wietie*, 1).

Pheto, Molefe. There is no Sun in Here (*The Gar*, 32, 1978).

Pieterse, Cosmo. *Present Lives Future Becomings* (with George Hallett et al., Richmond, Hickey Press, 1974); *Echoes and Choruses: Ballad of the Cells and Selected Shorter Poems* (Athens, Ohio, Ohio University Center for International Studies African Program, 1974).

Ruddin, Muhammed Omar. Tokologo (*Staffrider*, I,2, 1978).

Sepamla, Sidney Sipho. *Hurry Up to It* (Johannesburg, Ad. Donker, 1975); *The Blues is You in Me* (Johannesburg, Ad. Donker, 1976); *The Soweto I Love* (London, Rex Collings: Cape Town, David Philip, 1977).

Seroke, Jaki, Tragedy, Supermarket Bargains (III,1, 1980).

Serote, Wally Mongane. What's in this Black 'S---' (*Ophir*, 9, 1969); *Yakhal'inkomo* (Johannesburg, Renoster Books, 1972); *Tsetlo* (Johannesburg, Ad. Donker, 1974); No Baby Must Weep (Johannesburg, Ad. Donker, 1975); *Behold Mama, Flowers* (Johannesburg, Ad. Donker, 1978); Time has Run Out (*Staffrider*, II,4, 1979); The Kaffir and the Beast, In Some Kitchen, Ascension Day for a Boy—May 71, Maria, Listen to me . . . , Ofay Watcher-Blackwoman-Eternity (Matthews, ed. *Black Voices Shout! vide* anthologies); No More Stranger, Notes for a Fighter (*Peculef*, I, [undated]).

Setuke, Peter. Runner (*Staffrider*, II,4, 1979).

Small, Adam. *Black, Bronze, Beautiful: Quatrains* (Johannesburg, Ad. Donker, 1975); Body (*Contrast*, IV,3, 1967); Eternal Recurrence (*New Nation*, November 1967); There's Somethin' (Cope and Krige, eds. *Penguin Book of South African Verse, vide* anthologies).

Snyders, Peter. 'n Ordinary Mens (*Contrast*, 49, 1980).

Somhlahlo, Basil. Naked they Come (*New Coin*, Sept. 1971).

Soni, Ramanlal. Najur (*Izwi*, I,2, 1971); Vivasvan (*New Nation*, June, 1972).

Thomas, Gladys. *Cry Rage* (*vide* Matthews, James).

Tladi, Lefifi. The Death of a Poet (*New Classic*, I, 1975); Notes from an Afrikan Calabash (*Ophir*, 2, 1975).

Twala, James. Family Planning (*Staffrider*, II,3, 1979).

Van Wyk, Chris. *It is Time to Go Home* (Johannesburg and London, Ad. Donker, 1979); For You, Only Blacks Browse (*New Classic*, I, 1975); 'Blacks only' Blues (*New Classic*, 2, 1975); Mulatto, Praying for a Miracle (*The Voice*, February 11, 1978); from the Good Book (*The Voice*, February 18, 1978); Dreams Wither Slowly (*The Voice*, February 25, 1978); Words of Power (*The Voice*, March 18, 1978); We Can't Meet Here, Brother (*Staffrider*, I,2, 1978); Lavatory Coup (*New Classic*, 5, 1978).

Vilakazi, Paul. A Proud Servant, The Fortnight Terror (*UNISA English Studies*, XII,2, 1974); Our Worst Mornings, Portrait of an Intshumentshu (*Ophir*, 19, 1974).

wa Nthodi, Mothshile. *From the Calabash* (Johannesburg, Ravan Press, 1978).

Zungu, Sipho. Voices (*Staffrider*, I,3, 1978).

The Novel

Abrahams, Peter. *Songs of the City* (London, Dorothy Crisp, 1945); *Mine Boy* (London, Faber & Faber, 1946, Heinemann, 1963); *A Path of Thunder* (New York, Harper, 1948, London, Faber & Faber, 1952); *Wild Conquest* (New York, Harper, 1950, London, Faber & Faber, 1951); *A Wreath for Udomo* (London, Faber & Faber, 1956); *A Night of their Own* (London, Faber & Faber, 1965); *This Island Now* (Faber & Faber, 1966).

Boetie, Dugmore (with Barney Simon). *Familiarity is the Kingdom of the Lost* (London, Barrie and Rockcliff, the Cresset Press, 1969).

Carim, Enver. *A Dream Deferred* (London, W.H. Allen, 1973).

Dhlomo, R.R.R. *An African Tragedy* (Alice, Lovedale Press, undated).

Dikobe, Modikwe. *The Marabi Dance* (London, Ibadan, Nairobi, Heinemann, 1973).

Essop, Achmed. *The Visitation* (Johannesburg, Ravan Press, 1980).

Head, Bessie. *When Rain Clouds Gather* (London, Gollancz, 1969). *Maru* (London, Gollancz, 1971); *A Question of Power* (London, Heinemann, 1973).

Khafula, John J. *This Thing has Got to Stop* (Cape Town, African Bookman, 1946).

La Guma, Alex. *A Walk in the Night, vide A walk in the Night and Other Stories*—under short stories; *And A Threefold Cord* (London, Heinemann, 1964); *The Stone Country* (London, Heinemann, 1967); *In the Fog of the Season's End* (London, Heinemann, 1972); *Time of the Butcherbird* (London, Heinemann, 1979).

Matshoba, Mtutuzeli. 'The betrayal', excerpt from a novel in progress. (*Staffrider*, III,3, 1980).

Mopeli-Paulus, A.S. (with Peter Lanham), *Blanket Boy's Moon* (London, Collins, 1953).

Mphahlele, Ezekiel (Es'kia). *The Wanderers* (New York, Macmillan, 1970); *Chirundu* (Ravan Press, 1979).

Ngubane, Jordan K. (Khush). *Ushaba* (Washington D.C., Three Continents Press, 1974).

Peteni, R.L. *Hill of Fools* (Cape Town, David Phillip: London, Heinemann, 1976).

Plaatje, Solomon Tshekiso (Sol T.). *Mhudi* (Alice, Lovedale Press, 1957, London, Heinemann, 1978).

Rive, Richard. *Emergency* (London, MacMillan, 1964).

Sepamla, Sipho. *The Root is One.* (London, Rex Collings in association with David Phillip, Cape Town, 1979).

Serote, (Wally) Mongane. 'In the Sun', extract from a novel in progress (*Staffrider*, III,4, 1980).

Tlali, Miriam Masoli. *Muriel at Metropolitan* (Johannesburg, Ravan, 1975, London, Longman, 1979); *Amandla* (Johannesburg, Ravan, 1980).

Zwelonke, D.M. *Robben Island* (London, Heinemann, 1977).

Short Stories

Abrahams, Peter. *Dark Testament* (London, Allen & Unwin, 1942).

Choonara, I. A View from the Window (*Contrast*, 22, 1969).

Clarke, Peter (pseud. Peter Kumalo). The Departure (*Drum*, April, 1956); Death in the Sun (Hughes, ed., *An African Treasury, vide* anthologies); Pastorale (Gray, ed. *On the Edge of the World, vide* anthologies); Eleven O'Clock: the Wagons, the Shore (*New African*, Oct. 1962); Winter Shepherding (*Contrast*, III,2, 1964); Figures and Settings (*Contrast*, VI,4, 1970).

Dangor, Achmed. Waiting for Leila (Mutloatse, ed., *Forced Landing, vide* anthologies); The Wedding (*Wietie*, I).

Dhlomo, R.R. 20 Short Stories (*English in Africa* Special Issue, II,I, 1975, ed. and intro. T.J. Couzens).

Dikobe, Modikwe. *Vide* Ramitloa, Marks Dikobe.

Essa, Ahmed. The Prisoner (*The Literary Review*, XV,1, 1971).

Essop, Ahmed. *The Hajji and Other Stories* (Johannesburg, Ravan Press, 1978); Gemini (*Staffrider*, II,4, 1979); Two Dimensional (*Staffrider*, III,1, 1980); East/West (*Staffrider*, III,4, 1980).

Gwala, Mafika Michael (M) Pascal. Side Step (*Classic*, III,3, 1970).

Head, Bessie. *The Collector of Treasures and other Botswana Village Tales* (Cape Town, David Phillip, 1977); The Lovers (*Wietie*, 2).

House, Amelia. Awakening (*Staffrider*, II,I, 1979).

Hutchinson, Alfred. Washerwoman's Annie (*New Age*, Oct. 6, 1955); High Wind in the Valley (*New Age*, Dec. 25, 1958).

Johannesse, Fhazel. The Pot Plant (*Wietie*, I).

Jordan, A.C. *Tales from Southern Africa* (Berkeley, London, University of California Press, 1973).

Kumalo, Peter, pseud. *Vide* Clarke, Peter.

La Guma, Alex. *A Walk in the Night and Other Stories* (London, Heinemann, 1967); A Glass of Wine (*Black Orpheus*, 7, 1960); Slipper Satin (*Black Orpheus*, 8 [undated]); Blankets (*Black Orpheus*, 15, 1964, and Beier, *Political Spider*, vide anthologies).

Leshoai, B. (Benjamin, Bob). *Masilo's Adventures and Other Stories* (London, Longmans, 1968).

Maimane, J. Arthur. A Manner of Speaking (*Africa South in Exile*, IV,4, 1960); The Hungry Boy (*Following the Sun*, vide anthologies; also published as Hungry Flames, *New Classic*, 5, 1978); A Kaffer Woman (*Black Orpheus*, 12, 1963).

Makaza, Webster, The Last Room (*The New African*, Feb. 20, 1963); The Slave (*Classic*, II,3, 1967); Black Boy (*Classic*, III,3, 1970); Wheel of Justice (The Mob) (*Drum* short story contest 1962/3; *New African*, July 13, 1963).

Matshoba, Mtutuzeli. *Call Me Not a Man* (Johannesburg, Ravan Press, 1979); To Kill a Man's Pride (Mutloatse, ed. *Forced Landing*, vide anthologies).

Matthews, James. *The Park and Other Stories* (Athlone, Blac Publishing House, 1974); The Party (*Transition*, 10, 1962); A Case of Guilt (*Wietie*, I).

Mayet, Juby. The Informer (*The Voice*, Nov. 19, 1978).

Mkele, Nimrod. Devoted Leeches (*Drum*, May 1956).

Modisane, William (Bloke). The Dignity of Begging (*African Drum*, Sept. 1951); The Fighter that Wore Skirts (*Drum*, Jan. 1952); The Respectable Pickpocket (*Drum*, Jan. 1954); The Situation (Beier, ed. *Black Orpheus*, *vide* anthologies).

Molefe, Zulu. The Road to Evaton (*Bona*, April 1974).

Motsisi, Casey. *Casey & Co.*, Selected Writings of Casey 'Kid' Motsisi (ed. Mutloatse, Mothobi; Johannesburg, Ravan Press, 1978) (including Mita, Riot, Boy-Boy, and several sketches); Love in the Rain (*Drum*, Dec. 1955); A Very Important Appointment (*Classic*, I,1, 1963).

Mphahlele, Ezekiel (Es'kia, pseud., Esekie, Bruno). *Man Must Live* (Cape Town, African Bookman, 1946); *The Living and the Dead and Other Stories* (Ibadan, Ministry of Education, 1961); *In Corner B* (Nairobi, East African Publishing House, 1967); Blind Alley (*Drum*, Sept. 1953); Reef Train (*Drum*, August 1954, by Esekie, Bruno, pseud.); Across Down Stream (*Drum*, August 1955 and also as The Coffee-Court Girl, in *In Corner B*, *q.v.*); Down the Quiet Street (*Drum*, Jan. 1956); Lesane (*Drum*, Dec. 1956–April 1957).

Mutloatse, Mothobi. Old Man Motsamai's Philosophy (*New Classic*, I, 1975); Whither Now, Bundu Bulldozers, Enemies of the State, Madoda, Ijuba (*Bolt*, 12, 1975); While the Cat is Away (*Donga* April 1977); The Truth . . . Mama (*The Voice*, December 17, 1977); Mama Ndiyalila (*The Voice*, Jan. 7, 1978); Hell in Azania (*Okike*, 14, 1978); The Night of the Million Spears, Don't be Vague Insist on Human Rights (*Staffrider*, I,2, 1978); The Motherly Embrace (*Staffrider*, II,1, 1979); Face to Face (*New Classic*, 5, 1978); Mhalamhala 1981 (*Staffrider*, III,4, 1980/1).

Mzamene. *Mzala* (Johannesburg, Ravan Press, 1980).

Narain, Aiyer. The Cane is Singing (*Staffrider*, III,4, 1980/1).

Ndebele, Njabulo S. (Simakahle). The Music of the Violin (*Staffrider*, III,3, 1980).

Ngubane, Jordan (Kush). The Answer he wanted (*African Drum*, Dec. 1951); Man of Africa (*Drum*, August 1956).

Nkosi, Lewis. The Hotel Room (*Contrast*, II,3, 1963/4); The Prisoner (Mphahlele, Ezekiel, ed. *African Writing Today*, *vide* anthologies); Potgieter's Castle (*Transition*, IV,15, 1964).

Pitso, Randolph Ben. Nomoya of the Winds (*African Drum*, April 1951).

Ramitloa, Marks Dikobe (Dikobe, Modikwe). The Reverend Ndlovu (*Fighting Talk*, July 1962; also in Shore and Shore-Bos, eds., *Come Back Africa*, *vide* anthologies); Mobonga (*Fighting Talk*, December 1962).

Reddy, Jayapraga. The Slumbering Spirit (*Staffrider*, III,I, 1980).

Rive, Richard. *African Songs* (Berlin, Seven Seas Publishers, 1963); *Selected Writings* (Johannesburg, Ad. Donker, 1977); Middle Passage (*Contrast*, 21,VI,1, 1969); Riva (*Staffrider*, II,1, 1979); Black Macbeth (*Contrast*, XIII,1, 1980).

Sehume, Leslie. I'm Not a Tramp (*Classic*, I,1, 1963).

Sentso, Dyke H. The Harvest's Waiting (*African Drum*, June 1951); The Sun Stood Still (*Drum*, November 1951); Pay Back (*Drum*, May 1952); Other People's Goods (*Drum*, February 1954).

Sepamla, Sydney Sipho. Moffat (*Izwi*, II,14, 1973); King Taylor, Kenalemang (*New Classic*, I, 1975).

Serote, Mongane Wally. A Look at the Line (*Bolt*, 9, 1973).

Sigwili, Nokungcina. My dear Madam . . . (*Staffrider*, II,4, 1979/80).

Small, Adam. Gone to Canada (*New Nation*, February 1968).

Themba, Can. *The Will to Die* (Stuart, D. and Holland, R., eds., London, Heinemann, 1972); Passionate Stranger (*Drum*, March 1953); Mob Passion (*Drum* short story competition, 1953; Rutherfoord, ed., *Darkness and Light*, *vide* anthologies); Nice Time Girl (*Drum*, May 1954); Forbidden Love (*Drum*, November 1955); Marta (*Drum*, July 1956).

Tlali, Miriam. Point of No Return (*Staffrider*, I,2, 1978).

Tshabangu, Mango. Thoughts in a Train (Mutloatse, ed., *Forced Landing*, *vide* anthologies).

van Wyk, Christopher. Aunt Molly and the Girls (*Wietie*, I); Edward and Co. Consciousness Ltd (*The Voice*, March 3, 1978).

Autobiographical Writing

Abrahams, Peter, *Return to Goli* (London, Faber & Faber, 1953); *Tell Freedom* (London, Faber & Faber, 1954).

Hutchinson, Alfred, *Road to Ghana* (London, Gollancz, 1960).

Jabavu, Nontando (Noni), *Drawn in Colour* (London, Murray, 1960); *The Ochre People* (London, Murray, 1963).

Matshikiza, Todd, *Chocolates for my Wife* (London, Hodder & Stoughton, 1961).

Modisane, William (Bloke), *Blame Me on History* (London, Thames and Hudson, 1964).

Mokgatle, *The Autobiography of an Unknown South African* (Berkeley and Los Angeles, University of California Press, 1971).

Mphahlele, Ezekiel (Es'kia), *Down Second Avenue* (London, Faber & Faber, 1953).

Drama

Dhlomo, H.I.E. *The Girl Who Killed to Save* (Alice, Lovedale Press, 1935); *Dingana* (printed and bound at the University of Natal by the Library's Xerographic Photo Duplicating and Bindery Departments, 1954—30 copies); unpublished manuscripts presented to the University of Natal by R.R.R. Dhlomo on behalf of the Dhlomo family, October 1968: Dingana (as above), Cetewayo, Ntsikana, Men and Women, The Living Dead, Ruby, Malaria, The Expert, The Bazaar, The Pass, Umhlola Wasensimini, The Workers Part I, Moshesh.

Dike, Fatima. *The First South African* (Johannesburg, Ravan Press, 1978); The Sacrifice of Kreli (Gray, Stephen, ed. *Theatre One, vide* anthologies).

Fugard, Athol, Kani, John and Ntshona, Winston. *Statements; Three Plays* (London, Oxford, Cape Town, O.U.P., 1974) (incl. Sizwe Bansi is Dead and The Island).

Goro-X, S. *Shaka* (Johannesburg, Juta & Co., 1940).

Hutchinson, Alfred. The Rainkillers (Litto, ed. *Plays from Black Africa, vide* anthologies); Fusane's Trial (Pieterse, ed. *Ten One Act Plays, vide* anthologies).

Kente, Gibson. Too Late (extract, *S'ketsh*, Winter 1973).

La Guma, Alex. The Man in the Tree (*The Literary Review*, XV,1, 1971).

Leshoai, B.L. (Benjamin, Bob). *Wrath of the Ancestors and Other Plays* (Nairobi, East African Publishing House, 1972); The Weather Forecast (*S'ketsh*, Summer 1975); The Rendezvous (*S'ketsh*, Summer 1975); Lines Draw Monsters (extract, Pereira, ed. *Contemporary South African Plays, vide* anthologies).

Mabaso, Corney. *Vide* Mofokeng, Zakes.

Maimane, Arthur. The Opportunity (Pieterse, ed. *Ten One Act Plays, vide* anthologies).

Mda, Zanevula (Zakes). Dark Voices Ring (*S'ketsh*, Winter 1979).

Mekgoe, Shimane Solly. *Lindiwe* (Johannesburg, Ravan Press, 1978).

Mofokeng, Zakes, and Mabaso, Corney. Job Mava (*Staffrider*, III,4, 1980/81).

Mphahlele, Es'kia (Ezekie). Oganda's Journey (*Staffrider*, II,3, 1979).

Mqayisa, Khayalethu. *Confused Mhlaba* (Johannesburg, Ravan Press, 1974).

Nkosi, Lewis, *Rhythm of Violence* (London, O.U.P., 1964); We Can't All be Martin Luther King (typescript).

Ntshona, Winston, *vide* Fugard.

Pieterse, Cosmo. Ballad of the Cells (Pieterse, ed. *Short African Plays*, *vide* anthologies).

Rive, Richard. Resurrection (Pieterse, ed. *Short African Plays*, *vide* anthologies and *Selected Writings*, *vide* short stories); Make Like Slaves (Henderson, ed. *African Theatre*, *Eight Prize-Winning Plays*, *vide* anthologies).

van Wyk, Christopher. Night at Ebrahim's (*Staffrider*, I,2, 1978).

Critical Commentary

Abrahams, Cecil. Review of Richard Rive's *Selected Works* (*Research in African Literatures*, 10, 1979).

Abrahams, Peter. The Long View. The African Writer's Part in Battle Against Racial Prejudice (*African World*, June 1952).

Asvat, Farouk. Weapons of Words (*Wietie*, 1).

Brutus, Dennis. The New Un-African—Review of Noni Jabavu's *Drawn in Colour* (*The New African*, March 1962); In Memoriam: Arthur Nortje (*Research in African Literatures*, II,1, 1971); Protest against Apartheid (Pieterse, ed., *Protest and Conflict*, *vide* anthologies).

Dhlomo, H.I.E. *Literary Theory and Criticism*, ed. Visser, N.W. (*English in Africa*, IV,2, 1977, whole issue); Drama and the African (*South African Outlook*, October 1, 1936); African Drama and Poetry (*South African Outlook*, April 1, 1939); Why Study Tribal Dramatic Forms? (*Transvaal Native Education Quarterly*, March 1939); Three Famous African Authors I Knew (*Inkundla ya Banto*, 1st and 2nd fortnight, August 1946).

Essop, Achmed. Acceptance Speech for the Olive Schreiner Prize, 1979 (*English Academy Review* 1980).

Francis, Benjy. Untitled piece on writing for the theatre (*S'ketsh*, Winter 1979).

Head, Bessie. Let Me Tell a Story Now (*The New African*, September 1962); For a Friend, 'D.B.' (*Transition*, 11, 1963); Music (*Donga*, February 1977); Some Notes on Novel Writing (*New Classic*, 5, 1978).

House, Amelia. *Black South African Women Writers in English, a preliminary checklist* (Evanston, Program on Women, Northwestern University, 1980).

Gwala, Mafika Pascal, Workshop section in *Staffrider*, II,3, 1979; Review of *Just a Little Stretch of Road* by Neil Alwin and *The Rainmaker* by Fhazel Johannesse (*Staffrider*, III,1, 1980).

Jolobe, J.J.R. The Author (Paper read to Bantu Authors Conference, Atteridgeville, Pretoria, July 1939—Proceedings, typescript mimeo).

Jordan, A.C. Towards an African Literature (*Africa South*, 1958-1960); *Towards an African Literature: The Emergence of Literary Form in Xhosa* (Berkeley, Los Angeles, London, University of California Press, 1973).

Kgomongwe, Selaneng. Review of *Egoli* by Matsimela Manaka (*S'ketsh*, Winter 1979).

Kumalo, Alfred. Tribute to Todd Matshikiza (*The Classic*, III,1, 1969).

Kunene, Mazisi, Review of *Mhudi* by Sol Plaatje (*Research in African Literatures*, VIII,3, 1977); South African Oral Traditions (Heywood, ed. *Aspects of South African Literature*, vide anthologies).

Leshoai, Bob (Benjamin, B.L.). Theatre and the Common Man in Africa (*Transition*, IV,19, 1965); The Nature and Use of Oral Literature (*New Classic*, No 4, 1977).

Manaka, Matsemela. Theatre of the Dispossessed (*Staffrider*, III,3, 1980).

Manganyi, Noel Chabani. *Being-Black-in-the-World* (Spro-Cas/Ravan, Johannesburg, 1973); *Mashangu's Reverie and Other Essays* (Johannesburg, Ravan Press, 1977); The Censored Imagination (*English in Africa*, VI,2, 1979

Mashabela, Harry. Can Themba Remembered (*The Classic*, II,4, 1968).

Mayet, Juby. Can Themba Remembered (*The Classic*, II,4, 1968).

Melamu, Moteane. Bad Times, Sad Times (*New Classic*, 3, 1976).

Modisane, William (Bloke). Literary Scramble for Africa (*Contact*, July 12, 1962); Paper on the East African Short Story read to the Mbari Conference, pub., untitled *The New African*, October 1962).

Motjuwadi, Stanley. Can Themba Remembered (*The Classic*, II,4, 1968).

Motsisi, Casey. Can Themba Remembered (*The Classic*, II,4, 1968); Tribute to Todd Matshikiza (*The Classic*, III,4, 1969). Both in *Casey & Co, vide* Short Stories.

Mphahlele, Ezekiel (Es'kia). *The African Image* (London, Faber & Faber, 1962; revised edition 1973); *Voices in the Whirlwind and other Essays* (New York, Hill & Wang, 1972); The Syllabus and the Child (*The Good Shepherd*, November 1952); The Boycott that has Become a War (*Drum*, July 1956); The Non-European Character in South African English Fiction (Submitted to satisfy requirements for the degree of Master of Arts in the Department of English, University of South Africa, December 1956); The Evaton Riots (*Africa South*, January–March 1957); The African Intellectual (*Africa in Transition* ed. Prudence Smith, London, Reinhardt, 1958); The Dilemma of the African Elite (*Twentieth Century*, April 1959); Negro Culture in a Multi-Racial Society (*Présence Africaine*, Special issue, 24–25, 1959); The Real Africa (*Commonwealth Challenge*, VII,4, 1959); A South African in Nigeria (*Africa South*, III,4, 1959); Accra Conference (Hughes, *An African Treasury, vide* anthologies); Out of Africa (*Encounter*, April 1960); Black and White (*The New Statesman, September 10, 1960); The Cult of Negritude (Encounter*, March 1961); Travels on an Extramural Donkey (*Transition*, III,11, 1963); Langston Hughes (*Black Orpheus*, I,9, 1964); African Literature, What Tradition? (*Denver Quarterly*, II,2, 1967); Black Literature at the University of Denver (*Research in African Literatures*, III,1, 1972); Remarks on Negritude (Mphahlele, ed. *African Writing Today, vide* anthologies); Why I Teach my Discipline (*Denver Quarterly*, VIII,1, 1973); The Tyranny of Place (*New Letters*, 40,1, 1974); Reply to Addison Gayle, Jr (*Blackworld*, January 1974); The Function of Literature at the Present Time: The Ethnic Imperative (*Transition*, 45,IX,2, 1974); From the Black American World (*Okike*, 9, 1975, 2) 5, 1977, 3) 8, 1979); Reviews of *South African Voices* ed. Bernth Lindfors, *Strains* by Dennis Brutus and *The Present is a Dangerous Place to Live* by Keorapetse Kgositsile (*Okike*, 9, 1975); Notes from the Black American World, IX, Images of Africa in Afro-American Literature (*Okike*, 10, 1976); African Literature Surveyed (*The Journal of Commonwealth Literature*, XI,1, 1976); The Voice of Prophecy in African Poetry

(*English in Africa*, VI,1, 1979; *Weekend Argus*, April 7, 1979); Exile, the Tyranny of Place and the Literary Compromise (*UNISA English Studies*, XVII,1, 1979); Landmarks of Literary History in Southern Africa (*English Academy Review*, 1980).

Mtshali, Oswald. Black Poetry in Southern Africa: What it Means (Heywood, ed. *Aspects of South African Literature*, *vide* anthologies).

Mutloatse, Mothobi. Return Speech to the People (*The Voice*, November 3, 1977).

Mzamane, Mbulelo. The Study of Literature in Africa (*Donga*, September 1977), The Short Story Tradition in Black South Africa (*Donga*, September 1977); The Fifties and Beyond: An Evaluation (*New Classic*, 4, 1977); Literature and Politics Among Blacks in South Africa (*New Classic*, 5, 1978); Politics and Literature in Africa: A Review (*Staffrider*, III,4, 1980/81).

Nakasa, Nathaniel (Nat). Writing in South Africa (*The Classic*, I,1, 1963).

Nkosi, Lewis. *Home and Exile* (London, Longmans, 1963); *The Transplanted Heart* (Benin City, Nigeria, Ethiope Publishing Company, 1975); African Fiction, South Africa: Protest (*Africa Report*, VII,9,VII,11, 1962); African Writers of Today (*The Classic*, I,4, 1965); Against the Tribe (*The New African*, May 1965); White on Black (*The Observer*, April 1, 1962); A Question of Literary Stewardship (*Africa Report*, May–June, 1969); South Africa, Literature of Protest (Kitchen, ed., *Handbook of African Affairs*, *vide* anthologies); Interviews with Writers (*African Writers Talking* ed. Duerden and Pieterse, *vide* anthologies).

Patel, Essop. Review of *The Lahnee's Pleasure* by Govender (*S'ketsh*, Winter 1978).

Pieterse, Cosmo. Conflict in the Germ (*Protest and Conflict*, *vide* anthologies).

Rive, Richard. *Selected Writings* (Johannesburg, Ad. Donker, 1977) (contains Literature and Society, African Poets in Berlin, No Common Factor, Black Poets of the Seventies, Olive Schreiner: The Novels, Arthur Nortje: Poet, Taos in Harlem: An Interview with Langston Hughes, Senghor and Negritude, Three South Africans Abroad); Image of Drums and Tom-Toms (*Contrast*, III,1, 1964); Review of *Penguin Book of South African Verse* ed. Jack Cope and Uys Krige, (*Contrast*, VI,1, 1969); Olive Schreiner: A Checklist (*Studies in the Novel*, Summer 1972); An Infinite Compassion (*Contrast*, VIII,1, 1972); New Light on Olive Schreiner (*Contrast*, VIII,4, 1973); Race and Poetry (*Contrast*, IV,4, 1966); Ed. and Introduction to fragmentary manuscript of

Olive Schreiner and Selective bibliography (*English in Africa*, I,1, 1974, whole issue); No Place for Nat—review of *The World of Nat Nakasa* (*Contrast*, X,3, 1976); The Black Man and White Literature (*New Classic*, No 4, 1977); Black is Banned (*Speak*, I,3, 1978); Around the Back—review of *The Orange Earth* by Adam Small (*Speak*, I,5, 1978).

Sepamla, Sipho. A Tribute to the Late Jimmy Sabe (*S'ketsh*, Winter 1975); Review of The Train by James Mofokeng (*S'ketsh*, Winter 1975); The Black Writer in South Africa Today (*New Classic*, 3, 1976); The Urban Cultural Scene: Theatre (*S'ketsh*, Winter 1979); A Note on *New Classic* and *S'ketsh* (*English in Africa*, VII,2, 1980).

Small, Adam. Literature, Communication and South Africa (*New Classic*, 2, 1975).

Themba, Can. Through Shakespeare's Africa (*The New African*, September 21, 1963).

SECONDARY WORKS

Books

Abrahams, W.E. *The Mind of Africa* (London, Weidenfeld and Nicholson, 1962).

Ainslie, Roselynde. *The Press in Africa* (London, Gollancz, 1966).

Awoonor, Kofi. *The Breast of the Earth* (New York, Anchor Press/ Doubleday, 1975).

Barnett, Ursula A. *Ezekiel Mphahlele* (Boston, Twayne, 1976).

Beier, Ulli. *Introduction to African Literature* (London, Longmans, 1967, new edition, 1979).

Burgess, Donald. *Shaka King of the Zulus* (Washington, D.C., Three Continents Press, undated).

Cartey, Wilfred. *Whispers from a Continent* (New York, Random House, 1969).

Christie, Sarah, Hutchings, Geoffrey and Maclennon, Don. *Perspectives on South African Fiction* (Johannesburg, Ad. Donker, 1980).

Cook, Mercer and Henderson, Stephen E. *The Militant Black Writer in Africa* (Madison, Milwaukee and London, University of Wisconsin Press, 1969).

Daiches, David. *Companion to Commonwealth Literature* (Allen Lane and The Penguin Press, 1971).

Dathorne, Oscar Ronald. *The Black Mind: A History of African Literature* (Minneapolis, University of Minnesota Press, 1974).

De Mestral, Claude. *Christian Literature in Africa* (London, Christian Literary Council, 1959).

Egudu, R.N. *Modern African Poetry and the African Predicament* (London and Basingstoke, 1978).

Ferres, John H. and Tucker, Martin. *Modern Commonwealth Literature*, *vide* anthologies.

Gordimer, Nadine. *The Black Interpreters* (Johannesburg, Spro-Cas Ravan, 1973.

Graham-White, Anthony. *The Drama of Black Africa* (New York, Samuel French, 1974).

Gray, Stephen. *Sources of the First Black South African Novel in English: Solomon Plaatje's Use of Shakespeare and Bunyan in Mhudi* (Munger Africana Library Notes No 37. Pasadena, Munger Africana Library, California Institute of Technology, 1976).

Henderson, Stephen E. *Vide* Cook, Mercer.

Herdeck, Donald E. *African Authors: A Companion to Black African Writing 1900-1973 Vol I* (Washington, DC, Black Orpheus Press, 1973).

Heywood, Christopher, ed. *Perspectives on African Literature*, *vide* anthologies.

Hopkinson, Tom. *In the Fiery Continent* (London, Gollancz, 1962).

Jahn, Janheinz. *Muntu—An Outline of Neo-African Culture* (London, Faber & Faber, 1961) (original German edition 1958); with Ramsaran, John, *Approaches to African Literature* (Ibadan, Ibadan University Press, 1959); *A History of Neo-African Literature* (London, Faber & Faber, 1968), with Schild, Ulla and Nordmann, Almut. *Who's Who in African Literature* (Tübingen, Erdmann Verlag, 1972).

Larson, Charles R. *The Emergence of African Fiction* (Bloomingdale and London, Indiana University Press, 1971); *The Novel in the Third World* (Washington, DC, Inscape Publishers, 1976).

Lindfors, Bernth, ed., with Munro, Ian, Priebe, Richard and Sander, Reinhard. *Palaver—Interviews with Five African Writers in Texas* (Austin, Occasional Publication of the African and Afro-American Research Institute, The University of Texas at Austin, 1972).

Miller, G.M., with Sergeant, Howard. *A Critical Survey of South African Poetry in English* (Cape Town, Balkema, 1957).

Moore, Gerald. *Seven African Writers* (London, O.U.P., 1962, reprinted with corrections, 1966); *The Chosen Tongue: English Writing in the Tropical World* (London, Longmans, 1969); *Twelve African Writers* (London, Hutchinson, 1980).

Nathan, Manfred. *South African Literature—A General Survey* (Cape Town and Johannesburg, Juta, 1923).

Nordman, Almut. *Vide* Jahn.

Olney, James. *Tell Me Africa* (Princeton, Princeton University Press, 1973).

Oosthuyzen, G.C. *Shepherd of Lovedale* (Johannesburg, Hugh Keartland, 1970).

Paver, B.G. *Vide* Shepherd.

Priebe, Richard. *Vide* Lindfors.

Ramsaran, John. *Vide* Jahn.

Robinson, A.L. *None Daring to Make Us Afraid* (Cape Town, Maskew Miller, 1962).

Roscoe, Adrian. *Uhuru's Fire—*African Literature East to South (Cambridge, Cambridge University Press, 1977).

Rosenthal, Eric. *History of African Journalism* (South African Affairs Pamphlet No 14, 3rd series, Johannesburg, Society of Friends, undated).

Sampson, Anthony. *Drum* (London, Collins, 1956).

Sander, Reinhard. *Vide* Lindfors.

Sergeant, Howard. *Vide* Miller.

Shepherd, R.H.W. *Literature for the South African Bantu*: A Comparative Study of Negro Achievement (Pretoria, Carnegie Corporation Visitors' Grants Committee, 1936); *Lovedale and Literature* (Alice, Lovedale Press, 1945); *Bantu Literature and Life* (Alice, Lovedale Press, 1955); with Paver, B.G., *African Contrasts* (London, O.U.P., 1947).

Schild, Ulla. *Vide* Jahn.

Short, Alan Lennox, ed. *English and South Africa, vide* anthologies.

Snyman, J.P.L. *The South African Novel in English (1880-1930)* (Potchefstroom, University of Potchefstroom, *In U Lig* Series, for C.H.E., 1952).

Soyinka, Wole. *Myth, Literature and the African World* (Cambridge, Cambridge University Press, 1976).

Sulzer, Peter. *Schwarze Intelligenz* (Zurich and Freiburg, Atlantis Verlag, 1955).

Tibble, Anne. *African/English Literature—A Survey and Anthology*, *vide* anthologies.

Tucker, Martin. *Africa in Modern Literature: a survey of contemporary writers in English* (New York, Ungar, 1967); with Ferres, J.H. *Modern Commonwealth Literature, vide* secondary Ferres).

Wade, Michael. *Peter Abrahams* (London, Evans Brothers, 1972).

Wauthier, Claude. *The Literature and Thought of Modern Africa* (London, Pall Mall, 1966; Second English language edition, Washington, DC, Three Continents Press, 1979).

Papers, Essays and other short pieces

Abrahams, Lionel. Black Experience into English Verse (*The New Nation*, February 1970); The Blackness of Black Writing (*Jewish Affairs*, No 28, 1973); The Purple Renoster: An Adolescence (*English in Africa*, VII,2, 1980).

Armstrong, Robert G. The Role of Linguistics in African Studies (*Phylon*, XXV,2).

Barnett, U.A. Interview with Oswald Joseph Mtshali (*World Literature Written in English*, XII,1, 1976).

Beuchat, P.D. Do the Bantu Have a Literature? (Pretoria, Publication of the Institute for the Study of Man in Africa, No 7, typescript, undated).

Blair, Dorothy S. Black Writer—White Critic (*Contrast*, V,4, 1969).

Beard, Linda Susan. Bessie Head's *A Question of Power*: The Journey Through Disintegration to Wholeness (Colby Library Quarterly, December 1979).

Branford, William. Overseas Education—Paper on the University of Natal Medical Students Drama Group (London, Her Majesty's Stationery Office, 1956).

Cassirer, Thomas. Politics and Mystique—The Predicament of the African Writer (*African Forum*, III,1, 1967).

Charad, Linda. Kani the actor without a Script (*Sunday Times*, Colour Magazine, July 29, 1973).

Cope, Jack. The World of *Contrast* (*English in Africa*, VII,2, 1980).

Cordeau, Shirley. The B.B.C. African Services' Involvement in African Theatre (*Research in African Literature*, I,2, 1970).

Couzens, Tim (T.J.). Literature by Black Africans (*New Nation*, January 1971); ed. & introduction to 20 short stories by R.R.R. Dhlomo (*English in Africa*, II,1, whole issue); with Willan, Brian, Solomon Plaatje 1876–1932 An Introduction (ed. and introduction *English in Africa* Plaatje Centenary issue, III,2, 1976, whole issue); The Black Press and Black Literature in South Africa 1900–1950 (*English Studies in Africa*, XIX,2, 1976); The Continuity of Black Writing in English in South Africa before 1950 (ed. de Villiers, André, *English-Speaking South Africa Today*, London, O.U.P., 1976); Sol Plaatje's *Mhudi* (Parker, ed. *The South African Novel in English, vide* anthologies); The Social Ethos of Black Writing in South Africa (Heywood, ed. *Aspects of South African Literature, vide* anthologies).

Cullinan, Patrick. Announcement: The Bloody Horse (*English in Africa*, VII,2, 1980).

Dameron, Charles. Arthur Nortje: Craftsman for His Muse (Heywood, ed. *Aspects of South African Literature, vide* anthologies).

Egudu, R.N. Pictures of Pain: The Poetry of Dennis Brutus (Heywood, ed. *Aspects of South African Literature, vide* anthologies).

Gordimer, Nadine. *The English Novel in South Africa. The Novel and the Nation* (Series of lectures delivered at the Winter School of the National Union of South African Students at the University of the Witwatersrand, July 1959, ed. Levin, Hugh, Cape Town, NUSAS, 1959); The Novel and the Nation (*Times Literary Supplement*, August 11, 1961); Censored, Banned, Gagged (*Encounter*, June 1963); How Not to Know the African (*Contrast*, IV,3, 1967); Towards a Desk-Drawer Literature (*The Classic*, II,4, 1968); Note for its (*Contrast's*) Twentieth Anniversary (*Contrast*, XIII,2, 1980); Writers in South Africa: The New Black Poets (*Dalhousie Review*, LIII,4, 1973/74); Writers in South Africa: The New South African Poets (Smith, Rowland, ed. *Exile and Tradition, vide* anthologies).

Gray, Stephen. Plaatje's Shakespeare (*English in Africa*, IV,1, 1977); The Struggle—An Interview with Sipho Sepamla (*Contrast*, XI,3, 1977).

Jacobson, Dan. Out of Africa (*Encounter*, October 1959).

Kirkwood, Mike. *Staffrider*: An Informal Discussion (*English in Africa*, VII,2, 1980); The Colonizer: a critique of the English South African Culture Theory (Wilhelm and Polley, ed., *Poetry South Africa, vide* anthologies).

Lanham, L.W. English as a Second Language in Southern Africa since 1820 (de Villiers, ed. *English-Speaking South Africa Today*, *vide* anthologies).

Morris, Patricia. The Early Black South African Newspapers and the Development of the Novel (*Journal of Commonwealth Literature*, XV,1, 1980).

Odendaal, Welma. Donga: One Angry Voice (*English in Africa*, VII,2, 1980).

Parker, Kenneth. The South African Novel in English (Parker ed. *The South African Novel in English*, *vide* anthologies).

Partridge, A.C. The Novel of Social Purpose in South Africa (*S.A. P.E.N. Yearbook*, 1956–1957).

Povey, John. Conference on South African Writing (*Research in African Literatures*, I,1, 1970).

Ravenscroft, Arthur. The Novels of Bessie Head (Heywood, ed. *Aspects of South African Literature*, *vide* anthologies).

Roberts, Sheila V. South African Bilingual and Multilingual Drama of the 'Seventies (*Canadian Drama*, VI,1, 1980).

Simon, Barney. My Years with *The Classic*: A Note (*English in Africa*, VII, 2, 1980).

Ullyat, A.G. Dilemma in Black Poetry (*Contrast*, XI,4, 1977).

Visser, N.W. Towards an Edition of Literary Works of H.I.E. Dhlomo (*Research in African Literatures*, VII,2, 1976); H.I.E. Dhlomo, literary theory and criticism (ed. and introduction, *English in Africa*, IV,2, 1977, whole issue).

Wade, Michael. South Africa's First Proletarian Writer (Parker, ed. *The South African Novel in English*, *vide* anthologies); Art and Morality in Alex La Guma's *Walk in the Night* (Parker, as above).

Willan, Brian. *Vide* Couzens.

Anthologies (*primary contributors listed*).

Abrahams, Lionel, with Gordimer, Nadine, eds. *South African Writing Today*, *vide* Gordimer.

Abrahams, Lionel, and Saunders, Walter, eds. *Quarry, 1976* (Johannesburg, Ad. Donker, 1976; contributions by Sipho Sepamla, Bessie Head, Motshile Nthodi, Essop Patel, Lefifi Tladi, Ahmed Essop).

Abrahams, Lionel, and Saunders, Walter, eds. *Quarry, 1977* (Johannesburg, Ad. Donker, 1977; contributions by Motshile Nthodi, Mike Nicol).

Abrahams, Lionel, ed. *Quarry, '78-'79* (Johannesburg, Ad. Donker, 1979; contributions by Sipho Sepamla, Fhazel Johannesse, Christopher van Wyk).

Beier, Ulli, with Moore, Gerald, eds. *Modern Poetry from Africa*, vide Moore; *Black Orpheus*, An Anthology of New African and Afro-American Prose (London, Longmans, 1964; contributions by William (Bloke) Modisane, Alex La Guma); *Introduction to African Literature*—An Anthology of Critical Writing from *Black Orpheus* (London, Longmans, 1967; contributions by Ezekiel Mphahlele, Lewis Nkosi); *Political Spider* (New York, Africana Publishing Corporation, 1969; contribution by La Guma).

Breman, Paul, ed. *You Better Believe It—Black Verse in English* (Harmondsworth, Penguin, 1973; poems by Ezekiel Mphahlele, Dennis Brutus, Mazisi Kunene, Dollar Brand, Arthur Nortje).

Butler, Guy, and Mann, Chris, eds. *A New Book of South African Verse* (London, OUP, 1979; poems by J.J.R. Jolobe, H.I.E. Dhlomo, Mazisi Kunene, Sipho Sepamla, Adam Small, Oswald Mtshali, Arthur Nortje, Jennifer Davids, Pascal Mafika Gwala, Motshile Nthodi).

Clarke, Leon E. ed. *Through African Eyes* (New York, Praeger, 1971; contributions by Peter Abrahams, William (Bloke) Modisane, Richard Rive).

Cope, Jack, ed. *Seismograph*. Best South African writing from *Contrast* (Cape Town, Reijer Publishers, 1970; contributions by Richard Rive, Ahmed Essop, Lewis Nkosi, Jennifer Davids).

Cope, Jack, and Krige, Uys, eds. *The Penguin Book of South African Verse* (Harmondsworth, Penguin, 1968; contributions by Adam Small).

Dathorne, O.R., and Feuser, Willfried, eds. *Africa in Prose* (Harmondsworth, Penguin, 1969; contributions by R.R.R. Dhlomo, Casey Motsisi, Solomon Tshekedi Plaatje, Ezekiel Mphahlele, Alex La Guma).

Delahunty, Patrick, ed. *African Sun: An Anthology of Poetry from Africa and Other Lands* (London, Longmans, 1974; contributions by O.J. Ntshali (Mtshali), Peter Kumalo, Moses Kunene).

Denny, Neville, ed. *Pan African Short Stories* (London, Nelson, 1965; contributions by Richard Rive, Ezekiel Mphahlele, Casey Motsisi, Alex La Guma, James Matthews).

De Villiers, André, ed. *English Speaking South Africa Today.* Proceedings of the Conference of the 1820 Settlers National Monument Foundation (Cape Town, OUP, 1976).

Drachler, Jacob, ed. *African Heritage* (London, Crowell-Macmillan, 1964; contributions by Peter Abrahams, Alfred Hutchinson, Ezekiel Mphahlele).

Duerden, Dennis and Pieterse, Cosmo, eds. *African Writers Talking—* A Collection of Interviews (London, Heinemann, 1972. Writers interviewed by Pieterse and Lewis Nkosi include Dennis Brutus, Ezekiel Mphahlele).

Edwards, Paul, ed. *Through African Eyes* (Cambridge, CUP, 1966, 2 Vols; contributions by Peter Abrahams, Ezekiel Mphahlele); *Modern African Narrative* (London, Nelson, 1966; contributions by William (Bloke) Modisane, Peter Abrahams, Ezekiel Mphahlele).

Feinberg, Barry, ed. *Poets to the People* (London, Allen & Unwin, 1974, revised ed. London, Heinemann, 1980; poems by Dennis Brutus, A.N.C. Kumalo, Mazisi Kunene, Oswald R. Mtshali, Arthur Nortje, Cosmo Pieterse, Mongane Wally Serote, Lindiwe Mabuza, Ilva Mackay, Klaus Maphepha, Duncan Matlho, Rebecca Matlou, Victor Matlou, John Matshikiza, Victor Motapanyane).

Ferres, John A. and Tucker, Martin, eds. *Modern Commonwealth Literature:* A Library of Literary Criticism. Authors included: Peter Abrahams, Dennis Brutus, Alex La Guma, Ezekiel Mphahlele, Solomon T. Plaatje, Richard Rive; critical contributions by Dennis Brutus, Ezekiel Mphahlele, Lewis Nkosi.

Following the Sun (no ed.) (Berlin, Seven Seas Publishers, 1960; contributions by Mphahlele, Maimane).

Gordimer, Nadine and Abrahams, Lionel, eds. *South African Writing Today* (Harmondsworth, Penguin, 1967; contributions by Dugmore Boetie, Casey Motsisi, Ezekiel Mphahlele, Can Themba, Nathaniel Nakasa, Todd Matshikiza, Lewis Nkosi, Alex La Guma, Dennis Brutus).

Gray, Stephen, ed. *On the Edge of the World*—Southern African Stories of the Seventies (Johannesburg, Ad. Donker, 1974; contributions by Peter Clarke, Ahmed Essop, Bessie Head, James Matthews, Mbulelo Vizikhungo Mzamane, Sydney Sepamla, Mongane Wally Serote, Adam Small); *A World of Their Own*, Southern African Poets of the Seventies (Johannesburg, Ad. Donker, 1976; contributions by Oswald Mbuyiseni Mtshali, Sipho Sepamla, Mongane Wally Serote); *Theatre One*, New South African Drama (Johannesburg, Ad. Donker, 1978; Play by Fatima

Dike); *Modern South African Stories*, revised and expanded edition of *On the Edge of the World* (Johannesburg, Ad. Donker, 1980; contributions by Achmed Essop, Bessie Head, Bob Leshoai, James Matthews, Ezekiel Mphahlele, Mothobi Mutloatse, Mbulelo Mzamane, Richard Rive, Sipho Sepamla, Mongane Wally Serote, Adam Small, Christopher van Wyk).

Hannah, Donald, with Rutherford, Anna, eds. *Commonwealth Short Stories*, *vide* Rutherford.

Henderson, Gwyneth, ed. *African Theatre*, Eight Prize-Winning Plays for Radio (London, Heinemann, 1973; Play by Richard Rive).

Heywood, Christopher, ed. *Aspects of South African Literature* (London, Heinemann, 1976; contributions by Mazisi Kunene and Oswald Mtshali); *Papers on African Literature*, Sheffield University Seminar Series (Sheffield, Department of English Literature, The University, Sheffield in association with Africa Educational Trust, London, 1976; contributions by Lewis Nkosi).

Horn, Peter, with Saunders, Walter, eds. *It's Getting Late and Other Poems from Ophir*, *vide* Saunders.

Hughes, Langston, ed. *An African Treasury* (New York, Crown, 1960, London, Gollancz, 1961; contributions by Can Themba, Ntantula, Bloke Modisane, Ezekiel Mphahlele, Richard Rive);

Poems from Black Africa (Bloomington, Indiana University Press, 1963; poems by Peter Clarke, William (Bloke) Modisane, A.C. Jordan, Peter Abrahams, Ezekiel Mphahlele, Richard Rive).

Kgositsile, Keorapetse, ed. *The Word is Here* (New York, Anchor Books, 1973; contributions by Dennis Brutus, Keorapetse Kgositsile, Burns B. Machobane).

Kitchen, Helen, ed. *A Handbook of African Affairs*, London, Pall Mall, 1964 (contribution by Lewis Nkosi).

Komey, Ellis Ayitey and Mphahlele, Ezekiel, eds. *Modern African Stories* (London, Faber & Faber, 1964; contributions by Alfred Hutchinson, Casey Motsisi, Ezekiel Mphahlele, Can Themba, Alex La Guma, James Matthews, Richard Rive).

Krige, Uys, with Cope, Jack, eds. *The Penguin Book of South African Verse*, *vide* Cope.

Larson, Charles R., ed. *African Short Stories* (New York, Collier Books, 1970; contributions by James Matthews, Alex La Guma, Ezekiel Mphahlele); *More Modern African Stories* (London, Fontana/Collins, 1975; contributions by Bessie Head, Mbulelo V. Mzamane).

Lacy, Leslie. *Contemporary African Literature*, *vide* Makward.

Lawson, William, ed. *Yardbird Reader, Volume 4* (Berkeley, California, Yardbird Publishing, 1975; contribution by Keorapetse Kgositsile).

Lennox-Short, Alan, ed. *English and South Africa* (Cape Town, Nasou, 1973; separate section on Coloured and African Writing in English).

Lindfors, Bernth, ed. *South African Voices* (Austin, Texas, African and Afro-American Studies and Research Center in association with Harry Ransom Center, University of Texas, 1973; contributions by Dennis Brutus, Keorapetse Kgositsile, Mazisi Kunene, Oswald Mtshali, Cosmo Pieterse, Mongane Wally Serote); guest editor *Issue*, VI,1, 1976, Proceedings of the Symposium on Contemporary African Literature and First African Literature Association Conference (contributions by Mazisi Kunene, Daniel Kunene, Ezekiel Mphahlele, Mongane Wally Serote, Oswald Mtshali, Keorapetse Kgositsile, Dennis Brutus, Cosmo Pieterse).

Litto, Fred M., ed. *Plays for Black Africa* (New York, Hill & Wang, 1968; contributions by Lewis Nkosi, Alfred Hutchinson).

Macnab, Roy, ed. *Poets in South Africa* (Cape Town, Maskew Miller, 1958; contributions by J.J.R. Jolobe, H.I.E. Dhlomo, A.C. Jordan [translation of B.W. Vilakazi]).

Macnab, Roy and Gulston, Charles, eds. *South African Poetry, A New Anthology* (London, Collins, 1948; contribution by H.I.E. Dhlomo).

Makward, Edric and Lacy, Leslie, eds. *Contemporary African Literature* (New York, Random House, 1972; contributions by William (Bloke) Modisane, Ezekiel Mphahlele, Bessie Head, James Matthews, Richard Rive, Lewis Nkosi, Keorapetse Kgositsile, Dollar Brand).

Marquard, Jean, ed. *A Century of South African Short Stories* (Johannesburg, Ad. Donker, 1978; contributions by Peter Abrahams, A.C. Jordan, Can Themba, Bessie Head, Richard Rive, Ahmed Essop, James Matthews, Mbulelo Vizikhungo Mzamane).

Matthews, James, ed. *Black Voices Shout* (Athlone, Blac Publishing House, 1974; contributions by Austin Cloete, Christine Douts, Mike Dues, Pascal Gwala, Ilva Mackay, James Matthews, Wally Mongane Serote, Steven Smith, Ben Takavarasha).

McLears, Eva, with Oluwasanmi, Eva and Zell, Hans. *Publishing in Africa in the Seventies, vide* Oluwasanmi.

Moore, Gerald and Beier, Ulli, eds. *Modern Poetry from Africa* (Harmondsworth, Penguin, 1963; contributions by Mazisi Kunene,

William (Bloke) Modisane, Dennis Brutus, Keorapetse Kgositsile, Arthur Nortje).

Moore, Jane Anne, ed. *Cry Sorrow, Cry Joy!* (New York, Friendship Press, 1971; contributions by Lewis Nkosi, Arthur Maimane, Peter Abrahams, James Matthews, Ezekiel Mphahlele).

Mphahlele, Ezekiel, ed. *Modern African Stories* (with Komey, Ellis Ayitey, *vide* Komey); *African Writing Today* (Harmondsworth, Penguin, 1967; contributions by Mphahlele, Can Themba, Todd Matshikiza, Mazisi Kunene, Lewis Nkosi, Dennis Brutus, Richard Rive, Alex La Guma.

Mutloatse, Mothobi, ed. *Forced Landing*, African South: Contemporary Writings (Johannesburg, Ravan Press, 1980; contributions by Chicks Nkosi, Xolile Guma, Mbulelo Vizikhungo Mzamane, James Matthews, Moteane Melamu, Kaizer Ngwenya, Bereng Setuke, Mathatha Tsedu, Bessie Head, Sipho Sepamla, Ahmed Essop, Mafika Pascal Gwala, Mtutuzeli Matshoba, Bob Leshoai, Miriam Tlali, Mothobi Mutloatse, Mango Tshabangu, Ahmed Dangor, Mongane Wally Serote, Charles Rukuni, Obed Musi, Jacky Heyns, Black Stan Motjuwadi, Toivo Herman ja Toivo, Desmond Tutu).

Nolen, Barbara, ed. *Africa is People* (New York, Dutton, 1967; contributions by Noni Jabavu, Peter Abrahams); *More Voices of Africa* (New York, Scribner, 1972; contributions by Peter Abrahams, Ezekiel Mphahlele, Alex La Guma).

Oluwasanmi, Edwina, McLears, Eva, and Zell, Hans, eds. *Publishing in Africa in the Seventies*, Proceedings of an International Conference on Publishing and Book Development held at the University of Ife, Ife-Ife, Nigeria, December 1973 (Ife-Ife, University of Ife Press, 1974).

Okpaku, Joseph, ed. *New African Literature and the Arts I* (New York, Thomas Y. Crowell Company, undated, contributions copyrighted by *Journal of the New African Literature and the Arts* 1970, 1966, 1967; contributions by Dennis Brutus, Dollar Brand, K. William Kgositsile, Ezekiel Mphahlele); *New African Literature and the Arts II* (New York, Thomas Y. Crowell Company, as above, 1968, 1970; contributions by I. Choonara, Cosmo Pieterse).

Paton, J.S., ed. *The Grey Ones*, Essays on Censorship (Johannesburg, Ravan Press, 1974).

Parker, Kenneth, ed. *The South African Novel in English* (London, Macmillan, 1978).

Pereira, Ernest, ed. *Contemporary South African Plays* (Johannesburg, Ravan Press, 1977; play by Benjamin Leshoai.

Pieterse, Cosmo, ed. *Ten One Act Plays* (London, Heinemann, 1968); contributions by Alfred Hutchinson, Arthur J. Maimane); *Protest and Conflict in African Literature* (London, Heinemann, 1969; contributions by Pieterse, Dennis Brutus); *Seven South African Poets* (London, Heinemann, 1971; contributions by William Keorapetse Kgositsile, Dennis Brutus, Dollar Brand, I. Choonara, Arthur Nortje); *Short African Plays* (London, Heinemann, 1972; contributions by Richard Rive, Pieterse).

Polley, James A. with Wilhelm, Peter. *Poetry South Africa, vide* Wilhelm.

Reed, John, and Wake, Clive, eds. *A Book of African Verse* (London, Heinemann, 1964; contributions by J.J.R. Jolobe).

Rive, Richard, ed. *Modern African Prose* (London, Heinemann, 1964; contributions by Richard Rive, James Matthews, Ezekiel Mphahlele, Peter Abrahams, Alfred Hutchinson, Peter Clarke); *Quartet*, New Voices from South Africa (London, Heinemann, 1963; contributions by Richard Rive, James Matthews, Alex La Guma).

Royston, Robert, ed. *To Whom it May Concern* (Johannesburg, Ad. Donker, 1973; contributions by Casey Motsisi, Stanley Motjuwadi, Mongane Wally Serote, Mandlenkosi Langa, Njabulo S. Ndebele, Stanley Mogoba, M. Pascal Gwala, Mafika Mbuli, Oswald Mbuyiseni Mtshali, Basil Somhlahlo, Zuluboy Molefe, Sydney Sepamla).

Rutherfoord, Peggy, ed. *Darkness and Light* (Johannesburg, Drum Publications, 1958; published as *African Voices* An Anthology of Native African Writing, New York, Vanguard Press, 1958; contributions by Dyke Sentso, Can Themba, R.M. Mfeka translation of B.W. Vilakazi).

Rutherford, Anna, and Hannah, Donald, eds. *Commonwealth Short Stories* (London, Edward Arnold, 1971; contribution by Ezekiel Mphahlele).

Saunders, Walter and Horn, Peter, eds. *It's Getting Late and Other Poems from Ophir* (Johannesburg, Ravan Press, 1974; contributions by Oswald Mtshali, Wally Serote, Pascal Gwala, Mandlenkosi Langa).

Shore, Herbert L. and Shore-Bos, Megchelina, eds. *Come Back Africa* (Berlin, Seven Seas Publishers, 1968; contributions by Lewis

Nkosi, William Modisane, Alex La Guma, Dikobe Marks Ramitloa, Richard Rive, Ezekiel Mphahlele).

Shore-Bos, Megchelina, with Shore, Herbert L. *Come Back Africa*, *vide* Shore.

Smith, Rowland, ed. *Exile and Tradition*: Studies in African and Caribbean Literature (London, Longmans, and Dalhousie University Press, 1976).

Soyinka, Wole, ed. *Poems of Black Africa* (New York, Hill & Wang, 1975; contributions by Mazisi Kunene, Arthur Nortje, Keorapetse Kgositsile, Dennis Brutus, Oswald Mtshali.

Tibble, Anne, ed. *African-English Literature*, A Short Survey and Anthology of Prose and Poetry up to 1965 (London, Peter Owen, 1965; contributions by Peter Abrahams, Alfred Hutchinson, Noni Jabavu, Ezekiel Mphahlele, Solomon Tshekedi Plaatje, Alex La Guma, Dennis Brutus).

Tucker, Martin, with Ferres, John A., eds. *Modern Commonwealth Literature*, *vide* Ferres.

Wake, Clive, with Reed, John, eds. *A Book of African Verse*, *vide* Reed.

Whiteley, W.H., ed. *A Selection of African Prose* (London, OUP, 1964; contribution by Ezekiel Mphahlele).

Wilhelm, Peter, and Polley, James A., eds. *Poetry South Africa* (Johannesburg, Ad. Donker, 1976).

Zell, Hans, with Oluwasanmi, Edwina and McLears, Eva, eds. *Publishing in Africa in the Seventies*, *vide* Oluwasanmi.

Bibliographies

Abrash, Barbara. *Black-African Literature in English since 1952* (New York and London, Johnson Reprint Corporation, 1967).

Amosu, Margaret. *A Preliminary Bibliography of Creative African Writing in the European Languages* (Ibadan, Supplement to *African Notes*, Bulletin of the Institute of African Studies, Ibadan, University of Ibadan, 1964).

Astrinsky, Aviva. *A Bibliography of South African Novels, 1930–1960* (Cape Town, University of Cape Town School of Librarianship, typescript, 1965).

Courtney, Winifred, F. *The Reader Adviser No 1* (New York and London, R.R. Bowker & Co., 1968).

Couzens, Tim (T.J.) Annual Bibliography of Commonwealth Literature (*Journal of Commonwealth Literature*, XI,3, 1977; XII,3, 1978; XIII,3, 1979).

Dressler, Peter, with Jahn, Janheinz. *Bibliography of Creative African Writing, vide* Jahn.

Driver, Dorothy, and Smith, Judy. *Annual Bibliography of Commonwealth Literature* (*Journal of Commonwealth Literature*, XIV,2, 1979).

Driver, Dorothy. As above, XV,2, 1980.

Farmer, M.E. Bibliography of Books and Articles on English Language and Literature Published or Written in South Africa (Compiled in Gubbins Library of the University of the Witwatersrand, Johannesburg and published in March and September 1958, and each September thereafter till 1976 in *English Studies in Africa*).

Ganz, David L. *A Critical Guide to Anthologies of African Literature* (Waltham, Massachusetts, Literary Committee, African Studies Association, 1973).

Goldstein, Gillian. *Oswald Mbuyiseni Mtshali, South African Poet* (Johannesburg, University of the Witwatersrand, Department of Bibliography, Librarianship and Typography, 1974).

Greshoff, N.M. *Some English Writings by South African Bantu* (Cape Town, University School of Librarianship, 1943).

House, Amelia. *Black South African Women Writers in English*, preliminary checklist (Evanston, Program on Women, Northwestern University, 1980).

Jahn, Janheinz. *A Bibliography of Neo-African Literature* (London, André Deutsch, 1965); and Dressler, Peter, *Bibliography of Creative African Writing* (Liechtenstein, Kraus-Thomson, 1971); and Schild, Ulla, and Nordmann, Almut, *Who's Who in African Literature, vide* Secondary Works, Books.

Kiersen, S. *English and Afrikaans Novels on South African History* (Cape Town, University of Cape Town School of Librarianship, mimeographed, 1958).

Laredo, Ursula. Bibliography of South African Literature in English 1964–1968 (*The Journal of Commonwealth Literature*, 9, 1970); supplement to the above, June, 1971.

Lindfors, Bernth. *Short Fiction by Non-Europeans in South Africa between 1940 and 1964* (Boston, African Studies Centre, Boston University for African Studies Association, 1969); *Black African*

Literature in English—A Guide to Information Sources (Detroit, Gale, 1979).

Musiker, Reuben. *South African Bibliography* (London, Crosby, Lockwood and Son, 1970).

Nordmann, Almut, with Jahn, Janheinz and Schild, Ulla. *Who's Who in African Literature*, vide Jahn.

Our English Heritage—South African English Literature (Cape Town, City Libraries, mimeographed, 1962).

Ramsaran, John, *New Approaches to African Literature* (Ibadan, Ibadan University Press, 1963).

Schild, Ulla, with Jahn, Janheinz and Nordmann, Almut, *Who's Who in African Literature*, vide Jahn.

Schmidt, Nancy J. A Bibliography of African Dissertations and Theses on African Literature (*Research in African Literatures*, V,1, 1974).

Scott, Patricia, E. *James James Ranisi Jolobe* an Annotated Bibliography (Cape Town, Department of African Languages, Rhodes University, 1973).

Seary, E.R. *A Biographical and Bibliographical Record of South African Literature in English* (Grahamstown, tentative mimeographed edition, 1938).

Silbert, Rachel. *Southern African Drama in English 1900–1964* (Johannesburg, University of the Witwatersrand, Department of Bibliography, Librarianship and Typography, 1965).

Silver, Helene, vide Zell.

Smith, Judy, with Driver, Dorothy. *Annual Bibliography of Commonwealth Literature*, vide Driver.

South Africa in Print: Catalogue of an Exhibition of Books, Atlases and Maps held in the South African Library, Cape Town, 1 March till 5 April, 1952 (Cape, Town, South African Library, 1952).

Wilkov, A., *Some English Writings by Non-Europeans in South Africa* (Johannesburg, University of the Witwatersrand, Department of Bibliography, Librarianship and Typography, 1962).

Zell, Hans M., *Africana Centre Quarterly Catalogue* (New York, Africana Centre); *African Books in Print* (London, Mansell, 1978); with Helene Silver, and with contributions by Barbara Abrash, Gideon Cyros, M. Mutiso, *A Reader's Guide to African Literature* (London, Heinemann, 1972).

Index